Sociology of Education
Second Edition

sociology of education

a book of readings

second edition

edited by ronald m. pavalko

Florida State University

F. E. PEACOCK PUBLISHERS, INC. • ITASCA, ILLINOIS

CONTENTS

PREFACE

Education is currently receiving an unprecedented amount of attention and scrutiny from academicians and laymen alike. On the one hand, vast amounts of financial and manpower resources are being expended for educational research and development. On the other hand, debate over educational policy rages among public officials from City Hall to Capitol Hill and consumes an increasing amount of space in mass-circulation magazines.

Within American colleges and universities academicians from a range of disciplines have developed a variety of interests in the study of education. During the last three decades the study of education has emerged as a distinct field within the discipline of sociology, and courses on the sociology of education have been offered with increasing frequency by college and university sociology departments.

This book has been prepared to provide a body of material useful in the teaching of courses on the sociology of education at both the undergraduate and graduate levels. It consists of material previously published in scholarly journals.

In selecting the material for this book, I have made the assumption that those using it would have at least a minimal familiarity with and understanding of basic sociological concepts and terminology. I have not used the age of an article as a criterion for its inclusion. Rather, I have tried to select articles of significance and substance regardless of when they were originally published.

My goal has been to bring together a combination of research studies and theoretical discussions relevant to the sociological study of education and to the formulation of educational policy. While the majority of articles are authored by sociologists, the contributions of political scientists and specialists in education are also included.

The organization of articles into chapters attempts to accomplish two objectives. First, to present a fairly representative picture of the range of sociological research and writing on education. Second, to attempt to structure the field in terms of my own (hopefully not too idiosyncratic) view of the sociologist's major concerns in studying education. In this regard, chapter titles and the introductory material at the beginning of each chapter constitute my "outline for a sociology of education" and a framework for the future development of this field.

Ronald M. Pavalko

Part I

Introduction

Chapter One

Sociology of Education: Toward a Definition of the Field

"Education" means different things to different people. To some elementary and secondary school children it can be an exciting intellectual experience; to those poorly motivated or presented with a dull and unimaginative curriculum it can be a deadening ordeal; to college students education may be a means to acquiring the qualifications for a job, a way of escaping lowly social class origins, or a time for experimenting with a variety of social and personal identities; to parents education for their children may represent the realization of their own unfulfilled aspirations; to political officials education is something to be financed, often at the resistance of a penurious electorate; to those who operate the schools—teachers, principals, and administrators—education means a job, a place where career aspirations may be realized or thwarted, where viable relationships with colleagues and supervisors must be worked out. This list of the meanings of education could be expanded *ad infinitum*. However, it should be sufficient to illustrate the myriad meanings of education to people in various roles and subgroups in the society.

What does education mean to the sociologist? How does he begin to structure and make sense out of this multifaceted phenomenon called education? Basically, sociologists regard education as a distinctively social phenomenon or "institution" which, like other social phenomena, is amenable to objective scientific analysis. A sociological perspective on education requires that one "step back" from that which he is examining, set aside his personal and cultural biases, and take a long, hard look at the phenomenon of education. This is not an easy task. At times it is made more difficult by the fact that teachers, administrators, and concerned segments of the public may expect immediate answers to questions of policy and technique to emerge from the sociologist's research on education. Sociologists, on the other hand, are primarily concerned with building a body of verified knowledge about education and only secondarily with the problem of applying their findings and conclusions to the concerns of the educational practitioner. The conflicts and barriers to communication that often arise between sociologists and educators have been ably described elsewhere[1] and need not be reiterated here. However, it is tempting (and dangerous) to oversimplify this point, that is, to divide educators and sociologists into antagonistic camps. Though most research on education by sociologists has some policy implications, sociologists vary in the extent to which they spell out these implications in their work. Ultimately, the extent to which this is done is a matter of style and most sociologists have adopted a style in which policy implications are left implicit rather than one in which explicit programmatic statements and policy recommendations are made. The papers that comprise this book tend to fall toward the "implicit" end of the continuum. There are some notable exceptions to this statement but, in general, the reader is left to extract (if one cares to) the implications of the research and ideas presented for questions of policy and action.

The past several decades have been a period of increasing research and scholarly interest in education on the part of sociologists. While sociological research on education has taken a variety of directions and new issues continue to emerge, several major foci of attention have become discernible. Although the main purpose of this book is to bring together articles of significance and substance in-and-of themselves, a second and equally important task is to illustrate the nature of these directions. Thus, the chapter titles under which articles are grouped can be regarded as major concerns to which the sociologist of education is addressed. The three papers in this chapter are intended to illustrate the scope and variety of topics that might be of interest to the sociologist studying education.

The article by Brookover, published in 1949, was the first serious attempt by a sociologist to define the scope of this field and specify particular sub-topics for future research attention. That Brookover's outline for a sociology of education is as salient today as it was in 1949 is attested to by the articles of more recent vintage that comprise this book. Thus, this paper was directed primarily at sociologists in an attempt to sensitize them to the potential of education as a substantive sociological concern.

A somewhat different audience is the intended target of the second article of this chapter. Gross is concerned with illustrating the potential contribution of sociology to education for educational practitioners, that is, for teachers, principals, and other supervisory and administrative school personnel. It should be noted that virtually all the topics in this paper find close parallels in Brookover's outline for the sociology of education. This would seem to support the earlier comment that the more abstract interests of the sociologist do have implications for the more practical concerns of the educational practitioner.

The final article of this chapter is a critical review of the development of the sociology of *higher* education. Clark identifies several of the main thrusts that sociological work on higher education has taken, examines the direction that future work is likely to take, and suggests some additional topics and problems for sociologists to consider and explore. Several of the main topics that Clark identifies—equality of opportunity for education beyond the secondary level, the social psychological effects of college on students, and the organizational characteristics of higher education—are all dealt with in subsequent chapters of this book.

NOTES

1. Donald A. Hansen, "The Uncomfortable Relation of Sociology and Education," in Donald A. Hansen and Joel E. Gerstl (eds.), *On Education: Sociological Perspectives,* New York: John Wiley and Sons, Inc., 1967.

1.   WILBUR B. BROOKOVER

Sociology of Education: A Definition

In the minds of educators and sociologists, the concept, sociology of education, is associated with the concept, educational sociology. For that reason any discussion of a sociology of education which this paper proposes to define must take into consideration the development of educational sociology. At the turn

Reprinted from *American Sociological Review,* 14 (June, 1949), pp. 407–15, by permission of the author and the American Sociological Association.

This is a paper read at the annual meeting of the American Sociological Society held in Chicago, December 28–30, 1948.

of the present century, there was considerable enthusiasm for the development of a new discipline or at least a branch of sociology to be known as educational sociology. By 1914,[1] as many as sixteen institutions were offering courses called educational sociology. In the following period numerous books carrying some type of educational sociology title came off the press. These involved various concepts of the relationship between sociology and education.

By 1923 the "National Society for the Study of Educational Sociology"[2] was organized. This society met with both the American Sociological Society and the Department of Superintendents. Between 1923 and 1931 three yearbooks were issued by this organization, but such publications were discontinued and the *Journal of Educational Sociology,* founded in 1928 by E. G. Payne, became the official organ of the society. The independent existence of the society[3] ceased at about this time. Sociologists interested in problems of education have met as the educational section of the American Sociological Society at the annual meetings until 1948. The early demise of the National Society which was made up of both education specialists and sociologists is indicative of the divergence of interests in this group. The apparent demise of the educational sociology section suggests a lack of interest, among sociologists, in what has been known as educational sociology.

The same trend has been noted by various persons with regard to the college offerings in educational sociology. Herrington[4] found a decline in courses from 1926 to 1947. This decrease may be due in part to the substitution of other sociology courses for former educational sociology courses in schools of education and teachers colleges. It seems safe to say, however, that in the past few years relatively few sociologists have been interested in educational sociology, and apparently there has been no increase in interest in departments of education.

Before eliminating the area from further consideration, it may be desirable to examine the reasons for such a trend and to suggest an area in which sociologists who are interested in educational institutions can make an acceptable contribution. The purpose of this paper is, therefore, twofold. First, to examine what has been included under the rubrics educational sociology and sociology of education in order to understand the trends in the field. Second, to try to delineate an area of research involving educational processes and patterns in which sociologists are qualified to work and in which considerable numbers have shown some interest.

AREAS OF STUDY BY EDUCATIONAL SOCIOLOGISTS

The study by Lee[5] in 1927 indicated that educational sociology courses had little similarity to one another in content. They gave the appearance of being merely a hodgepodge of subjects which instructors in sociology and education might put together for the training of teachers and others interested in education. The study of the aims of educational sociology by Moore[6] in 1924 indicated a similar variety of content. An examination of the literature in educational sociology including books with this or a related title, as well as the periodical literature in which the field is defined or delineated, leads to a similar conclusion. It may be worth while to examine very briefly several conceptions or definitions of the area of educational sociology at this point. They are not mutually exclusive categories, but indicate the widely different although somewhat related ideas of the field.

Analysis of Education as the Means of Social Progress

Several of the early sociologists thought of educational sociology as a field which would provide the basis for social progress and the solution of social evils. This probably stems from the early work of Lester F. Ward[7] in which he looked upon education as an ameliorative process whose main function is the improvement of society. Ward's emphasis on education as the means to progress in society is also seen in the works of Good,[8] Ellwood,[9] and Kinneman.[10] These men expressed the idea that the school might succeed in teaching the people to exercise social control in such an intelligent fashion that culture would progress to the highest level possible. Others have set similar tasks for educational sociology, but these indicate the nature of this conception of the field.

Educational Sociology as Providing the Aims for Education

A second conception of educational sociology can be recognized in the contributions of those who were concerned with social determination of the aims or objectives of education. Finney,[11] Snedden,[12] Peters,[13] Clements,[14] and Kinneman,[15] all in various degrees thought of educational sociology as the objective analysis of the aims or purposes of education. In this sense they were attempting to arrive at a social philosophy of education which would be based on an analysis of society and the needs of people in society.

Application of Sociology to Education

Quite a number of students in the field have defined educational sociology as the application of sociology to educational problems. Most of the men mentioned in the previous paragraph discussed the application of sociology to curriculum development. Many of the persons who gave this catch-all definition of educational sociology also discussed specific problems. Among these are Smith,[16] Zorbaugh,[17] and Kulp.[18] More recently Brown encompassed the whole area of applications of sociology to education when he said that "The educational sociologist utilizes all that has been learned in both fields but joins them in a new science by applying sociological principles to the whole process of education."[19] In addition to his emphasis on the idea of a sociological curriculum Zeleny[20] in his paper read before the educational sociology section of the American Sociological Society, a year ago, took the position that "Educational sociology cannot be a pure science; it must be applied to the control of education." Viewed in this light, educational sociology is strictly technology and not a science at all.

We turn now to consideration of somewhat different concepts of the educational sociology program. Viewed in one light, the following two approaches to educational sociology are almost as comprehensive as sociology in general.

The Educational Process as the Socializing Process

Prior to the more recent emphasis by sociologists and social psychologists on the development of personality, some educational sociologists viewed the entire process of socializing a child as the area of educational sociology. That part of the field of social experience in which the individual is affected by the social group was considered the field of cultivation for educational sociologists. Important in this group were Ellwood,[21] Smith,[22] and more recently, Brown.[23] Brown presents this view in quoting from Dodson: "Educational sociology is interested in the impact of the total cultural milieu in which and through which experience is acquired and organized. It is interested in the school, but recognizes it as a small part of the total. Educational sociology is particularly interested in finding out how to manipulate the educational process to achieve better personality development."

Sociology Training for Educational Workers and Training for Educational Research

The point of view expressed by Brown and Dodson is similar to that expressed by Payne[24] when he says, "by educational sociology we mean the science which describes and explains . . . the social relationships in which or through which the individual gains and organizes his experience." He also indicates "that educational sociology is interested in social behavior and the principles of its control." At various points he looks upon educational sociology as a comprehensive study of all aspects of education from a technological or applied science point of view. When this is examined in the light of New York University's very extensive sociology offerings in the School of Education we recognize that, for Payne, educational sociology included anything in the field of sociology which could be related to the learning or socializing process and anything in education that was subject to sociological analysis. This all-inclusive view plus the opportunity to develop a separate department at N.Y.U. led to a varied and multiple conception of the field of educational sociology. Primary emphasis throughout, however, if I understand it correctly, is on the need to provide teachers, research workers, and others interested in education with an adequate and effective training in sociology and its contributions to the understanding of the educational process.

In this sense the work being done at Ohio State University is similar to that at N.Y.U. Although a part of the sociology department, a staff of sociologists provide several courses in sociology for teacher trainees at this institution. It is understood that prospective teachers take educational sociology along with the general introductory course as the requirement in sociology. The emphasis at this institution is upon the understanding of the community and the total social scene in which the child is socialized. The nature of this work is indicated by Cook[25] and Greenhoe.[26] In both of the institutions mentioned, and perhaps in many others, educational sociology rather than other sociology courses are offered to teacher trainees. In many other institutions the teacher trainees receive similar contact with sociology but do so through the same courses offered to other students. Many of the books which were written as educational sociology texts reflect the desire to provide a survey of sociology as a general background for teachers.

The outline of trends in educational sociology made by Zeleny[27] in 1948 suggests a new departure in this field of training for teachers. He emphasized the contribution that sociologists, trained in social drama and role-taking procedures, could make to the techniques of teaching. He also emphasized the contribution which sociologists could make in socializing other techniques of classroom instruction.

Role of Education in Society

A more recent development in the field of educational sociology and quite different from the earlier orientations is the analysis of the role of education in the community and society generally. In his book, *Community Backgrounds of Education,* Cook has placed some emphasis upon the function of educational institutions in the community and has analyzed the social relationship between the school and other aspects of the community. Many of the rural sociologists have delineated rural communities and neighborhoods in relation to high-school and elementary-school attendance areas. Somewhat different but classifiable in the same general category is the analysis of the function of the school in the status structure of society with particular reference to the local community structure. The work of Warner[28] and his associates is significant in this area. The emphasis in all of them is on the analysis of the community and society with particular reference to the function of education. For this reason it is hardly appropriate to call this by the same name as the previous categories of educational sociology which placed much more emphasis on the idea of application.

Patterns of Social Interaction within the School and between the School and the Community

Closely related to the above and similarly recent has been an attempt to analyze the patterns of social interaction and social roles within the school society and the relation of personalities within the school to outside groups. The work of Waller[29] was the first major attempt to analyze the role of teachers both in relation to their students and to the communities in which they teach. Greenhoe's[30] study of community contacts and participation of a nationwide sample of school teachers is also significant. In this same general area are the analyses of the roles of teachers on the higher education level by Znaniecki[31] and Wilson.[32] Warren[33] has also made a study of teachers in his analysis of social roles. The studies of clique structure, leadership, and rejections have also been contributions to a sociology of the social groups within the school. Major contributions in this field have been made by Cook[34] and Smucker.[35] Here again it is hardly accurate to list this approach as educational sociology if that rubric is to contain the variety of other work that has been described above.

Summary of Various Approaches to Educational Sociology

The range of differences among persons who call themselves educational sociologists has been apparent throughout the half-century of the concept's existence and was recognized by Lee in his 1926 study.[36] The practice of calling anything that anyone might want to include in a course for teachers educational sociology may be a factor in the decline of emphasis upon that type of course. Competent sociologists could hardly continue to have respect for such a hodgepodge of content. This becomes particularly evident when the emphases on value judgments, educational technology, and other materials foreign to the scientific analysis of social interaction are considered.

This apparent decline in interest in educational sociology among sociologists is not, however, an indication that sociology is no longer considered an important part of the training for prospective teachers. Although no evidence is immediately available to illustrate trends, there is some indication that teacher training institutions are offering many more sociology courses, other than educational, than they previously did. The study by Landis[37] which found 1,022 sociology courses listed in the catalogs of 162 teacher colleges would substantiate the assumption that teacher training institutions are offering a considerable number of courses. This seems to be much greater than the number offered twenty years ago. This may mean that directors of teacher training programs have come to feel that teachers can get better training in sociology from other courses than those specifically designated educational sociology. This may account in part for the decline in the number of courses of the latter type.

The more recent interest of sociologists in the analysis of the educational system as a pattern of social interaction and its relation to other social systems suggests a new and different role for sociology in relation to education. It is this to which we now turn our attention.

SOCIOLOGY OF EDUCATION: SCIENTIFIC ANALYSIS OF THE HUMAN RELATIONS IN EDUCATION

The foregoing survey of various approaches to educational sociology may lead some to the conclusion that there is no place for a sociological analysis of education. It is our purpose here to note that there is not only such a place, but that it is one of the more important tasks that the sociologist is equipped to do. Furthermore, the stage of scientific development has arrived wherein a major contribution can be made to the educational system in our society. It should, however, be made clear at this point that there is no intention to disagree with those who wish to deal in the philosophy of education or the development of the goals or objectives of education from sociological data. Neither is there any wish to discredit those who, like Zeleny,[38] wish to apply sociological information and principles to the construction of the school curriculum or to the improvement of teaching methods. It is submitted that these concepts of educational sociology either do not contribute to the scientific analysis of human relations—thus are not sociology—or that they are attempts to include all sociology under this rubric.

The fundamental and increasing importance of the educational process and the system of social relations associated with that process certainly makes it of such importance that the sociologist should turn his attention and abilities to the analysis of this aspect of the society. It is doubtful if those who wish to apply sociological principles and information to the school administration can make rapid progress until we understand the nature of the human relations within the school, and the social structure within which the schools operate in the community. Just as sociologists have turned their attention to the analysis of human relations in the family, industry, religion, politics, the community, or in any other system of social interaction, so it is appropriate for those trained in this field to determine the patterns of interaction in the educational system. Furthermore, this approach can meet the most rigorous requirements of scientific investigation. It can also make as much contribution to an understanding of the total society as the analysis of any other portion of society.

It should be pointed out that such a delineation of a field which we would designate the sociology of education is not new. Some years ago Angell[39] made a significant and valid definition of the field. He took the position that an educational sociologist should be simply a sociologist who specializes in his thoughts and research on the educational process. Furthermore, he maintained that in this light "educational sociology is then merely a branch of the pure science of sociology." He stated that he preferred to call this area of the discipline *Sociology of Education,* because the approach was through the school as a source of data which could be analyzed rather than as something to be acted upon, which is implied in the traditional concept of educational sociology. Angell further pointed out that an applied science of educational sociology is impossible because the application of sociology alone to the educational process does not supply all that is necessary to administer and determine the policy of educational systems. The school administrator faced with the necessity of organizing and directing an educational system must draw upon the information provided by psychology, political science, economics, and many other disciplines. For this reason, as Angell pointed out, the problems of school administration involve a broad technology.

Somewhat later Reuter[40] made a similar delineation of the field when he pointed out that "The interests of the educational sociologist differ from that of the general sociologist only in the fact that he works with a specially selected set of materials. . . . He is interested to understand education's forms, functions and developments in diverse situations, to understand the behavior and ideologies of school men, to discover the effect of school on existing institutions and its influence on personality." Reuter further recognized the fact that his definition of educational sociology eliminated much that had gone by that name: "educational sociologists have for the most part been concerned with other than sociological material. . . . Even that labeled as sociological commonly deals with social, practical, and moral topics or with questions of educational objectives and curricular content rather than with sociological problems."

Unfortunately neither Angell nor Reuter followed up his delineation of the sociology of education with an extensive analysis in the field. In fact, only a limited number of contributions are found in the literature which can be included in the area outlined by these men. There is, however, a rapidly growing body of research data which makes possible the organization of a rather extensive and significant sociological analysis of the educational system in American society.

In summarizing the reflections on the earlier contributions to the so-called field of educational sociology and the more carefully defined concepts of what might preferably be called sociology of education, some criteria, both negative and positive, for delineating the latter field are suggested. First, it will *not* include all of sociology simply because sociology is good training for teachers. If the latter is true, then teachers should be trained in sociology. Having prospective teachers studying courses in sociology does not make that sociology a science of educational sociology. Second, sociology of education is *not* a technology of education. Certainly it is to be hoped that the educational administrator will know sociology and will use it in the administration of the school. It is also hoped that he will know more than sociology and that he will not be primarily a researcher in the social relations within the school.

Third, on the positive side, the sociology of education *is* the scientific analysis of the social processes and social patterns involved in the educational system. This assumes that education is a combination of social acts and that sociology deals with the analysis of human interaction. Such analysis of the human interaction in education may include both the formal education occurring in other places as well as the school and the multitude of informal communication processes which serve educational functions. It is also assumed that such an analysis would lead to development of scientific generalizations about human relations in the educational system. Finally, any adequate sociology of education must present hypotheses concerning such human relations which will provide the body of theory to be tested in research.

Although only limited segments of the area have been analyzed and few if any supportable generalizations are available, there is a rapidly increasing number of contributions to a scientific analysis of the educational social system. There is no wish to withhold this information from the educator who wishes to improve the organization and administration of the educational system. In fact, it is hoped that the end result or goal of this area of sociological analysis will be just that. On the other hand, it is maintained that improvement in the school system can move forward much more rapidly if based upon a scientific analysis of the educational system when such is available. This is the task of the sociologist who is sufficiently interested to turn his abilities and attention to the social relations involved in the educational processes and patterns.

AN OUTLINE OF THE SOCIOLOGY OF EDUCATION

The present state of research and analysis of the educational system makes it possible to indicate a tentative outline of a sociology of education. Because of personal interest and experience the outline will be limited to the areas of analysis that can now be recognized in the formal aspects of the educational system. These areas will provide the subject matter for a forthcoming book in the field of sociology of education.[41]

The Relation of the Educational System to Other Aspects of Society

There is now available a considerable amount of evidence upon which to develop some theories about the relation of the educational system, particularly the schools, to other aspects of American society. This division of the sociology of education would include several subdivisions. Among them would be: (1) the relationship of the educational system to the processes of social and cultural change or the maintenance of the status quo, (2) the functioning of the formal educational system in the process of social reform in such areas of human relationships as those between racial, cultural, and other groups, (3) functions of the educational system in the process of social control, (4) the relationship of education to the social class or status system, (5) the relation of the educational system to public opinion, and (6) the significance of education as a symbol of faith in democratic culture. There is no attempt to make an inclusive outline of all possible topics in the area, but to indicate those in which some analyses have been made. These will indicate something of the scope of this area without a bibliography of the contributions or a more detailed outline.

Human Relations within the School

The second area of the sociology of education which is receiving increasing attention and to which many significant contributions have been made is the analysis of the social structure within the school. It has been pointed out that the cultural patterns within the school system are significantly different from other aspects of society, but much remains to be done to describe and analyze the nature of this school culture. A considerable number of studies have been made of the patterns of interaction among the persons in the school situation. This makes it possible to suggest several types of sociological analysis that would be included in this area. Among these are: (1) the nature of the school culture, particularly as it differs from the culture outside the school, (2) the nature of the patterns of stratification within the school, (3) the relationships between teachers and pupils, (4) the analysis of the clique and congeniality group structure in the school system, and (5) the nature of the leadership patterns and power structure in the school groups. There are no doubt other types of analysis in this area, but these will suggest the nature of the area and many of the contributions that have been made to it.

The Relation between the School and Community

A third area that has been the focus of attention for a number of sociologists is the analysis of the patterns of interaction between the school and other social groups in the immediate community. In this field one might include: (1) the delineation of the community as it affects school organization,[42] (2) the analysis of the community power structure as it impinges on the school, and (3) analysis of the relation between the school system and other social systems in the community. All of these are significant aspects of the increasingly accepted concept of the community school which is intended to achieve an educational system that is better integrated with the life of the community which it serves. Sociological analyses can well provide the type of knowledge that is essential for the achievement of this end.

The Impact of the School on the Behavior and Personality of Its Participants

The last major division of the sociology of education to be mentioned might be considered a social psychology of the educational system. In this we are interested in analyzing the nature of the behavior patterns or personality that result from the participation of teachers, pupils, and others in the total educational system. Psychologists and educationists have devoted considerable research and theorizing to the problem of the impact of the school on the pupils. Sociologists and social psychologists can also make contributions by noting the significance of the social roles the child plays in relation to teachers and other pupils in the school society. Just as human relations in the school have the effect of defining the roles and behavior of the children, so do they define the roles and behavior of teachers. Thus the development of teacher personality is a significant aspect of an overall sociology of education.

Some of the analyses that can be mentioned in this area are: (1) the social roles of the teacher, (2) the nature of the teacher's personality, (3) the impact of the teacher's personality on the behavior of students, (4) the role of the school in the growth, adjustment, and/or maladjustment of children, and (5) the nature of behavior resulting from varying degrees of authoritarian or democratic school situations.

Others would no doubt subdivide the sociology of education into other segments, but, in terms of the criteria indicated earlier, it would seem that these are the more significant areas in which some analyses have been made and for which there is some research evidence to support hypotheses and tentative theories. There is, however, a tremendous amount of research to be done before an adequate sociology of education can be said to exist.

SUMMARY

A review of the contributions to the field traditionally known as educational sociology indicates a wide variety of subject matter and concepts of the field. It further indicates that there has been an apparent decline of interest in educational sociology as such. This has been associated, however, with an increasing emphasis upon sociological analysis as the means of understanding schools and the educational processes. This suggests the necessity for a comprehensive analysis of the human relations in the educational system and between the educational system and other aspects of society. These, with the impact of such human relations on the behavior of individual human beings, are suggested as the areas for research and analysis to be pursued in the sociology of education. The growing body of research and increasing interest suggests the advisability of distinguishing it from the earlier applied educational sociology. Although the apparent demise of the educational sociology section of the American Sociological Society suggests that this paper may be an elegy for educational sociology, it is hoped that it may be a part of the initiation ceremony for a robust sociology of education.

NOTES

1. D. H. Kulp, *Educational Sociology* (New York: Longmans Green, 1932), p. 536.
2. *Ibid.,* p. 554.
3. *Ibid.,* p. 555.
4 G. S Herrington, "The Status of Educational Sociology Today," *Journal of Educational Sociology,* 21 (November, 1947), p. 129.
5. H. Lee, *Status of Educational Sociology* (Monograph, New York University Press Bookstore, 1927).
6. C. B. Moore, "Aims of Educational Sociology," *Education,* 45, pp. 159–70.
7. L. F. Ward, "Education as the Proximate Means of Progress," in his *Dynamic Sociology,* 1883.
8. Alvin Good, "Sociology and Education," *Harpers,* 26 (1926), p. 25.
9. C. A. Ellwood, "What Is Educational Sociology?" *Journal of Educational Sociology,* 1 (September, 1927), pp. 25–30.
10. John A. Kinneman, *Society and Education* (New York: Macmillan, 1932), p. 49.
11. Ross L. Finney, "Divergent Views of Educational Sociology," *Journal of Educational Sociology,* 1 (October, 1927), p. 100.
12. David Snedden, *Sociology for Teachers* (New York: Century, 1924), p. 33.
13. C. C. Peters, *Foundation of Sociology* (New York: Macmillan, 1935).
14. S. C. Clement, "Educational Sociology in Normal Schools and Teachers Colleges," *Journal of Educational Sociology,* 1 (1927), p. 33.
15. Kinneman, *op. cit.,* p. 48.
16. W. R. Smith, *Principles of Educational Sociology* (Boston: Houghton-Mifflin, 1928), p. 6.
17. Harvey Zorbaugh, "Research in Educational Sociology," *Journal of Educational Sociology,* 1 (1927), pp. 18–19.
18. Kulp, *op. cit.,* p. 71.
19. Francis Brown, *Educational Sociology* (New York: Prentice-Hall, 1947), pp. 35–36.
20. Leslie Zeleny, "The Sociological Curriculum," *Journal of Educational Sociology,* 13, especially p. 45, and "New Directions in Educational Sociology and the Teaching of Sociology," *American Sociological Review,* 13 (June, 1948), pp. 336–41.
21. C. A. Ellwood, *op. cit.,* pp. 25–30.
22. C. R. Smith, *loc. cit.*
23. Francis Brown, *op. cit.,* pp. 35–36.
24. E. G. Payne, *Principles of Educational Sociology* (New York: New York University Press, 1928), p. 20.
25. L. A. Cook, *Community Backgrounds of Education* (New York: McGraw-Hill, 1938), p. 19.
26. Florence Greenhoe, "Community Sociology and Teacher Training," *Journal of Educational Sociology,* 13 (April, 1940), pp. 463–70.
27 Zeleny, *op. cit.*

28. W. L. Warner, R. J. Havighurst, and M. B. Loeb, *Who Shall Be Educated?* (New York: Harper, 1944).

29. Willard Waller, *Sociology of Teaching* (New York: Wiley, 1932).

30. Florence Greenhoe, *Community Contacts and Participation of Teachers* (Washington, D.C.: American Council on Public Affairs, 1941).

31. Florian Znaniecki, *Social Roles of the Man of Knowledge* (New York: Columbia University Press, 1940).

32. Logan Wilson, *Academic Man* (London: Oxford University Press, 1942).

33. Roland Warren, unpublished manuscript which has been made available to the writer.

34. L. A. Cook, "An Experimental Sociographic Study of a Stratified 10th Grade Class," *American Sociological Review,* 10 (April, 1945), pp. 250–61.

35. O. C. Smucker, "The Campus Clique As an Agency of Socialization," *Journal of Educational Sociology,* 21 (*3*), pp. 163–69; and "Prestige Status Stratification on a College Campus," *Journal of Applied Anthropology,* 6 (1), pp. 20–27.

36. Harvey Lee, "The Status of Educational Sociology in . . . Schools . . . Colleges . . . and Universities" (New York University Press Bookstore; summary in Payne, *Readings in Educational Sociology,* Vol I, [New York: Prentice-Hall, 1939], pp. 2–8.)

37. Judson T. Landis, "The Sociology Curriculum and Teacher Training," *American Sociological Review,* 12 (February, 1947), pp. 113–16.

38. Zeleny, *op. cit.*

39. Robert Cooley Angell, "Science, Sociology, and Education," *Journal of Educational Sociology,* 1 (March, 1928), pp. 406–13.

40. E. B. Reuter, "The Problem of Educational Sociology," *Journal of Educational Sociology,* 9 (September, 1935), pp. 15–22.

41. Wilbur B. Brookover, *A Sociology of Education* (New York: American Book Company, 1955).

42. See J. F. Thaden and Eben Mumford, "High School Communities in Michigan," *Special Bulletin* 289 (January, 1938), Agricultural Experiment Station, Michigan State College, East Lansing.

2.   NEAL GROSS

Some Contributions of Sociology to the Field of Education

The purpose of this paper is to delineate *for the educational practitioner* some specific contributions of sociological analysis to the field of education. We propose to focus on a limited set of substantive sociological contributions that teachers, supervisory personnel, school principals, or school superintendents may find of value in dealing with their work environment in a more realistic and effective manner.

Of the many approaches possible in describing some "practical contributions" of sociology to the field of education, the following procedure has been adopted. Specific contributions will be discussed under three headings that constitute sociological perspectives in the examination of school systems as functioning social systems. The first is that educational relationships occur in the context of a formal organizational setting. Students, teachers, supervisors, principals, and school superintendents interact as incumbents of positions in a social system which has an organizational goal, the education of children. To accomplish this task the work that goes on in a school must be assigned, coordinated, and integrated. Educational practice involves a number of people in a complicated division of labor; this necessitates networks of role relationships within an organizational environment. The second perspective derives from the fact that the basic work of the school, the educational transaction, takes place primarily in a relatively small social system, the classroom. The third perspective emerges from an observation that the sociologist would make about the school as social system: Like all organizations, it is influenced by forces external to it. The impact of these external factors on the functioning of the school therefore comes under his scrutiny as a focal point of inquiry. It is from these three limited perspectives[1]—the school system as a formal organization, the classroom as a social system, and the external environment of the schools—that we propose to delineate some contributions of sociology to practitioners in the field of education.

Reprinted from *Harvard Educational Review,* 29 (Fall, 1959), pp. 275–87, by permission of the author and the Harvard Educational Review. Copyright © 1959 President and Fellows of Harvard College.

THE SCHOOL SYSTEM AS A FORMAL ORGANIZATION

A school system from a sociological point of view shares many common characteristics with other kinds of large-scale organizations. Two of these are of special relevance for our purpose. The first is that a school system, like business firms and hospitals, has an organizational objective. It is a goal-directed social system. Second, it contains a network of interrelated positions (for example, teachers, supervisors, and administrators) that are directly linked to the accomplishment of the organizational goal.

According to the "organizational model" for public schools, the business of the school is to impart knowledge and skills to students and therefore teachers are employed for this purpose. The function of supervisors is to help teachers to do a more effective job, and the formal duties of school administrators are to coordinate and integrate the diverse activities of the school. The incumbents of these positions have certain rights and obligations in their relationships with incumbents of other positions with whom they interact. Implicit in discussions of these aspects of the organizational structure of the school are two assumptions that deserve empirical examination. The first is that there is basic agreement on the organizational objective of the schools. The second is that there is agreement on the rights and obligations associated with the various positions in education. Sociological analysis suggests that both assumptions may in fact be tenuous in many school systems, and that lack of agreement on educational objectives and role definition may constitute major dysfunctional elements in the functioning of the school and may affect the gratification educators derive from their jobs.

The formal organizational goal of public school systems is vague and is characterized by ambiguity. This observation emerges from a comparison of school systems with other types of organizations, for example, a business firm. The formal organizational goal of a business firm is unambiguous: to produce products or services for a profit. Labor unions may fight with management over the distribution of profits, but typically there is no quarrel over the organizational goal itself. The situation is quite different, however, when an effort is made to specify the organizational objective of a school system. "To educate children" is a largely meaningless statement unless the purposes of the education are specified. And here lies the difficulty.

The specification of educational purposes invokes value issues such as the respective responsibilities of the home and the school or the meaning of a "good education." Whether the schools should give greater primacy to the intellectual, social, or emotional development of the child; whether or not they have the responsibility to impart moral values; whether the schools have different obligations to the "typical" and "atypical" child; whether they should encourage or discourage the questioning of the status quo; whether driver education, physical education, and courses in home economics and family living are legitimate or illegitimate functions of the school—each of these is a value question on which there may be contradictory points of view within and outside of school systems. An unpublished Harvard study involving personnel at different levels in eight New England school systems revealed dramatic differences in the beliefs teachers hold about educational goals and revealed that principals and teachers frequently do not share common views about educational objectives. Striking disagreements between superintendents and school boards have also been uncovered in regard to certain eductional objectives.[2] Research evidence[3] further indicates that one of the major sources of pressures to which school administrators are exposed consists in conflicting viewpoints in their communities about school objectives and programs. Educational practitioners need to recognize that a fundamental source of controversy within the schools may be related to basic and unrecognized value conflicts over its organizational objectives. These differences in beliefs are infrequently brought to the surface for frank and open discussion. They may constitute basic blocks to effective group action and harmonious social relationships.

The second "organizational assumption," that there is agreement on the role definition for educational positions, also appears to be suspect. Although textbooks in education glibly speak about the role of the teacher and of the school administrator as if everybody agreed on what they are, and many educational practitioners make this assumption, the organizational fact in many school systems may be that those people who work together frequently do not share similar views about the rights and obligations associated with their positions.

Should teachers be expected to attend PTA meetings regularly? Does the teacher's job include the counseling function? What are the teacher's obligations to the especially bright or especially dull child? Or the problem child? What are the teacher's obligations in handling discipline problems? Should teachers be expected to participate in inservice training programs? Does the teacher have the right to expect that the administrator will always support him when parents complain about his behavior? On these and many other phases of a teacher's job there may be considerable disagreement between principals and teachers as well as among teachers.

The findings of a study concerned with the role definition of approximately 50 per cent of the superintendents and school board members in Massachusetts revealed a basic lack of agreement over the division of labor between them.[4] On the issue of hiring new teachers, seven out of ten superintendents interviewed reported that the arrangement they desired was this: when a new teacher was to be hired, the school board should act *solely* on the nominations of the superintendent. But only one out of five of the school board members agreed with them. How about the selection of textbooks? Nearly nine out of ten superintendents felt that the school board should always accept the recommendation of the superintendent in choosing a textbook. But less than one-half of the school board members agreed. What about teacher grievances? Nearly 90 per cent of the superintendents believe that teachers should always bring their grievances to the superintendent before they went to the school board. Only 56 per cent of the school board members agreed. What should the procedure be when a community group wishes to use school property? Nine out of ten school superintendents thought that this decision should be the superintendent's responsibility. Nearly one-half of the school board members, however, felt that these decisions should be made by the school board. What about recommendations for salary increases for school system employees? Over two-thirds of the superintendents felt that the superintendent should make all such recommendations. Only one-third of the school board members agreed with them. These findings imply that in many school systems disagreements over the rights and obligations associated with educational positions may constitute basic sources of stress in the school system. They also suggest that intra-role conflicts appear to be "built into" many educational positions.

By an intra-role conflict we mean conflicting expectations to which an individual is exposed as a consequence of his occupancy of a *single* position. Teachers are frequently exposed to conflicting expectations from their principal and supervisors, from guidance personnel and their principal, from parents and administrators, and even from students in their classrooms. School principals are exposed to conflicting expectations from their superintendent and their staff over such matters as the supervision of classroom instruction and the handling of discipline problems. School administrators are confronted with conflicting expectations among their school staff. For example, some teachers expect their principal to make all important decisions affecting their welfare, but other teachers expect to participate in such decisions.[5] In addition, parents and teachers frequently hold contradictory expectations for the principal's behavior in regard to student promotion and discipline practices. It is the school superintendent, however, who probably is exposed most frequently to intra-role conflict. A major source of these conflicting expectations arises from the differential views held by his school board and his staff for his behavior. Whose views should he support when the school board and the staff hold conflicting expectations for his behavior on such issues as the size of the school budget or promotion policies? Superintendents, like school principals, must also frequently deal with differential expectations among the teaching staff. And their most difficult problems may emerge from conflicting expectations held by their school board members for their performance.

To sum up: Viewing school systems as organizations from a sociological perspective suggests major organizational barriers to their effective functioning. We have emphasized two of these blocks: lack of agreement on organizational goals and lack of consensus on the role definitions associated with educational positions.

THE CLASSROOM AS A SOCIAL SYSTEM

Parsons, in a recent paper, presents a provocative theoretical analysis of the school class as a social system from the viewpoint of its functions for American society.[6] Coleman's analysis of the structure of competition in the high school and its influence on academic achievement clearly has implications for isolating forces that influence the "academic output" of the classroom.[7] These analyses, plus those of sociologists like Gordon[8] and Brookover,[9] suggest the importance of a sociological perspective in examining the structure and functioning of the classroom as a social system.

At this stage of sociological and socio-psychological inquiry on the classroom as a social system, the major empirical contributions of the sociologist have undoubtedly been to draw attention to the sociometric structure of the classroom and to isolate basic sources of strain and tension to which teachers are exposed in the classroom. Sociometric studies reveal that classrooms typically contain "stars" and "isolates," and they have uncovered factors that affect student interpersonal relations in the school class.[10] Of especial importance to educators is the finding that teachers appear to misperceive frequently the interpersonal relationships among students in their classrooms.[11] They do not show high sensitivity to the way children actually react to each other, and they frequently allow their own biases toward students to hinder a correct assessment of the "sociometric facts of life."

A second sociological contribution to the understanding of classroom behavior stems from the isolation of some potential sources of strain for the classroom teacher. One source of stress is the collision between the authority structure of the school and the professional status of the teaching staff. A school system must provide for the coordination and integration of the work of its members. Someone has to assign responsibilities, see that tasks are accomplished, and have the power to sanction teachers and students for deviant behavior. The elementary school principal, for example, as the formal leader of his school has to make room assignments and final decisions about the disposition of discipline problems. He must also see that the educational experiences of the child in the first grade are integrated with those he receives in the second and third grades. This requires some type of control over the work content and work output of teachers at each of these levels. Their classroom behavior is part of his concern. The authority structure, however, conflicts with another characteristic of school organization—the school is staffed with professional personnel. A professional worker is supposed to have autonomy over his own activities. This implies that the teacher should have considerable freedom in the manner in which he conducts his classes and in skills and knowledge which he imparts to his students. It is this built-in source of strain that in part accounts for the "social distance" that frequently exists between school principals and their teachers and for the charge—by teachers —that administrators upset "their" classes. The clash between the authority structure and the professional status of teachers is also undoubtedly reflected in the latent and overt opposition of teachers to the introduction of new educational practices.

A second source of strain derives from the differential norms held by teachers and students for the student's behavior. Gordon's analysis[12] of a high school suggests the differential frames of reference that may be operating in many classrooms. His analysis indicates that teachers expected students to perform in a manner that approximated their knowledge and ability potential. But students' expectations were in part based on the informal social structure and values of the students. He indicates that student stereotypes had an important influence on the "roles" students assigned each other and played themselves, and that these stereotypes therefore affected their role performance. When student-defined and teacher-defined roles and values were incompatible, the net result was strain for the teacher in his transactions with students.

Another contribution of a sociological perspective on classroom behavior is demonstrated by the current work of Lippitt and his associates at the University of Michigan on the "socially unaccepted" child in the classroom. In addition to showing the need for a typology of such children, their studies suggest the power group forces operating on the unaccepted child. The major barriers to changing his behavior may be in the classroom, rather than or in addition to forces within the child. This finding has important implications for teachers and also for school guidance practices which are usually based on the assumption that individual counseling is the only way to change a student's behavior. The observation that the attributes and stereotypes of classmates as well as the teacher are barriers to behavior changes is one demanding rigorous exploration.

In addition, sociological analysis strongly suggests that the attitudes and behavior of the individual are strongly linked to those groups to which he belongs or aspires. These reference groups constitute "anchoring points" which have to be considered in inducing changed behavior. For the classroom teacher, the important consequence of this observation is that to deal effectively with a child may require isolating group forces that are constraining his behavior and inducing changes in clique norms and values.

THE EXTERNAL ENVIRONMENT OF THE SCHOOL

A school system does not exist in a vacuum. Its existence and functioning depend in part on its outside world, its external environment. This sociological point of view has many implications for the analysis of school systems.

One implication is that changes in the larger social system of the community materially affect the composition of the student body in a school system, and therefore may require modifications in the curriculum. The heavy migration of the rural population in the South to metropolitan centers implies that many large city school systems need to undertake a critical review of the ability of their school program to meet the needs of the school's changed clientele. The empty school buildings in the center of many cities and the needed new school buildings in suburban areas, associated with the recent "flight to the suburbs," suggest the need for a metropolitan approach to school planning, a concept infrequently considered in education circles. In short, the educational implications of demographic studies require considerably greater attention by educators.

A second aspect of the external environment of public school systems to which sociologists have given considerable attention is the social class structure of communities. Studies in this area[13] reveal that most aspects of school functioning are influenced by social class phenomena. Research on social class strongly supports the notion that teacher grading practices and the criteria which teachers apply to children are related to the social class placement of the child and the teacher. The mobility aspirations of children, the drop-out rate, participation in extracurricular activites, dating behavior, and friendship patterns are in part accounted for by the socioeconomic characteristics of the child's family.

A third "external environment" factor that has important implications for the public schools is the power structure or structures of the community.[14] School systems absorb a large portion of the local tax dollar and the influence of informal and formal power agents in the community on educational budgetary decisions is without doubt a basic influence on the quality of the staff and the program of a school system. It is not surprising that national meetings of educational administrators usually have sessions devoted to "techniques for studying community power structure" and that sociologists are invited to participate in them.

A fourth contribution of sociology to the understanding of the external environment of the schools is the analysis of the basic link between the community and the schools—the school board. Charters has questioned the assumption, frequently found in the educational literature, that the disproportionate incidence of school board members from upper socioeconomic strata results in "a conservative bias" in public education.[15] Sociological research has demonstrated the impact of the behavior of school board members and of their motivation for seeking election to this position on the superintendent's job satisfaction and his job performance. The effect of such factors as religion, occupation, and income on the school board member's behavior as well as the pressures to which school administrators are exposed by their school boards have also been examined. These findings lead to the general conclusion that a crucial, but frequently neglected, variable influencing the operation of the school is the behavior of the small group of laymen who are its official policy-makers.[16] This conclusion has had many important ramifications, one of which is the National School Board Association's current effort to improve the "quality" of school board members.

A fifth sociological contribution emerges from the analysis of inter-role conflicts to which educational personnel are exposed as a consequence of their occupancy of positions in schools and in other social systems. Getzels and Guba[17] found that many of the expectations linked to the teacher's position conflict with other positions he occupies, and that some of these conflicts are a function of local school and community conditions.

The school superintendent's position is especially exposed to inter-role conflict. His job and the way he carries it out influence in some way virtually all members of the community. In dealing with him, members of his church, his personal friends, members of other organizations to which he may belong, and, of course, his wife and family, are inclined to identify him not only as a fellow church member, for example, but as a fellow church member who is at the same time the superintendent of schools.

Some unpublished findings of the School Executive Studies[18] shed light on the kinds of inter-role conflicts to which school superintendents are exposed. Twenty per cent of the superintendents reported that they faced incompatible expectations, deriving from their simultaneous occupancy of positions in the *educational and religious systems*. The formal leaders and certain members of their church expected them to act in one way regarding certain issues, while other individuals and groups expected contrary behavior. One Catholic superintendent said that he faced situations like this all the time:

> Sometimes, the situation gets pretty touchy. I want to keep good relations with the Church. Don't forget—most of my school committee members and the local politicans belong to my church. Take this for example: one of the Catholic groups wanted to let the kids out early from school. They were having some special meetings, and they wanted the kids to be there. I knew that wouldn't be right. It wasn't fair to the other kids. So what did I do? I refused to give an official o.k. to the request, but at the time I simply winked at it [letting them out early]. I would have offended them if I'd stopped the kids from going, and I just couldn't

afford to do that. It really left me bothered. Should I have stopped it? Legally, I could and I would have been right. But I know I would have had hell to pay.

Another superintendent, a Protestant, told the interviewer:

[My] minister wants all kinds of special favors because I am a member of his church. He expected me to turn over our gym to the church basketball team. He wanted me to support his idea of giving out a Bible to each public school child. He told me that he thought I ought to see that more of "our people" get jobs in the school. None of these are fair requests. I'm supposed to represent all the people, and I want to use the criterion of "what's best for the schools," not "what's best for my church." I might give him the gym, but it would be worth my job to give in on the Bibles in this community. I try not to play favorites, but sometimes it's hard to know what is the right thing to do.

Of perhaps as great personal and emotional significance to superintendents are the role conflicts arising from the expectations of their *personal friends* which are incompatible with those held by other individuals and groups in the community. Thirty-five percent of the superintendents reported conflicts of this kind.

Although some superintendents said that their "personal friends" expected special consideration in the areas of personnel decisions and the allocation of school contracts, more often the superintendents said that their friends expected special consideration for their children. These included requests that teachers be reprimanded for treating their children unfairly, that their children be transferred to a school in another district, that transportation be provided for children who are not entitled to it, that their children be promoted against the best judgment of the teacher and principal involved, and so on. Each of these "special consideration" expectations is incompatible with procedures and principles which the superintendent is expected to follow and which are set by the school board, by the teachers, and by PTA groups. Undoubtedly there are many requests of this kind which superintendents automatically ignore or refuse and which they did not mention in the interview; it is when these requests come from personal friends and when these friends expect the superintendent to make particular concessions, that the superintendents decribe them as "role conflict" situations.

One superintendent said:

[One of the] nastiest aspects of my job is bus transportation. Good friends of of mine have the nerve to telephone me, the superintendent of schools, and ask that a bus pick up their children, when they know, and I know, and the bus driver knows, that they live within the one-mile limit. I tell them I don't drive the bus. I'm just superintendent of schools. Talk to the bus driver. They think I'm saying okay, and I guess I am if you come right down to it. Someday I guess I'll get into trouble when someone who doesn't have the gall to come to me goes to the committee and says, "so and so, the superintendent's friend, has his kids picked up. Why can't I have mine?" It's all in the game and sometimes the game is rough.

A third role conflict situation frequently mentioned involved the *superintendency and the father positions.* Forty-eight per cent of the superintendents described conflicts of this type.

The superintendents reported a wide variety of situations in which their children expected one thing and others expected something quite different. One superintendent who was greatly troubled by problems in this area described his situation in this way:

> You know one of the worst things about this job that you never think of before you get into it is its effect on your children. You don't have time for your children. You have to be out every night and it just isn't fair to them. They don't like it; they resent it. And then the kids have a cross to bear. Either they get especially soft or especially rough treatment by the teachers. And the teachers are just waiting for you to throw your weight around.
>
> For example, my boy has told me certain things about one of his teachers—the way she behaves in the classroom. He's an honest youngster so I have no reason to doubt him, and if I were not the superintendent you can be darn sure I'd raise a lot of cain. But as the superintendent I'm not supposed to invade a teacher's classroom. So I try to support the teacher even though I know she is in the wrong. I feel pretty mean about this, but what else can I do? I hope my boy will understand the situation better later on.

Eighteen per cent of the superintendents mentioned inter-role conflicts stemming from incompatible expectations held for their behavior as a *member of a local community association and as the superintendent.* For example, in many communities certain local organizations to which the superintendent belonged expected him to allow them to use the time of students and staff to achieve their own organizational objectives, whereas the professional school staff expected him to protect the schools from this type of "invasion." School superintendents are exposed to requests for school children to be active in fund-raising activities, for the school band to play in parades, and for the schools to participate in youth activities. Local community groups expect the superintendent to facilitate their use of these school resources. On the other hand, many superintendents know that one of the major complaints of their faculty is that this type of activity frequently disrupts classroom activities and planned school programs. This constitutes a difficult area of decision making, especially when the organization in question has a powerful voice in community affairs.

These findings support the proposition that inter-role conflicts stemming from occupancy of positions in the school system and in the environment external to it constitute a basic source of potential stress for the educator.

SUMMARY

There are dangers to be avoided as well as benefits to be derived from the closer alignment between the fields of sociology and education. One of these dangers is to overgeneralize sociological research findings that apply to a single case or a small population to American education or American society when there is no logical basis for such induction. Sociologists as well as educators have erred in this respect. A second pitfall is the uncritical acceptance of unverified pronouncements of sociologists as verified propositions. There are many statements to be found in textbooks of educational sociology that are speculative in nature and which are not based on rigorous research evidence. Hunches and speculations need to be distinguished from verified propositions. A third danger is the acceptance of sociological research findings without critical examination of their assumptions, the adequacy of their research methods, and their conclusions. The literature on the influence of social class structure in American education is permeated with each of these, as well as other, pitfalls in the sociology-education mating process. The educational practitioner needs to be aware of these difficulties in his utilization of sociological analyses of educational problems.

These precautionary observations lead to the consideration of the major contribution of the sociologist to educational practitioners. The teacher or school administrator must constantly bear in mind that he is working in a complex environment in which many variables are at play. The forces are multidimensional and his environment, although it shares common features with the situation confronting other educational practitioners, has many unique features. The sociologist, however, usually defines his problem so that he is working with one or a few independent variables (for example, social class or leadership structure) and one dependent variable (for example, academic achievement or sociometric choice), and he attempts to control other variables that may be influencing the relationships he is investigating. Of necessity he must simplify his problem so he can deal with it. He usually assumes multiple causation but his methodological tools allow him to deal with only a very limited number of the forces that may account for the phenomena he is trying to explain. He never deals with *all* the variables that the practitioner probably needs to take into account in his decision-making. Further, the research findings of the sociologist may not be applicable to the particular set of conditions confronting the practitioner. Research findings based on a sample of suburban school systems may not hold for city school systems. These considerations lead to the following point of view about the sociologist's major contribution to the educational practitioner. What the sociologist has to offer is basically a series of sensitizing and analytic concepts and ideas based on theoretical and empirical analysis that will allow the practitioner to examine in a more realistic and more incisive way the multiple forces operating in his social environment. The sociologist cannot make the educational practitioner's decisions for him, nor can the sociologist's research findings based on one population be applied to any educational population indiscriminately. The practitioner's task is to assess the various forces that have a bearing on the achievement of his objectives, assign them relative weights, and make a decision based on these calculations. The basic sociological contribution is to add to the educator's kit of intellectual tools a set of sociological insights and concepts that will allow him to take account in his decision-making organizational, cultural, and interpersonal factors at work in his environment.

NOTES

1. For other perspectives and an examination of needed research in the sociology of education see Orville G. Brim, Jr., *Sociology and the Field of Education* (New York: Russell Sage Foundation, 1958), and Neal Gross, "The Sociology of Education," in Robert K. Merton, Leonard Broom, and Leonard S. Cottrell, Jr. (eds.), *Sociology Today* (New York: Basic Books, 1959).

2. Neal Gross, *Who Runs Our Schools?* (New York: Wiley, 1958), pp. 113–25.

3. *Ibid.,* pp. 45–60.

4. Neal Gross, Ward S. Mason, and Alexander W. McEachern, *Explorations in Role Analysis: Studies of the School Superintendency Role* (New York: Wiley, 1958), p. 124.

5. Melvin Seeman, "Role Conflict and Ambivalence in Leadership," *American Sociological Review,* 18 (August, 1953), pp. 373–80; also see Charles E. Bidwell, "The Administrative Role and Satisfaction in Teaching," *Journal of Educational Sociology,* 29 (September, 1955), pp. 41–47.

6. Talcott Parsons, "The School Class as a Social System: Some of Its Functions in American Society," *Harvard Educational Review,* 29 (Fall, 1959), pp. 297–318.

7. James S. Coleman, "Academic Achievement and the Structure of Competition," *Harvard Educational Review,* 29 (Fall, 1959), pp. 330–51.

8. C. Wayne Gordon, *The Social System of the High School: A Study in the Sociology of Adolescence* (Glencoe, Ill.: The Free Press, 1957).

9. Wilbur B. Brookover, "The Social Roles of Teachers and Pupil Achievement," *American Sociological Review,* 8 (August, 1943), pp. 389–93.

10. See Lloyd A. Cook, "An Experimental Sociographic Study of a Stratified 10th Grade Class," *American Sociological Review,* 10 (April, 1945), pp. 250–61; Otto H. Dahlke and Thomas O. Monahan, "Problems in the Application of Sociometry to Schools," *School Review,* 57 (April, 1949), pp. 223–34; Robert J. Havighurst and Bernice L. Neugarten, *Society and Education* (Boston: Allyn and Bacon, 1957); and August B. Hollingshead, *Elmtown's Youth* (New York: Wiley, 1949).

11. Merl E. Bonney, "Sociometric Study of Agreement between Teacher Judgments and Student Choices: In Regard to the Number of Friends Possessed by High School Students," *Sociometry,* 10 (May, 1947), pp. 133–46; and Norman E. Gronlund, "The Accuracy of Teachers' Judgments Concerning the Sociometric Status of Sixth-Grade Pupils," *Sociometry,* 13 (August, 1950), part I, pp. 197–225; part 2, pp. 329–57.

12. Gordon, *op. cit.*

13. For a summary of these studies see Wilbur B. Brookover, *A Sociology of Education* (New York: American Book Co., 1955); and Havighurst and Neugarten, *op. cit.* For a critical appraisal of some of this literature see Neal Gross, "Social Class Structure and American Education," *Harvard Educational Review,* 23 (Fall, 1953), pp. 298–329.

14. See, for example, Robert E. Agger, "Power Attributions in the Local Community," *Social Forces,* 34 (May, 1956), pp. 322–31; Floyd Hunter, *Community Power Structure: A Study of Decision Makers* (Chapel Hill: University of North Carolina Press, 1953); Peter Rossi, "Community Decision Making," *Administrative Science Quarterly,* 1 (March, 1957), pp. 415–41; and Robert O. Schulze, "The Role of Economic Dominants in Community Power Structure," *American Sociological Review,* 23 (February, 1958), pp. 3–9.

15. W. W. Charters, Jr., "Social Class Analysis and the Control of Public Education," *Harvard Educational Review,* 23 (Fall, 1953), pp. 268–83.

16. For a report of the specific findings leading to this conclusion, see Gross, *Who Runs Our Schools?, op. cit.*

17. J. W. Getzels and E. G. Guba, "The Structure of Roles and Role Conflict in the Teaching Situation," *Journal of Educational Sociology,* 29 (September, 1955), pp. 30–40.

18. For other findings of the School Executive Studies, see Gross, Mason, and McEachern, *op. cit.;* and Gross, *Who Runs Our Schools?, op. cit.*

3.   BURTON R. CLARK

Development of the Sociology
of Higher Education

My purposes here are to review the development to date of the sociological study of higher education and, upon that base, to assess the strengths and weaknesses of current research and to point the prospects for the future. The review is selective and the assessment biased by personal perception and preference. I would like to err in being open and catholic, since there are so many ways that sociological study of colleges and universities can render us more sensitive in coping with immediate problems as well as contribute to theory and method in sociology. But, in a limited essay, it is necessary to categorize roughly the work of the past and to highlight the more salient work. It is also realistic to face the fact of limited talent and resources as we turn to the future and to emphasize one or two perspectives that might best correct the defects of our current efforts.

THE PAST AND THE PRESENT

The emergence and substantial growth of a sociology of higher education have followed from the extensive educational expansion of the period since the end of World War II especially that of the last decade, in semi-developed and developed nations around the world. The higher learning became problematic to social analysts as it became more important to the general population as well as to economic and governmental elites. The move toward mass participation in higher education has strained the traditional internal ordering of educational affairs. New demands have caused great problems of adapting externally to fast-changing sectors of society. The various demands, new and old, often pull in opposite directions: a dynamic, advanced economy, fueled by governmental concern about national strength, presses for a rationalization of training while a highly-volatile culture of youth, fueled by the needs of the mass media and a youth industry, argues against such technical rationality, prefer-

Reprinted from *Sociology of Education,* 46 (Winter, 1973), pp. 2–14, by permission of the author and the American Sociological Association.

ring a logic of sentiment and identity. Such strains, seemingly basic and reflected in various conflicts and disturbances, have led scholars to turn with wonderment, and often with some anguish, to the serious study of their own world. The 1960s saw a revitalization of the study of education in economics, political science, history, organizational analysis—and sociology.

We need only to look back a few years to see how recent is our concern. In the United States, we have had colleges since colonial days and universities since the last quarter of the nineteenth century. General sociology developed about the turn of the century and was a viable enterprise with a number of sub-fields by the 1920s. But among the sub-fields the sociology of education was a fragile enterprise until at least the 1950s; and within it, thought and analysis centered on the elementary and secondary levels. In its early state, the field was called "Educational Sociology" and its main journal was *The Journal of Educational Sociology.* It was based in teachers colleges and the social foundations divisions of schools of education at the universities where its task was to aid in the preparation of teachers and administrators for the public schools. One historical review of sociological inquiry in education in the period 1917 to 1940 speaks of three sub-groups: a general sociology group, concerned with the development of sociology; a policy group, interested in setting educational values and effecting social reform through the training of teachers and administrators; and a social technology group, seeking to develop a practitioner role around technical prescription on educational methods (Richards, 1969). Not one of these groups was successful in developing a prominent position either within education or sociology; and, of note for our purposes, none paid serious attention to higher education. The proper subject matter was the school, not the college and university.

We may connect two types of pre-World War II literature to the modern sociology of higher education. For one, broad statements in sociology and anthropology offered an undifferentiated view of education of all levels and types as a means of cultural transmission, socialization, social control or social progress. (Durkheim, 1922; Cooley, 1956; Ross, 1928; Ward, 1906.) Of the broad approaches, Durkheim's seemingly conservative view of education as a dependent element in a slowly evolving web of institutions has been the most noted: education is "a collection of practices and institutions that have been organized slowly in the course of time, which are comparable with all the other social institutions and which express them, and which, therefore, can no more be changed at will than the structure of the society itself" (Durkheim, 1922:65). Such statements, elaborating the basic sociological truth of the interdependence of social institutions, now seem both more appropriate, in the round, for 1900 than 1970 and for the elementary school than the university. Their import lay in establishing the terms of discussion for a long period and even today they remain useful in recalling the specialist to the broadest conceptions of the social functions of education. Secondly, certain specific statements about higher education became established as classics but stood for decades in lonely isolation. The foremost instance in the basic theoretical literature is composed of Max Weber's statements on "Science as a Vocation" and "The 'Rationalization' of Education and Training," in which, following from his general insight on the rise of bureaucracy and specialization, he portrayed the tension between the generalist and the specialist—"the struggle of the 'specialist type of man' against the older type of 'cultivated man' "—as basic to many modern educational problems (Weber, 1936:243). In retrospect, a highly useful line of inquiry could have developed three or four decades ago from the Weberian perspective on education, bureaucracy, and culture; but instead we have a notable instance of discontinuity in social research. The second instance of the striking specific classical statement was Thorstein Veblen's angry blast at the influence of businessmen and their mentality in the control and administration of colleges and universities, in his *The Higher Learning in America,* originally published in 1918 (Veblen, 1954). Veblen apparently was not followed for thirty years, until Hubert P. Beck's work, *Men Who Control Our Universities,* appeared in 1947 (Beck, 1947). Noting this discontinuity, we can well wish that Veblen had taken apprentices or had attracted followers whose work in turn would have established momentum in the analysis of power and control in higher education. A third instance of work that stood by itself for a long time was Logan Wilson's dissertation on university professors, published in 1942 as *The Academic Man: A Study in the Sociology of a Profession* (Wilson, 1942). There was no follow-up on this promising topic for a decade and a half, until Caplow and McGee's *the Academic Marketplace,* 1958, and still today we do not have a book-length treatment of the university professor that is as serious and systematic as Wilson's effort of almost thirty years ago.

It is not until the 1960s that we discern a serious sociology of higher education in the sense of a sub-field with a steady flow of writing and a specialty in which students take training, pursue it for a number of years and accept a professional label. Two main directions of effort have become firmly institutionalized in these few short years, each representing a convergence of a sociological concern and a practical problem. The first stream is the study of inequality in education beyond the high school, particularly the search for the sources of inequality in social class, race, ethnicity, and sex. Inequality remains the root concern in the sociology of education around the world.

In American sociology, the basic field of stratification, concerned with class and race, was the base from which there developed a disciplined, empirically-minded thrust into the study of education. In the 1930s and 1940s, a series of now-classic community studies (Lynd, 1929, 1937; Warner, 1941; Hollingshead, 1949), dramatized the impact of social class on the mobility of the young in the elementary and secondary school, including who finished high school and thus qualified for college. This sociological concern developed in the 1950s and 1960s into a serious tradition of statistical analysis (for example, see the work of William Sewell and his students—Sewell, 1966, 1967) and this concern followed mass education up into the college level. We now have an extensive journal literature of the social determinants of aspiration and achievement that includes the collegiate as well as the secondary and elementary levels of education, with increasing refinement around the issues germane to open admission and differentiation of institutions and tracks within a mass system, for example, who goes to what kind of college and who completes the various degree levels. Here ideas on various overt and covert forms of channeling students and hence affecting seriously their social mobility have enlivened the literature and anticipated some current criticisms of schooling, for example, the cooling-out function of certain practices in colleges (Clark, 1960), the difference between sponsored and contest forms of formal selection in educational systems (Turner, 1968) and the effects of counselors' categories of thought as labels placed on the young (Cicourel and Kitsuse, 1963).

The second stream is the study of the effects of the college years on the character, belief, and thought of students. An early study here was T. M. Newcomb's analysis of the effect of Bennington College on its girls (Newcomb, 1943), a classic work in social psychology. The topic was picked up again in the 1950s when Nevitt Sanford and his associates attempted a longitudinal examination of personality development in Vassar girls, a study that was only weakly sociological (Sanford, 1962); and a group of Cornell sociologists compared the attitudes and values of students at eleven colleges and universities, noting some differences between public and private institutions in inputs and apparent effects (Goldsen, et al., 1960). Since 1960, there has been a rapidly growing body of sociological writing, beginning with the study of Howard Becker and colleagues on the subculture of medical students (Becker, et al., 1961) and the essay by Clark and Trow on types of undergraduate subcultures (see Newcomb and Wilson, 1966). Among the best studies reported later in the decade were the analysis of Becker, Geer, and Hughes of students' orientations to making the academic grade (1968) and the remarkable re-analysis of Bennington College by Newcomb a quarter century after his first study (1967). The study of life inside the campus and of its effects on the values, attitudes, and achievements of the student has become established rapidly, fueled by practical concerns of professors and administrators as well as the professional influence of senior investigators on colleagues and students. Research in this area also converges with that of psychologists who have been developing an even more extensive and intensive literature of the effect—or non-effect—of college on students (see Feldman and Newcomb, 1970).

Bordering on, and often converging with, this interest in student life is the late great concern with the causes of student disturbances. Stemming from the growing sense of academic crisis in the years since 1964, the writings on student unrest have come in waves from successively embattled campuses as all factions leaped to their pens and have been therefore long on ideology and short on research. This interest may yet find steady and creative academic bases in political sociology, for example, in the comparative study of student movements (Lipset, 1966; Martinelli and Cavalli, 1970), and in the study of student life as related to the organization and governance of the college and university (Yamamoto, 1968; Kruytbosch and Messinger, 1970). But militant student action is a highly volatile phenomenon—witness the relative quiet of 1970–71—and its academic pursuit remains unsteady. A concern that escalated rapidly with the front-page headlines also may subside rapidly if student news becomes relegated again to the page behind the want ads or is assigned low priority as a campus problem when such matters as finance and faculty rights come to the fore.

Beyond these two main lines of inquiry, each of which centers on students, we may note two additional efforts that are otherwise focused. One is the study of "academic man," or higher education as a profession. Here we have the early study of Logan Wilson, noted above; some thoughts by Riesman on academic disciplines as power groups (1956); the efforts of Lazarsfeld and Thielens in *The Academic Mind* to study social scientists in a time of crisis (1958); the reflections of Caplow and McGee on the vagaries of the academic marketplace (1958); the delineation by John D. Donovan of *The Academic Man in the Catholic College* (1964); and the current, largely unpublished work of Talcott Parsons and Gerald M. Platt on "The American Academic Profession." Work is going forward in this line in other countries; for example, the extensive investigation undertaken in the mid-1950s in West Germany, reported in Plessner (1956) and the study by Halsey and Trow of the academic man in Britain. Most past work in this line has been conceptually ad hoc; but since there is now a thriving sociology of occupations and professions, the study of academic man can play effectively against this literature, for example, on the strain between professional and bureaucratic orientations and the tensions common to the roles of professional men in complex organizations (cf. Clark, 1966).

The second subsidiary path takes the organizations of higher education as the units for study. Here conceptual leads have come from the literature on organization theory to which all the social sciences have contributed and the sociological field of complex organizations. The work includes the study of the dilemmas of the open door college (Clark, 1960); the analysis of university goals (Gross and Grambsch, 1968); the creation of new perspectives on academic authority and power, including that of a subculture of administrators (Lunsford, 1970; Baldridge, 1971); the tensions of public experimental colleges (Riesman, Gusfield, and Gamson, 1970); and developmental analysis of organizational character and institutional self-belief (Clark, 1970). The organizational studies commonly are case studies oriented to exploration and discovery rather than to validation. Varying in rigidity, they shade off into journalistic vignettes and the writings of administrators and students of higher education that are not particularly sociological in intent or style.

This line of inquiry also extends at a more macrocosmic level into the organizations of sets of colleges and universities, including national systems of higher education. Here our appetites were whetted early by the skillful and provocative essays of Joseph Ben David, the Israeli sociologist, on the effects of major structural differences among the systems of the most advanced industrial societies on flexibility, innovation and change (Ben David, 1962). Riesman has portrayed the rank-ordering and imitating propensities of the American system as a snake-like procession (Riesman, 1956); and Jencks and Riesman, within a wide-ranging description of the variety of colleges and universities in the American system, have interpreted the rise to power of professional scholars and scientists as the fundamental academic revolution of recent times (Jencks and Riesman, 1968). We have had an occasional illuminating country case study of a country outside of the advanced nations, as in Philip Foster's analysis of education and social status in Ghana (Foster; 1965). An educational literature on national systems has grown rapidly in the 1960s but much of it remains in the general terms of manpower need, quantitative educational expansion, and national planning. The surveys of national systems have at least provided basic descriptive information comparatively assembled, on an ever larger number of systems of higher education (e.g., OECD, 1970), providing a base for more conceptually-focused comparative inquiry.

THE FUTURE

Relatively young and unformed fields of study often are torn between intensive effort in one or two main lines of research and a desire to wander around testing the ground to find new and more sensitive approaches. The intensive effort allows us to refine empirically a few concepts and improve a few methods, with the possibility that we may finally pin something down. The wandering effort allows us to leapfrog from one idea to another, accelerating the conceptual game, with the possibility that we will come up with an exciting idea. These contradictory approaches are evident in the sociology of higher education and each, with its evident virtues, carries its own dangers for the decade or two ahead.

The first approach has the danger of an inbred tradition of work, with increasing tunnel vision riveted on the trivial. The two most established lines of research mentioned earlier, those of educational inequality and college impact, will face this danger in the 1970s. The study of educational inequality is fast becoming a detailed and technical business in which only a few analysts, equipped with the latest statistical techniques, are competent. A tricky and complex problem does indeed call for the greatest possible methodological sophistication. But down that road also comes the career devoted to improving the reliability and validity of instruments of highly specific application. Our colleagues in educational psychology can attest to the stultifying and deadend pitfalls of that particular academic procession.

In the study of college impact, we already have a relatively massive but trivial literature (cf. Feldman and Newcomb's review of 1500 studies). If at last we have stopped attempting to measure the effects of specific courses on students, we seemingly still are stuck with a commitment to measure ever more carefully the year-by-year effect of one college after another—or perhaps several hundred of them simultaneously—on a host of specific attitudes. But the effort to sort out the determinants and the outcomes, particularly to comprehend the interactions between student inputs and campus structures, is increasingly costly in time and money. Is it worth it? Is it worth it for social science? It is helpful to stand back and recall that a fundamental if not the basic effect of college is to make college graduates out of high school graduates. Here the change is one hundred per cent in the surviving cohort: none of those entering college but all those receiving the degree are socially defined as college graduates. As John Meyer has put it, this is what colleges socially are chartered to do, to alter social statuses with this particular self- and public definition (Meyer, 1972). The consequences of the definition are enormous. In Meyer's terms: "Whether or not the student has learned anything—[and, we might add, become a little less religious or a little more liberal]—his job prospects, income potential, access to political and civil service positions, marital prospects, and other opportunities, are greatly altered" (Meyer, 1972:110). Here the fundamental sociological thesis is that college effects occur primarily not at the level of attitudes and values but in the allocation of statuses and roles. This plausible argument should give some pause to those who would spend research fortunes on highly sophisticated, five-year, input-throughput-output analyses of small changes in specific values. In any event, the more sustained lines of work in the sociology of higher education already need this kind of direct challenging of their relative importance and possible contribution.

The second approach, that of the wandering analytical gypsy, will carry in the 1970s the danger of a game of vignettes. For many of us, it is more fun to go find another interesting case about which to write an interpretive story than to plug along in one vein seeking replication or the hard data of comparison. The result of drifting too far in this direction is a maximum of zig and zag, a minimum of accumulation, and even a reduction of scholarly discipline to journalistic play. The temptation is to be clever, even sardonic: The provocative phrase, rather than the truth, will set us free. Thus we are right on one page and wrong on the next and only a few informed people are able to distinguish the one from the other. We shall see much of this form of quasi-sociological writing in the 1970s and what at one time is a fresh and useful ethnography can become a tiresome description of an endless number of tribes and a tangle of uncorrected interpretations. The ethnography will need conceptual focus and the hard criticism of those who insist on some systematic data.

The research of the 1970s clearly will include much comparative analysis, in line with the general drift of sociology toward comparative study, a development that should help correct the myopia that comes from too many days spent on scale reliability or on vignettes of the American college. The comparative work will entail a variety of analytical interests, for example, inequalities in access, student life, institutional resilience and change, and governance and management of national systems. We also will gain from more historical investigation. The written history of higher education has been improving rapidly (cf. Hofstadter and Metzger, 1955; Rudolph, 1962; Veysey, 1965); there are young scholars who seem equally at home in sociology and history; and general sociology is clearly no longer uncomfortable with historical perspectives and materials. Historical studies instruct us about educational systems of the past, connections between educational trends and change in other sectors of society, and, most important for sociologists, the past-to-present development of existing systems. Developmental analysis carried out over decades of time can highlight fundamental institutional trajectories and hence suggest the potentialities and limitations of current institutional forms as they face new demands.

As one attempts to estimate the future for the lines of inquiry identified above, a latent common problem in approach and perspective becomes more manifest: how can the sociology of higher education take cues from, and make returns to, the concerns of educational practitioners without becoming a managerial sociology? It is not that we are so easily bought but that we are so much involved. Since education prepares the young for later life and professor-researchers are part of the training corps, we tend to perceive and define education in instrumental terms. Like administrators and reformers, we want to know who gets in and who gets out, what the students have learned and whether their personal character has been affected. Educational questions not only too easily set the sociological questions, but they also become voiced around immediate needs of administration and public policy, for example, what specific issues are disturbing the students and hence what manipulations of structure and procedure will be advantageous? Even when our attitude is critical of present practice, we are still in the stance of defining the ends of educational work and arranging practices to be effective means to those ends.

One way to contain this tendency in part is to see higher education through the definitions presented by students and other subordinate actors, an approach practiced by Howard Becker and others in the symbolic interaction school of thought. A second way is to play against instrumental terms by seeking the expressive aspects of the system. Though colleges and universities begin as purposive formal organizations, they become, in varying degree, social institutions heavy with affect and non-rational involvement. For faculty and administrators, there are loyalties and life-styles of the employing institution and the national discipline. For students, there are the feelings of group attachment or detachment that are constructed in the meeting of personal and institutional character. Research on attitudes and values of students and professors catches some of the personal side of expressive phenomena. What lags is research on institutional and system capacities to embody certain values in the thought and life styles of an evolving group. Macro-system analysis need not be limited to inputs and outputs and managerial manipulation of administrative structure. Compared to most other classes of complex organizations, colleges and universities apparently have a high propensity to order themselves through normative bonds and emotional commitment. We move toward a fuller understanding of their nature as we bring into view their variations as systems that at a given time are ends in themselves. We seek then for the evolution of value systems that give meaning to the lives of participants. We seek how the organized social system unconsciously absorbs the individual into a collectivity, promoting personal satisfaction in return. We seek group and institutional identities.

In historical connection, the present natural interest in effective delivery of educational services links well with the Weberian interest in bureaucratic rationality and the role of education in the certification of training. The corrective perspective emphasized here, in contrast, is rooted more in the Durkheimian concern with the role of morality and sentiment in social order. Durkheim saw schools as miniature societies that have their own particular moralities, ones developed over time as institutional character emerges as a reaction to institutional function. If colleges and universities as well as schools are places where society recreates (and develops) itself in the young, then their values, traditions, and collective identities appropriately can be placed at the center of sociological attention.

REFERENCES

Astin, A. "The methodology of research on college impact," Part One and Part Two. *Sociology of Education* 1970, 43, 3 and 4:223–254, 437–448.

Baldridge, J. V. *Power and Conflict in the University.* New York: Wiley, 1970.

Beck, H. P. *Men Who Control Our Universities.* New York: King's Crown Press, 1947.

Becker, H. S., B. Geer, E. C. Hughes, and A. L. Strauss. *Boys in White: Student Culture in Medical School.* Chicago: University of Chicago Press, 1961.

Becker, H. S., B. Geer, and E. C. Hughes. *Making the Grade: The Academic Side of College Life.* New York: Wiley, 1968.

Ben David, J., and A. Sloczower. "Universities and academic systems in modern societies." *European Journal of Sociology,* 1962, 3:45–84.

Caplow, T., and R. J. McGee. *The Academic Marketplace.* New York: Basic Books, 1958.

Cicourel, A. V., and J. I. Kitsuse. *The Educational Decision-makers.* Indianapolis: Bobbs-Merrill, 1963.

Clark, B. R. *The Open Door College.* New York: McGraw-Hill, 1960.

———. "Organizational adaptation to professionals," in H. M. Vollmer and D. L. Mills (eds.), *Professionalization.* Englewood Cliffs, N.J.: Prentice-Hall, 1966, 282–291.

———. *The Distinctive College: Antioch, Reed, and Swarthmore.* Chicago: Aldine, 1970.

Cooley, C. H. *Two Major Works: Social Organization* and *Human Nature and the Social Order.* Glencoe, Illinois: The Free Press, 1956 (originally published in 1909 and 1902).

Donovan, J. D. *The Academic Man in the Catholic College.* New York: Sheed and Ward, 1964.

Durkheim, E. *Education and Society.* Translated by Sherwood D. Fox. Glencoe, Illinois: The Free Press, 1956 (originally published in 1922).

Feldman, K. A., and T. M. Newcomb. *The Impact of College on Students.* Vols. 1 and 2. San Francisco: Jossey-Bass, 1970.

Foster, P. *Education and Social Change in Ghana.* Chicago: University of Chicago Press, 1965.

Goldsen, K., and M. Rosenberg, R. M. Williams, and E. A. Suchman. *What College Students Think.* New York: D. Van Nostrand Co., Inc., 1960.

Gross, E. G., and P. V. Grambsch. *University Goals and Academic Power.* Washington, D.C.: American Council on Education, 1968.

Halsey, A. H., and M. A. Trow. *The British Academics.* Cambridge, Mass.: Harvard University Press, 1971.

Hofstadter, R., and W. P. Metzger. *The Development of Academic Freedom in the United States.* New York: Columbia University Press, 1955.

Hollingshead, A. B. *Elmtown's Youth.* New York: Wiley, 1959.

Jencks, C., and D. Riesman. *The Academic Revolution.* Garden City, N.Y.: Doubleday & Co., Inc., 1968.

Kruytbosch, C. E., and S. L. Messinger (eds.). *The State of the University: Authority and Change.* Beverly Hills, Calif.: Sage Publications, 1970.

Lazarsfeld, P. F., and W. Thielens, Jr. *The Academic Mind.* New York: The Free Press of Glencoe, 1958.

Lipset, S. M. (ed.). Special Issue on Student Politics, *Comparative Education Review,* 1966, 10 (June).

Lunsford, F. "Authority and ideology in the administered university," in C. E. Kuytbosch and S. L. Messinger (eds.), *The State of the University: Authority and Change.* Beverly Hills, Calif.: Sage Publications, 1970.

Lynd, S., and H. M. Lynd. *Middletown.* New York: Harcourt, Brace, 1929.

———. *Middletown in Transition.* New York: Harcourt, Brace, 1937.

Martinelli, A., and A. Cavalli. "Toward a Conceptual Framework for the Comparative Analysis of Student Movements." Paper presented at 7th World Congress of Sociology, Varna, Bulgaria, 1970.

Meyer, J. W. "The effects of the institutionalization of colleges in society," in K. A. Feldman (ed.), *College and Student: Selected Readings in the Social Psychology of Higher Education.* New York: Pergamon, 1972, 109–126.

Newcomb, T. M. *Personality and Social Change.* New York: Dryden, 1943.

Newcomb, T. M., and E. K. Wilson (eds.). *College Peer Groups.* Chicago, Aldine, 1966.

Newcomb, T. M., K. E. Koenig, R. Flacks, and D. P. Warwick. *Persistence and Change: Bennington College and Its Students After Twenty-Five Years.* New York: Wiley, 1967.

OECD (Organisation for Economic Co-operation and Development). *Development of Higher Education, 1950–1967. Statistical Survey.* Paris: OECD, 1970.

Parsons, T., and G. M. Platt. "The American Academic Profession: A Pilot Study." Unpublished paper, 1969.

Plessner, H. (ed.). *Untersuchungen zur Lage der Deutschen Hochschullehrer.* Gottingen: Vandenhoeck und Ruprescht.

Richards, R. R. "Perspectives on Sociological Inquiry in Education, 1917–1940." Unpublished Ph.D. dissertation. University of Wisconsin, 1969.

Riesman, D. *Constraint and Variety in American Education.* Lincoln, Nebraska: University of Nebraska Press, 1956.

Riesman, D., J. Gusfield, and Z. Gamson. *Academic Values and Mass Education: The Early Years of Oakland and Monteith.* Garden City, N.Y.: Doubleday, 1970.

Ross, E. *Social Control.* New York: Macmillan, 1928 (originally published in 1901).

Rudolph, F. *The American College and University.* New York: Alfred A. Knopf, 1962.

Sanford, N. (ed.). *The American College.* New York: Wiley, 1962.

Sewell, W. H., and J. M. Armer. "Neighborhood context and college plans." *American Sociological Review,* 1966, 31:159–168.

Sewell, W. H., and V. P. Shah. "Socioeconomic status, intelligence, and the attainment of higher education." *Sociology of Education,* 1967, 40:1–23.

Turner, Ralph H. "Sponsored and contest mobility and the school system." *American Sociological Review,* 1960, 25:855–867.

Veblen, T. *The Higher Learning in America.* Stanford, Calif.: Academic Reprints, 1954 (originally published in 1918).

Veysey, L. R. *The Emergence of the American University.* Chicago: University of Chicago Press, 1965.

Ward, L. F. *Applied Sociology.* Boston: Ginn & Co., 1906.

Warner, W. L., and P. S. Lunt. *The Social Life of a Modern Community.* New Haven: Yale University Press, 1941.

Weber, M. *From Max Weber: Essays in Sociology.* Translated and edited by H. H. Gerth and C. Wright Mills. New York: Oxford, 1946.

Wilson, L. *The Academic Man: A Study in the Sociology of a Profession.* New York: Oxford, 1942.

Yamamoto, K. (ed.). *The College Student and His Culture: An Analysis.* Boston: Houghton Mifflin, 1968.

Part II

Some Functions of Education

Chapter Two

Social Selection: Determinants of Educational Aspiration and Attainment

One extensively used mode of analysis in sociological inquiry is to approach a social institution with the question: "What functions does this institution perform both for the society and for individuals, and what is its relationship to other social institutions?" Thus, a major function of the family is seen to be the regulation of sexual activity and the socialization of the young; similarly, political institutions function as a means of collective decision-making and a mechanism of social control. Addressing ourselves to the functions of education is simply a matter of extending this functional orientation to the institution of education.

While a number of educational functions have been enumerated, they have not all received an equal amount of research attention. For example, the role of education in transmitting the culture from one generation to the next has been extensively noted but relatively little research has been devoted to this topic.[1] Likewise, only modest attention has been paid to the innovative function of education—the process whereby new knowledge is created and added to the culture.[2] Consequently, these two sometimes conflicting functions of education—culture transmission and innovation—remain relatively unexplored.

What has been called the "social selection and allocation" function of education has received an extensive amount of attention from sociologists. In modern industrial societies the task of allocating persons to occupational roles and levels of the stratification system has become one of the major functions of educational institutions. Indeed, education has come to play a primary role in determining the destination of individuals in the class structure. Since university training has become a crucial determinant of occupational and class destination, sociological research in this area has focused on determinants of access to higher education.

On what basis is social selection for higher education made? The egalitarian ideology of western democratic societies implies that schools will select, process, and allocate their students on the basis of achieved rather than ascribed qualities, for example, on the basis of such characteristics as intellectual ability, achievement, and promise rather than social class background. A large number of studies conducted over a number of years in a variety of geographic areas have consistently demonstrated the importance of such factors as sex, social class background, rural-urban residence, ability, and peer group influences as major determinants of the educational aspiration and attainment of high school youth. That is, boys are more likely than are girls to aspire to and attend college; the higher a student's social class background the more likely he (or she) is to plan on and attend college; students from larger urban areas are more likely to plan on and attend college than are those from small towns and rural areas; the higher a student's measured intelligence and academic performance in high school the more likely the student is to plan to go to college and actually to do so; and students whose friends plan to go to college are more likely to aspire to and attend college themselves than are those whose friends do not plan on college. While ability (as measured by intelligence and school performance) is itself related to educational aspiration and attainment, it has been found that among students of *comparable* ability, such factors as sex, social class background, rural-urban residence, and peer influence continue to be related to educational aspirations in the manner described above.

Thus, aspiration for higher education is clearly patterned. The chances of acquiring a college education (and, perhaps more importantly, gaining access to the more prestigious and better-paying jobs that accrue to the college-trained person) are clearly *unequally* distributed in society. They are to a great extent a consequence of the accidents of birth—one's sex, the position of one's family in the social class structure, and the size of the community in which one is reared.

Findings such as these have given rise to concern about "talent loss" or "talent wastage" in the educational system. What is referred to by these terms is the fact that we are in all likelihood under-educating vast numbers of highly able rural and working class youth. The implication is that acquisition of a college education by these young people would represent not only a personal but also a social gain in the sense of a greater pool of trained manpower and a higher level of productivity.

Women constitute a special topic of concern in any discussion of talent loss and waste. As a result of the failure of many young women of substantial intellectual ability to acquire a college education and the failure of many if not most college-trained women to utilize their education directly, women may represent the largest single source of talent loss. The sources of this phenomenon lie deep in the values and appropriate sex-role conceptions of American culture. Despite the fact that young women today are more likely to plan on an occupational career outside the home than they were two generations ago, the commitment to the traditional wife-and-mother role rather than to a career remains strong. When women do work, either full-time prior to marriage or after their children are in school, it is typically in those occupations culturally defined as appropriate for women, such as nursing, teaching, social work, or minor clerical tasks. In contrast to many societies, particularly those of Eastern and Central Europe, few women enter professional and managerial occupations. In other words, our cultural conception of "women's place" and "woman's work" is in itself an underlying source of talent loss.

The articles in this chapter include both theoretical discussions and representative examples of the research that has been done on the relationship of the above-mentioned variables to the educational aspiration and attainment of youth.

The first article in this chapter is a theoretical discussion of the relationship between educational institutions and cultural norms about social mobility. Distinguishing between "sponsored" and "contest" mobility, Turner deals with the way in which the social selection function of educational systems is performed in England and the United States.

In the second article Sewell summarizes the findings of one of the major studies of educational aspiration and attainment conducted in the United States and discusses its policy implications for the issue of equal opportunity for access to higher education. Although this article deals with one study it should be emphasized that the findings summarized here are typical of those reported in dozens of comparable studies conducted over a number of years and in a variety of communities and states.

The third selection in this chapter deals with the issue of peer influence in the educational aspiration process. Using data from their study of Canadian high school students, Pavalko and Bishop demonstrate that while peer influence on aspiration for a college education exists, the magnitude of this influence is different for males and females and for students of different ability levels and socioeconomic backgrounds.

Clearly, not all those who aspire to a higher education are able to attain it, and many students who enter college are unable to complete their education. Given an educational system influenced by the norm of "contest mobility" described by Turner, there are both winners and losers in the competition for higher education. Thus, institutions of higher education have come to perform the function of assisting losers in the competition to adapt to failure. In the final article of this chapter Clark identifies the "junior" or "community" college as one such institution and elaborates and discusses some of the mechanisms that exist to facilitate this adaptation and minimize the consequent stress for both students and the educational system.

NOTES

1. See Burton R. Clark, *Educating the Expert Society,* San Francisco: Chandler Publishing Company, 1962, Chapter 1.
2. A notable exception is Fritz Machlup, *The Production and Distribution of Knowledge in the United States,* Princeton, N.J.: Princeton University Press, 1962.

4. RALPH H. TURNER

Sponsored and Contest Mobility and the School System

This paper suggests a framework for relating certain differences between American and English systems of education to the prevailing norms of upward mobility in each country. Others have noted the tendency of educational systems to support prevailing schemes of stratification, but this discussion concerns specifically the manner in which the *accepted mode of upward mobility* shapes the school system directly and indirectly through its effects on the values which implement social control.

Reprinted from *American Sociological Review,* 25 (December, 1960), pp. 855–67, by permission of the author and the American Sociological Association.

This is an expanded version of a paper presented at the Fourth World Congress of Sociology, 1959, and abstracted in the *Transactions* of the Congress. Special indebtedness should be expressed to Jean Floud and Hilde Himmelweit for helping to acquaint the author with the English school system.

Two ideal-typical normative patterns of upward mobility are described and their ramifications in the general patterns of stratification and social control are suggested. In addition to showing relationships among a number of differences between American and English schooling, the ideal-types have broader implications than those developed in this paper: they suggest a major dimension of stratification which might be profitably incorporated into a variety of studies in social class; and they readily can be applied in further comparisons between other countries.

THE NATURE OF ORGANIZING NORMS

Many investigators have concerned themselves with rates of upward mobility in specific countries or internationally,[1] and with the manner in which school systems facilitate or impede such mobility.[2] But preoccupation with the *extent* of mobility has precluded equal attention to the predominant *modes* of mobility. The central assumption underlying this paper is that within a formally open class system that provides for mass education the organizing folk norm which defines the accepted mode of upward mobility is a crucial factor in shaping the school system, and may be even more crucial than the extent of upward mobility. In England and the United States there appear to be different organizing folk norms, here termed *sponsored mobility* and *contest mobility,* respectively. *Contest* mobility is a system in which elite[3] status is the prize in an open contest and is taken by the aspirants' own efforts. While the "contest" is governed by some rules of fair play, the contestants have wide latitude in the strategies they may employ. Since the "prize" of successful upward mobility is not in the hands of an established elite to give out, the latter cannot determine who shall attain it and who shall not. Under *sponsored* mobility elite recruits are chosen by the established elite or their agents, and elite status is *given* on the basis of some criterion of supposed merit and cannot be *taken* by any amount of effort or strategy. Upward mobility is like entry into a private club where each candidate must be "sponsored" by one or more of the members. Ultimately the members grant or deny upward mobility on the basis of whether they judge the candidate to have those qualities they wish to see in fellow members.

Before elaborating this distinction, it should be noted that these systems of mobility are ideal types designed to clarify observed differences in the predominantly similar English and American systems of stratification and education. But as organizing norms these principles are assumed to be present at least implicitly in people's thinking, guiding their judgments of what is appropriate on many specific matters. Such organizing norms do not correspond perfectly with the objective characteristics of the societies in which they exist, nor are they completely independent of them. From the complex interplay of social and economic conditions and ideologies people in a society develop a highly simplified conception of the way in which events take place. This conception of the "natural" is translated into a norm—the "natural" becomes what "ought" to be—and in turn imposes a strain toward consistency upon relevant aspects of the society. Thus the norm acts back upon the objective conditions to which it refers and has ramifying effects upon directly and indirectly related features of the society.[4]

In brief, the conception of an ideal-typical organizing norm involves the following propositions: (1) The ideal types are not fully exemplified in practice since they are normative systems, and no normative system can be devised so as to cope with all empirical exigencies. (2) Predominant norms usually compete with less ascendant norms engendered by changes and inconsistencies in the underlying social structure. (3) Though not fully explicit, organizing folk norms are reflected in specific value judgments. Those judgments which the relevant people regard as having a convincing ring to them, irrespective of the logic expressed, or which seem to require no extended argumentation may be presumed to reflect the prevailing folk norms. (4) The predominant organizing norms in one segment of society are functionally related to those in other segments.

Two final qualifications concerning the scope of this paper: First, the organizing folk norm of upward mobility affects the school system because one of the latter's functions is the facilitation of mobility. Since this is only one of several social functions of the school, and not the most important function in the societies under examination, only a very partial accounting of the whole set of forces making for similarities and differences in the school systems of United States and England is possible here. Only those differences which directly or indirectly reflect the performance of the mobility function are noted. Second, the concern of this paper is with the current dynamics of the situation in the two countries rather than with their historical development.

DISTINCTIONS BETWEEN THE TWO NORMS

Contest mobility is like a sporting event in which many compete for a few recognized prizes. The contest is judged to be fair only if all the players compete on an equal footing. Victory must be won solely by one's own efforts. The most satisfactory outcome is not necessarily a victory of the most able, but of the most deserving. The tortoise who defeats the hare is a folk-prototype of the deserving sportsman. Enterprise, initiative, perseverance, and craft are admirable qualities if they allow the person who is initially at a disadvantage to triumph. Even clever manipulation of the rules may be admired if it helps the contestant who is smaller or less muscular or less rapid to win. Applied to mobility, the contest norm means that victory by a person of moderate intelligence accomplished through the use of common sense, craft, enterprise, daring, and successful risk-taking[5] is more appreciated than victory by the most intelligent or the best educated.

Sponsored mobility, in contrast, rejects the pattern of the contest and favors a controlled selection process. In this process the elite or their agents, deemed to be best qualified to judge merit, choose individuals for elite status who have the appropriate qualities. Individuals do not win or seize elite status; mobility is rather a process of sponsored induction into the elite.

Pareto had this sort of mobility in mind when he suggested that a governing class might dispose of persons potentially dangerous to it by admitting them to elite membership, provided that the recruits change character by adopting elite attitudes and interests.[6] Danger to the ruling class would seldom be the major criterion for choice of elite recruits. But Pareto assumed that the established elite would select whom they wished to enter their ranks and would inculcate the attitudes and interests of the established elite in the recruits.

The governing objective of contest mobility is to give elite status to those who earn it, while the goal of sponsored mobility is to make the best use of the talents in society by sorting persons into their proper niches. In different societies the conditions of competitive struggle may reward quite different attributes, and sponsored mobility may select individuals on the basis of such diverse qualities as intelligence or visionary capability, but the difference in principle remains the same.[7]

Under the contest system society at large establishes and interprets the criteria of elite status. If one wishes to have his status recognized he must display certain credentials which identify his class to those about him. The credentials must be highly visible and require no special skill for their assessment, since credentials are presented to the masses. Material possession and mass popularity are altogether appropriate credentials in this respect, and any special skill which produces a tangible product and which can easily be assessed by the untrained will do. The nature of sponsored mobility precludes these procedures, but assigns to credentials instead the function of identifying elite members to one another.[8] Accordingly, the ideal credentials are special skills that require the trained discrimination of the elite for their recognition. In this case, intellectual, literary, or artistic excellencies, which can be appraised only by those trained to appreciate them, are fully suitable credentials. Concentration on such skills lessens the likelihood that an interloper will succeed in claiming the right to elite membership on grounds of the popular evaluation of his competence.

In the sporting event there is special admiration for the slow starter who makes a dramatic finish, and many of the rules are designed to insure that the race should not be declared over until it has run its full course. Contest mobility incorporates this disapproval of premature judgments and of anything that gives special advantage to those who are ahead at any point in the race. Under sponsored mobility, fairly early selection of only the number of persons necessary to fill anticipated vacancies in the elite is desirable. Early selection allows time to prepare the recruits for their elite position. Aptitudes, inherent capacities, and spiritual gifts can be assessed fairly early in life by techniques ranging from divination to the most sophisticated psychological test, and the more naive the subjects at the time of selection the less likely are their talents to be blurred by differential learning or conspiracy to defeat the test. Since elitists take the initiative in training recruits, they are more interested in the latters' capabilities than in what they will do with them on their own, and they are concerned that no one else should first have an opportunity to train the recruits' talents in the wrong direction. Contest mobility tends to delay the final award as long as practicable to permit a fair race; sponsored mobility tends to place the time of recruitment as early in life as practicable to insure control over selection and training.

Systems of sponsored mobility develop most readily in societies with but a single elite or with a recognized elite hierarchy. When multiple elites compete among themselves the mobility process tends to take the contest pattern, since no group is able to command control of recruitment. Sponsored mobility further depends upon a social structure that fosters monopoly of elite credentials. Lack of such monopoly undercuts sponsorship and control of the recruitment process. Monopoly of credentials in turn is typically a product of societies with well entrenched traditional aristocracies employing such credentials as family line and bestowable title which are intrinsically subject to monopoly, or of societies organized on large-scale bureaucratic lines permitting centralized control of upward social movement.

English society has been described as the juxtaposition of two systems of stratification, the urban industrial class system and the surviving aristocratic system. While the sponsored mobility pattern reflects the logic of the latter, our impression is that it pervades popular thinking rather than merely coexisting with the logic of industrial stratification. Patterns imported into an established culture tend to be reshaped, as they are assimilated, into consistency with the established culture. Thus it may be that changes in stratification associated with industrialization have led to alterations in the rates, the specific means, and the rules of mobility, but that these changes have been guided by the but lightly challenged organizing norm of sponsored mobility.

SOCIAL CONTROL AND THE TWO NORMS

Every society must cope with the problem of maintaining loyalty to its social system and does so in part through norms and values, only some of which vary by class position. Norms and values especially prevalent within a given class must direct behavior into channels that support the total system, while those that transcend strata must support the general class differential. The way in which upward mobility takes place determines in part the kinds of norms and values that serve the indicated purposes of social control in each class and throughout the society.

The most conspicuous control problem is that of ensuring loyalty in the disadvantaged classes toward a system in which their members receive less than a proportional share of society's goods. In a system of contest mobility this is accomplished by a combination of futuristic orientation, the norm of ambition, and a general sense of fellowship with the elite. Each individual is encouraged to think of himself as competing for an elite position so that loyalty to the system and conventional attitudes are cultivated in the process of preparation for this possibility. It is essential that this futuristic orientation be kept alive by delaying a sense of final irreparable failure to reach elite status until attitudes are well established. By thinking of himself in the successful future the elite aspirant forms considerable identification with elitists, and evidence that they are merely ordinary human beings like himself helps to reinforce this identification as well as to keep alive the conviction that he himself may someday succeed in like manner. To forestall rebellion among the disadvantaged majority, then, a contest system must avoid absolute points of selection for mobility and immobility and must delay clear recognition of the realities of the situation until the individual is too committed to the system to change radically. A futuristic orientation cannot, of course, be inculcated successfully in all members of lower strata, but sufficient internalization of a norm of ambition tends to leave the unambitious as individual deviants and to forestall the latters' formation of a genuine subcultural group able to offer collective threat to the established system. Where this kind of control system operates rather effectively it is notable that organized or gang deviancy is more likely to take the form of an attack upon the conventional or moral order rather than upon the class system itself. Thus the United States has its "beat-niks"[9] who repudiate ambition and most worldly values and its delinquent and criminal gangs who try to evade the limitations imposed by conventional means,[10] but very few active revolutionaries.

These social controls are inappropriate in a system of sponsorship since the elite recruits are chosen from above. The principal threat to the system would lie in the existence of a strong group, the members of whom sought to *take* elite positions themselves. Control under this system is maintained by training the "masses" to regard themselves as relatively incompetent to manage society, by restricting access to the skills and manners of the elite, and by cultivating belief in the superior competence of the elite. The earlier that selection of the elite recruits is made, the sooner others can be taught to accept their inferiority and to make "realistic" rather than fantasy plans. Early selection prevents raising the hopes of large numbers of people who might otherwise become the discontented leaders of a class challenging the sovereignty of the established elite. If it is assumed that the difference in competence between masses and elite is seldom so great as to support the usual differences in the advantages accruing to each,[11] then the differences must be artificially augmented by discouraging acquisition of elite skills by the masses. Thus a sense of mystery about the elite is a common device for supporting in the masses the illusion of a much greater hiatus of competence than in fact exists.

While elitists are unlikely to reject a system that benefits them, they must still be restrained from taking such advantage of their favorable situation as to jeopardize the entire elite. Under the sponsorship system the elite recruits —who are selected early, freed from the strain of competitive struggle, and kept under close supervision—may be thoroughly indoctrinated in elite culture. A norm of paternalism toward inferiors may be inculcated, a heightened sensitivity to the good opinion of fellow-elitists and elite recruits may be cultivated, and the appreciation of the more complex forms of aesthetic, literary, intellectual, and sporting activities may be taught. Norms of courtesy and altruism easily can be maintained under sponsorship since elite recruits are not required to compete for their standing and since the elite may deny high standing to those who strive for position by "unseemly" methods. The system of sponsorship provides an almost perfect setting for the development of an elite culture characterized by a sense of responsibility for "inferiors" and for preservation of the "finer things" of life.

Elite control in the contest system is more difficult since there is no controlled induction and apprenticeship. The principal regulation seems to lie in the insecurity of elite position. In a sense there is no "final arrival" because each person may be displaced by newcomers throughout his life. The limited control of high standing from above prevents the clear delimitation of levels in the class system, so that success itself becomes relative: each success, rather than an accomplishment, serves to qualify the participant for competition at the next higher level.[12] The restraints upon the behavior of a person of high standing, therefore, are principally those applicable to a contestant who must not risk the "ganging up" of other contestants, and who must pay some attention to the masses who are frequently in a position to impose penalties upon him. But any special norm of paternalism is hard to establish since there is no dependable procedure for examining the means by which one achieves elite credentials. While mass esteem is an effective brake upon overexploitation of position, it rewards scrupulously ethical and altruistic behavior much less than evidence of fellow-feeling with the masses themselves.

Under both systems, unscrupulous or disreputable persons may become or remain members of the elite, but for different reasons. In contest mobility, popular tolerance of a little craftiness in the successful newcomer, together with the fact that he does not have to undergo the close scrutiny of the old elite, leaves considerable leeway for unscrupulous success. In sponsored mobility, the unpromising recruit reflects unfavorably on the judgments of his sponsors and threatens the myth of elite omniscience; consequently he may be tolerated and others may "cover up" for his deficiencies in order to protect the unified front of the elite to the outer world.

Certain of the general values and norms of any society reflect emulation of elite values by the masses. Under sponsored mobility, a good deal of the protective attitudes toward and interest in classical subjects percolates to the masses. Under contest mobility, however, there is not the same degree of homogeneity of moral, aesthetic, and intellectual values to be emulated, so that the conspicuous attribute of the elite is its high level of material consumption —emulation itself follows this course. There is neither effective incentive nor punishment for the elitist who fails to interest himself in promoting the arts or literary excellence, or who continues to maintain the vulgar manners and mode of speech of his class origin. The elite has relatively less power and the masses relatively more power to punish or reward a man for his adoption or disregard of any special elite culture. The great importance of accent and of grammatical excellence in the attainment of high status in England as contrasted with the twangs and drawls and grammatical ineptitude among American elites is the most striking example of this difference. In a contest system, the class order does not function to support the *quality* of aesthetic, literary, and intellectual activities; only those well versed in such matters are qualified to distinguish authentic products from cheap imitations. Unless those who claim superiority in these areas are forced to submit their credentials to the elite for evaluation, poor quality is often honored equally with high quality and class prestige does not serve to maintain an effective norm of high quality.

This is not to imply that there are no groups in a "contest" society devoted to the protection and fostering of high standards in art, music, literature, and intellectual pursuits, but that such standards lack the support of the class system which is frequently found when sponsored mobility prevails. In California, the selection by official welcoming committees of a torch singer to entertain a visiting king and queen and "cancan" dancers to entertain Mr. Khrushchev illustrates how American elites can assume that high prestige and popular taste go together.

FORMAL EDUCATION

Returning to the conception of an organizing ideal norm, we assume that to the extent to which one such norm of upward mobility is prevalent in a society there are constant strains to shape the educational system into conformity with that norm. These strains operate in two fashions: directly, by blinding people to alternatives and coloring their judgments of successful and unsuccessful solutions to recurring educational problems; indirectly, through the functional interrelationships between school systems and the class structure, systems of social control, and other features of the social structure which are neglected in this paper.

The most obvious application of the distinction between sponsored and contest mobility norms affords a partial explanation for the different policies of student selection in the English and American secondary schools. Although American high school students follow different courses of study and a few attend specialized schools, a major educational preoccupation has been to avoid any sharp social separation between the superior and inferior students and to keep the channels of movement between courses of study as open as possible. Recent criticisms of the way in which superior students may be thereby held back in their development usually are nevertheless qualified by the insistence that these students must not be withdrawn from the mainstream of student life.[13] Such segregation offends the sense of fairness implicit in the contest norm and also arouses the fear that the elite and future elite will lose their sense of fellowship with the masses. Perhaps the most important point, however, is that schooling is presented as an opportunity, and making use of it depends primarily on the student's own initiative and enterprise.

The English system has undergone a succession of liberalizing changes during this century, but all of them have retained the attempt to sort out early in the educational program the promising from the unpromising so that the former may be segregated and given a special form of training to fit them for higher standing in their adult years. Under the Education Act of 1944, a minority of students has been selected each year by means of a battery of examinations popularly known as "eleven plus," supplemented in varying degrees by grade school records and personal interviews, for admission to grammar schools.[14] The remaining students attend secondary modern or technical schools in which the opportunities to prepare for college or to train for the more prestigeful occupations are minimal. The grammar schools supply what by comparative standards is a high quality of college preparatory education. Of course, such a scheme embodies the logic of sponsorship, with early selection of those destined for middle-class and higher-status occupations, and specialized training to prepare each group for its destined class position. This plan facilitates considerable mobility, and recent research reveals surprisingly little bias against children from manual-laboring-class families in the selection for grammar school, when related to measured intelligence.[15] It is altogether possible that adequate comparative study would show a close correlation of school success with measured intelligence and a lesser correlation between school success and family background in England than in the United States. While selection of superior students for mobility opportunity is probably more efficient under such a system, the obstacles for persons not so selected of "making the grade" on the basis of their own initiative or enterprise are probably correspondingly greater.

That the contrasting effects of the two systems accord with the social control patterns under the two mobility norms is indicated by studies of student ambitions in the United States and in England. Researches in the United States consistently show that the general level of occupational aspiration reported by high school students is quite unrealistic in relation to the actual distribution of job opportunities. Comparative study in England shows much less "fantasy" aspiration, and specifically indicates a reduction in aspirations among students not selected following the "eleven-plus" examination.[16] One of the by-products of the sponsorship system is the fact that at least some students from middle-class families whose parents cannot afford to send them to private schools suffer severe personal adjustment problems when they are assigned to secondary modern schools on the basis of this selection procedure.[17]

This well-known difference between the British sorting at an early age of students into grammar and modern schools and the American comprehensive high school and junior college is the clearest application of the distinction under discussion. But the organizing norms penetrate more deeply into the school systems than is initially apparent. The most telling observation regarding the direct normative operation of these principles would be evidence to support the author's impression that major critics of educational procedures within each country do not usually transcend the logic of their respective mobility norms. Thus the British debate about the best method for getting people sorted according to ability, without proposing that elite station should be open to whosoever can ascend to it. Although fear of "Sputnik" in the United States introduced a flurry of suggestions for sponsored mobility schemes, the long-standing concern of school critics has been the failure to motivate students adequately. Preoccupation with motivation appears to be an intellectual application of the folk idea that people should *win* their station in society by personal enterprise.

The functional operation of a strain toward consistency with the organizing norms of upward mobility may be illustrated by several other features of the school systems in the two countries. First, the value placed upon education itself differs under the two norms. Under sponsored mobility, schooling is valued for its cultivation of elite culture, and those forms of schooling directed toward such cultivation are more highly valued than others. Education of the non-elite is difficult to justify clearly and tends to be half-hearted, while maximum educational resources are concentrated on "those who can benefit most from them"—in practice, this means those who can learn the elite culture. The secondary modern schools in England have regularly suffered from less adequate financial provision, a higher student-teacher ratio, fewer well trained teachers, and a general lack of prestige in comparison with the grammar schools.[18]

Under contest mobility in the United States, education is valued as a means of getting ahead, but the contents of education are not highly valued in their own right. Over a century ago Tocqueville commented on the absence of an hereditary class "by which the labors of the intellect are held in honor." He remarked that consequently a "middling standard is fixed in America for human knowledge."[19] And there persists in some measure the suspicion of the educated man as one who may have gotten ahead without really earning his position. In spite of recent criticisms of lax standards in American schools, it is in keeping with the general mobility pattern that a Gallup Poll taken in April, 1958, reports that school principals are much more likely to make such criticisms than parents. While 90 per cent of the principals thought that ". . . our schools today demand too little work from the students," only 51 per cent of the parents thought so, with 33 per cent saying that the work was about right and 6 per cent that schools demanded too much work.[20]

Second, the logic of preparation for a contest prevails in United States schools, and emphasizes keeping everyone in the running until the final stages. In primary and secondary schools the assumption tends to be made that those who are learning satisfactorily need little special attention while the less successful require help to be sure that they remain in the contest and may compete for the final stakes. As recently as December, 1958, a nationwide Gallup Poll gave evidence that this attitude had not been radically altered by the international situation. When asked whether or not teachers should devote extra time to the bright students, 26 per cent of the respondents replied "yes" and 67 per cent, "no." But the responses changed to 86 per cent "yes" and only 9 per cent "no" when the question was asked concerning "slow students."[21]

In western states the junior college offers many students a "second chance" to qualify for university, and all state universities have some provision for substandard high school students to earn admission.

The university itself is run like the true contest: standards are set competitively, students are forced to pass a series of trials each semester, and only a minority of the entrants achieve the prize of graduation. This pattern contrasts sharply with the English system in which selection is supposed to be relatively complete before entrance to university, and students may be subject to no testing whatsoever for the first year or more of university study. Although university completion rates have not been estimated accurately in either country, some figures are indicative of the contrast. In American institutions of higher learning in 1957–58, the ratio of bachelor's and first-professional degrees to the number of first-time degree-credit enrollments in the fall four years earlier was reported to be .610 for men and .488 for women.[22] The indicated 39 and 51 per cent drop-out rates are probably underestimates because transfers from two-year junior colleges swell the number of degrees without being included in first-time enrollments. In England, a study of the careers of individual students reports that in University College, London, almost 82 per cent of entering students between 1948 and 1951 eventually graduated with a degree. A similar study a few years earlier at the University of Liverpool shows a comparative figure of almost 87 per cent.[23] Under contest mobility, the object is to train as many as possible in the skills necessary for elite status so as to give everyone a chance to maintain competition at the highest pitch. Under sponsored mobility, the objective is to indoctrinate elite culture in only those presumably who will enter the elite, lest there grow a dangerous number of "angry young men" who have elite skills without elite station.

Third, systems of mobility significantly affect educational content. Induction into elite culture under sponsored mobility is consistent with an emphasis on school *esprit de corps* which is employed to cultivate norms of intra-class loyalty and elite tastes and manners. Similarly, formal schooling built about highly specialized study in fields wholly of intellectual or aesthetic concern and of no "practical" value serves the purpose of elite culture. Under contest mobility in the United States, in spite of frequent faculty endorsement of "liberal education," schooling tends to be evaluated in terms of its practical benefits and to become, beyond the elementary level, chiefly vocational. Education does not so much provide what is good in itself as those skills, especially vocational skills, presumed to be necessary in the competition for the real prizes of life.

These contrasts are reflected in the different national attitudes toward university students who are gainfully employed while in school. More students in the United States than in Britain are employed part-time, and relatively fewer of the American students receive subsidies toward subsistence and living expenses. The most generous programs of state aid in the United States, except those applying to veterans and other special groups, do not normally cover expenses other than tuition and institutional fees. British maintenance grants are designed to cover full living expenses, taking into account parental ability to pay.[24] Under sponsored mobility, gainful employment serves no apprenticeship or testing function, and is thought merely to prevent students from gaining the full benefit of their schooling. L. J. Parry speaks of the general opposition to student employment and asserts that English university authorities almost unanimously hold that "... if a person must work for financial reasons, he should never spend more than four weeks on such work during the whole year."[25]

Under contest mobility, success in school work is not reviewed as a sufficient test of practical merit, but must be supplemented by a test in the world of practical affairs. Thus in didactic folk tales the professional engineer also proves himself to be a superior mechanic, the business tycoon a skillful behind-the-counter salesman. By "working his way through school" the enterprising student "earns" his education in the fullest sense, keeps in touch with the practical world, and gains an apprenticeship into vocational life. Students are often urged to seek part-time employment, even when there is no financial need, and in some instances schools include paid employment as a requirement for graduation. As one observer describes the typical American view, a student willing to work part-time is a "better bet" than "the equally bright student who receives all of his financial support from others."[26]

Finally, training in "social adjustment" is peculiar to the system of contest mobility. The reason for this emphasis is clear when it is understood that adjustment training presumably prepares students to cope with situations for which there are no rules of intercourse or for which the rules are unknown, but in which the good opinions of others cannot be wholly ignored. Under sponsored mobility, elite recruits are inducted into a homogeneous stratum within which there is consensus regarding the rules, and within which they succeed socially by mastering these rules. Under contest mobility, the elite aspirant must relate himself both to the established elite and to the masses, who follow different rules, and the elite itself is not sufficiently homogeneous to evolve consensual rules of intercourse. Furthermore, in the contest the rules may vary according to the background of the competitor, so that each aspirant must successfully deal with persons playing the game with slightly different rules. Consequently, adjustment training is increasingly considered to be one of the important skills imparted by the school system.[27] That the emphasis on such training has had genuine popular support is indicated by a 1945 *Fortune* poll in which a national sample of adults was asked to select the one or two things that would be very important for a son of theirs to get out of college. Over 87 per cent chose "Ability to get along with and understand people;" and this answer was the second most frequently chosen as the *very* most important thing to get out of college.[28] In this respect, British education may provide better preparation for participation in an orderly and controlled world, while American education may prepare students more adequately for a less ordered situation. The reputedly superior ability of "Yankees" to get things done seems to imply such ability.

To this point the discussion has centered on the tax-supported school systems in both countries, but the different place and emphasis of the privately supported secondary schools can also be related to the distinction between sponsored and contest mobility. Since private secondary schools in both countries are principally vehicles for transmitting the marks of high family status, their mobility function is quite tangential. Under contest mobility, the private schools presumably should have little or no mobility function. On the other hand, if there is to be mobility in a sponsored system, the privately controlled school populated largely with the children of elite parents would be the ideal device through which to induct selectees from lower levels into elite status. By means of a scholarship program, promising members of lesser classes could be chosen early for recruitment. The English "public" schools, in fact, have incorporated into their charters provisions to insure that a few boys from lesser classes will enter each year. Getting one's child into a "public" school, or even into one of the less prestigeful private schools, assumes an importance in England relatively unknown in the United States. If the children cannot win scholarships, the parents often make extreme financial sacrifices in order to pay the cost of this relatively exclusive education.[29]

How much of a role private secondary schools have played in mobility in either country is difficult to determine. American studies of social mobility usually omit information on private versus tax-supported secondary school attendance, and English studies showing the advantage of "public" school attendance generally fail to distinguish between the mobile and the nonmobile in this respect. However, during the nineteenth century the English "public" schools were used by *nouveaux riches* members of the manufacturing classes to enable their sons to achieve unqualified elite status.[30] In one sense, the rise of the manufacturing classes through free enterprise introduced a large measure of contest mobility which threatened to destroy the traditional sponsorship system. But by using the "public" schools in this fashion, they bowed to the legitimacy of the traditional system—an implicit acknowledgement that upward mobility was not complete without sponsored induction. Dennis Brogan speaks of the task of the "public" schools in the nineteenth century as "the job of marrying the old English social order to the new."[31]

With respect to mobility, the parallel between the tax-supported grammar schools and the "public" schools in England is of interest. The former in important respects have been patterned after the latter, adopting their view of mobility but making it a much larger part of their total function. Generally the grammar schools are the vehicle for sponsored mobility throughout the middle ranges of the class system, modeled after the pattern of the "public" schools which remain the agencies for sponsored mobility into the elite.

EFFECTS OF MOBILITY ON PERSONALITY

Brief note may be made of the importance of the distinction between sponsored and contest mobility with relation to the supposed effects of upward mobility on personality development. Not a great deal is yet known about the "mobile personality" nor about the specific features of importance to the personality in the mobility experience.[32] However, today three aspects of this experience are most frequently stressed: first, the stress or tension involved in striving for status higher than that of others under more difficult conditions than they; second, the complication of interpersonal relations introduced by the necessity to abandon lower-level friends in favor of uncertain acceptance into higher-level circles; third, the problem of working out an adequate personal scheme of values in the face of movement between classes marked by somewhat variant or even contradictory value systems.[33] The impact of each of these three mobility problems, it is suggested, differs depending upon whether the pattern is that of the contest or of sponsorship.

Under the sponsorship system, recruits are selected early, segregated from their class peers, grouped with other recruits and with youth from the class to which they are moving, and trained specifically for membership in this class. Since the selection is made early, the mobility experience should be relatively free from the strain that comes with a series of elimination tests and long-extended uncertainty of success. The segregation and the integrated group life of the "public" school or grammar school should help to clarify the mobile person's social ties. (One investigator failed to discover clique formation along lines of social class in a sociometric study of a number of grammar schools.[34]) The problem of a system of values may be largely met when the elite recruit is taken from his parents and peers to be placed in a boarding school, though it may be less well clarified for the grammar school boy who returns each evening to his working-class family. Undoubtedly this latter limitation has something to do with the observed failure of working-class boys to continue through the last years of grammar school and into the universities.[35] In general, then, the factors stressed as affecting personality formation among the upwardly mobile probably are rather specific to the contest system, or to incompletely functioning sponsorship system.

It is often taken for granted that there is convincing evidence to show that mobility-oriented students in American secondary schools suffer from the tendency for cliques to form along lines predetermined by family background. These tendencies are statistically quite moderate, however, leaving much room for individual exceptions. Furthermore, mobility-oriented students usually have not been studied separately to discover whether or not they are incorporated into higher-level cliques in contrast to the general rule. Nor is it adequately demonstrated that the purported working-class value system, at odds with middle-class values, is as pervasive and constraining throughout the working class as it is conspicuous in many delinquent gangs. The model of contest mobility suggests, then, that there is more serious and continuing strain over the uncertainty of attaining mobility, more explicit and continued preoccupation with the problem of changing friendships, and more contradictory learning to inhibit the acquisition of a value system appropriate to the class of aspiration than under sponsored mobility. But the extent and implications of these differences require fuller understanding of the American class system. A search for personality-forming experiences specific to a sponsorship system, such as the British, has yet to be made.

CONCLUSION: SUGGESTIONS FOR RESEARCH

The foregoing discussion is broadly impressionistic and speculative, reflecting more the general impression of an observer of both countries than a systematic exploration of data. Relevant data of a variety of sorts are cited above, but their use is more illustrative than demonstrative. However, several lines of research are suggested by this tentative analysis. One of these is an exploration of different channels of mobility in both England and the United States in an attempt to discover the extent to which mobility corresponds to the mobility types. Recruitment to the Catholic priesthood, for example, probably strictly follows a sponsorship norm regardless of the dominant contest norm in the United States.

The effect of changes in the major avenues of upward mobility upon the dominant norms requires investigation. The increasing importance of promotion through corporation hierarchies and the declining importance of the entrepreneurial path of upward mobility undoubtedly compromise the ideal pattern of contest mobility. The growing insistence that higher education is a prerequisite to more and more occupations is a similar modification. Yet, there is little evidence of a tendency to follow the logic of sponsorship beyond the bureaucratic selection process. The prospect of a surplus of college-educated persons in relation to jobs requiring college education may tend to restore the contest situation at a higher level, and the further possibility that completion of higher education may be more determined by motivational factors than by capacity suggests that the contest pattern continues within the school.

In England, on the other hand, two developments may weaken the sponsorship system. One is positive response to popular demand to allow more children to secure the grammar school type of training, particularly by including such a program in the secondary modern schools. The other is introduction of the comprehensive secondary school, relatively uncommon at present but a major plank in the Labour party's education platform. It remains to be determined whether the comprehensive school in England will take a distinctive form and serve a distinctive function, which preserves the pattern of sponsorship, or will approximate the present American system.

Finally, the assertion that these types of mobility are embedded in genuine folk norms requires specific investigation. Here, a combination of direct study of popular attitudes and content analysis of popular responses to crucial issues would be useful. Perhaps the most significant search would be for evidence showing what courses of action require no special justification or explanation because they are altogether " natural" and "right," and what courses of action, whether approved or not, require special justification and explanation. Such evidence, appropriately used, would show the extent to which the patterns described are genuine folk norms rather than mere by-products of particular structural factors. It would also permit determination of the extent to which acceptance of the folk norms is diffused among the different segments of the populations.

NOTES

1. A comprehensive summary of such studies appears in Seymour M. Lipset and Reinhard Bendix, *Social Mobility in Industrial Society* (Berkeley and Los Angeles: University of California Press, 1959).

2. *Cf.* C. A. Anderson, "The Social Status of University Students in Relation to Type of Economy: An International Comparison," *Transactions of the Third World Congress of Sociology* (London, 1956), V, pp. 51–63; J. E. Floud, *Social Class and Educational Opportunity* (London: Heinemann, 1956); W. L. Warner, R. J. Havighurst, and M. B. Loeb, *Who Shall Be Educated?* (New York: Harper, 1944).

3. Reference is made throughout the paper to "elite" and "masses." The generalizations, however, are intended to apply throughout the stratification continuum to relations between members of a given class and the class or classes above it. Statements about mobility are intended in general to apply to mobility from manual to middle-class levels, lower-middle to upper-middle class, and so on, as well as into the strictly elite groups. The simplified expressions avoid the repeated use of cumbersome and involved statements which might otherwise be required.

4. The normative element in an organizing norm goes beyond Max Weber's *ideal type,* conveying more of the sense of Durkheim's *collective representation; cf.* Ralph H. Turner, "The Normative Coherence of Folk Concepts," *Research Studies of the State College of Washington,* 25 (1957), pp. 127–136. Charles Wagley has developed a similar concept which he calls "ideal pattern" in his as yet unpublished work on Brazilian kinship. See also Howard Becker, "Constructive Typology in the Social Sciences," *American Sociological Review,* 5 (February, 1940) pp. 40–55.

5. Geoffrey Gorer remarks on the favorable evaluation of the successful gamble in American culture: "Gambling is also a respected and important component in many

business ventures. Conspicuous improvement in a man's financial position is generally attributed to a lucky combination of industry, skill, and gambling, though the successful gambler prefers to refer to his gambling as 'vision.' " *The American People* (New York: Norton, 1948), p. 178.

6. Vilfredo Pareto, *The Mind and Society* (New York: Harcourt, Brace 1935), 4, 1796.

7. Many writers have noted that different kinds of societies facilitate the rise of different kinds of personalities, either in the stratification hierarchy or in other ways. Cf. Jessie Bernard, *American Community Behavior* (New York: Dryden, 1949), 205. A particularly interesting statement is Martindale's exploration of "favored personality" types in sacred and secular societies. Don Martindale and Elio Monachesi, *Elements of Sociology* (New York: Harper, 1951), pp. 312–78.

8. At one time in the United States a good many owners of expensive British Jaguar automobiles carried large signs on the cars identifying the make. Such a display would have been unthinkable under a sponsored mobility system since the Jaguar owner would not care for the esteem of persons too uninformed to tell a Jaguar from a less prestigious automobile.

9. See, e.g., Lawrence Lipton, *The Holy Barbarians* (New York: Messner, 1959).

10. Cf. Albert K. Cohen, *Delinquent Boys: The Culture of the Gang* (Glencoe, Ill.: The Free Press, 1955).

11. D. V. Glass, ed., *Social Mobility in Britain* (Glencoe, Ill.: The Free Press, 1954), pp. 144–45, reports studies showing only small variations in intelligence between occupational levels.

12. Gorer, *op. cit.,* pp. 172–87.

13. See e.g., *Los Angeles Times,* May 4, 1959, Part I, p. 24.

14. The nature and operation of the "eleven plus" system are fully reviewed in a report by a committee of the British Psychological Society and in a report of extensive research into the adequacy of selection methods. See P. E. Vernon, editor, *Secondary School Selection: A British Psychological Inquiry* (London: Methuen, 1957); and Alfred Yates and D. A. Pidgeon, *Admission to Grammar Schools* (London: Newnes Educational Publishing Co., 1957).

15. J. E. Floud, A. H. Halsey, and F. M. Martin, *Social Class and Educational Opportunity* (London: Heinemann, 1956).

16. Mary D. Wilson documents the reduction in aspirations characterizing students in British secondary modern schools and notes the contrast with American studies revealing much more "unrealistic" aspirations; see "The Vocational Preferences of Secondary Modern School-children," *British Journal of Educational Psychology,* 23 (1953), pp. 97–113. See also Ralph H. Turner, "The Changing Ideology of Success," *Transactions of the Third World Congress of Sociology, 1956* (London), V, esp. p. 37.

17. Pointed out by Hilde Himmelweit in private communication.

18. Less adequate financial provision and a higher student-teacher ratio are mentioned as obstacles to parity of secondary modern schools with grammar schools in *The Times Educational Supplement,* February 22, 1957, p. 241. On difficulties in achieving prestige comparable with grammar schools, see G. Baron, "Secondary Education in Britain: Some Present-Day Trends," *Teachers College Record,* 57 (January, 1956), pp. 211–21; and O. Banks, *Parity and Prestige in English Secondary Education* (London: Routledge and Kegan Paul, 1955). See also Vernon, *op. cit.,* pp. 19–22.

19. Alexis de Tocqueville, *Democracy in America* (New York: Knopf, 1945), I, p. 52.

20. An earlier Gallup Poll had disclosed that 62 per cent of the parents opposed

stiffened college entrance requirements while only 27 per cent favored them. Reported in *Time,* April 14, 1958, p. 45.

21. Reported in the *Los Angeles Times,* December 17, 1958, Part I, p. 16.

22. U.S. Department of Health, Education, and Welfare, Office of Education, *Earned Degrees Conferred by Higher Education Institutions, 1957–1958* (Washington, D.C.: Government Printing Office, 1959), p. 3.

23. Nicholas Malleson, "Student Performance at University College, London, 1948–1951," *Universities Quarterly,* 12 (May, 1958), pp. 288–319.

24. See, e.g., C. A. Quattlebaum, *Federal Aid to Students for Higher Education* (Washington, D.C.: Government Printing Office, 1956); and "Grants to Students: University and Training Colleges," *The Times Educational Supplement,* May 6, 1955, p. 446.

25. "Students' Expenses," *The Times Educational Supplement,* May 6, 1955, p. 447.

26. R. H. Eckelberry, "College Jobs for College Students," *Journal of Higher Education,* 27 (March, 1956), p. 174.

27. Adjustment training is not a necessary accompaniment of contest mobility. The shift during the last half century toward the increased importance of social acceptability as an elite credential has brought such training into correspondingly greater prominence.

28. Reported in Hadley Cantril, ed., *Public Opinion 1935–1946* (Princeton, N.J.: Princeton University Press, 1951), p. 186.

29. For one account of the place of "public" schools in the English educational system, see Dennis Brogan, *The English People* (New York: Knopf, 1943), pp. 18–56.

30. A. H. Halsey of Birmingham University has called my attention to the importance of this fact.

31. *Op. cit.,* pp. 24–25.

32. Cf. Lipset and Bendix, *op. cit.,* pp. 250 ff.

33. See, e.g., August B. Hollingshead and Frederick C. Redlich, *Social Class and Mental Illness* (New York: Wiley, 1958); W. Lloyd Warner and James C. Abegglen, *Big Business Leaders in America* (New York: Harper, 1955); Warner *et al., Who Shall Be Educated?, op. cit.;* Peter M. Blau, "Social Mobility and Interpersonal Relations," *American Sociological Review,* 21 (June, 1956), pp. 290–300.

34. A. N. Oppenheim, "Social Status and Clique Formation among Grammar School Boys," *British Journal of Sociology,* 6 (September, 1955), pp. 228–45. Oppenheim's findings may be compared with A. B. Hollingshead, *Elmtown's Youth* (New York: Wiley, 1949), pp. 204–42. See also Joseph A. Kahl, *The American Class Structure* (New York: Rinehart, 1957), pp. 129–38.

35. Floud *et al., op. cit.,* pp. 115 ff.

5.   WILLIAM H. SEWELL

Inequality of Opportunity for Higher Education

INTRODUCTION

Higher education in American society gains only a part of its significance from the personal satisfactions and self-realization that come from general learning and the mastery of high-level skills. More importantly, higher education confers increased chances for income, power, and prestige on people who are fortunate enough to obtain it.[1] In modern technological societies the allocation of social position is increasingly dependent on higher education. Entrance into an ever enlarging range of valued occupations is restricted to those whose educational attainments beyond secondary school are presumed to have given them the habits of thought, attitudes, and special skills that these occupations require (Sorokin, 1927:169–172, 187–193; Lenski, 1966:389–395; Blau and Duncan, 1967:401–441; Miller and Roby, 1970:119–141; Hauser, 1970).

It has long been accepted that training for the higher professions should be an almost exclusive monopoly of colleges and universities. More recently this near monopoly has been extended to include many subprofessional and technical occupations as well. Even the training required for the skilled blue-collar and lower level white-collar occupations—which formerly was acquired on the job, through apprenticeships, or in vocational curricula in high schools—has increasingly been shifted to post-secondary institutions.

Recently there has been a good deal of criticism of the overemphasis on credentialism and the certification role that colleges and other educational institutions perform (Miller and Reissman, 1969; Berg, 1970; Newman *et al.*, 1971:38–43). This criticism is particularly persuasive whenever it can be shown

Reprinted from *American Sociological Review,* 36 (October, 1971), pp. 793–809, by permission of the author and the American Sociological Association.

Presidential Address, 66th Annual Meeting of the American Sociological Association, August 30, 1971, Denver, Colorado. The research reported herein was supported by grants from the National Institutes of Health, U.S. Public Health Service (M–6275) and the Social and Rehabilitation Service, Social Security Administration (CRD–314). I wish especially to thank Robert M. Hauser for his critical comments and suggestions and for his contribution to the analytical work reported here. David Mechanic and Bryant E. Kearl made valuable suggestions for the revision of an earlier draft of this paper. I wish also to acknowledge the contributions of my professional associates on this project over the years: Archibald O. Haller, Kenneth G. Lutterman, Vimal P. Shah, Janet A. Fisher, Ronald M. Pavalko, Robert M. Hauser, J. Michael Armer, Alan M. Orenstein, Eldon L. Wegner, Alejandro Portes, George W. Ohlendorf, Herschel Shosteck, Victor Jesudason, Dorothy M. Ellegaard, and Ruth M. Gasson.

that the educational requirements for entry into an occupation have little bearing on the activities of that occupation. It is especially unfortunate that when such requirements are artificially high, many otherwise qualified persons from disadvantaged backgrounds are excluded from desirable occupations. However, with high school graduation becoming almost universal in the United States and with the level of technology increasing, it seems quite likely that the trend will be toward more, not less, dependence on post-secondary institutions to select, train, and certify people for an enlarging variety of occupations.[2] Those who fail to obtain this training, for whatever reasons, will be severely disadvantaged in the competition for jobs and in many other areas of social life as well.

With occupational selection, training, and certification carried out mainly through the schools, and particularly in post-secondary institutions, life chances will not be equal until opportunities for advanced education are equal. The extent to which opportunities for higher education are contingent on characteristics of social origin that are not relevant to learning—most notably sex, socioeconomic origins, race and ethnic background—is a matter of great importance to the study of social stratification and a pressing problem to a society that stresses equality of opportunity as a national goal.[3]

The purpose of this paper is to review the research my associates and I have been doing on this subject,[4] and to suggest some of its implications for public policy. First, I will summarize briefly our findings, then discuss some of the results of our efforts to elucidate the complex relationships between socioeconomic background and educational attainment, and finally I will consider their policy implications.

Our research has been based on a longitudinal study of approximately 9,000 randomly selected Wisconsin high school students who have been successfully followed since they were high school seniors in 1957.[5] Our data provide information not only on socioeconomic origins, sex, academic ability, and post-high school educational and occupational attainments, but also on such matters as the student's performance in high school, the expectations of parents and teachers and peers, and the student's educational and occupational aspirations. With these data we have examined in detail inequalities in opportunities for higher education and have also devised explanatory models for the educational attainment process.

INEQUALITIES IN HIGHER EDUCATION

Using such measures of socioeconomic status as parental income, father's and mother's educational attainment, and father's occupation—either singly

or in combination—we have found enormous differences in educational opportunities among the various socioeconomic groups and between the sexes. These
differences are great regardless of what socioeconomic indices are used and
regardless of how restrictively or broadly opportunity for higher education is
defined—whether it is taken to mean college entry, college graduation, professional or graduate study, or simply continuation in any kind of formal education beyond high school.[6]

   To illustrate. When we divide our cohort into quarters ranging from low to
high on an index based on a weighted combination of our indicators of socio-
economic status, we estimate that a high SES student has almost a 2.5 times
as much chance as a low SES student of continuing in some kind of post-high
school education. He has an almost 4 to 1 advantage in access to college, a 6
to 1 advantage in college graduation, and a 9 to 1 advantage in graduate or
professional education. In the middle SES categories the rates are consistently
between these extremes: the lower the SES group, the more limited the opportunities at each higher level of education.

   These socioeconomic differentials in educational attainment hold for both
sexes. However, the educational chances of males are uniformly greater than
those of females at every SES level. For example, in the bottom SES category
males have a 26 per cent advantage over females in obtaining any further
schooling, a 58 per cent advantage in attending college, an 86 per cent advantage in completing college, and a 250 per cent advantage in attending graduate
or professional school. Likewise, in the top SES category males have an 8 per
cent advantage over females in obtaining any further schooling, a 20 per cent
advantage in attending college, a 28 per cent advantage in completing college,
and a 129 per cent better chance of attending graduate or professional school.
Thus, the advantage of males is greatest in the lower SES categories and least
in the top SES category.

   Even when we control for academic ability by dividing our sample into
fourths according to the students' scores on standardized tests,[7] we find that
higher SES students have substantially greater post-high school educational
attainment than lower SES students. For example, among students in the
lowest fourth of the ability distribution, those in the highest SES category have
a 2.5 times advantage over those in the lowest SES category in their chances
to go on to some form of post-high school education. For students in the
highest ability fourth, the chances of continuing their schooling are 1.5 times
greater if they are from the highest rather than the lowest SES category.
Similarly, in the lowest ability fourth the rate of college attendance is 4 times
greater for the highest SES group than for the lowest SES group. Among the
top quarter of students in ability, a student from the lowest SES category is
only about half as likely to attend college as a student from the highest SES
category. A similar pattern holds for the chances of graduating from college,

where corresponding ratios range from 9 to 1 among low ability students to 2 to 1 among high ability students. At the level of graduate or professional school entry, where we would expect ability considerations to be determinant, the odds are 3.5 to 1 in favor of high SES over low SES students, even in the high ability category.

The patterns we have described hold for both women and men. When SES and ability are both controlled, women have lower probabilities of obtaining any further schooling, of attending college, of graduating from college, and of entering graduate or professional school. The differences in rates of attainment between the sexes tend to be lower at the higher levels of attainment and in the higher SES groups, but are still marked at all educational levels and in all SES categories.

Our findings lead inexorably to the conclusion that in their opportunities for higher education the members of this sample cohort seldom escape the influence of their social origins. The selective influences of socioeconomic background and sex operate independently of academic ability at every stage in the process of educational attainment. Social selection is most vividly apparent in the transition from high school to college, but it is operative at every other transition point as well. Those who overcome the handicap of origin status or of sex at one level of the system find themselves again disadvantaged in moving on to the next level.

The results presented thus far do not fully indicate the numerical magnitude of the educational inequalities suffered by women and low socioeconomic status members of this cohort, consisting of approximately 36,000 persons. For this purpose we present an estimate obtained by assuming that the members of each SES and ability category, regardless of sex, should have had the same educational opportunities as high SES males of equal ability. Had this goal been realized, there would have been an increase of 8,800 or 32 per cent more students continuing their schooling beyond high school graduation; 10,089 or 43 per cent more students entering college; and 5,770 or 47 per cent more students graduating from college.

Socioeconomic origin contributes more than sex to the failure of all students to enjoy the same educational opportunities, but even so the result of equalizing women's opportunities would have been to increase by 1,176 or 28 per cent the number of women who would have obtained some further schooling beyond high school; by 2,157 or 52 per cent the number who would have attended college; and by 1,455 or 68 per cent the number who would have graduated from college.

Despite Wisconsin's proud record of providing public and private scholarships and low tuition rates in its diverse system of public higher education, by any standard these figures represent a massive failure to provide equality of opportunity for higher education to qualified students of all SES levels and both sexes. The results are that the state and the nation suffer a great loss in potential, high-level manpower and the young people involved pay through reduced life chances.

Our study reveals still other inequities suffered by students from low SES groups in their quest for higher education. Holding academic ability constant, low SES persons are less likely to go to college immediately after high school graduation, much less likely to attend or to be graduated from high quality colleges, more likely to drop out of college if they enter, less likely to return if they drop out, and more likely to have their college careers interrupted by military service. On all of these dimensions except military service, women fare worse than men.

It is indeed regrettable that generally comparable and adequate data on inequality of opportunity for higher education are not available for large and representative samples for the nation as a whole.[8] The data that exist on national samples, particularly the badly flawed data from Project Talent,[9] remarkably parallel the trends in our data whenever similar analysis has been undertaken (Folger *et al.*, 1970:305–324). We have no basis for making estimates of national parameters, but to the extent that our data are representative they furnish solid documentation for the claim that there is substantially reduced opportunity for higher education in America for those of lower socioeconomic origins and for women, and that this inequality cannot be explained by differences in academic ability. Despite the spectacular increase in the numbers attending college during the past decade, there is no good reason to believe that socioeconomic differentials in opportunity for higher education have altered appreciably.[10]

It is also unfortunate that no comparable data or analyses exist for blacks, Chicanos, Puerto Ricans, or American Indians. These groups are overrepresented in the lower socioeconomic levels of our society, and they suffer disadvantages due to racial and ethnic discrimination over and above those that characterize the poor in the overwhelmingly white population of Wisconsin (Duncan and Duncan, 1968; Duncan, 1968). We do know that in 1970 only 65 per cent of blacks aged 20–24 had graduated from high school, in contrast to 83 per cent of whites. Only 23 per cent of blacks in the same age cohort had even completed a year of college, in contrast to 39 per cent of the whites. In the cohort aged 25–29, only 7 per cent of all blacks had college degrees, in contrast to 17 per cent of whites. And only slightly over 1 per cent of the blacks in this same age cohort had completed as much as one year of professional or graduate education, compared with 6 per cent of the whites.[11] The current enrollment situation at the undergraduate and the graduate and professional levels is still heavily unbalanced. In 1970 only 7 per cent of the students enrolled in colleges and universities in the United States were black, and blacks made up only 2 per cent of current graduate school enrollments and less than

2.5 per cent of enrollments in medical schools, although blacks were approximately 12 per cent of the affected age cohorts (Wright, 1970). The situation of Puerto Rican, Mexican, and Indian Americans is less well known, but may be as bad. We believe that if data comparable with those for our study were available on black and other disadvantaged minorities, the relationships would be even more marked.

THE EDUCATIONAL ATTAINMENT PROCESS

In addition to the descriptive analysis reported thus far, we have attempted to understand more fully the process of higher educational attainment. We have identified a number of experiences that young people undergo in their formative years which have an important bearing on post-high school educational outcomes. These include level of performance in high school, whether significant others encourage or discourage aspirations for higher education, and whether one actually develops high educational and occupational aspirations. All of these experiences intervene between the social origins, academic ability, and sex characteristics of the individual and become the mechanism through which these background characteristics transmit their influence. In addition, these same experiences have direct and indirect effects of their own, quite independent of the background characteristics.

This complex multivariate process has been the focus of much of our recent research, and we have been developing and testing linear causal models to further explicate the process of attainment. Building on the work of Blau and Duncan (1967:163–205), we have devised and published a linear recursive model that attempts to elaborate and explain the effects of socioeconomic origins and academic ability on educational achievements and occupational attainments as these influences are mediated by social psychological processes (Sewell et al., 1969; Sewell et al., 1970).

Recently we have further elaborated our model by disaggregating socioeconomic status into its component parts—parents' income, mother's education, father's education, and father's occupation—and by decomposition of "significant others' influence" into parental encouragement, teachers' encouragement, and peers' plans.[12] This enables us to obtain estimates of the individual role of each of these variables in the educational attainment process.[13]

Because this analysis is quite complicated, we shall present only the major findings for the total sample, making references to sex differences where they are especially large or interesting.

We begin the analysis with a very simple model that includes only the four socioeconomic background variables. We find that these four socioeconomic background variables taken together account for 18 per cent of the total variance in years of post-high school educational attainment. Whether we look at linear or nonlinear effects, each of the four has an approximately equal, direct influence on educational attainment and on all other intervening variables in the model. This approximate equality of effects of such stratification variables as parental education, occupation, or income suggests that there may be little merit in the efforts of some social scientists to interpret all social inequalities in terms of any particular stratification variable.

What is impressive is not so much the extent to which socioeconomic status governs the life chances of any particular individual, but rather the extent to which it reduces the aggregate or average educational achievements of those from the lower strata. For example, each year of parental education, father's or mother's, was worth one-tenth of a year of higher education for their child —after the effects of father's occupational status and family income were taken into account. Thus, the children of parents with only grade school education obtained on the average one and one-half years less education than the children of parents who were both college graduates—even if their fathers had similar jobs and their families had similar incomes.

Likewise, a thousand dollar increase in the annual income of a family on the average yielded an increase of .08 of a year in the educational attainment of their child—slightly less than an additional year of education of either parent. Thus, a shift in income from the poverty level of $3,000—below which 18 per cent of those in the Wisconsin sample fell—to the median income at that time, $6,000, increased the average years of schooling by a quarter of a year when the effects of parental education and occupation were taken into account. A shift from the poverty line to $10,000—which was exceeded by only 11 per cent of the families in the Wisconsin sample—led to an increase of more than half an additional year of post-secondary schooling.

When we add academic ability to the model, the explained variance in higher educational attainment is increased from 18 to 30 per cent. The additional 12 per cent represents a large component of the variance in educational attainment that is completely independent of socioeconomic origins. An important component, varying between 20 and 30 per cent, of the effects of each of the socioeconomic status variables is mediated by academic ability. At the same time the influence of ability on attainment is clearly not spurious. Only one-fifth of the association of academic ability with educational attainment may be attributed to its association with socioeconomic background. Whether one thinks of measured ability as a valid psychological trait or as an administratively convenient basis for social selection, it seems apparent that the effects of ability on schooling are not merely a reflection of one's SES background. We think this is particularly germane to current discussions of the social role of testing.[14]

Next, in order to explain more completely the ways in which socioeconomic status origins influence post-high school attainment, we further complicate the model by adding three sets of social psychological intervening variables: (1) high school performance, (2) significant others' influence, and (3) educational and occupational aspirations. We believe that these variables intervene in the order indicated to mediate the effects of socioeconomic status and academic ability on higher educational attainment. Taken as a whole, these intervening variables account for a large part of the effects of each socioeconomic status variable on post-high school educational attainment. Some 85 to 90 per cent of the total association of each socioeconomic status variable with attainment is mediated by the variables in the model, of which about 75 per cent is mediated by the social psychological variables, leaving only 10 to 15 per cent to be explained by other variables not in the model, by measurement error, and by socioeconomic discrimination. Still, even with this powerful model which explains over 55 per cent of the variance in higher educational attainment, socioeconomic origins continue to influence directly one's chances for educational attainment.

The extent to which our model explains the effects of socioeconomic origin on ultimate educational attainment is remarkable in light of the fact that none of our intervening variables pertains to the post-secondary experience of the cohort. Even for young persons who succeed in graduating from high school, the effect of social background on later educational achievement is largely explicable in terms of events which took place during the high school years.

Again, with this more complex model it is noteworthy that the interpretations for total associations are very similar for each of the SES variables. About 12 per cent of the influence of each SES variable on higher educational attainment is direct. About 16 per cent is due to the association with the other SES variables, about 11 per cent is ultimately mediated by academic ability and high school performance, about 23 per cent is eventually mediated by significant others' influence, and about 38 per cent is ultimately mediated by educational and occupational aspirations.

Not only does the model interpret the various ways in which SES variables influence higher educational attainment, but also it interprets the effects of academic ability. Of the total association between academic ability and educational attainment, 18 per cent is due to the unmediated effect of ability, 21 per cent is due to the relationship between academic ability and socioeconomic background, and the remaining 61 per cent is mediated by the social psychological variables in our model. This indicates that the influence of academic ability can only in a minor way be attributed to SES considerations, but rests more solidly on its direct and pertinent influence on academic performance, and its direct and indirect influences on significant others and on educational and occupational aspirations. In this context it is also pertinent that the model indicates that SES has no effect on performance in high school independent of academic ability.

Next, in the analysis of our full model, we introduce the effects of parental encouragement, teachers' encouragement, and the educational plans of friends. In looking at the effects of these significant others on educational attainment, we are struck by the evidence that parental encouragement and friends' plans depend heavily on the student's socioeconomic origin. Teachers' encouragement, on the other hand, depends much more heavily on ability and academic performance. Indeed, teachers are not perceived to engage in direct socioeconomic status discrimination as parents and peers apparently do, but rather depend mainly on judgments of student academic ability, particularly as it is validated by school performance.

We find that the influence of parents on educational and occupational aspirations and ultimately on attainment of higher education is about twice that of teachers, and the influence of friends only slightly less than that of parents. Holding constant all of the other factors we have included in the model up to this point (SES, academic ability, school performance, parental encouragement, and friends' plans), we find that teachers' encouragement is worth an additional 0.3 of a year of schooling—whereas the net values of parental encouragement and friends' plans are 0.9 of a year and 0.7 of a year, respectively. While all three variables have important effects on students' educational attainments, we are led to conclude that teachers' expectations of students are not a powerful mediating factor in the process of educational stratification. But far from reflecting overt or covert status discrimination, on the whole teachers' expectations seem to be based on academic ability and performance, and as such they make a fundamental though modest contribution to the equalization of opportunities.

Although our model is quite successful in accounting for socioeconomic differentials in educational attainment, it is less successful in accounting for sex differences—which favor men by approximately one-half year of educational attainment on the average. Our analysis indicates that women are most seriously disadvantaged relative to men in levels of teachers' and parents' encouragement and in their own levels of educational aspirations. They enjoy some advantage over men in that they get higher grades in high school and have slightly higher perceptions of their friends' plans and somewhat higher occupational aspirations. Our model tends to predict higher average educational attainments for women than they actually achieve. This may be due to its failure to represent crucial aspects of women's high school experiences, or it may be that the primary sources of the lower attainments of women must be sought in the months and years immediately following the completion of high school. We are inclined toward the latter view, for the effects of socialization in the family and in the school are already manifest in women's levels of school performance, of significant others' influence, and of aspiration.

POLICY IMPLICATIONS

What bearings do our findings have for policies designed to reduce inequality in higher education? Certainly, in this large cohort there is striking evidence of its pervasiveness. Although socioeconomic origin plays an important part in inequality in higher education, our analysis indicates that its role is far from simple and direct. Its effects tend to be mediated largely by social psychological factors, which in turn also have independent influences on the processes of educational attainment. Moreover, when we look at the components of socioeconomic status—father's and mother's education, father's occupation, and family income—we find that no one of them plays any unique part in the causal system explaining attainment in higher education. This is unfortunate from the standpoint of policy considerations. One would have wished that family income might have had a larger and a more special set of effects because it is the aspect of socioeconomic background most readily amenable to change.[15] But our evidence raises doubt that programs based on family income supplementation alone will result in any rapid and marked reduction in inequality in higher education. This is not to deny the importance of income in obtaining access to higher education, but it is to warn that family income programs, however desirable they may be for reducing other social inequalities, will not bring quick or dramatic results in overcoming inequality in higher education.[16] Certainly we should not rely on this means alone to bring about equalization of opportunity for higher education.

Rather, I would argue for a more targeted economic approach.[17] I believe that programs specifically limited to financing post-secondary educational costs based strictly on student need would be the most effective and equitable approach to the problem. Besides making it possible for needy students to continue their education, such a grants program might have desirable indirect effects on the educational aspirations and achievements of the disadvantaged. For example, if students and parents became aware that it was national policy to make grants to cover the full cost of post-secondary schooling for qualified students whose families had incomes too low to bear these costs themselves, it is entirely conceivable that this knowledge would lead to better performance in school because now performance would have a greater likelihood of being rewarded. Parents and teachers might then give more attention to the student's academic growth, with consequent favorable effects on the development of the student's self-conceptions, ambitions, and aspirations. All of this might lead to a greater likelihood that the student would continue education beyond high school and be more successful in post-high school studies.

I advocate that all new subsidy programs be limited to those who need the subsidy. There is mounting evidence that existing subsidy programs for higher education do not go primarily to needy students. Not only do federal moneys for training and research go mainly to institutions that are attended primarily by middle- and high-income students, but also most other forms of institutional aid go to high-prestige colleges and universities. Even student-aid moneys are not primarily concentrated in the community colleges, city colleges, and less prestigious colleges that serve the poor (Rivlin, 1970:9). Moreover, in their recent analysis of the distribution of subsidy for public higher education in California, Hansen and Weisbrod (1969a; 1969b) argue that because higher-income students are more likely to go to college, to attend the most expensive public institutions, and to stay in college longer, their families are in effect receiving a much greater educational subsidy from the state than are low income families.[18] Probably the same trend would be revealed and possibly accentuated in states with less availability of public higher education. Consequently, new programs for the subsidy of higher educational opportunity should be limited to students who need the subsidy in order to continue their education beyond high school.

Most of the funds should go directly to students rather than to institutions.[19] Nor should subsidy programs be limited to those who go to four-year colleges, but rather should include also those whose interests and aptitudes lead them to select community colleges and vocational training schools. Neither would I argue that funds should go only to students of proven academic ability and achievement. Motivated students with qualities that make them admissible to various types of institutions should be given equal opportunity to pursue their education in other appropriate ways. For this group there must be institutions located in all larger communities with open admission policies, programs to remedy prior academic deficiencies, flexible scheduling, pacing and credit loads, and special tutoring and counseling programs (Willingham, 1970:217–223; Gordon, 1971). The grants given should be sufficient to enable the student to attend any post-secondary institution—public or private—to which he could gain admission. In the case of the poor, the grants should cover full costs —tuition, books, board, lodging, travel, and even a modest amount for incidental personal expenses—and should be in effect as long as the student makes satisfactory progress in school.

The low propensity of the families in our sample to trade family income for education leads me to believe that other funding schemes such as the education opportunity bank, various other loan schemes, and tax credit plans are likely to be much less effective in encouraging low-income students to continue their education. Their families are already burdened with debt, and they fear longtime loans—even at low interest or no interest rates—that are likely to run into thousands of dollars before the student has completed his education. Tax credit schemes are likely to appeal greatly to the middle classes who pay heavy income taxes, but not to the poor. In fact, if our goal is to equalize opportunity for post-high school education, it may be necessary, in order to release funds for direct help to students from lower income groups, to reduce current subsidies to students whose parents can afford to pay for their education.

This should not be interpreted as an endorsement for schemes that call for the support of public higher education on the basis of full-cost tuition fees so that all public subsidies for higher education would go only to those who can demonstrate need.[20] I believe that tuitions should be kept as low as possible to encourage all motivated students—especially women—to continue their education beyond high school. But even if there were no tuition fees charged for higher education, access to it would, I think, still be painfully inequitable. Consequently, new resources need to be directed at special and extraordinary steps to attract and serve those groups now least well represented in our colleges and universities.[21] I believe that a grants program along the lines outlined is administratively feasible and could be put into operation rapidly so that its effects would be apparent in the immediate future.

For those not now in the educational pipeline there must be increased opportunities for recurrent education, including part-time study, work-study programs, education on the job, and various other types of continuing education of both general and technical character (Organization for Economic Cooperation and Development, 1971; Newman, 1971: Carnegie Commission on Higher Education, 1971). These will also require special financing and will be expensive, but our evidence suggests that there are millions of disadvantaged youth and adults now in the labor force who dropped out of the educational process early and who have the capacity to profit from such programs. Both as a matter of equity and of intelligent manpower policy, they should be given the opportunity to continue their education.

I do not believe that economic programs alone will be sufficient to overcome inequality in opportunities for higher education. Our analysis also indicates that we must give a good deal of attention to such social psychological factors as the development of cognitive skills, academic performance, the influence of significant others, and the stimulation of educational and occupational aspirations. All of these variables have direct and indirect influences on educational achievement that are quite independent of socioeconomic background. Consequently, any strategies that can be suggested for increasing their strength should be investigated, developed, and given intensive trials in the hope that ways can be found to overcome the deficits in these areas from which so many disadvantaged children suffer.

Particular attention must be given to programs designed to increase the academic ability and performance of lower SES children. Evidence from the Coleman report and other research suggests that many children from disadvantaged homes enter school with a deficit in learning skills that tends to increase steadily throughout the school years, with the consequence that by twelfth grade many lower class children are well behind higher status children in academic skills and achievement (Coleman *et al.* 1966:20–21). The fact that these academic deficits seem to increase over the years of schooling suggests that special programs designed to develop cognitive and affective skills, beginning in the preschool period and continuing throughout the grades, will be necessary to enlarge the personal and academic potential of socioeconomically disadvantaged children so that they can compete successfully with higher status children.

Unfortunately, current large-scale attempts to improve the cognitive development of socially disadvantaged children have not thus far had promising results (Gordon and Wilkerson, 1966:156–189; Williams and Evans, 1969), despite a good deal of evidence from more restricted laboratory and field studies indicating the possibility of rather large and lasting gains.[22] However, the stakes are so great that rather than give up this line of attack, a great deal more ingenuity and effort must be devoted to devising more effective programs, including interventions which involve the family and peers, as well as the school. This will require much research, experimental programing, and structural changes in schools. All of this will be expensive and it may take much more time than we once optimistically thought, but our research suggests that the potential payoffs are very significant, are likely to be largely above and beyond those resulting from economic programs, and are essential if we do not want the early handicaps of disadvantaged children to prevent them from realizing their potential for later academic achievement (Carnegie Commission on Higher Education, 1970a).

Our analysis suggests, also, that programs designed to influence the significant others of disadvantaged students would have important effects on the student's educational aspirations and achievements. One immediately thinks of the possible role that teachers and counsellors might play in programs of this kind. If socioeconomically disadvantaged students with good academic potential were discovered early and high school teachers and counsellors were alerted to the students' potential for development so that they might provide special guidance and encouragement, modest gains might accrue in the students' educational aspiration and attainment levels. On the basis of our data, we would not expect gains of great magnitude because our model does not show teachers' influence to be a very powerful determinant of educational attainment. Still other ways should be sought to involve teachers more actively in the academic and career plans of disadvantaged students. This is important because teachers, unlike parents and peers, are relatively free from socioeconomic bias in stimulating and encouraging promising students.

At the same time there must be programs to acquaint parents with the academic potential of their child, to get them interested in his educational development, to make them aware of the importance of academic achievement to later educational and occupational opportunities, and to make sure that they know about scholarship and grants programs that would enable their child to continue in post-high school education. I am not optimistic that such programs could effectively provide the encouragement for educational aspirations and achievements that higher status families give their children in the normal course of their socialization. But, again, our research shows that parental influences are so crucial that every effort must be made to utilize this avenue to reduce educational inequalities.

I have no innovative ideas about how peers could be used to stimulate the educational aspirations and achievements of lower status children, but I do believe that their peer culture might be shifted toward educational achievement through programs designed to make school a more interesting and challenging place—by emphasizing competent and sensitive teaching, by restructuring the school around students' interest, by changing the authority patterns in the schools, by elimination of socioeconomic and racial segregation, and by similar innovations. More direct interventions are also possible. Coleman (1965:72–87) has emphasized the use of adolescent peer structures to stimulate intellectual values and performance through intergroup competition. Others have stressed monetary rewards to motivate academic achievement (Effrat *et al.*, 1969). Spilerman (1971) has recently suggested a combination of material inducements with a reward structure emphasizing peer group attainment as a strategy for motivating lower class adolescents. As yet these suggestions have not been tested in large-scale practical programs. However, possible programs along these lines and further research should be encouraged because of the important role that peers play in the educational attainment process.

What does our research tell us about the special problem of equality of opportunity for higher education for women? Our analysis indicates that women make better grades in high school than men. Yet, they are disadvantaged at every level of higher education. Our data do not bear directly on all of the sources of these disadvantages, but they do suggest that parents are less likely to encourage high educational aspirations among their daughters than their sons, and that whenever family funds are short, parents are more likely to spend them on the sons' education. We also know that women have lower educational aspirations than men. This is no doubt in part due to their uncertainty about career and marriage opportunities and plans. But these factors do not fully account for the lower educational attainments of women. We suspect that a narrow sex-role training that stresses household and family roles for women over educational and occupational opportunities—and which becomes most salient when young women for the first time face the realities of discrimination in higher education and the job market—plays a major part in depressing the women's post-secondary educational attainments.

I endorse the policy recommendations which women have frequently suggested for achieving equality of opportunity for women in higher education, such as requirements that all scholarships, fellowships, part-time jobs, assistantships, and admission to all types of training must be equally open to women and men. Existing rules covering residency, full-time enrollment, and credit transfers should be revised to accommodate the needs of women, and child care centers should be established at all institutions. Also there should be courses in the schools to broaden the conceptions of male and female roles, to reduce prejudice toward women's full participation in all institutional areas, and, particularly, to further encourage women to form (and men to accept) a life-long commitment to educational and occupational achievement. Educational institutions should also lead the way in equal employment programs. All positions, including top administrative jobs, must be equally open to women and men. Women should receive equal pay for equal rank and be considered for faculty tenure on the same standards as men. Also, educational institutions and other organizations must show greater imagination and flexibility in facilitating part-time professional involvement and rewarding careers for women who choose to combine occupational careers with child rearing. Programs to change public attitudes, and particularly those of parents toward female children, doubtless will be necessary, too, if women are not to be discriminated against in higher education and in most other areas of American life.

Finally, special programs will need to be undertaken to increase the participation of blacks, Chicanos, Puerto Ricans, and American Indians in higher education. The measures designed for the poor, if applied without discrimination, would go a long way to reduce the problems of minorities because these minorities are disproportionately represented among low-income families. But we also know that these minorities suffer added disadvantages of discrimination in housing, employment, health care, and in most other areas of American life, and in their personal relations with whites. Discrimination has left many of them not only disadvantaged educationally, but with a well-merited distrust of American institutions and promises of equality in the future. They are likely to distrust educational programs that are planned and carried out by the white majority, and they may also question the relevance of many existing programs of higher education for their personal and community needs. Much joint effort will have to be devoted to revision of existing programs and the establishment of more relevant programs for special needs of minorities. These programs must include ways of making the adjustment to academic life less difficult and should provide opportunities for minority group students to maintain contacts with their communities. Also, much more effort will have to be devoted to recruitment programs designed for the early discovery of potentially talented persons from minority groups and to maximize the development of their abilities and their opportunities. Special efforts must be made to increase the representation of disadvantaged minorities in such professional training programs as law, medicine, and dentistry, and in all graduate training areas. Institutions of higher education must also actively recruit minority staff, faculty, and administrators. And certainly, if increased opportunity for higher education is not to be a sham and a delusion for minority people, it must be accompanied by equal opportunity to participate fully in every aspect of American life.

I would have liked to end this discussion on a note of optimism regarding the immediate prospects for equality of opportunity in higher education. I cannot do so. Our research has shown that the process of higher educational attainment is an exceedingly complex one, and that there are no simple and easy prescriptions for attaining equality of opportunity. Many avenues must be tried, but our knowledge of how to mount successful programs, even in the areas we know are important, is far from perfect. Moreover, political problems abound, and national, state, and local priorities do not currently favor increased expenditures for higher education—and particularly not for novel programs. Many colleges and universities are in severe financial difficulties (Cheit, 1971) and may find it necessary to cut their current inadequate levels of expenditure for opportunity programs of all kinds. In the current emergency many of them are increasing tuition without providing additional scholarship opportunities for needy students. Most experts agree that it will take added annual expenditures running into the billions to provide equality of opportunity for higher education, and that the federal government must provide an increasing proportion of the necessary funds.[23]

On the other hand, pressures are mounting, especially from disadvantaged minorities and from many educators and other citizens. The Carnegie Commission on Higher Education, composed of a number of distinguished citizens and educators, recently announced the following national goals: "That (by 1976) the economic barriers to higher education be removed" and "That (by 2000) all remaining barriers to equality of opportunity which are subject to public policy be removed so that ability, motivation, and choice are the only determinants of college attendance" (Carnegie Commission on Higher Education, 1968, 1970a, 1970b). That these are financially feasible goals is documented in their reports, but the pace of the action must be stepped up considerably if either goal is to be achieved. To date, the Congress and the Administration have fallen far short on legislation and appropriations to equalize educational opportunities.

It is a sociological truism that great gaps often exist between stated goals and their implementation. Americans of all political persuasions have expressed the view that equality of educational opportunity is an essential prerequisite for a well-functioning, democratic society. The programs I have discussed detail some measures necessary to begin to implement this essential need. I urge you as citizens to join me in working for their implementation and as sociologists to join me in pursuing further research which will more clearly specify the most effective alternative programs.

NOTES

1. There is a vast literature on the economic benefits of education which shows that those with advanced education enjoy much higher annual and lifetime earnings than those with lesser education. See especially Schultz (1963), Morgan and David (1963), Becker (1964), Innes *et al.* (1965), Weisbrod and Karpoff (1968), and Bowman (1971). Our own unpublished results indicate that, even when we control for ability, average annual earnings of college graduates are considerably higher than the earnings of those who obtained less post-high school education. These results are based on 1967 data, and these earning differentials doubtless will increase over the years as those in the professions and business enter the more productive phases of their careers.

2. We find it difficult to come up with a better alternative to heavy reliance on the educational system for the training and certification function. We agree that other ways to qualify for jobs must remain open and should be expanded, but we would question seriously the equity and efficiency of relying heavily on the selection and training procedures of the many thousands of employers in the job market. Incidentally, some of the criticism of credentialism, insofar as it deals with racial minorities, seems to be misplaced because our best evidence indicates that a large fraction of the disadvantage of these minorities in occupation and income accrues to those who have obtained the right educational credentials but are still discriminated against in the job market (Duncan, 1968).

3. Recent concern with inequality of opportunity in higher education has resulted in a number of reports and recommendations for national policy. Among the most prominent of these are the Reports of the Carnegie Commission on Higher Education (see especially 1968, 1970a, 1970b) and the Report of the U.S. Department of Health, Education, and Welfare (1969). Other references are given in later footnotes. For a provocative discussion of the evolution of the concept inequality of educational opportunity, see Coleman (1968). For an outstanding statement on inequality and opportunity, see Duncan (1969).

4. The most directly pertinent publications from our research are: Sewell (1964); Sewell and Haller (1965); Sewell and Armer (1966a and 1966b); Sewell and Shah (1967, 1968a and 1968b); Sewell *et al.* (1969); Wegner and Sewell (1970); and Sewell *et al.* (1970).

5. The original 1957 sample consisted of 10,321 students who were followed up in 1964 by means of mailed questionnaires and telephone interviews. Follow-up data were obtained for 9,007 or 87.2 per cent of those in the original sample. Since that time additional information on the earnings of the students has been obtained periodically, but these data are used only incidentally in this paper. Extensive comparisons of the characteristics of the original and follow-up sample show little if any bias in the follow-up sample. For a description of the original survey, see Little (1958:1–6). A brief description of the follow-up survey is given in Sewell and Shah (1967:6–8). Much more complete information on the data and procedures used in the analysis reported in this paper will be available in a book currently in preparation (Sewell *et al.,* forthcoming).

6. The detailed tables on which the conclusions in this section of the paper are based are given in Sewell *et al.* (unpublished). They have also been presented in somewhat different form in Sewell and Shah (1967:9–16).

7. Academic ability—its definition, its dimensions, its causes, and its measurement —presents vexing questions to social scientists. There is a long history of debate on these issues which has not led to universal agreement on any of them (Goslin, 1963:123–151; Bloom, 1964:52–94; Jensen, 1969). We take the position that by the end of high school the widely used tests of academic ability yield essentially valid measures of individual potential for success in the system of higher education (Lavin, 1965:42–63; Eckland, 1967). In this study we have used a single standardized measure of academic ability, the Henmon-Nelson Test of Mental Maturity, obtained in the junior year of high school (Henmon-Nelson, 1954). This test, like similar tests, has been said to be culture-bound and, therefore, unfair to lower class respondents (Eells *et al.*, 1950; Lefever, 1959). Whatever the merits of that argument, any class bias in the test will lead us to underestimate the independent influence of socioeconomic background on educational attainments. Since our interest lies in demonstrating that socioeconomic background has an effect independent of academic ability on the completion of every stage of post-high school education, the test bias, if any, will have a conservative effect on our conclusions. If significant social class differences in educational attainment are still in evidence when measured ability is controlled, there will be no doubt about the existence of unequal opportunities in higher education.

8. Among the national studies in which some attempt has been made to follow up high school students are: the Educational Testing Service (1957) study of college plans and enrollment; Project Talent (Flanagan *et al.*, 1962a, 1962b; Flanagan *et al.*, 1964, 1966; Shaycroft *et al.*, 1963; Shaycroft, 1967); the Trent and Medsker (1968) study of 10,000 high school graduates; the Nam and Cowhig (1962) study of factors related to college attendance of high school graduates; the Bureau of the Census and Bureau of Applied Social Research study of factors related to high school graduation and college attendance (U.S. Bureau of Census, 1969); and study of educational and occupational experiences of male youth by Parnes *et al.* (1970) and Zeller *et al.* (1970). Another national study—The Institute for Social Research study of adolescent boys—which will have follow-up data eventually, is "Youth in Transition," by Bachman *et al.* (1969). Unfortunately, there is little uniformity in the sampling, variables, follow-up procedures, or data analysis in these studies, thus making impossible anything but gross comparison of results. Also it is unfortunate that the design of the Equality of Educational Opportunity Study (Coleman *et al.*, 1966) will not permit any follow-up of the over 600,000 students included in that national survey.

9. The most glaring defects of the Project Talent Study were its very low response rate (32 per cent) in the five-year follow-up study and high rates of nonresponse to items on the questionnaire. A small nonrandom subsample of nonrespondents to the mailed questionnaire was interviewed, and weighting procedures based on this subsample were employed to make estimates for the larger sample and eventually for the population studied (Folger *et al.*, 1970:Appendix B). We believe that this technique was not adequate to compensate for bias due to nonresponse, e.g., computations we have made using Project Talent data for the 1965 panel (Folger *et al.*, 1970:Appendix B, Table B2) indicate that 36 per cent of the males in their sample graduated from college, whereas the census of 1970 data shows that only 26 per cent of U.S. males in the age cohort 25–29 (the age cohort most comparable with their sample) had completed four or more years of college (U.S. Bureau of Census, 1970).

10. The booming college enrollments of the Sixties have led many to believe that opportunities for higher education must have become much more widespread during the decade. This is in part true but, from computations we have made using information on the college experiences of persons 20–24 years old in 1960 and 1970 (U.S. Bureau of Census, 1960, 1970), we found that 34 per cent of the increased college experience in the decade was due to the growth in the size of the age cohort, 30 per cent due to the increased rate of high school graduation, and 36 per cent due to increase in the rate of college entry. Unfortunately, we know of no evidence that would permit us to draw a firm conclusion as to whether the increased rate of college enrollment has resulted in a higher rate of college going among high school graduates from the lower SES groups. One calculation we have made, using data from a U.S. sample, indicates that the proportion of students of manual and service origins enrolled in college increased by 7 per cent during the decade, while the proportion of white-collar students increased by less than 2 per cent (U.S. Bureau of Census, 1961, Current Population Reports, P–20, No. 110, Table 5, and 1971, P–20, No. 222, Table 7). This is a notable increase, but is not likely to have had any marked effect on the validity of the general pattern of socioeconomic differentials in educational opportunity revealed by the Wisconsin data. The fact that the pattern we have described has been quite stable over the years is indicated by Spady's analysis of the data from the 1962 current population supplement, "Occupational Changes in a Generation," showing that SES differences in college attendance had increased over the decades covered in that study (Spady, 1967).

11. These figures are based on computations from data included in Current Population Reports (U.S. Bureau of the Census, 1970 and 1971).

12. The operational definitions of the variables used in the models discussed in this section of the paper are basically the same as given in Sewell *et al.* (1970:1017) except that educational attainment for parents and students has been recoded into approximate years of schooling rather than the four broad categories used in that report. For further details, see Sewell *et al.* (unpublished).

13. The tables and formulae for the computations summarized in this section would require several printed pages to reproduce. Consequently they are not presented here but will be given in full in Sewell *et al.* (unpublished).

14. Critics of the use of tests for selection for higher education have often overlooked the fact that many poor children of all races score well on the tests and (*through family sacrifices and their own efforts and often*) with the help of student-aid programs are freed from the handicaps of their social origins. We would not wish to see any reorganization of testing in our society that would overlook this valuable function in efforts to eliminate any undesirable side effects of testing. An interesting result of recent criticisms of testing has been a broadened conception of the responsibility of the major testing services to seek other valid methods of discovering the potential of disadvantaged students and to help disadvantaged students find appropriate educational institutions in which to develop their talents.

15. For a provocative discussion of the use of policy variables, see Cain and Watts (1970) and replies by Coleman (1970) and Aigner (1970).

16. Rainwater (1970:398–425) has presented a strong case for a national policy of income redistribution as the most effective way of reducing social inequality. In this connection he argues that it is unlikely that educational outcomes for poor children can be greatly improved without increasing the incomes of their families. Masters (1969) presents evidence that although the short-run effects of income transfer programs on educational retardation and dropout may be small, the long-run effects may be quite important.

17. Financial programs have been stressed by many economists. For a comprehensive review of the various plans, see the papers by Robert E. Bolton, W. Lee Hansen and Burton A. Weisbrod, Alice Rivlin and Jeffrey H. Weiss, Andre Daniere, Clark Kerr, Howard R. Bowen, Jerrold R. Zacharias, and Roger Freeman in a report on financing higher education submitted to the Joint Economic Committee of the Congress of the United States (1969). See also the papers by Theodore W. Schultz, Mary Jean Bowman, W. Lee Hansen and Burton A. Weisbrod, Howard R. Bowen, Robert W. Hartman, Roger A. Freeman, Robert L. Farrell and Charles J. Andersen, John P. Mallan, and M. E. Orwig in Orwig (1971a).

18. Hansen and Weisbrod's analysis (1969a, 1969c) has drawn critical substantive and methodological comment from Pechman (1970), which in turn has been answered by Hartman (1970). Pechman (1971) has recently made further comments and has been replied to by Hansen and Weisbrod (1971a).

19. We would agree with the Kerr and Rivlin reports that there should be a cost-of-education allowance to help institutions meet the costs of special services that federally aided students might require and for new facilities necessary to accommodate the additional students (Carnegie Commission on Higher Education, 1968; U.S. Department of Health, Education, and Welfare, 1969). For a full discussion of the debate now going on between those who advocate fuller funding of existing institutional programs and those favoring direct payments to students, see Mallan (1971) and Orwig (1971b:331–360).

20. Hansen and Weisbrod (1971b) have proposed such a plan for Wisconsin.

21. The basic political issues in federal funding of the various aid-to-higher-education proposals are well covered in Mallan (1971).

22. For comprehensive reviews of research and theory in this area, see especially Deutsch and Associates (1967) and Hess and Bear (1968).

23. The Kerr Commission estimates that expenditures for higher education must be increased from 17.2 billions in 1967–68 to 41 billions in 1976–77 if equality of opportunity for higher education is to be broadly extended and quality is to be maintained. This would require an increase in federal expenditures from 3.5 to 13.0 billions. The Commission estimates that this would be less than one-seventh of the projected increase in federal revenues in the next several years (Carnegie Commission on Higher Education, 1968, 1970b).

REFERENCES

Aigner, D. J. "A comment on problems in making inferences from the Coleman Report." *American Sociological Review* 35 (March, 1970), pp. 249–252.

Bachman, Jerald G., Robert L. Kahn, Martha T. Mednick, *et al. Youth in Transition,* Volume 1. Ann Arbor: Institute for Social Research, The University of Michigan, 1969.

Becker, Gary S. *Human Capital.* New York: Columbia University Press, 1946.

Berg, I. *Education and Jobs: The Great Training Robbery.* New York: Praeger, 1970.

Blau, Peter M. and Otis Dudley Duncan. *The American Occupational Structure.* New York: Wiley, 1967.

Bloom, Benjamin S. *Stability and Change in Human Characteristics.* New York: Wiley, 1964.

Bowman, Mary Jean. "Economics of education." Pp. 37–70 in Orwig (ed.), *Financing Higher Education: Alternatives for the Federal Government.* Iowa City: American College Testing Program, 1971.

Cain, Glen G. and Harold W. Watts. "Problems in making policy inferences from the Coleman Report." *American Sociological Review,* 35 (April, 1970), pp. 228–242.

Carnegie Commission on Higher Education. *Quality and Equality: New Levels of Federal Responsibility for Higher Education.* New York: McGraw-Hill, 1968.

———. *A Chance to Learn: An Action Agenda for Equal Opportunity in Higher Education.* New York: McGraw-Hill, 1970.(a)

———. *Quality and Equality: Revised Recommendations, New Levels of Federal Responsibility for Higher Education.* New York: McGraw-Hill, 1970.(b)

———. *Less Time, More Options: Education Beyond the High School.* New York: McGraw-Hill, 1971.

Cheit, Earl F. *The New Depression in Higher Education: A Study of Financial Conditions at 41 Colleges and Universities.* New York: McGraw-Hill, 1971.

Coleman, J. S. *Adolescents and the Schools.* New York: Basic Books, 1965.

———. "The concept of equality of educational opportunity." *Harvard Educational Review,* 38 (Winter, 1968), pp. 7–22.

———. "Equality of educational opportunity: Reply to Cain and Watts." *American Sociological Review,* 35 (April, 1970), pp. 242–249.

Coleman, J. S., Ernest Q. Campbell, Carl F. Hobson, *et al. Equality of Educational Opportunity.* Washington: U.S. Office of Education, 1966.

Deutsch, Martin and Associates. *The Disadvantaged Child.* New York: Basic Books, 1962.

Duncan, Beverly and Otis Dudley Duncan. "Minorities and the process of stratification." *American Sociological Review,* 33 (June, 1968), pp. 356–364.

Duncan, Otis Dudley. "Inheritance of poverty or inheritance of race?" Pp. 85–110 in Daniel P. Moynihan (ed.), *On Understanding Poverty.* New York: Basic Books, 1968.

———. "Inequality and opportunity." *Population Index,* 35 (October–December, 1969), pp. 361–366.

Eckland, Bruce. "Genetics and sociology: A reconsideration." *American Sociological Review,* 32 (April, 1967), pp. 173–194.

Educational Testing Service. *Background Factors Relating to College Plans and College Enrollment Among Public High School Students.* Princeton, New Jersey: Educational Testing Service, 1957.

Eells, Kenneth, Allison Davis, Robert Havighurst, *et al. Intelligence and Cultural Differences.* Chicago: University of Chicago Press, 1950.

Effrat, Andrew, Roy Feldman, and Harvey M. Sapolsky. "Inducing poor children to learn." *The Public Interest,* 15 (Spring, 1969), pp. 106–112.

Flanagan, J. C., W. W. Cooley, P. R. Lohnes, *et al. Project Talent One-Year Follow-up Studies.* Final report to the U.S. Office of Education, Cooperative Research Project No. 2333. Pittsburgh: Project Talent Office, University of Pittsburgh, 1966.

Flanagan, J. C., J. T. Dailey, Marion F. Shaycoft, *et al. The Talents of American Youth.* Volume 1. *Design for a Study of American Youth.* Boston: Houghton Mifflin, 1962.(a)

———. *Studies of the American High School.* Final Report to the U.S. Office of Education, Cooperative Research Project No. 226. Washington: Project Talent Office, University of Pittsburgh, 1962.(b)

Flanagan, J. C., F. B. Davis, J. T. Dailey, *et al. The American High-School Student.*

Final report to the U.S. Office of Education, Cooperative Research Project No.
635. Pittsburgh: Project Talent Office, University of Pittsburgh, 1964.

Folger, John K., Helen S. Astin, and Alan Bayer. *Human Resources and Higher
Education.* New York: Russell Sage Foundation, 1970.

Gordon, Edmund W. "Programs and practices for minority group youth in higher
education." Pp. 109–126 in Stephen W. Wright (ed.), *Barriers to Higher Education.* New York: College Entrance Examination Board, 1971.

Gordon, Edmund W. and Doxey A. Wilkerson. *Compensatory Education for the Disadvantaged.* New York: College Entrance Examination Board, 1966.

Goslin, David A. *The Search for Ability.* New York: Russell Sage Foundation, 1963.

Hansen, W. Lee and Burton A. Weisbrod. "The distribution of costs and direct benefits
of public higher education: The case of California." *Journal of Human Resources,*
4 (Spring, 1969), pp. 176–191.

———. "The search for equality in the provision and finance of higher education." Pp.
107–123 in *The Economics and Financing of Higher Education in the United States.*
Washington: U.S. Government Printing Office, 1969.(b)

———. *Benefits, Costs, and Finance of Higher Education.* Chicago: Markham, 1969.(c)

———. "On the distribution of costs and benefits of public higher education: Reply."
Journal of Human Resources, 6 (Summer, 1971), pp. 363–374.(a)

———. "A new approach to higher education finance." Pp. 117–142 in Orwig (ed.),
Financing Higher Education: Alternatives for the Federal Government. Iowa City:
American College Testing Program, 1971.(b)

Hartman, Robert W. "A comment on Pechman-Hansen-Weisbrod controversy." *Journal of Human Resources,* 5 (Fall, 1970), pp. 519–523.

Hauser, Robert M. "Educational stratification in the United States." *Sociological Inquiry,* 40 (Spring, 1970), pp. 102–109.

Henmon, V. A. C. and M. J. Nelson. *The Henmon-Nelson Test of Mental Ability:
Manual for Administration.* Chicago: Houghton-Mifflin, 1954.

Hess, Robert D. and Roberta Meyer Bear (eds.). *Early Education.* Chicago: Aldine,
1968.

Innes, J. T., P. B. Jacobson and R. J. Pellegrin. *The Economic Returns to Higher
Education: A Survey of Findings.* Eugene: The Center for Advanced Study of
Educational Administration, University of Oregon, 1965.

Jensen, Arthur R. "How much can we boost IQ and school achievement?" *Harvard
Educational Review,* 39 (Winter, 1969), pp. 1–123.

Joint Economic Committee, Congress of the United States. *The Economics and Financing of Higher Education in the United States.* Washington: U.S. Government
Printing Office, 1969.

Lavin, David E. *The Prediction of Academic Performance.* New York: Russell Sage
Foundation, 1965.

Lefever, D. Welty. "Review of Henmon-Nelson test of mental ability." Pp. 470–472
in Oscar Krisen Buros (ed.), *The Fifth Mental Measurement Year Book.* Highland
Park, New Jersey: Gryphon Press, 1959.

Lenski, Gerhard. *Power and Privilege: A Theory of Social Stratification.* New York:
McGraw-Hill, 1966.

Little, J. Kenneth. *A Statewide Inquiry into Decisions of Youth About Education Beyond
High School.* Madison: School of Education, University of Wisconsin, 1958.

Mallan, John P. "Current proposals for federal aid to higher education: Some political
implications." Pp. 303–330 in Orwig (ed.), *Financing Higher Education: Alternatives for the Federal Government.* Iowa City: American College Testing Program,
1971.

Masters, Stanley H. "The effects of family income on children's education: Some findings on inequality of opportunity." *Journal of Human Resources,* 4 (Spring, 1969), pp. 158–175.

Miller, S. M. and F. Reissman. "The credentials trap." Pp. 69–78 in S. M. Miller and F. Reissman (eds.), *Social Class and Social Policy.* New York: Basic Books, 1969.

Miller, S. M. and Pamela Roby. *The Future of Inequality.* New York: Basic Books. 1970.

Morgan, James N. and Martin H. David. "Education and income." *Quarterly Journal of Economics* (August, 1963), pp. 423–437.

Nam, Charles B. and James D. Cowhig. "Factors related to college attendance of farm and nonfarm high school graduates: 1960." U.S. Department of Commerce, U.S. Department of Agriculture, Farm Population, Series Census—ERS (P-27) 32 (June). Washington: U.S. Government Printing Office, 1962.

Newman, Frank (ed.). *Report on Higher Education.* Washington: U.S. Government Printing Office, 1971.

Organization for Economic Cooperation and Development. *Equal Educational Opportunity.* Paris: OECD, Center for Educational Research and Innovation, 1971.

Orwig, M. D. (ed.). *Financing Higher Education: Alternatives for the Federal Government.* Iowa City: American College Testing Program, 1971.(a)

———. "The federal government and the finance of higher education." Pp. 331–360 in Orwig (ed.), *Financing Higher Education: Alternatives for the Federal Government.* Iowa City: American College Testing Program, 1971.(b)

Parnes, Herbert S., Robert C. Miljus, Ruth S. Spitz and Associates. *Career Thresholds: A Longitudinal Study of the Educational and Labor Market Experience of Male Youth,* Volume 1. Washington: U.S. Department of Labor, Manpower Administration, 1970.

Pechman, Joseph A. "The distributional effects of public higher education in California." *Journal of Human Resources,* 5 (Summer, 1970), pp. 361–370.

———. "The distribution of costs and benefits of public higher education." *Journal of Human Resources,* 6 (Summer, 1971), pp. 375–376.

Rainwater, Lee. *Behind Ghetto Walls: Black Family Life in a Federal Slum.* Chicago: Aldine, 1970.

Rivlin, Alice M. "Equality of Opportunity and Public Policy." Pp. 6–11 in College Entrance Examination Board, *Financing Equal Opportunity in Higher Education.* New York: College Entrance Examination Board, 1970.

Schultz, Theodore W. *The Economic Value of Education.* New York: Columbia University Press, 1963.

Sewell, William H. "Community of residence and college plans." *American Sociological Review,* 29 (February, 1964), pp. 24–38.

Sewell, William H. and J. Michael Armer. "Neighborhood context and college plans." *American Sociological Review,* 31 (April, 1966), pp. 159–168.(a)

———. "Response to Turner, Michael and Boyle." *American Sociological Review,* 31 (October, 1966), pp. 707–712.(b)

Sewell, William H. and Archibald O. Haller. "Educational and occupational perspectives of farm and rural youth." Pp. 149–169 in Lee G. Burchinal (ed.), *Rural Youth in Crisis: Facts, Myths, and Social Change.* Washington: U.S. Government Printing Office, 1965.

Sewell, William H., Archibald O. Haller, and George W. Ohlendorf. "The educational and early occupational status achievement process: Replication and revision." *American Sociological Review,* 35 (December, 1970), pp. 1014–1027.

Sewell, William H., Archibald O. Haller, and Alejandro Portes. "The educational and early occupational attainment process." *American Sociological Review,* 34 (February, 1969), pp. 82–92.

Sewell, William H., Robert M. Hauser, and Vimal P. Shah. Social Status and Higher Education. Unpublished, n.d.

Sewell, William H. and Vimal P. Shah. "Socioeconomic status, intelligence, and the attainment of higher education." *Sociology of Education,* 40 (Winter, 1967), pp. 1–23.

_____. "Social class, parental encouragement, and educational aspirations." *American Journal of Sociology,* 73 (March, 1968), pp. 559–572.(a)

_____. "Parents' education and children's educational aspirations and achievements." *American Sociological Review,* 33 (April, 1968), pp. 191–209.(b)

Shaycoft, Marion F. *The High School Years: Growth in Cognitive Skills.* Interim Report 3 to the U.S. Office of Education, Cooperative Research Project No. 3051. Pittsburgh: Project Talent Office, American Institutes for Research and University of Pittsburgh, 1967.

Shaycoft, Marion F., J. T. Dailey, D. B. Orr, *et al. Studies of a Complete Age Group —Age 15.* Final report to the U.S. Office of Education, Cooperative Research Project No. 635. Pittsburgh: Project Talent Office, University of Pittsburgh, 1963.

Sorokin, Pitirim. *Social Mobility.* New York: Harper & Brothers, 1927.

Spady, William G. "Educational mobility and access: Growth and paradoxes." *American Journal of Sociology,* 73 (November, 1967), pp. 273–279.

Spilerman, Seymour. "Raising academic motivation in lower class adolescents: A convergence of two research traditions." *Sociology of Education,* 44 (Winter, 1971), pp. 103–118.

Trent, James W. and Leland L. Medsker. *Beyond High School.* San Francisco: Jossey-Bass, 1968.

U.S. Bureau of the Census. *Census of Population 1960,* Volume 1. *Characteristics of the Population,* Part I, U.S. Summary, Table 173 and *Current Population Reports,* Population Characteristics, Series P-20, No. 207, Table 1. Washington: U.S. Government Printing Office, 1960.

_____. "School enrollment, and education of young adults and their fathers: October 1960." *Current Population Reports,* P-20, 110 (July). Washington: U.S. Government Printing Office, 1961.

_____. "Factors related to high school graduation and college attendance: 1967." *Current Population Reports,* Series P-20, 185 (July). Washington: U.S. Government Printing Office, 1969.

_____. "Educational Attainment: March 1970." *Current Population Reports,* Series P-20, 207 (November). Washington: U.S. Government Printing Office, 1970.

_____. "School Enrollment: October 1970." *Current Population Reports,* Series P-20, 222 (June). Washington: U.S. Government Printing Office, 1971.

U.S. Department of Health, Education, and Welfare, Office of Assistant Secretary for Planning and Education. *Toward a Long Range Plan for Federal Support for Higher Education (A Report to the President).* Washington: U.S. Government Printing Office, 1969.

Wegner, Eldon and William H. Sewell. "Selection and context as factors affecting the probability of graduation from college." *American Journal of Sociology,* 75 (January, 1970), pp. 665–679.

Weisbrod, Burton A. and Peter Karpoff. "Monetary returns to college education, student ability, and college quality." *Review of Economics and Statistics* (November, 1968), pp. 491–497.

Williams, Walter and John W. Evans. "The political evaluation: The case of Head Start." *The Annals,* 385 (September, 1969), pp. 118–132.

Willingham, Warren (ed.). *Free Access Higher Education.* New York: College Entrance Examination Board, 1970.

Wright, Stephen J. "The financing of equal opportunity in higher education: The problem and the urgency." Pp. 1–5 in College Entrance Examination Board, *Financing Equality of Educational Opportunity in Higher Education.* New York: College Entrance Examination Board, 1970.

Zeller, Frederick A., John R. Shea, Andrew I. Kohen, Jack A. Meyer. *Career Thresholds: A Longitudinal Study of the Educational and Labor Market Experience of Male Youth,* Volume 2. Columbus, Ohio: The Ohio State University Center for Human Resource Research, 1970.

6.   RONALD M. PAVALKO and DAVID R. BISHOP

Peer Influences on the College Plans of Canadian High School Students

During the past decade sociologists have been making extensive studies of the factors affecting the plans of high school youth to go to college. This large and growing body of research findings has been highly consistent in demonstrating that socio-economic status, rural-urban residence, measured intelligence, and sex are related to plans to go to college.

Recently, several studies have focused on what might be called the "sociometry of the high school social system" as an influence on post-high school education plans.[1] These studies have demonstrated that a student's status in the subculture of the high school, and the educational plans of close friends, exert an influence on his plans to go to college. Our primary concern is to examine the relationship between the student's own plans for college and the educational plans of his close friends, and the way in which this relationship

Reprinted from *The Canadian Review of Sociology and Anthropology,* 3:4 (1966), pp. 191–200, with deletions, by permission of the authors and the Canadian Sociology and Anthropology Association.

is affected by considerations such as sex, measured intelligence, and socio-economic status.

Data for the study were obtained by means of a self-administered questionnaire completed by grade 12 students in six of the seven high schools of Port Arthur and Fort William, Ontario, during February, 1965. All students present on the days the questionnaire was administered are included in the study; however, students for whom any data required for the present analysis were missing or incomplete are excluded from the analysis.

The major hypothesis we are testing here is that students whose friends plan to go to college will be more likely to plan on college themselves than will students whose friends do not plan to go to college. Given the findings of other studies, as well as a previous analysis of the present sample,[2] that sex, measured intelligence, and socio-economic status are related to plans to go to college, it is necessary to guard against the possibility of a spurious relationship by controlling for the effect of these three variables. While rural-urban residence is also related to college plans, the present sample is entirely urban and it can be argued that this variable is, in effect, taken into account.

Our strategy will be first to examine the relationship between a student's college plans and those of his friends; secondly, to examine this relationship by controlling *separately* for the effect of sex, measured intelligence, and socio-economic status; thirdly, to examine this relationship by controlling two variables simultaneously (sex and measured intelligence, sex and socio-economic status, measured intelligence and socio-economic status); finally, to examine this relationship with sex, measured intelligence, and socio-economic status simultaneously controlled. In this procedure, our concern is to see if the original relationship between an individual's plans to go to college and those of his friends can be reduced or eliminated by introducing the control variables into the analysis singly and in combination. In this way the *independent* effect of friends' plans can be assessed.

The operational definition of the dependent variable, college plans, was obtained from responses to questions such as, "Do you plan to enter university after you graduate from high school?" Those students who responded that they definitely planned to enter university were classified as having college plans, as were those who indicated elsewhere in the questionnaire that they planned to enter a teachers' college or a three-year technical institute. Students who said that they had tentative plans for university, or definitely did not plan to go to university or a teachers' college or technical institute, are regarded as not having college plans.

Data on the independent variable, post-high school educational plans of friends, were obtained from the student's response to the following questionnaire item: "Most of my close friends are planning to . . ." followed by a checklist. Students who indicated that most of their close friends were planning to "go to university" are defined as having friends who plan on college. All students who indicated that their close friends plan to do something other than go on to university, such as "get a job," or "go into military service," are defined as having friends who do *not* plan to go to college.[3]

Information on the control variable, sex, was provided by the student on the questionnaire.

Data for the second control variable, measured intelligence, were obtained from the files of the six participating schools. It was found that four different intelligence tests had been used by the schools. No one test had been used exclusively by any of the schools. Records indicated that, on the average, students received an intelligence test during grade 9. The intelligence test scores were based on the Dominion Test of Mental Maturity,[4] the Otis Quick Scoring Mental Ability Test,[5] the Henmon-Nelson Test of Mental Ability,[6] and the Vocational Guidance Centre Test.[7] A method for standardizing the scores on the different tests was used so that scores on the Dominion and Henmon-Nelson were equated with the Otis, the test which the largest number of students had taken.[8] No data were available on the mean and standard deviation for the V.G.C. test. Since the number of respondents with a V.G.C. score was small[9] compared to the total size of the sample and because there was a broad range of scores on this test, the V.G.C. scores were included in the distribution of standardized scores at face value. The mean score was 108.5. The distribution of measured intelligence scores was divided into approximately equal sixths. For purposes of this analysis, the three low sixths were designated as the low measured intelligence group, and the three high sixths were designated as the high measured intelligence group.

Socio-economic status, the final control variable, was obtained from information on father's occupation provided by the student. For purposes of analysis, socio-economic status was dichotomized into high and low. The low socio-economic status category consists of manual occupations and includes craftsmen, operatives, farmers,[10] service workers, and labourers. The high socio-economic status category consists of non-manual occupations and includes professional-technical, managers, proprietors and officials, clerical, and sales. Those students for whom no data were available on father's occupation (N = 8) were categorized by father's education. They were classified as high if the father had junior matriculation or higher formal education, and low if the father had less than junior matriculation.

It is apparent from Table 1 (Total column) that a strong relationship exists between the plans of close friends and the plans of these students to go to college. While 41.3 per cent of all students plan to go to college, those whose friends plan on college are themselves more likely to plan to go to college (55.7 per cent) than are those whose friends do not (27.4 per cent).

The impact of friends' educational plans on the college plans of both boys

TABLE 1

Percentage of Grade 12 Boys and Girls with College Plans
by Plans of Friends

Friends' Plan	Boys	Girls	Totals
To go to college	63.7 (262)*	43.6 (172)	55.7 (434)
Not to go to college	32.7 (223)	22.4 (232)	27.4 (455)
Total	49.5 (485)	31.4 (404)	41.3 (889)

*In this table and successive tables, numbers in parentheses indicate the number of cases on which the percentage is based.

and girls can also be seen in Table 1. To begin with, a larger proportion of boys than girls plan to go to college (Total row). However, among both boys and girls, those whose friends plan to go to college are more likely to plan on college themselves than are those whose friends do not. Controlling on sex reduces the relationship between the independent and dependent variables among girls and increases it slightly among boys. Thus, the relationship of friends' plans to college plans persists when sex is controlled.

Table 2 indicates that measured intelligence also has a strong independent effect on the plans of these students to go to college. Among students who are

TABLE 2

Percentage of Grade 12 Students With College Plans, by Measured
Intelligence and Plans of Friends

Friends' Plan	Measured Intelligence		
	High	Low	Total
To go to college	63.8 (257)	44.1 (177)	55.7 (434)
Not to go to college	36.2 (177)	21.9 (278)	27.4 (455)
Total	52.5 (434)	30.5 (455)	41.3 (889)

TABLE 3

Percentage of Grade 12 Students With College Plans, by Socio-economic Status and Plans of Friends

Friends' Plan	Socio-economic Status		
	High	Low	Total
To go to college	67.2 (204)	45.7 (230)	55.7 (434)
Not to go to college	27.9 (129)	27.3 (326)	27.4 (455)
Total	52.0 (333)	34.9 (556)	41.3 (889)

high in measured intelligence, 22.0 per cent more plan on college than among those who are low in measured intelligence. Nevertheless, within both the high and low measured intelligence categories, those whose friends plan on college are more likely to have college plans themselves than are those whose friends do not plan on college. The magnitude of the relationship is not changed in the high intelligence group but is reduced slightly in the low intelligence group. In other words, the plans of friends have an effect on college plans that is independent of the effect of measured intelligence.

The relationship between socio-economic background and college plans is evident in Table 3 (Total row). Students who are from high socio-economic backgrounds are more likely to plan to go to college than those who are low on this variable. Yet, as with sex and measured intelligence, the effect of friends' plans on college plans persists within each socio-economic level. The relationship is increased in the high socio-economic status group and reduced, but by no means eliminated, in the low socio-economic status group.

Given that sex, measured intelligence, and socio-economic status are all singly related to college plans, it is possible that by controlling these variables in combination the effect of friends' plans on college plans may be reduced or eliminated altogether even though the effect of friends' plans remains when they are controlled separately.

In Table 4 the relationship between friends' plans and college plans is presented controlling for both sex and measured intelligence. In all cases, that is, among both boys and girls at both high and low measured intelligence levels, educational plans of friends continue to be related to college plans. This relationship is strongest among boys of high intelligence and weakest among girls of low intelligence.

Controlling for sex and socio-economic status, the relationship between

TABLE 4

**Percentage of Grade 12 Boys and Girls With College Plans,
by Measured Intelligence and Plans of Friends**

Friends' Plan	Measured Intelligence		
	High	Low	Total
Boys			
To go to college	71.4 (154)	52.8 (108)	63.7 (262)
Not to go to college	38.0 (92)	29.0 (131)	32.7 (223)
Girls			
To go to college	52.4 (103)	30.4 (69)	43.6 (172)
Not to go to college	34.1 (85)	15.6 (147)	22.4 (232)
Total	52.5 (434)	30.5 (455)	41.3 (889)

friends' plans for college and college plans is presented in Table 5. Here, the effect of friends' plans persists among boys irrespective of socio-economic status but only among girls of high socio-economic status. Among the latter, the relationship between friends' plans and college plans is the strongest of all four sex-socio-economic status sub-groups, while the relationship virtually disappears among girls of low socio-economic status.

When measured intelligence and socio-economic status, our final pair of

TABLE 5

**Percentage of Grade 12 Boys and Girls With College Plans,
by Socio-economic Status and Plans of Friends**

Friends' Plan	Socio-economic Status		
	High	Low	Total
Boys			
To go to college	70.4 (125)	57.7 (137)	63.7 (262)
Not to go to college	35.5 (62)	31.7 (161)	32.7 (223)
Girls			
To go to college	62.0 (79)	28.0 (93)	43.6 (172)
Not to go to college	20.9 (67)	23.0 (165)	22.4 (232)
Total	52.0 (333)	34.9 (556)	41.3 (889)

TABLE 6

Percentage of Grade 12 Students With College Plans, by Socio-economic Status, Measured Intelligence and Plans of Friends

Friends' Plan	Socio-economic Status		
	High	Low	Total
Intelligence High			
To go to college	76.2 (130)	51.2 (127)	63.8 (257)
Not to go to college	33.9 (59)	37.3 (118)	36.2 (177)
Intelligence Low			
To go to college	51.4 (74)	38.8 (103)	44.1 (177)
Not to go to college	22.9 (70)	21.6 (208)	21.9 (278)
Total	52.0 (333)	34.9 (556)	41.3 (889)

control variables, are introduced (Table 6), educational plans of friends continue to be related to college plans. That is, among both high and low intelligence students of both high and low socio-economic status, those whose friends plan to go to college are more likely to plan on college themselves. The effect of friends' plans is strongest among those who are high on both intelligence and socio-economic status, and weakest among those of high intelligence but low on socio-economic status; however, even among the high intelligence-low socio-economic status subgroup, 13.9 per cent *more* of those whose friends plan on college also plan to go to college than do those whose friends do not.

The relationship of friends' educational plans to individual college plans with sex, measured intelligence, and socio-economic status simultaneously controlled is presented in Table 7.

Plans of friends to go to college continue to be related to the college plans of individuals, with two exceptions. The relationship disappears among both high and low intelligence girls of low socio-economic status. Thus, among girls of high intelligence and high socio-economic status, those whose friends plan to go to college are much more likely to plan on college themselves (43.0 per cent difference) than are those whose friends do not plan to go to college. This same pattern holds for high socio-economic status girls of low intelligence. However, among girls of low socio-economic status whether of high or low measured intelligence, this relationship disappears. For them, the plans of

TABLE 7

Percentage of Grade 12 Boys and Girls With College Plans, by Socio-economic Status, Measured Intelligence, and Plans of Friends

Friends' Plan	Socio-economic Status		
	High	Low	Total
Boys Intelligence High			
To go to college	79.7 (79)	62.7 (75)	71.4 (154)
Not to go to college	40.0 (30)	37.1 (62)	38.0 (92)
Boys Intelligence Low			
To go to college	54.3 (46)	51.6 (62)	52.8 (108)
Not to go to college	31.3 (32)	28.3 (99)	29.0 (131)
Girls Intelligence High			
To go to college	70.6 (51)	34.6 (52)	52.4 (103)
Not to go to college	27.6 (29)	37.5 (56)	34.1 (85)
Girls Intelligence Low			
To go to college	46.4 (28)	19.5 (41)	30.4 (69)
Not to go to college	15.8 (38)	15.6 (109)	15.6 (147)
Total	52.0 (333)	34.9 (556)	41.3 (889)

friends do not have an influence on college plans. All boys, irrespective of socio-economic status and measured intelligence, are more likely to plan to go to college if their friends also plan to do so than if their friends do not plan to go to college.

This analysis provides a good deal of support for the hypothesis that the post-high school educational plans of young people are greatly influenced by the plans of their friends. It is also clear that while this hypothesis generally holds when other variables related to college plans are controlled, some important qualifications must be noted. Specifically, among girls of low socio-economic status, plans of close friends have virtually no effect on their plans to go to college (Table 5). Furthermore, this lack of relationship persists when measured intelligence is controlled (Table 7). That is, plans of friends have no effect on the college plans of girls of low socio-economic status even if they are of high ability, as evidenced by measured intelligence.

These findings suggest that peer influence on educational aspirations may not operate uniformly across all socio-economic status and sex groups. That is, the dynamics of peer influence on plans may be quite different among high school boys than among girls, and different among girls of high than girls of low socio-economic status. Whatever non-intellectual attractions going to college may offer girls—be it increased prestige within the high school status system or greater access to young men of potentially high occupational status —the plans of their close friends do not mitigate the depressing effect of low socio-economic status on planning to go to college even among girls of high intelligence and, by implication, with a high probability of academic success in college.

Another implication of this study bears on the view of some that peer influences have a generally negative or lowering effect on educational aspiration and achievement. Rather than supporting this thesis, our findings suggest that peer influences can be either positive or negative, depending on their content. In support of this notion, we refer to the fact that the gross rate of college planning for students in this study is 41.3 per cent, that is, without regard to sex, measured intelligence, or socio-economic status. However, the data in Table 7 indicate that among boys at each socio-economic status and measured intelligence level, those whose friends plan to go to college plan on college themselves at rates above 41.3 per cent; and those whose friends do not plan to go to college plan on college at lower rates. The same holds true for girls of high socio-economic status, the exception being girls of low socio-economic status discussed above.

Clearly, generalizing that "youth subculture," or peers generally, have a lowering effect on educational aspirations without taking into account the content of subcultural or peer group norms involves a good deal of imprecision. Our findings point to a need for investigating the dynamics of peer influence among different kinds of adolescent subgroups identified on the basis of (among possibly other characteristics) sex, intelligence, and socio-economic background.

A related problem raised by this analysis is precisely how subgroups of students differentiated by sex, measured intelligence, and socio-economic status, come to place different values on higher education. While we have documented the existence of a relationship between the plans of peers and the student's own educational plans, an explanation of *how* such homogeneity of goals comes into being is not possible with the data available in this study.

NOTES

1. The most important representatives of this line of inquiry are C. Norman Alexander, Jr., and Ernest Q. Campbell, "Peer Influences on Adolescent Educational Aspirations and Attainments," *American Sociological Review,* 29 (August, 1964), 568–575; A. O. Haller and C. E. Butterworth, "Peer Influences on Levels of Occupational and Educational Aspiration," *Social Forces,* 38 (May, 1960), 289–295; Edward L. McDill and James Coleman, "High School Social Status, College Plans, and Interest in Academic Achievement: A Panel Analysis," *American Sociological Review,* 28 (December, 1963), 905–918; and Edward L. McDill and James Coleman, "Family and Peer Influences in College Plans of High School Students," *Sociology of Education,* 38 (Winter, 1965), 112–126. Although it deals with the plans of college students for graduate work, a study by Wallace is also relevant here; see Walter L. Wallace, "Peer Influences and Undergraduates' Aspirations for Graduate Study," *Sociology of Education,* 38 (Fall, 1965), 375–392.

2. Ronald M. Pavalko and David R. Bishop, "Socio-economic Status and College Plans: A Study of Canadian High School Students," *Sociology of Education,* 39 (Summer, 1966), pp. 288–298.

3. It should be kept in mind that this variable refers to the student's *perception* of the educational plans of his close friends. It is possible that if actual reported plans of friends were used to measure this variable, relationships different from those reported here might be found.

4. *The Dominion Tests,* Department of Educational Research, Ontario College of Education, Toronto, 1939.

5. A. S. Otis, *Otis Quick-Scoring Mental Ability Tests,* World Book Company, 1939.

6. V. A. C. Henmon and M. J. Nelson, *The Henmon-Nelson Test of Mental Ability* (Chicago, 1942).

7. V. G. C., The Guidance Centre, Ontario College of Education, University of Toronto. (This test is apparently no longer used according to Fort William guidance personnel and officials of the Guidance Centre.)

8. The technique used is discussed in "The Army General Classification Test with Special Reference to the Construction and Standardization of Forms la and lb," *Journal of Educational Psychology,* 38 (November, 1947), 385–420. (See especially pp. 403–404.) The equation for transforming a set of scores Y having a given mean and standard deviation into an equivalent set of scores X having some other arbitrary mean and standard deviation may be written:

$$X = Y\frac{SD_x}{SD_y} - \overline{X}_y\frac{SD_x}{SD_y} + \overline{X}_x$$

9. The total number of students who had taken the Vocational Guidance Centre Test is only 17 or 1.9 per cent of the sample.

10. Although this is an urban sample and all the high schools are located in the cities, a few students (1.6 per cent) live outside the city limits and have fathers who are farmers.

7.   BURTON R. CLARK

The "Cooling-Out" Function in Higher Education

A major problem of democratic society is inconsistency between encouragement to achieve and the realities of limited opportunity. Democracy asks
individuals to act as if social mobility were universally possible; status is to be
won by individual effort, and rewards are to accrue to those who try. But
democratic societies also need selective training institutions, and hierarchical
work organizations permit increasingly fewer persons to succeed to ascending
levels. Situations of opportunity are also situations of denial and failure. Thus
democratic societies need not only to motivate achievement but also to mollify
those denied it in order to sustain motivation in the face of disappointment and
to deflect resentment. In the modern mass democracy, with its large-scale
organization, elaborated ideologies of equal access and participation, and
minimal commitment to social origin as a basis for status, the task becomes
critical.

The problem of blocked opportunity has been approached sociologically
through means-ends analysis. Merton and others have called attention to the
phenomenon of dissociation between culturally instilled goals and institution-
ally provided means of realization; discrepancy between ends and means is
seen as a basic social source of individual frustration and recalcitrance.[1] We
shall here extend means-ends analysis in another direction, to the responses
of organized groups to means-ends disparities, in particular focusing attention
on ameliorative processes that lessen the strains of dissociation. We shall do
so by analyzing the most prevalent type of dissociation between aspirations and
avenues in American education, specifying the structure and processes that
reduce the stress of structural disparity and individual denial. Certain components of American higher education perform what may be called the cooling-
out function,[2] and it is to these that attention will be drawn.

Reprinted from *The American Journal of Sociology,* 65 (May, 1960), pp. 569–76, by permission
of the University of Chicago Press. Copyright © 1960 by the University of Chicago.

This article is a revised and extended version of paper read at the Fifty-fourth Annual Meeting
of the American Sociological Association, Chicago, September 3–5, 1959. The author is indebted
to Erving Goffman and Martin A. Trow for criticism and to Sheldon Messinger for extended
conceptual and editorial comment.

THE ENDS-MEANS DISJUNCTURE

In American higher education the aspirations of the multitude are encouraged by "open-door" admission to public-supported colleges. The means of moving upward in status and of maintaining high status now include some years in college, and a college education is a prerequisite of the better positions in business and the professions. The trend is toward an ever tighter connection between higher education and higher occupations, as increased specialization and professionalization insure that more persons will need more preparation. The high-school graduate, seeing college as essential to success, will seek to enter some college, regardless of his record in high school.

A second and allied source of public interest in unlimited entry into college is the ideology of equal opportunity.[3] Strictly interpreted, equality of opportunity means selection according to ability, without regard to extraneous considerations. Popularly interpreted, however, equal opportunity in obtaining a college education is widely taken to mean unlimited access to some form of college: in California, for example, state educational authorities maintain that high school graduates who cannot qualify for the state university or state college should still have the "opportunity of attending a publicly supported institution of higher education," this being "an essential part of the state's goal of guaranteeing equal educational opportunities to all its citizens."[4] To deny access to college is then to deny equal opportunity. Higher education should make a seat available without judgment on past performance.

Many other features of current American life encourage college-going. School officials are reluctant to establish early critical hurdles for the young, as is done in Europe. With little enforced screening in the pre-college years, vocational choice and educational selection are postponed to the college years or later. In addition, the United States, a wealthy country, is readily supporting a large complex of colleges, and its expanding economy requires more specialists. Recently, a national concern that manpower be fully utilized has encouraged the extending of college training to more and different kinds of students. Going to college is also in some segments of society the thing to do; as a last resort, it is more attractive than the army or a job. Thus ethical and practical urges together encourage the high-school graduate to believe that college is both a necessity and a right; similarly, parents and elected officials incline toward legislation and admission practices that insure entry for large numbers; and educational authorities find the need and justification for easy admission.

Even where pressures have been decisive in widening admission policy, however, the system of higher education has continued to be shaped partly by other interests. The practices of public colleges are influenced by the academic personnel, the organizational requirements of colleges, and external pressures other than those behind the open door. Standards of performance and graduation are maintained. A commitment to standards is encouraged by a set of values in which the status of a college, as defined by academicians and a large body of educated laymen, is closely linked to the perceived quality of faculty, student body, and curriculum. The raising of standards is supported by the faculty's desire to work with promising students and to enjoy membership in an enterprise of reputed quality—college authorities find low standards and poor students a handicap in competing with other colleges for such resources as able faculty as well as for academic status. The wish is widespread that college education be of the highest quality for the preparation of leaders in public affairs, business, and the professions. In brief, the institutional means of the students' progress toward college graduation and subsequent goals are shaped in large part by a commitment to quality embodied in college staffs, traditions, and images.

The conflict between open-door admission and performance of high quality often means a wide discrepancy between the hopes of entering students and the means of their realization. Students who pursue ends for which a college education is required but who have little academic ability gain admission into colleges only to encounter standards of performance they cannot meet. As a result, while some students of low promise are successful, for large numbers failure is inevitable and *structured.* The denial is delayed, taking place within the college instead of at the edge of the system. It requires that many colleges handle the student who intends to complete college and has been allowed to become involved but whose destiny is to fail.

RESPONSES TO DISJUNCTURE

What is done with the student whose destiny will normally be early termination? One answer is unequivocal dismissal. This "hard" response is found in the state university that bows to pressure for broad admission but then protects standards by heavy dropout. In the first year it weeds out many of the incompetent, who may number a third or more of the entering class.[5] The response of the college is hard in that failure is clearly defined as such. Failure is public; the student often returns home. This abrupt change in status and in access to the means of achievement may occur simultaneously in a large college or university for hundreds, and sometimes thousands, of students after the first semester and at the end of the freshman year. The delayed denial is often viewed on the outside as heartless, a slaughter of the innocents.[6] This excites public pressure and anxiety, and apparently the practice cannot be extended indefinitely as the demand for admission to college increases.

A second answer is to sidetrack unpromising students rather than have them fail. This is the "soft" response: never to dismiss a student but to provide him with an alternative. One form of it in some state universities is the detour to an extension division or a general college, which has the advantage of appearing not very different from the main road. Sometimes "easy" fields of study, such as education, business administration, and social science, are used as alternatives to dismissal.[7] The major form of the soft response is not found in the four-year college or university, however, but in the college that specializes in handling students who will soon be leaving—typically, the two-year public junior college.

In most states where the two-year college is a part of higher education, the students likely to be caught in the means-ends disjuncture are assigned to it in large numbers. In California, where there are over sixty public two-year colleges in a diversified system that includes the state university and numerous four-year state colleges, the junior college is unselective in admissions and by law, custom, and self-conception accepts all who wish to enter.[8] It is tuition-free, local, and under local control. Most of its entering students want to try for the baccalaureate degree, transferring to a "senior" college after one or two years. About two-thirds of the students in the junior colleges of the state are in programs that permit transferring; but, of these, only about one-third actually transfer to a four-year college.[9] The remainder, or two out of three of the professed transfer students, are "latent terminal students": their announced intention and program of study entails four years of college, but in reality their work terminates in the junior college. Constituting about half of all the students in the California junior colleges, and somewhere between one-third and one-half of junior college students nationally,[10] these students cannot be ignored by the colleges. Understanding their careers is important to understanding modern higher education.

THE REORIENTING PROCESS

This type of student in the junior college is handled by being moved out of a transfer major to a one- or two-year program of vocational, business, or semiprofessional training. This calls for the relinquishing of his original intention, and he is induced to accept a substitute that has lower status in both the college and society in general.

In one junior college[11] the initial move in a cooling-out process is pre-entrance testing: low scores on achievement tests lead poorly qualified students into remedial classes. Assignment to remedial work casts doubt and slows the student's movement into bona fide transfer courses. The remedial courses are, in effect, a subcollege. The student's achievement scores are made part of a counseling folder that will become increasingly significant to him. An objective record of ability and performance begins to accumulate.

A second step is a counseling interview before the beginning of the first semester, and before all subsequent semesters for returning students. "At this interview the counselor assists the student to choose the proper courses in light of his objective, his test scores, the high school record and test records from his previous schools."[12] Assistance in choosing "the proper courses" is gentle at first. Of the common case of the student who wants to be an engineer but who is not a promising candidate, a counselor said: "I never openly countermand his choice, but edge him toward a terminal program by gradually laying out the facts of life." Counselors may become more severe later when grades provide a talking point and when the student knows that he is in trouble. In the earlier counseling the desire of the student has much weight; the counselor limits himself to giving advice and stating the probability of success. The advice is entered in the counseling record that shadows the student.

A third and major step in reorienting the latent terminal student is a special course entitled "Orientation to College," mandatory for entering students. All sections of it are taught by teacher-counselors who comprise the counseling staff, and one of its purposes is "to assist students in evaluating their own abilities, interests, and aptitudes; in assaying their vocational choices in light of this evaluation; and in making educational plans to implement their choices." A major section of it takes up vocational planning; vocational tests are given at a time when opportunities and requirements in various fields of work are discussed. The tests include the "Lee Thorpe Interest Inventory" ("given to all students for motivating a self-appraisal of vocational choice") and the "Strong Interest Inventory" ("for all who are undecided about choice or who show disparity between accomplishment and vocational choice"). Mechanical and clerical aptitude tests are taken by all. The aptitudes are directly related to the college's terminal programs, with special tests, such as a pre-engineering ability test, being given according to need. Then an "occupational paper is required of all students for their chosen occupation"; in it the student writes on the required training and education and makes a "self-appraisal of fitness."

Tests and papers are then used in class discussion and counseling interviews, in which the students themselves arrange and work with a counselor's folder and a student test profile and, in so doing, are repeatedly confronted by the accumulating evidence—the test scores, course grades, recommendations of teachers and counselors. This procedure is intended to heighten self-awareness of capacity in relation to choice and hence to strike particularly at the latent terminal student. The teacher-counselors are urged constantly to "be alert to the problem of unrealistic vocational goals" and to "help students to accept their limitations and strive for success in other worthwhile objectives that are within their grasp." The orientation class was considered a good place "to talk tough," to explain in an *impersonal* way the facts of life for the overambitious student. Talking tough to a whole group is part of a soft treatment of the individual.

Following the vocational counseling, the orientation course turns to "building an educational program," to study of the requirements for graduation of the college in transfer and terminal curriculum, and to planning of a four-semester program. The students also become acquainted with the requirements of the college to which they hope to transfer, here contemplating additional hurdles such as the entrance examinations of other colleges. Again, the hard facts of the road ahead are brought to bear on self-appraisal.

If he wishes, the latent terminal student may ignore the counselor's advice and the test scores. While in the counseling class, he is also in other courses, and he can wait to see what happens. Adverse counseling advice and poor test scores may not shut off his hope of completing college; when this is the case, the deterrent will be encountered in the regular classes. Here the student is divested of expectations, lingering from high school, that he will automatically pass and, hopefully, automatically be transferred. Then, receiving low grades, he is thrown back into the counseling orbit, a fourth step in his reorientation and a move justified by his actual accomplishment. The following indicates the nature of the referral system:

> *Need for Improvement Notices* are issued by instructors to students who are doing unsatisfactory work. The carbon copy of the notice is given to the counselor who will be available for conference with the student. The responsibility lies with the student to see his counselor. However, experience shows that some counselees are unable to be sufficiently self-directive to seek aid. The counselor should, in such cases, send for the student, using the Request for Conference blank. If the student fails to respond to the Request for Conference slip, this may become a disciplinary matter and should be referred to the deans.
>
> After a conference has been held, the Need for Improvement notices are filed in the student's folder. *This may be important* in case of a complaint concerning the fairness of a final grade.[13]

This directs the student to more advice and self-assessment, as soon and as often as he has classroom difficulty. The carbon-copy routine makes it certain that, if he does not seek advice, advice will seek him. The paper work and bureaucratic procedure have the purpose of recording referral and advice in black and white, where they may later be appealed to impersonally. As put in an unpublished report of the college, the overaspiring student and the one who seems to be in the wrong program require "skillful and delicate handling. An accumulation of pertinent factual information may serve to fortify the objectivity of the student-counselor relationship." While the counselor advises delicately and patiently, but persistently, the student is confronted with the record with increasing frequency.

A fifth step, one necessary for many in the throes of discouragement, is probation: "Students [whose] grade-point averages fall below 2.0 [C] in any semester will, upon recommendation by the Scholarship Committee, be placed on probationary standing." A second failure places the student on second probation, and a third may mean that he will be advised to withdraw from the college altogether. The procedure is not designed to rid the college of a large number of students, for they may continue on probation for three consecutive semesters; its purpose is not to provide a status halfway out of the college but to "assist the student to seek an objective (major field) at a level on which he can succeed."[14] An important effect of probation is its slow killing-off of the lingering hopes of the most stubborn latent terminal students. A "transfer student" must have a C average to receive the Associate in Arts (a two-year degree) offered by the junior college, but no minimum average is set for terminal students. More important, four-year colleges require a C average or higher for the transfer student. Thus probationary status is the final blow to hopes of transferring and, indeed, even to graduating from the junior college under a transfer-student label. The point is reached where the student must permit himself to be reclassified or else drop out. In this college, 30 per cent of the students enrolled at the end of the spring semester, 1955–56, who returned the following fall were on probation; three out of four of these were transfer students in name.[15]

This sequence of procedures is a specific process of cooling-out;[16] its effect, at the best, is to let down hopes gently and unexplosively. Through it students who are failing or barely passing find their occupational and academic future being redefined. Along the way, teacher-counselors urge the latent terminal student to give up his plan of transferring and stand ready to console him in accepting a terminal curriculum. The drawn-out denial when it is effective is in place of a personal, hard "No"; instead, the student is brought to realize, finally, that it is best to ease himself out of the competition to transfer.

COOLING-OUT FEATURES

In the cooling-out process in the junior college are several features which are likely to be found in other settings where failure or denial is the effect of a structured discrepancy between ends and means, the responsible operatives or "coolers" cannot leave the scene or hide their identities, and the disappointment is threatening in some way to those responsible for it. At work and in training institutions this is common. The features are:

1. Alternative Achievement. Substitute avenues may be made to appear not too different from what is given up, particularly as to status. The person destined to be denied or who fails is invited to interpret the second effort as more appropriate to his particular talent and is made to see that it will be the less frustrating. Here one does not fail but rectifies a mistake. The substitute status reflects less unfavorably on personal capacity than does being dismissed and forced to leave the scene. The terminal student in the junior college may appear not very different from the transfer student—an "engineering aide," for example, instead of an "engineer"—and to be proceeding to something with a status of its own. Failure in college can be treated as if it did not happen; so, too, can poor performance in industry.[17]

2. Gradual Disengagement. By a gradual series of steps, movement to a goal may be stalled, self-assessment encouraged, and evidence produced of performance. This leads toward the available alternatives at little cost. It also keeps the person in a counseling milieu in which advice is furnished, whether actively sought or not. Compared with the original hopes, however, it is a deteriorating situation. If the individual does not give up peacefully, he will be in trouble.

3. Objective Denial. Reorientation is, finally, confrontation by the facts. A record of poor performance helps to detach the organization and its agents from the emotional aspects of the cooling-out work. In a sense, the overaspiring student in the junior college confronts himself, as he lives with the accumulating evidence, instead of the organization. The college offers opportunity; it is the record that forces denial. Record-keeping and other bureaucratic procedures appeal to universal criteria and reduce the influence of personal ties, and the personnel are thereby protected. Modern personnel record-keeping, in general, has the function of documenting denial.

4. Agents of Consolation. Counselors are available who are patient with the overambitious and who work to change their intentions. They believe in the value of the alternative careers, though of lower social status, and are practiced in consoling. In college and in other settings counseling is to reduce aspiration as well as to define and to help fulfill it. The teacher-counselor in the "soft" junior college is in contrast to the scholar in the "hard" college who simply gives a low grade to the failing student.

5. Avoidance of Standards. A cooling-out process avoids appealing to standards that are ambiguous to begin with. While a "hard" attitude toward failure generally allows a single set of criteria, a "soft" treatment assumes that many kinds of ability are valuable, each in its place. Proper classification and placement are then paramount, while standards become relative.

IMPORTANCE OF CONCEALMENT

For an organization and its agents one dilemma of a cooling-out role is that it must be kept reasonably away from public scrutiny and not clearly perceived or understood by prospective clientele. Should it become obvious, the organization's ability to perform it would be impaired. If high school seniors and their families were to define the junior college as a place which diverts college-bound students, a probable consequence would be a turning-away from the junior college and increased pressure for admission to the four-year colleges and universities that are otherwise protected to some degree. This would, of course, render superfluous the part now played by the junior college in the division of labor among colleges.

The cooling-out function of the junior college is kept hidden, for one thing, as other functions are highlighted. The junior college stresses "the transfer function," "the terminal function," etc., not that of transforming transfer into terminal students; indeed, it is widely identified as principally a transfer station. The other side of cooling-out is the successful performance in junior college of students who did poorly in high school or who have overcome socioeconomic handicaps, for they are drawn into higher education rather than taken out of it. Advocates of the junior college point to this salvaging of talented manpower, otherwise lost to the community and nation. It is indeed a function of the open door to let hidden talent be uncovered.

Then, too, cooling-out itself is reinterpreted so as to appeal widely. The junior college may be viewed as a place where all high-school graduates have the opportunity to explore possible careers and find the type of education appropriate to their individual ability; in short, as a place where everyone is admitted and everyone succeeds. As described by the former president of the University of California:

> A prime virtue of the junior college, I think, is that most of its students succeed in what they set out to accomplish, and cross the finish line before they grow weary of the race. After two years in a course that they have chosen, they can go out prepared for activities that satisfy them, instead of being branded as failures. Thus the broadest possible opportunity may be provided for the largest number to make an honest try at further education with some possibility of success and with no route to a desired goal completely barred to them.[18]

The students themselves help to keep this function concealed by wishful unawareness. Those who cannot enter other colleges but still hope to complete four years will be motivated at first not to admit the cooling-out process to consciousness. Once exposed to it, they again will be led not to acknowledge it, and so they are saved insult to their self-image.

In summary, the cooling-out process in higher education is one whereby systematic discrepancy between aspiration and avenue is covered over and stress for the individual and the system is minimized. The provision of readily available alternative achievements in itself is an important device for alleviating the stress consequent on failure and so preventing anomic and deviant behavior. The general result of cooling-out processes is that society can continue to encourage maximum effort without major disturbance from unfulfilled promises and expectations.

NOTES

1. "Aberrant behavior may be regarded sociologically as a symptom of dissociation between culturally prescribed aspirations and socially structured avenues for realizing these aspirations" (Robert K. Merton, "Social Structure and Anomie," in *Social Theory and Social Structure* [rev. ed.; Glencoe, Ill.: The Free Press, 1957], p. 134). See also Herbert H. Hyman, "The Value Systems of Different Classes: A Social Psychological Contribution to the Analysis of Stratification," in Reinhard Bendix and Seymour M. Lipset (eds.), *Class, Status and Power: A Reader in Social Stratification* (Glencoe, Ill,: The Free Press, 1953), pp. 426–42; and the papers by Robert Dubin, Richard A. Cloward, Robert K. Merton, and Dorothy L. Meier, and Wendell Bell, in *American Sociological Review*, 24 (April, 1959).

2. I am indebted to Erving Goffman's original statement of the cooling-out conception. See his "Cooling the Mark Out: Some Aspects of Adaptation to Failure," *Psychiatry*, 15 (November, 1952), 451–63. Sheldon Messinger called the relevance of this concept to my attention.

3. Seymour Martin Lipset and Reinhard Bendix, *Social Mobility in Industrial Society* (Berkeley: University of California Press, 1959), pp. 78–101.

4. *A Study of the Need for Additional Centers of Public Higher Education in California* (Sacramento: California State Department of Education, 1957), p. 128. For somewhat similar interpretations by educators and laymen nationally see Francis J. Brown (ed.), *Approaching Equality of Opportunity in Higher Education* (Washington, D.C.: American Council on Education, 1955), and the President's Committee on Education beyond the High School, *Second Report to the President* (Washington, D.C.: Government Printing Office, 1957).

5. One national report showed that one out of eight entering students (12.5 per cent) in publicly controlled colleges does not remain beyond the first term or semester; one out of three (31 per cent) is out by the end of the first year; and about one out of two (46.6 per cent) leaves within the first two years. In state universities alone, about one out of four withdraws in the first year and 40 per cent in two years (Robert E. Iffert, *Retention and Withdrawal of College Students* [Washington, D.C.: Department of Health, Education, and Welfare, 1958], pp. 15–20). Students withdraw for many reasons, but scholastic aptitude is related to their staying power: "A sizable number of students of medium ability enter college, but . . . few if any of them remain longer than

two years" (*A Restudy of the Needs of California in Higher Education* [Sacramento: California State Department of Education, 1955], p. 120).

6. Robert L. Kelly, *The American Colleges and the Social Order* (New York: Macmillan, 1940), pp. 220–21.

7. One study has noted that on many campuses the business school serves "as a dumping ground for students who cannot make the grade in engineering or some branch of liberal arts," this being a consequence of lower promotion standards than are found in most branches of the university (Frank C. Pierson, *The Education of American Businessmen* [New York: McGraw-Hill, 1959], p. 63). Pierson also summarizes data on intelligence of students by field of study which indicate that education, business, and social science rank near the bottom in quality of students (*ibid.,* pp. 65–72).

8. Burton R. Clark, *The Open Door College: A Case Study* (New York: McGraw-Hill, 1960), pp. 44–45.

9. *Ibid.,* p. 116.

10. Leland L. Medsker, *The Junior College: Progress and Prospect* (New York: McGraw-Hill, 1960), Chapter IV.

11. San Jose City College, San Jose, Calif. For the larger study see Clark, *op. cit.*

12. San Jose Junior College, Handbook for Counselors, 1957–58, p. 2. Statements in quotation marks in the next few paragraphs are cited from this.

13. *Ibid.,* p. 20.

14. Statement taken from unpublished material.

15. San Jose Junior College, "Digest of Analysis of the Records of 468 Students Placed on Probation for the Fall Semester, 1956," September 3, 1956.

16. Goffman's original statement of the concept of cooling-out referred to how the disappointing of expectations is handled by the disappointed person and especially by those responsible for the disappointment. Although his main illustration was the confidence game, where facts and potential achievement are deliberately misrepresented to the "mark" (the victim) by operators of the game, Goffman also applied the concept to failure in which those responsible act in good faith *(op. cit., passim).* "Cooling-out" is a widely useful idea when used to refer to a function that may vary in deliberateness.

17. *Ibid.,* p. 457; cf. Perrin Stryker, "How To Fire an Executive," *Fortune,* 50 (October, 1954), 116–17 and 178–92.

18. Robert Gordon Sproul, "Many Millions More," *Educational Record,* 39 (April, 1958), 102.

Chapter Three

Socialization: The "People-Changing" Function of Education

A universal function of education is the socialization of the young into the culture of the society. No matter how small or large, how simple or complex, some kind of "education" is found in all societies, although the form or structure that such education can and does take varies tremendously.

In simple, preliterate, preindustrial societies education is indistinguishable from other life activities. As Clark has commented, "in preliterate societies education was (and is) concentrated in the family, the tribe, and the other social groupings within which the young were raised. The earliest 'educational systems' were no more than a woman instructing a daughter or a man and a boy walking, talking, and working together. In the Stone Age, we may bet, there were no elementary classes in flint chipping; a boy learned to chip flints by watching adults. Where there was little lore and skill to transmit, and the life of the society was lived out before a child's eyes, education was blended with other activities."[1]

Formal schooling as we know it in the second half of the twentieth century is largely a response to the increasingly complex cultures of urban-industrial societies. Profound changes in social structure, precipitated by the Industrial Revolution but beginning much earlier, have had far-reaching implications for the organization of education. The most important of these was the separation of economic activity from family life. In contrast to a primarily agrarian society, the family was no longer the basic unit of production. Coupled with an explosive increase in technical knowledge and a demand for ever more diversified and specialized occupational skills, this meant that the family could no longer adequately perform what was becoming a much more complicated socialization function. Not only were male (and often female) adults physically separated from children in their work activities (in factories and workshops) but parents also simply became incompetent to teach all the knowledge and skills that their children would need in the new industrial order.

Thus, formal schooling emerged to perform a socialization function that could no longer be performed by individual family units. The socialization function of the family has by no means disappeared, however. Indeed, the family is usually the first socializing influence upon children, and the school and family may sometimes be in conflict in terms of what they are trying to teach.

While schools have become the primary agents of socialization with regard to the transmission of technical knowledge and skills, their effect upon students is not limited to these concerns. Schools are also concerned with "moral socialization," that is, with the transmission of values, norms, and "appropriate" social attitudes. Moral socialization can at times be very intentional and explicit (as it usually is in elementary and secondary schools) or accidental and unintentional (as it often is in universities and colleges). In a sense, contemporary schools perform a "people-changing" function. If we may be permitted an industrial analogy, the school can be looked at as an organization that takes in and processes a raw material (i.e. students) and turns out a certain product (i.e. persons with certain amounts and kinds of education). What happens during the "production process" is that the raw material is changed considerably. With varying degrees of effectiveness, new skills are transmitted and new values, norms, and attitudes are imparted.

Two very broad interests in this socialization process have emerged among both educators and social sientists. On the one hand there has been an interest in studying the "methods of production" (pedagogic techniques, instructional materials, student testing, etc.) with an eye to maximizing efficiency in the teaching process. This has largely been an interest of educational researchers and educational psychologists. On the other hand sociologists and political scientists have been primarily interested in the effect of schools on the moral, ideological, and political socialization of students. Within this area of concern a great deal of interest has been focused on the effect of higher education on student political, social, and economic values.

Two overarching issues—and topics of continuing debate—have emerged from the work of sociologists on the impact of the college experience on student values. The first issue regards the extent to which the college experience actually changes students—that is, changes their values, attitudes, and, ultimately, their behavior. The second issue deals with whether the college experience produces homogeneity or diversity in student values. Both of these issues remain unsettled. Conflicting findings and conclusions abound amidst a variety of methodological difficulties.

One of the best known and most controversial studies in this area is that done by Philip E. Jacob in the mid-1950's.[2] After reviewing the existing literature on the influence of curriculum and the impact of teachers on student values, Jacob concluded that "basic values remain largely constant through college".[3] The only factor that seemed to make any difference in student values was the "climate" of certain small, private, liberal arts colleges. While Jacob found studies showing changes in students, he concluded that these changes were superficial and did not represent changes in basic value orientations. He says, "The changes which do occur bring greater consistency into the value-patterns of the students and fit these patterns to a well-established standard of what a college in American society is expected to believe and do. But the college graduate is not front-runner in a broad forward movement of values within the culture at large. If anything the 'typical' college graduate is a cultural rubber-stamp for the social heritage as it stands rather than the instigator of new patterns of thought and new standards of conduct".[4]

Detractors of the "Jacob Report" have cautioned against uncritical acceptance of these conclusions. For example, David Riesman has pointed out that Jacob failed to differentiate between studies of varying quality. In effect, the same "weight" is given to those studies that are poorly done as to those that are more adequately done.[5] Allen H. Barton has also criticized Jacob for failing to clearly define and distinguish between "basic values" and "superficial attitudes" and for failing to critically evaluate the adequacy of the research he reviewed.[6] Clearly, the extent to which colleges have an impact on the values of students will depend upon such factors as the extent to which value change is defined as a legitimate and desirable goal by the college or segments within the college. Furthermore, a great deal of selectivity occurs when students decide where to go to college. Colleges and universities vary a great deal in the intellectual quality, receptivity, and interests of the students they attract. Variation in entrance standards and the "public image" of schools undoubtedly results in student populations that differ in their readiness and willingness to give up old values and take on new ones.

The first article of this chapter deals directly with the impact of higher education on student values. The research on students at the University of Georgia presented here by Crotty is especially important because it presents a comparison with the findings of an earlier study done at the University of California, Berkeley, thereby permitting longitudinal as well as geographic comparisons.

In the second article, three political scientists, Grove, Remy, and Zeigler, focus on high school students and deal with the effect of a variety of factors, including political socialization experiences, on student dissatisfaction and discontent.

NOTES

1. Burton R. Clark, *Educating the Expert Society,* San Francisco: Chandler Publishing Company, 1962, p. 12.
2. Philip E. Jacob, *Changing Values in College,* New York: Harper and Row, 1957.
3. *Ibid.,* p. 38
4. *Ibid.,* p. 38.
5. David Riesman, "The Jacob Report," *American Sociological Review,* 23 (December, 1958), pp. 732–738.
6. Allen H. Barton, *Studying the Effects of College Education,* New Haven: The Edward W. Hazen Foundation, 1959.

8.   WILLIAM J. CROTTY

Democratic Consensual Norms and the College Student

American political values are products of the seventeenth and eighteenth century philosophers whose arguments influenced the Founding Fathers and served to justify the Revolution. A statement of these core values can be found in the Declaration of Independence, the Constitution, and the oral and written pronouncements of governmental leaders over the years. They include such concepts as ". . . consent, accountability, limited or constitutional government,

Reprinted from *Sociology of Education,* 40 (Summer, 1967), pp. 200–218, by permission of the author and the American Sociological Association.

These data were collected by Professor Willard Range who graciously made them available to me for analysis. I am grateful also to the Center for the Advanced Study of Educational Administration at the University of Oregon for the opportunity to develop the implications of the material.

representation, majority rule, minority rights, the principle of political opposition, freedom of thought, speech, press, and assembly, equality of opportunity, religious toleration, equality before law, the rights of juridical defense, and individual self-determination over a broad range of personal affairs."[1]

A number of agencies within the society are charged with the responsibility of inculcating within the individual acceptance of the system's norms. The most important socializing agencies are the family and the school.[2] This study focuses on one aspect of the socializing process—the impact of higher education on the student's acceptance of democratic beliefs. The popular expectation is that the university plays an important role in *reorienting* the individual's ideas, that is, the university sensitizes the student to a broader range of intellectual stimuli which "liberalize" his political views. This is debatable, but it can be argued that the university offers the first serious challenge to the student's previously unquestioned views which were ingrained through family and pre-university school experience.

Belief in the liberalizing influence of higher education is partly based on the famed Bennington study done in 1935–1939 by Theodore Newcomb.[3] Briefly, Newcomb convincingly illustrated the profound impact of a liberal faculty on girls from conservative, higher income, typically Republican families. A follow-up study of the sample conducted during the 1960's showed that changes in attitudes persisted over time. However, many commentators have pointed out that the Newcomb study was selective and that the results lacked generality.[4] Other studies since show conflicting results and question whether the college experience has any impact on basic student values.[5] In general, research on political socialization in higher education has been disjointed and inconclusive. Whatever the effect of college experiences on student attitudes, college students, as Philip Jacob has rightly pointed out, are the forerunners of major cultural and ethical change.[6] Understanding student attitudes is thus important in the study of larger social trends.

THE PRESENT STUDY

The present study is concerned with acceptance of democratic norms among students in a Southern state university. The research is an outgrowth of similar studies conducted on different populations by Stouffer, Mack, and Selvin and Hagstrom.[7] The study uses a revised measure of the libertarian index devised by Hanan Selvin and Warren Hagstrom and applied to a sample of 894 students at the University of California at Berkeley. It is related to the work of Stouffer and to similar studies conducted at the University of Wisconsin and Northwestern University.

In May of 1963, a slightly modified[8] version of the Selvin-Hagstrom libertarian index was administered to a sample of 904 students at the University of Georgia, a state university in the reputedly least democratic section of the nation.[9] As in the Selvin and Hagstrom study, those chosen were not a random probability sample of the Georgia student body. Rather, the sample reflects major groups within the student population.

The college community represents a distinctive subculture or "value climate" within the larger society. More than most private schools, state universities such as the University of Georgia reflect their geographical and cultural environments. Their students are mostly natives of the state, they mature within the same social and intellectual milieu, they are seldom exposed to or encouraged to explore unconventional ideas in their predominately public school training, and they reach the university having shared much the same cultural experiences.

At the time of the study, Georgia had a student enrollment of just under 10,000, predominately in-state residents. The University, like the state and region as a whole, was rapidly changing. The University's enrollment grew, and an increased emphasis on higher education by the state government, an expanding graduate school, and broader faculty recruitment influenced the school's intellectual climate. Still, the political atmosphere, while covering the broad spectrum of political beliefs, was moderately conservative and the University, to borrow Riesman and Jencks' phrase, remained in the "romantic" stage of evolution, with a sports-minded alumni, adequate social activities for the interested student, and big-time athletics.[10]

This, then, was the setting at the time the questionnaire was administered.

SUPPORT FOR LIBERTARIAN VALUES

Table 1 presents the response to the libertarian items by the Georgia students and compares their support scores with the relevant responses from the Selvin-Hagstrom California study. As expected, support for libertarian values among Georgia students is well below that of California; the average difference per item was 12 per cent. We can see the difference more clearly by dividing the two samples into "high" and "low" libertarian responses.[11]

The comparison favors the California students, 80 per cent of whom are "high libertarian" as against only 52 per cent of the Georgia students.

Differences in the pattern and the priority of democratic beliefs favored show up in the comparison between rank orderings of the two studies.[12] The individual rights are divided into two categories—procedural and substantive (Table 2), and in both categories, the California sample scores high (61 per cent

TABLE 1

Support for Democratic Norms Among Georgia and California College Students[1]

Item	Percent Giving Libertarian Responses [2]		Rank [3]	
	Georgia	California	Georgia	California
a. It unduly hampers the police in their efforts to apprehend criminals when they have to have a warrant to search a home.	80%	84%	1	4
b. The police are justified in holding a man wtih a long criminal record until they have enough evidence to indict him.	77	80	2	5
c. The circulation of Russian or Chinese newspapers in this country should be restricted to scholars.	75	87	3	1
d. State governments should have the power to pass laws making it illegal to speak against racial or religious groups.	71	85	4	3
e. It is reasonable to suspect the loyalty of a lawyer who represents accused Communists before a Congressional Committee.	65	79	5	6
f. The government should have the right to prohibit any group of persons who disagree with our form of government from holding public meetings.	63	85	6	2
g. Crime comic books should be screened by some government agency before publication.	51	47	7	10
h. If new evidence is found after a person is acquitted of a crime, he should be retried.	47	39	8	11
i. Legislative committees should not investigate the political beliefs of a university faculty member.	35	61	9	7
j. It is wrong for government investigators to take pictures of people listening to a street-corner speech.	29	56	10	9

[1] Statements are ranked by the strength of libertarian support in the Georgia student body, not in relation to how they appeared on the questionnaire.

[2] An acceptance of statements d, i, and j and a rejection of the others represents a libertarian response. Percentages are rounded.

[3] Questions used in Georgia (and not in California) and the percentage giving libertarian answers were: "Public libraries should not have subversive literature on their shelves," 69 percent; "Refusal to issue parade permits is a deterrent to the right of assembly," 34 percent; "The government is acting properly in refusing permission to a Communist entering the United States," 14 percent. The data from the last item were faulty and they were omitted from the analysis to follow.

TABLE 1 (continued)

Item	Percent Giving Libertarian Responses [2]		Rank [a]	
	Georgia	California	Georgia	California
k. The government should have the right to withhold relevant F.B.I. files from defendants in criminal cases, when opening the files to them might reveal the names of confidential informants.	28	24	11	12
l. A former member of the Communist Party who refuses to reveal the names of Party members he had known should not be allowed to teach in a university.	27	60	12	8
$\overline{X}$ Item Score	54%	66%	..	..
N	904	894	..	..

and 69 per cent respectively), with somewhat stronger support given to substantive rights. In the Georgia study, the differences are slightly more pronounced, and the direction is reversed. Selvin and Hagstrom demonstrate that the highest incidence of support was for items embodying references to the freedoms of press, assembly, and speech, in that order. Since these findings are identical with similar studies of Wisconsin and Northwestern students, they hypothesize that this may represent a universal ordering of values among students. Apparently this is not the case. Those particular items ranked third, sixth, and fourth respectively in the Georgia sample. The Southern students showed a much greater appreciation for procedural than for substantive rights. The average Georgian's support for procedural rights was about equivalent to the Californian's, 59 per cent as against 61 per cent scoring in the high libertarian category, and well above the Georgia student's own average support for substantive rights. On two procedural items, the retrial of once-acquitted individuals and the advisability of making F.B.I. files available to the accused, the Georgia students actually outscored the Californians. On only one other item, the censorship of comic books, did the Georgia students do as well.

Perhaps high esteem for procedural guarantees is not unusual in a society in which the pursuit of law is a time-honored profession and where the voter is asked to decide on policy questions couched in intricate legal terminology. Debates concerning legal rights of states within the constituted framework of the Union, implications and counter-arguments of Supreme Court decisions, and legal stipulations on regulations regarding the power of office-holders, combined with a keen sensitivity to the nuances of the spoken and written word and a deep-seated respect for tradition and authority are staples of the South-

TABLE 2

Comparative Support of Georgia and California Students for Procedural and Substantive Rights

Items	Georgia	California
Procedural Rights		
1. Police warrant	80%	84%
2. Indictment	77	80
3. Right to counsel for Communist	65	79
4. Retrial of acquitted individual	47	39
5. F.B.I. files available to defendants	28	24
$\overline{X}$ Item Score	59%	61%
Substantive Rights		
1. Restrict circulation of Communist newspapers	75%	87%
2. State regulation of speech	71	85
3. Government prohibit public meetings	63	85
4. Censorship of comic books	51	47
5. Investigate beliefs of faculty members	35	61
6. Prohibit former Communist from teaching	27	60
7. Government photograph individuals at speech*	29	56
$\overline{X}$ Item Score	50%	69%

* This item could be considered either procedural (guilt-by-association without fair hearing) or substantive (right to assembly). The latter seemed more directly relevant.

ern political environment. On the stump as well as in the courtroom, the language of the law has been the traditional language of Southern politics.

But the pattern among the Georgia responses is not entirely consistent. Georgia students are considerably less willing to extend any safeguards—procedural or otherwise—to persons demonstrably unfriendly to the established social order. If proximity of the danger or severity of the threat to the established order can be posited as the twin stress conditions that pose the iron test of democratic principles, then the Georgia students fare poorly. For the rights of Communists in particular, these students evidence little sympathy. Only 65 per cent of the Georgia sample, in comparison to 79 per cent of the California students, disagreed with the statement that questioned the loyalty of a counsel for an accused Communist; one out of four Georgians *would* prohibit libraries from making available "subversive" literature; and only 35 per cent of the Georgia students, as against 61 per cent of the California students, would quarrel with the right of the legislature to investigate the ideological beliefs of a college faculty member. Georgians also strongly (64 per cent) supported the view that a repentant Communist party member who refused to reveal the identity of his former associates should be barred from teaching. Just as emphatically, the California students (60 per cent) disagreed with the statement. On this point there is better than a 2:1 ratio of difference between the two groups, and in the areas of Communism and subversion in general, the two student bodies are the most seriously divided.

The explanation may lie within the Southern culture. The socially and intellectually homogeneous environment of the South has bred a very low level of tolerance for diversity, not atypical in a traditional society. A distrust of the unfamiliar plus a generally poorly developed appreciation of the less technical, more philosophically abstract individual rights have combined to encourage within the Southerner an impatience with ideas or individuals (here Communist) which in some way threaten existing institutions. There is an unwillingness to extend to such people the safeguards of the system. These tendencies, reflected in the Georgia sample, have been commented on by others. Stouffer, for example, in reporting the high level of intolerance in the South refers to a series of other surveys that identify the South as containing the highest percentages of people with "authoritarian personality" syndromes. Kirsch not only finds in the South a lack of sympathy for Negroes and Communists but also a generalized intolerance that extends to Catholics and Jews. He believes that a knowledge and appreciation of democratic principles, low in the South, correlates positively with an emphasis on social distance (intolerance) towards Negroes and deviant religious groups.[13]

Concerning the other substantive rights, the *pattern* of response, although not the intensity of support, is substantially the same among Georgia and Berkeley students. The Southerners are more inclined to allow the government to withhold the privilege of conducting public meetings from individuals who "disagree with our form of government," at best a nebulous mandate to guide official action. Overall, the Georgia students are willing to permit a more heavy-handed exercise of governmental authority in restricting individual rights—a position theoretically inconsistent with their emphasis on Jeffersonian political principles and their rigid, if selective, adherence to legalistic individual protections.

LIBERTARIANISM AND ACADEMIC MAJOR

It is reasonable to expect: (1) that there will be differences in level of support for democratic norms by students in various disciplines; and (2) that the attitude development of the student during his four years in college will be influenced by the subject matter he is exposed to.

Some evidence indicates that personality is an important variable in the initial selection of an academic major.[14] A series of studies have shown the possibility of isolating and comparing distinctive psychological characteristics associated with students in various disciplines. In one study of anti-democratic attitudes in a midwestern university, departments were ranked on various dimensions of authoritarianism. On this basis, students in Psychology, Sociology, English, and Art showed the least prejudice, and Administration, Pharmacy, Physical Education, Military Science, Agriculture, and Education were the most intolerant of the departments listed.[15] From his summation of works employing the "F-Scale," an index of authoritarianism, on college populations, Jacob concluded that authoritarians were attracted to "instrumental" vocational majors in college, such as engineering, medicine, and business administration, and that non-authoritarians gravitated towards "consummatory" vocations, exemplified by teaching, the arts, and social service.[16] While there was evidence in the studies he analyzed of attitudinal differences that divided along departmental lines, the variations were small and failed to show any generalized or powerful trends. Edelstein, in his summary analysis of the literature, reports on a series of studies supporting the belief that the curriculum affects students' political ideas. For example, Drucker and Remmers controlled for situational factors in an experiment with science and engineering students and found that personality may act as a filter in choosing a major field.[17]

In addition to psychological selectivity, interaction with colleagues in the same discipline can pressure attitudes into conformity with the group. The selective influence of others in the same major field may be most pronounced in larger universities with their more compartmentalized and semiautonomous divisions. The Bennington study suggests that in a small college where there is a freer interaction and exchange of ideas among students in all courses of study, the effect of any one major on an individual's political views is minimized.

The subject matter within each discipline could also help shape an individual's political perspective.[18] If, as in the humanities and the social sciences, the academic focus is on social and political problems and the student is forced to think through the ramifications of ideas in more abstract, nonvocationally oriented terms, his understanding of and appreciation for democratic values may increase. Finally, the faculty may guide the student's intellectual development towards goals the faculty values. Through a personal identification with favored professors and broader exposure to their views and a more willing acceptance of their values, a student's own belief structure can change.[19] Where faculty values have "captured" control of the student environment student socialization to the prevailing views would be more pronounced.[20]

Georgia students in each major subject area were distinguished by their support for fundamental democratic tenets (Table 3). The rankings of major areas by support for democratic values produces some surprises. Journalism had the highest percentage of high libertarians. Sensitivity to social problems and inquisitiveness about individual concerns may direct students at Georgia

TABLE 3

Support for Democratic Norms among Georgia Students, by Major Subject Area

Category	Rank	Major Subject	High	Low	(N)
I	1	Journalism	71%	39%	(59)
	2	Law	69	31	(58)
	3	Social Science	66	34	(44)
	4	Humanities	62	38	(107)
II	5	Business	50	50	(171)
	6	Natural Science *	46	54	(282)
	7	Education	43	57	(144)
	8	Home Economics	36	64	(39)

* Natural Science includes Life and Physical Sciences and agriculture and forestry students.

into this area of study. Appreciation of formalized safeguards among Georgia law students ranks them second. The social sciences and the humanities follow. These latter two majors rank at the top of the California sample.[21]

After humanities students, there is an abrupt break that in effect distinguishes a higher (Category I) and a lower (Category II) clustering of disciplinary support for libertarian values. The second grouping is led by students in business—last in the California rankings—and students in the natural sciences. The lowest support for democratic values was found among education and home economics majors, the majority of whom intend to marry, or teach or both. Since the family and the school are major socializing agencies, this is a disturbing finding—especially since this is not an isolated or regional phenomena. In the California study, education majors ranked above only business majors in their failure to support democratic beliefs.[22]

It is possible to analyze major areas of study by year in the university in order to find if, for example, freshmen in the humanities are initially more likely to support democratic norms than first year education majors. If there is a change in support for libertarian values through the four years, which way does it go? Primarily because of delay in choosing a major during the first two years of college, the number of respondents when subdivided by year and major is too small in some cases for meaningful comparison. So we divided the major areas of study into categories, as in Table 3, in order to analyze differences in initial acceptance of democratic norms, and differences in rate and direction of change among the four classes (Table 4).

The freshmen in Category I show a decidedly higher average acceptance of democratic norms than do the freshmen in Category II. The extent of the discrepancy between the two groupings declines among sophomores. The two

TABLE 4

Percentage Distribution of High Libertarian Scores by Category of Major Area and Year in College

| Major Area | Year in College | | | |
	Freshman	Sophomore	Junior	Senior
Category I	69% (N=33)	49% (N=57)	60% (N=91)	76% (N=46)
Category II	42% (N=139)	44% (N=122)	49% (N=153)	51% (N=109)
Total	47% (N=172)	46% (N=179)	53% (N=244)	59% (N=155)

second year classifications are closer together in the distribution of reponses primarily because of the decrease in the percentage of Category I students classified as strong libertarians. Support for democratic norms increases among juniors with their majors in Category I; among the seniors three out of four are high libertarians. Consistent differences in libertarianism persist between the two categories of majors in all four classes; particularly striking differences appear between the two groups of freshmen and seniors. Category II majors progress each year more consistently, though undramatically, towards a higher proportion of libertarians. A minority of Category II freshmen score as high libertarians, and support increases by two points with sophomores. Juniors and seniors about split their support with a shade more of Category II seniors high libertarians.

Of the individual substantive majors, the most pronounced variations appear among students in business school. Vocationally-oriented, perhaps unconcerned with the content and implications of democratic principles, these freshmen have the highest percentage (71 per cent) of low libertarians of any year in any discipline in the study. Support for basic governmental principles increases among second year business students; 43 per cent classify as high libertarians. Fifty-five per cent of juniors are high libertarians and 60 per cent of seniors are high libertarians. There is a difference of slightly over 80 per cent in the division of the freshmen and senior business students on the libertarian index. Apparently the college experience profoundly affects this group. In the other individual major subject scores, the students in each succeeding year show higher libertarian support scores, but the differences are not great. One point bears repeating. Since this is a cross-sectional study, class differences can only suggest a progressive modification of attitudes during college.

Some of the apparent differences between the California and Georgia students may result from conditions found within the universities' subcultures. For example, a good proportion of business school students at the University of Georgia are exposed to courses and faculty in the social sciences. Business school students, unlike education majors, enrolled regularly in political science courses. To some extent, the aim was vocational. The Political Science Department had a well-developed series of courses in public administration, but the same students often supplemented these courses with others in the Department. Perhaps this exposure moderates some students' attitudes. Nonetheless, those initially most insensitive to the subtleties of democratic ideology are the ones most likely to change.

Students most involved with immediate social problems and desirous of articulating positions on these did appear to gravitate to the journalism school. Many of these students maintained a dual major in journalism and a social science content area, usually either political science or sociology.

The University of Georgia Law School was another factor influencing the findings. The Law School was considered the best of its kind in the state. As with many state university law schools, its graduates predominated in the more prestigious public positions, and a degree from the Law School was a valued stepping-stone to either a private or public career. The Law School was becoming increasingly selective in its admissions and the faculty more involved with and articulate about social problems confronting the broader community. Possibly this image influenced those who wished to attend it. It may be that the University of Georgia Law School graduates as a *group* are more tolerant than graduates of the state's other law schools. Overall the prestige of the degree, the past public success of its graduates, and the more forceful stands on social issues taken by its faculty and administration may well encourage future developments within the state.

We take a closer look at education majors because of their political importance as conduits for the very values they modestly support and because our findings are similar to those reported by Selvin and Hagstrom. Among education majors, the size of the home community (over or under 10,000) or association with a fraternity or sorority is unrelated to libertarianism. Catholics held roughly a 2:1 edge over Protestants, and, surprisingly, both fared better than Jews in their support for libertarian values. Good students (B+ to A) and those a little better than average (C+ to B) showed a somewhat higher although still modest support for democratic norms, with 50 per cent and 40 per cent respectively classified as high libertarians. There was a decisive difference between the above average and better education majors and those with low scholastic achievement (D to C) in sensitivity to applied democratic values. Only 19 per cent of the latter group were high libertarians. Males were more libertarian than women (55 per cent as against 41 percent high libertarians). Finally, there was nothing to indicate increasing acceptance of democratic views in each of the four years among education majors.[23] Education majors are less attuned to democratic values initially and nothing within their college curriculum, their interaction with students who share predominantly similar views, or their relationship with the faculty encourages them to cultivate a deeper appreciation of democratic principles.

LIBERTARIANISM, COLLEGE CLASS, AND GRADE AVERAGE

College students modify many of their attitudes during the college years. H. Webster and associates indicate that freshmen tend to be politically conservative. During their stay at the university, their values become more diverse, their tolerance for diversity increases, they develop intellectual skills that enable them to deal comfortably with the ramifications of abstractions, and they become more liberal.[24]

Libertarianism is related to membership in one of the four college classes. In the two first years, a majority of students at Georgia were not "libertarian." The average for freshmen and sophomores is stable—if anything with a very slight drop in support among the sophomores. Yet approximately six out of ten graduating seniors classify as high libertarians. There is a difference of 12 percentage points between freshmen and seniors which suggest that there may be change during the college years towards an increasing appreciation of applied democratic values. These findings are consistent with the California study.[25]

There is a relationship between libertarianism and grade average; the greater the evidence of scholastic achievement, the greater the indication of libertarian support. There is a 20 per cent difference in high libertarian support between good and poor students. Intelligence, as evidenced by scholastic grades, apparently does equip an individual with the tools necessary and perhaps even the motivation to explore the implications of democratic theory and eventually to accept and to support some of its applications.

A clearer understanding of the dynamics of the process emerges when democratic support scores are analyzed in relation to both years in college and scholastic achievement (Table 5). There are strong indications of a developing consensus among students towards an acceptance of *college* norms on libertarian issues. While there may be a great disparity in libertarianism between good and poor students in the freshman year (26 per cent), there is a progressive modification of the extremes, with the exception of the D—C students in the sophomore years,[26] in the search for a set of core values on democratic beliefs. The gap, for example, among seniors is but two percentage points. In each year, the better students show a steady *decrease* in libertarian support.

TABLE 5

**Percentage of Georgia Students Classified as High Libertarian Supporters,
by Year in College and Grade Average**

| | Grade Average | | |
Year in College	D—C	C+—B	B+—A
Freshman	42%	45%	68%
Sophomore	24	50	68
Junior	50	51	63
Senior	57	59	59
$\overline{X}$	44%	51%	63%
N	134	494	121

The average to somewhat better than average increase from 45 per cent high libertarian among freshmen to 59 per cent for seniors. Similarly, poorer students show a 15 per cent differential between seniors and freshmen in libertarian support. The evidence indicates a "homogenization" of the college population in support of democratic values.

Another interpretation is possible. Possibly the attrition rate among classes filters out poorer students, and those left in each succeeding year and their libertarianism scores may be more a product of scholastic achievement than general exposure. However, available data indicate that change in libertarian support is associated with cumulative college experience. The University of Georgia uses a standardized admissions policy that takes into account a combination of high school grade averages and scores on college admissions examinations. The majority of entrants are in-state residents with broadly similar high school curricula and approximately consistent high school achievement levels. All incoming students meet a minimum level of pre-college scholastic accomplishment, yet roughly one out of four freshmen in this study did not return for their sophomore year. (This was the highest attrition rate among the eligible classes studied.) Previous academic accomplishments do not help predict those most likely to continue after admittance.[27] Many students in good academic standing withdrew from the University, and the underlying reasons are not clear. Beyond the more obvious explanations volunteered by those who have left by choice,[28] it may be that students most isolated from the value climate of the University or those most unwilling or unable to modify their views are the most likely to withdraw. At any rate, the nonacademic motivations leading to withdrawal need to be intensively explored as do the attitudinal differences between those who finish the four year course and those who could do college level work but do not want to continue. Such a personality profile would help us understand attitudinal change and the factors asso-

ciated with it more than do present indicators of academic potential. The most
direct evidence of college influence on the student, independent of scholastic
achievement, is supplied by Table 5. The poor and average students show (with
one exception) a progressively greater acceptance of democratic values while
the better students substantially decline in libertarian support over the four
year period. These findings suggest that the college environment has an independent effect on the acceptance of democratic values.

LIBERTARIANISM BY POPULATION OF HOME COMMUNITY, MEMBERSHIP IN A SORORITY OR FRATERNITY, RELIGION AND SEX

Stouffer concluded from his research that there was a consistent difference
in levels of tolerance that was related to urban-rural residence, independent of
region of the country, and which persisted when other variables were controlled.[29] At a cursory glance, the Georgia data reveal a similar finding.
Fifty-five per cent of students from communities of over 10,000 population are
high libertarians, contrasted with 48 per cent from communities under 10,000
population.

When year in college is controlled, however, we see more clearly the forces
at work (Table 6). On initial entry to college, the Georgia students from less
urbanized areas are 11 percentage points below those from more urbanized
areas in their average support for libertarian values. Six out of ten students

TABLE 6

**Percentage of Georgia Students Classified as High Libertarian Supporters
According to Size of Home Community and Membership in a
Fraternity or Sorority, by Year in College**

Year in College	Home Community Population		Fraternity–Sorority	
	10,000+	Less than 10,000	Member	Non-Member
Freshman	51%	40%	37%	55%
Sophomore	48	40	43	48
Junior	54	52	58	49
Senior	61	55	61	56
X̄	55%	48%	51%	53%
N	558	283	364	385

from small towns and rural areas qualify as low libertarians. There is a slight drop-off in libertarian support among sophomores and then an increase in libertarianism among juniors and seniors. The difference in rate of increase is more marked among those from smaller communities; the biggest single difference (12 per cent) was between sophomores and juniors from the less populous areas. In the senior year, there is even stronger support for democratic norms among the students from larger cities, but what was once an 11 percentage point difference has been almost halved. The changes evident in the students at each level from the small town and rural areas are impressive. Fifteen per cent more of the seniors from these areas are classified as high libertarians than are the freshmen. Thus, attitudes consistently change over the years towards greater support for democratic values. Those less exposed to a heterogeneity of ideas and individual types in their home environment do show a greater understanding and tolerance of these differences in each succeeding class in college. Coming from backgrounds that encourage little individuality in thought or in action, the small-town and rural students, nonetheless, can adapt their ideas when cast into a different environment and subject to different intellectual and social stimuli. While their support for applied examples of democratic ideological beliefs is not exceedingly high, it is at least consistent with the college community of which they are a part.

Fifty-one per cent of fraternity-sorority members are high libertarians.[30] Fraternities and sororities have a popular image of being discriminatory, status-conscious, academically frivolous, and clannish. The qualities assigned to these institutions are frequently associated with their members. Yet the difference in high libertarian support between members and non-members (53 per cent), is only two percentage points. The real differences in the dynamics of socialization appear when we contrast members and non-members in each year in college. Freshmen "Independents" show a libertarianism which would make them immediately comfortable within the University community. There are differences among class years, but senior and freshmen Independents show essentially the same division and an average approximately the same as that of the school as a whole. The freshman fraternity-sorority members rank among the most intolerant groups—63 per cent are low libertarians. Yet libertarian support increases among fraternity-sorority members during the four years of college. The most noticeable change, a difference of 15 per cent, occurs between the sophomores and juniors. Seniors have an above-campus average of 61 per cent high libertarians. It is unclear whether this is the result of a simple reaction, or over-reaction, of a deviant group within a college community or whether the fraternity-sorority system liberalizes students. These findings,[31] if confirmed by other studies, may call for a reassessment of the influence of fraternities and sororities. It may be that the influence of these institutions in support of libertarian values is a regional idiosyncracy. Whether fraternities or sororities liberalize students may depend on the cultural norms of the region and the university in question.

The South is as consistent in its religious identification as in its political preferences. The vast majority of Southerners are of some Protestant affiliation. This is reflected in the Georgia study: 84 per cent of the population samples were Protestant, seven per cent were Jewish, and five per cent were Catholic. (The remaining four per cent had no religious affiliation or one that fell outside of the major classifications.) The discrepancy in numbers here is decisive and the small sample of Jews (62) and Catholics (47) make any comparisons tenuous. On the libertarian index, the Protestants with 52 per cent high libertarian fell intermediate between the Catholics and Jews. Nationally Jews are the most consistent supporters of liberal causes and candidates,[32] but they score the lowest of all the religious groups in libertarian support at Georgia. Only 45 per cent of Jewish students are high libertarians. Surprisingly, Catholics, who are often considered more authoritarian and conservative than the other two groups, have the highest percentage (57 per cent) of strong libertarians. The type of fundamentalist Protestant denominations that prevail in the South tend to bring down the libertarian scores of Protestants in general.

Finally, libertarianism is slightly higher among males than females and in the expected direction; 53 per cent of men and 49 per cent of women are highly libertarian.[33]

CONCLUSIONS

This study is a selective discussion of the degree to which students at the University of Georgia accept an applied index of democratic norms. We examined student acceptance of certain procedural and substantive civil rights presented to the respondents within a "stress" context that necessitated a reaction to a specific application and a weighing of priorities. Variations in the support scores of various groups in each of the four college classes were identified and analyzed.

The results in part confirm findings of a number of other scholars. Regionalism is a factor in both the *intensity* and the *type* of applied principle supported. Academic grade average and urban residence are positively related to libertarian views. There was an apparent selectivity exercised by students of different ideological persuasions in the choice of a major area of concentration. There was evidence also of an increasing acceptance of libertarian attitudes by each class year until a level of University consensus was achieved. Fraternity-sorority membership and sex per se (with the exception of the over-representation of women among the extreme non-libertarians) were not distinguishing factors in acceptance of libertarian values. There may be something within the dynamics of the fraternity-sorority process, however, that influences intolerant students to modify their beliefs. In the four classes, freshman fraternity-sorority members were less likely to be libertarian while the senior fraternity-sorority members exceeded the University average for high libertarianism. The number of non-Protestants in the sample was relatively small, but our major religious divisions showed an atypical (for the country) distribution of acceptance of democratic beliefs. The differential support among students from one class year to another was indicative primarily of an adjustment toward a college value pattern.

The groups apparently the most susceptible to change during college were those composed of individuals—specifically freshman fraternity-sorority members and students from rural-small town areas—who initially evidenced the most rigid rejection of democratic norms. It may be hypothesized that those whose acceptance of democratic norms is the least subject to examination in the pre-college period are the most likely to undergo value change once in college.[34]

The South is undergoing fundamental change.[35] It no longer has the monolithic political, social, or economic order that for generations had been accepted as immutable. The students analyzed represent the emerging leadership of one state in the region. Overall, the differences among the college classes indicate a trend during college toward a greater sensitivity to the prevalent national norms. Further, that consensus with national norms, while still allowing for some regional variations, will probably increase. This country may be witnessing a dialogue over the relation of the individual to his government and the extent and limits of his rights that will result in a broader understanding and acceptance of democratic principles—an acceptance that will be manifested in a nationalization of ideological perspectives, a decrease in the distinctiveness of selective regional interpretations of democratic principles, and an increasing consensus as to the goals and value priorities of the society as a whole.

NOTES

1. Herbert McClosky, "Consensus and Ideology in American Politics," *American Political Science Review,* 58 (June, 1964), p. 462. In addition to McClosky's article, discussions of consensus relevant to this presentation can be found in: James W. Prothro and Charles M. Grigg, "Fundamental Principles of Democracy: Basis of Agreement and Disagreement," *Journal of Politics,* 22 (March, 1960), pp. 276–294; and McClosky, Paul J. Hoffman, and Rosemary O'Hara, "Issue Conflict and Consensus

Among Party Leaders and Followers," *American Political Science Review,* 54 (June, 1960), pp. 406–427. Both the Prothro and Grigg and the McClosky selections provide a good discussion of the problem of consensus within a philosophic perspective and the difficulties encountered in attempting an empirical study of the topic. Also relevant is Philip E. Converse, "The Nature of Belief Systems in Mass Publics," in David E. Apter, editor, *Ideology and Discontent,* New York: The Free Press, 1964, pp. 206–261.

2. There is a rich and expanding literature on the impact of the family and the educational process on political socialization. For a summary analysis of the works, consult: Herbert Hyman, *Political Socialization,* Glencoe, Ill.: The Free Press, 1959; and Robert E. Lane, *Political Life,* Glencoe, Ill.: The Free Press, 1959. For an introduction to the research on family socialization see: Herbert McClosky and Harold E. Dahlgren, "Primary Group Influence on Party Loyalty," *American Political Science Review,* 53 (September, 1959), pp. 757–776; Robert E. Lane, "Fathers and Sons: Foundations of Political Belief," *American Sociological Review,* 24 (August, 1959), pp. 502–511; Eleanor E. Maccoby, Richard E. Matthews, and Alton S. Morton, "Youth and Political Change," *Public Opinion Quarterly,* 18 (Spring, 1954), pp. 23–39; and Martin L. Levin, "Social Climates and Political Socialization," *Public Opinion Quarterly,* 25 (Winter, 1961), pp. 596–606. Representative of the research being done on pre-college socialization are: Fred I. Greenstein, *Children and Politics,* New Haven: Yale University Press, 1965; and the Easton-Hess-Dennis nationwide study, exemplified by David Easton and Jack Dennis, "The Child's Image of Government," in Roberta Sigel, editor, *Political Socialization: Its Role in the Political Process,* Philadelphia: The Annals of the American Academy of Political and Social Sciences, September, 1965, pp. 40–57; and Robert D. Hess and Judith V. Torney, *The Development of Basic Attitudes and Values Toward Government and Citizenship During the Elementary School Years,* Chicago: University of Chicago, 1965.

3. Theodore M. Newcomb, *Personality and Social Change,* New York: Dryden Press, 1943; and Newcomb, "Persistence and Regression of Changed Attitudes: Long-Range Studies," *Journal of Social Issues,* 19 (Number 4), pp. 3–14.

4. Philip E. Jacob, *Changing Values in College,* New York: Harper & Row, 1957; Allen H. Barton, *Studying the Effects of College Education,* New Haven: The Edward W. Hazen Foundation, 1959; and Alex S. Edelstein, "Since Bennington: Evidence of Change in Student Political Behavior," *Public Opinion Quarterly,* 26 (Winter, 1962), pp. 564–577.

5. Edelstein traces the studies generally related to the Bennington research, *ibid.* Relevant projects that report often conflicting findings are: Karl C. Garrison, "World-minded Attitudes of College Students in a Southern University," *Journal of Social Psychology,* 54 (June, 1961), pp. 147–153; Neva Allman, "A Study of Social Attitudes of College Students," *Journal of Social Psychology,* 53 (February, 1961), pp. 33–51; Albert Somit, Joseph Tanenhaus, Walter H. Wilke, and Rita W. Cooley, "The Effect of the Introductory Political Science Course on Student Attitudes Toward Personal Participation," *American Political Science Review,* 52 (December, 1958), pp. 1129–1132; Philip Nogee and Murray B. Levin, "Some Determinants of Political Attitudes Among College Voters," *Public Opinion Quarterly,* 22 (Winter, 1958), pp. 449–463; Richard W. Dodge and Eugene S. Uyeki, "Political Affiliation and Imagery Across Two Related Generations," *Midwest Journal of Political Science,* 6 (August, 1962), pp. 266–276; Charles G. McClintock and Henry A. Turner, "The Impact of College Upon Political Knowledge, Participation, and Values," *Human Relations,* 15 (May, 1962), pp. 163–176; and Harold Webster, Marvin Freedman, and Paul Heist, "Personality Change in College Students," in Nevitt Sanford, editor, *The American College,* New York: Wiley, 1962, pp. 810–846.

6. Jacob, *op. cit.,* pp. 47–49.

7. Samuel A. Stouffer, *Communism, Conformity, and Civil Liberties,* Garden City, N.Y.: Doubleday, 1955; Raymond Mack, "Do We Really Believe in the Bill of Rights?", *Social Problems,* 3 (April, 1956), pp. 264–269; and Hanan G. Selvin and Warren O. Hagstrom, "Determinants of Support for Civil Liberties," *British Journal of Sociology,* 11 (1960), pp. 51–73.

8. The changes were made because some of the items in the original Selvin-Hagstrom index, applied in December, 1957, related to issues at the level of public awareness in the mid-1950's and were not as relevant to a college population in the 1960's. The Georgia questionnaire consisted of nine questions taken directly from the Selvin-Hagstrom study, three slightly modified from the original, and three new questions. One item in the final analysis of the Georgia data (see below) was dropped because the information was felt to be unreliable. Selvin and Hagstrom, *ibid.*

9. Stouffer, *op. cit.,* p. 112. Stouffer's findings are consistent with the results of other national surveys—many of which he refers to in his book. In a more recent research piece on "Social Distance," Arthur D. Kirsch still ranks the South last in his discussion of regional variations and offers some explanations for the predominant Southern attitudes, in "Social Distance and Some Related Variables in Voting Behavior," in H. H. Remmers, editor, *Anti-Democratic Attitudes in American Schools,* Evanston, Ill.: Northwestern University Press, 1963, pp. 91–96. Jacob, in reviewing the data available on social and political attitudes, found the Southern universities (North Carolina and Texas) in the studies he reports on to represent the extreme of the continuum—or as he refers to them, the "strongholds of conformity." Jacob, *op. cit.,* pp. 102–116.

10. David Riesman and Christopher Jencks, "The Viability of the American College," in Sanford, *op. cit.,* p. 116.

11. Selvin and Hagstrom divided their sample into "high," "moderate," and "low" on the basis of the response to a set number of questions (15). In Georgia the "high" scores were so few that in effect the "moderate" and "high" categories have been combined. Thus in the analysis to follow, "high" libertarian scores had eight or more "correct" responses (out of a possible 14), "low" scores, seven or less. Hereinafter the "high" and "low" dichotomy employed refers to the Georgia division of the items.

12. The Kendall's Tau correlation measure of association in Table 1 yields a relatively low .58.

13. Stouffer, *op. cit.,* p. 128; and Kirsh, *op. cit.,* pp. 91–95. See also the discussion by Prothro and Grigg, *op. cit.,* of the differences between their Northern (Ann Arbor, Michigan) and Southern (Tallahassee, Florida) samples. Jacob, *op. cit.,* Table 9, pp. 30–31, presents in summary form the attitudes of students in a number of colleges to questions gauging prejudice and toleration. Again, the two Southern Universities in the sample, the University of North Carolina and the University of Texas, are consistently deviant from the attitudes of the others.

14. Webster, *et al., op. cit.*

15. See Elmer L. Struening, "Anti-Democratic Attitudes in Midwest University," in Remmers, *op. cit.,* p. 246; and the literature cited therein (pp. 210–258).

16. Jacob, *op. cit.,* p. 123.

17. Edelstein, *op. cit.,* pp. 569–570.

18. Selvin and Hagstrom, *op. cit.,* p. 65; and Jacob, *op. cit.,* p. 69–70.

19. The latter argument presupposes a difference in political viewpoints among the professors in the various disciplines. In the report of a study in progress conducted at "a large university," Alex Gottfried supplies information to support this belief. Gottfried found substantially more support in 1956 and 1960 for the Democratic presidential nominee among professors in the arts and sciences than among professors in

professional and vocational departments. In the latter cases, the tendency among faculty members was to support the Republican candidate but with somewhat lesser intensity. Alex Gottfried, "Professor in Politics," *Western Political Quarterly,* 14 (September, 1961), Supplement, p. 44. Using their own index of "conservatism-permissiveness," Lazarsfeld and Thielens endorsed the idea that there are politically relevant and distinctive views common to professors in each of the academic majors they analyzed. Paul F. Lazarsfeld and Wagner Thielens, Jr., *The Academic Mind,* Glencoe, Ill.: The Free Press, 1958, pp. 113–158.

20. This is what happened at Bennington. Newcomb found, for example, that initial choice of major was only slightly related to the original liberal-conservative orientations of students and that attitude change was only marginally associated with course of study. He concluded that the overall academic environment and not the specific major was the factor most conducive to encouraging a redefinition of values. Newcomb, *op. cit.,* p. 148.

21. The California listings were, in order of libertarian support: Applied Social Sciences; Social Sciences; Humanities; Life Sciences; Physical Sciences (and Mathematics); Engineering and Other Applied Physical Sciences; Education; and Business Administration.

22. Selvin and Hagstrom, *op. cit.,* p. 67.

23. The percentage of education majors that scored as high libertarians in each of the college years is: freshmen, 42 per cent; sophomores, 39 per cent; juniors, 47 per cent; and seniors, 43 per cent.

24. Webster et al., *op. cit.* Jacob argues that college primarily socializes the individual to values that will mark him as a member in good standing of the "American college alumni." Among the views that distinguish the college educated from those of less education are: a concern with status and prestige; a distaste for socio-economic welfare policies and centralized government; a greater tolerance for unconventional ideas; less prejudice; an absence of a preoccupation with subversion within colleges and among teachers; more religious independence; a greater feeling of mastery over environment; and a more conservative political outlook on policy questions in general. Jacob, *op. cit.,* pp. 4–5. A number of studies have demonstrated a positive correlation between the amount of formal education an individual receives and his understanding of democratic principles. Stouffer and McClosky find political leaders, for example, to be characterized by greater educational achievement and a correspondingly more sophisticated ideological awareness than the electorate in general. Stouffer, *op. cit.;* McClosky, *op. cit.;* and McClosky, Hoffman, and O'Hara, *op. cit.*

25. Selvin and Hagstrom, *op. cit.,* p. 69.

26. For no apparent reason the sophomore D—C students decline drastically in libertarian support. The difference between these students and the junior D—C students in terms of increased libertarian support is just as pronounced.

27. A series of studies dealing with factors related to attrition have been undertaken by Donald W. Irvine, Department of Guidance, College of Education, University of Georgia and by the Institute of Higher Education, University of Georgia, Galen M. Drewry, Director. Among the more relevant of these reports are: Donald W. Irvine, "Multiple Prediction of College Graduation from Pre-Admission Data," *Journal of Experimental Education,* 35 (Fall, 1966), pp. 84–89; Irvine, "Graduation and Withdrawal: An Eight Year Follow-Up," *College and University,* 41 (Fall, 1965), pp. 32–40, Irvine, "Graduation Rate of 1959 Female Freshmen," (Unpublished Memorandum, University of Georgia, April 14 (1965); and Irvine, "Freshman Persistence by Levels of Predicted Average," Unpublished Memorandum, University of Georgia, May 25, 1964).

A follow-up study in this area would do well to include not only students who progress from freshman to senior year, but those who leave school for assorted reasons, and those in the same age range who never attended college. Placed in a comparative perspective, an understanding of the independent influence of college on attitudinal change as well as the more general patterns of attitude change in the post-high school period would be greatly advanced.

28. Donald W. Irvine, "University Drop-Outs in Good Standing," (University of Georgia, Office of Admissions, Report No. 63–13, July, 1963).

29. Stouffer, *op. cit.*, p. 130.

30. See Barton, *op. cit.*, p. 61.

31. The trend remains the same when the other variables are controlled. Both sorority and fraternity members exhibit the same patterns and directions of change. These results differ from Selvin and Hagstrom, *op. cit.*, p. 69.

32. Angus Campbell, Philip E. Converse, Warren E. Miller, and Donald E. Stokes, *The American Voter*, New York: Wiley, 1960, Table 12–2, p. 306; Philip E. Converse and Donald E. Stokes, "Stability and Change in 1960: A Reinstating Election," *American Political Science Review*, 55 (June, 1961), pp. 269–280; Lawrence H. Fuchs, "American Jews and the Presidential Vote," *American Political Science Review*, 49 (June, 1955), pp. 385–401; Fuchs, *The Political Behavior of American Jews*, Glencoe, Ill.: The Free Press, 1956; and Nogee and Levin, *op. cit.*, p. 462. The comparative results in the Selvin and Hagstrom California study on proportion high libertarian were: Jews, 49 per cent; Protestants, 32 per cent; and Catholics, 30 per cent. Selvin and Hagstrom, *op. cit.*, p. 64. The Fuchs' book in particular focuses on and attempts to explain the cultural reasons underlying the high degree of Jewish liberalism and tolerance in the United States.

From empirically unsubstantiated follow-ups on this problem, it would appear that there is a selective Jewish representation at the University of Georgia. As a group, they are not among the best high school graduates, they tend to come from middle to lower class families in which the father is engaged in some form of self-owned small business, and they tend to deemphasize formal associations with and manifestations of Jewish religious identity (Hillel membership, for example).

33. The 112 individuals in the sample from whom four or fewer libertarian responses were elicited were isolated for further analysis. The characteristics of these non-libertarians were then compared with the rest of the sample. It was found that seniors, the better students, men, and Protestants and Catholics were underrepresented among the extreme non-libertarians. Population of home community or membership in a fraternity or sorority showed no difference in proportionate breakdown from the sample as a whole. The three characteristics with which the non-libertarians were most identified were: women (overrepresented by ten per cent); Jews (overrepresented by five per cent); and the poorest students academically (overrepresented by five per cent).

34. Selvin and Hagstrom suggest a similar explanation in a different context. In hypothesizing reasons for leaders' more tolerant attitudes in comparison with group members—an area not explored in this study, they write: ". . . a leader is exposed to a more diverse assortment of people than in his own group. Experience with people unlike those with whom one has previously associated is often a key factor in the acquisition of libertarian attitudes." *Op. cit.*, p. 72.

35. Evaluations of the contemporary mood of the South can be found in: Avery Leiserson, editor, *The American South in the 1960's*, New York: Frederick A. Praeger, 1964; Allan P. Sindler, editor, *Change in the Contemporary South*, Durham, N.C.: Duke University Press, 1963; and Donald R. Matthews and James W. Prothro, *Negroes and the New Southern Politics*, New York: Harcourt, Brace and World, 1966.

9.   D. JOHN GROVE, RICHARD C. REMY, and L. HARMON ZEIGLER

Political Socialization and Political Ideology as Sources of Educational Discontent

The extent of student dissatisfaction with high school education is, we are told, widespread. A recent survey by the Purdue Opinion Panel has shown that over 40 per cent of high school students agree with the radical critique of education.[1] Student unrest in high schools is increasing in scope, frequency and violence.[2] In response to this student discontent, a proliferation of alternative educational models (such as voucher systems, decentralization, and community control) have been suggested as possible strategies to make education more "responsive" to its clientele—students. However, in order to make informed judgments on the selection of responsive models, it would seem imperative that the major sources of educational discontent in high schools be defined.

During the 1960's youth emerged as an active political force in society. Indeed, during the last decade commentators frequently hailed or decried the emergence of a new kind of political awareness and self-consciousness among youth. In response to contemporary social and political problems, students attempted to mobilize public opinion and to bring political and moral pressure to bear on the governmental system. Students in the 1970's, on the other hand, appear to be entering a new phase of turning inward and concern with their immediate environment.[3] If we are entering a new phase of student dissent, then we should find the primary sources of student discontent taking on different dimensions in the 1970's—dimensions which would reflect a shift of students' concern from the total society to the smaller systems of their high schools.

Reprinted from *Social Science Quarterly*, 55 (September, 1974), pp. 411–424, by permission of the authors and the Southwestern Social Science Association.

The authors wish to acknowledge the support of the Research and Development Division, Center for Educational Policy and Management, during a portion of the time they devoted to the preparation of this paper. The Center for Educational Policy and Management is funded under a contract with National Institute of Education, Department of Health, Education and Welfare. The research reported in this paper was conducted as part of the research and development of the Center.

Data for this study were collected under the auspices of the American Political Science Association's Committee on Pre-Collegiate Education. Financial support for collection and processing of the data came from the Department of Health, Education and Welfare, U.S. Office of Education, Contract # OEG-0-70-2023 (725) and from the Spencer Foundation—Northwestern University Program for Interdisciplinary Research in Education.

This study employs data from a national sample of 1,811 high school student leaders to empirically assess the extent to which the political socialization experience in high school is a major source of educational discontent. In addition, we will examine the contribution of political ideology as a source of educational discontent. If various aspects of the school-based political socialization experience are primary sources of educational dissatisfaction, then alternative educational models designed to alleviate the causes of student unrest must take this factor into account. If, on the other hand, political beliefs are a primary source, then a different set of models becomes important.

SOURCES OF EDUCATIONAL DISCONTENT

Political Socialization

A major thesis of this paper is that a potentially important source of educational discontent lies in the nature of students' political experiences within their high schools—that is, in their political socialization. While schools are not the only source of political socialization in society, they rank with the family, peer groups and mass-media as important agents of political socialization for several reasons.[4]

Formal instruction about politics through social studies and civics curricula is mandated in one form or another in practically every high school in the nation.[5] Dawson and Prewitt argue that in modern societies this curriculum "is potentially one of the major sources of political socialization."[6] However, as any analysis of textual material will show, the curriculum is formalistic, descriptive, weakly linked to reality, devoid of analytical concepts except legalistic ones and noncontroversial.[7] In fact, few changes have occurred over the last half-century.[8]

Consequently, research finds the impact of high schools' civics courses is minimal for white, middle-class youth. Blacks, on the other hand, particularly those of low- and middle-class origins, did show significant increases in political knowledge, toleration, efficacy and the desire to participate in politics.[9] Extra-curricular activities also have a limited impact on student political values.[10] In fact, Merelman concludes that the high school experience apparently increases neither adolescent support for nor understanding of democratic values.[11] Indeed, there is even some evidence that the school alienates bright twelfth graders from democratic values.[12] An impoverished formal political education curriculum may itself be an important factor and, as we will note shortly, it may also be related to educational dissatisfaction in a more complex manner.

Political socialization in schools, however, is not confined to the formal curriculum. A number of researchers have noted that the social climate, and political culture and organization of schools—the "informal curriculum"—is importantly related to the development of students' political orientations.[13] Indeed, from an analytical perspective schools may be seen as political systems of which the students, teachers and administrators are members.

With respect to the informal curriculum, there is evidence that high school students are beginning to perceive power as a key variable in determining the quality of life in school. Wittes' study of crisis-torn high schools indicates that students' perception of their ability to influence school policy has important implications for the desire to achieve academic success.[14] Coleman's nationwide survey of schools found that feelings of being able to control one's own environment were related more highly to differences in academic achievement of students than all of the other school characteristics put together.[15] Unfortunately, the sociopolitical organization of schools is not democratic, and student participation in the structure and processes of school governance is minimal. In a study of 7,000 high school students Westin concluded that students see their schools as undemocratic institutions with the consequence that they "report increased levels of dissatisfaction, tension, frustration and anger with schools as a whole."[16] The quality and character of the political socialization experience embodied in the "informal curriculum," then, is also a potentially important source of educational discontent.

Finally, the incongruities between the ideals of participation, critical thinking, rational inquiry and political awareness espoused in the formal curriculum and the realities of the sociopolitical organization of schools as experienced daily by students is a potentially major factor in student dissatisfaction. As Merelman explains, "curricular offerings and student activities that are incongruent with the actual structure of school governance as students experience it will not have the desired effect."[17] Simply put, if the school does not serve as a model for the values it purveys, then student unrest would seem likely to increase in scope and frequency.

Political Ideology

Students' beliefs about the wider political system beyond their high schools may be related both to their attitudes toward their political socialization experience and to their level of educational discontent. Unfortunately, a great deal of research on student dissent has confounded political ideology with activism. The general reference to radical activists has confused the issue. The general dimensions of attitude and activism are conceptually independent.

Individuals with any ideological position may be active or inactive towards the realization of goals. Block, Haan and Smith originally set up the framework for the separate analysis of attitudes and activism; unfortunately, much of the research still continues to confound the two.[18] A number of recent studies support the separation of political ideology and activism, which suggests that previous research on radical activists is really characteristic of all students who act on their political beliefs.[19] Clark and Egan found that a large proportion of the demonstrators are liberal or middle-of-the-road in their political beliefs.[20] Therefore, whether political ideology in any way influences educational discontent is an empirical question; conceptually, political beliefs should be independent of other forms of dissent.

METHOD OF THE STUDY

We have argued that the school-based political socialization experience of students and their political ideology may be important sources of educational discontent. Our dependent variable is educational discontent measured in terms of students' acceptance of the radical view of education. There are five independent variables. Four measure various aspects of students' school-based political socialization experience: attitudes towards the civics curricula, political activism in school, and political alienation from the sociopolitical structure of the school measured in terms of powerlessness and normlessness. The fifth independent variable is political ideology measured in terms of students' degree of acceptance of pluralist, elitist or democratic theory.

Our procedure will be to first present profiles of the distribution of responses for the sample for each variable. This will allow us to examine the pattern of student attitudes. We will then test the interrelationship between the four sources and assess the relative contribution of each source through regression analysis. The resulting predictive model will allow us to focus on certain independent variables which substantially contribute to educational discontent.

Data Base

The data analyzed in this study come from a paper and pencil questionnaire administered to 1,811 high school seniors from all 50 states attending a non-governmental educational program in Washington, D.C., in the Winter of 1971. The sample consists of predominantly white, college bound, academically successful students who frequently participated in student organizations and government in their high schools.[21] The survey represents a national sample of a pool of American youth who are not only possible future elites but who are also likely to define the sources of student unrest.[22]

The attitudes and behavior of this stratum of American youth have been left largely uninvestigated in previous political socialization research. Yet the utility of employing this type of sample is pointed out by David Marsh in his recent review of the implicit assumptions of socialization research. Marsh observes that:

> An elementary study of any nation will show that not all individuals' political behavior and attitudes have equal influence. . . . Yet most students of political socialization study the attitudes and behavior of groups of children who ideally would represent a cross section of all types of combinations of demographic characteristics. If their major interest is in the operation of the political system and some peoples' behavior is more influential in affecting that system than that of others, then this concentration or aim to achieve a representative national sample would seem misguided. . . . Bearing in mind the purpose of political socialization research we should study the . . . elite (not the entire population) as their behavior is likely to have most influence on the operation of the political system.[23]

FINDINGS

Operationalization and Profiles of Variables

The profiles of educational discontent, alienation, activism, political ideology and curricular attitudes are presented below. These profiles are distributions of a number of scaled items. As the items within each profile are of equal difficulty, and following Rutherford's contention that the true scores are more closely approximated by additive rather than Guttman techniques, the scale scores were computed.[24]

1. Educational Discontent. One indicator of educational discontent is the radical view of education. A resolution adopted by the Students for a Democratic Society Council, University of Colorado, October, 1969, states that: "Schools are in need of drastic change, change is described as the overthrow of the system by direct confrontation."[25] To determine the extent of radical attitudes toward the high school, the students were asked to respond to the accuracy/inaccuracy of six radical statements on a four point scale (the score of 1 is accurate and 4 is inaccurate).[26]

The distribution of the high school students along the educational discontent continuum is surprisingly normal with approximately 16 percent accepting the radical position, 36.3 per cent partially accepting, 34.8 per cent partially rejecting and 13.1 per cent rejecting the radical assessment of American education. This distribution indicates the extent of educational discontent in high school. Over 50 per cent of the sample agrees, partially or totally, with the radical critique of education. This is a significant number of dissatisfied students. Out of the 16 per cent who accept the radical critique, only 23 per cent (or 4 per cent of the sample) consistently accepted *all* six radical items. Likewise, 17.1 per cent of those rejecting the radical critique (or 2.2 per cent of the sample) responded with a rejection on all six radical items. The distribution indicates the extent of educational discontent in American high schools; one out of every two high school students is dissatisfied. This represents a 10 per cent increase over the Purdue Opinion Poll data.

2. *Alienation.*   Most definitions of alienation include the notion of trust or confidence in the system or institution. Schacht divides the focus of alienation into four categories: "alienation from work, alienation from self or others, alienation from events and structures, and alienation from culture and society."[27] In this study our concern is with the students' alienation from the events or structures (the sociopolitical organization) of their schools as measured by the concepts of political powerlessness and political normlessness.[28]

Powerlessness implies the perceived inability of the individual to maintain effective control over his or her life and destiny within the school. It is the conclusion that people do not shape decisions but are shaped by the decisions. Opportunities for high school participation in decision-making are limited and often depend on the sociopolitical organization of the high school. In order to measure the perceived influence that students have on a number of relevant issues, students were asked to respond to six questions concerning their influence on different types of high school policy, on an agree/disagree 1 to 5 continuum.

Most students assume a norm of equal and considerate treatment by school officials. Lack of congruence between this norm and actual behavior may be considered an indication of deterioration in the normative structure. Accordingly, the subjective assessment of the existence of this state can be interpreted as a condition of perceived normlessness. "That is, the individual who thinks that he would receive inequal treatment is making this judgment with reference to a state of affairs that he thinks should exist because it is affirmed by the political culture."[29] In order to assess students' perceived normlessness in the high school system, students were asked three questions concerning the equality of treatment by school officials and teachers on a three-point scale of fair/unfair.

The profile shows a heavily skewed distribution with approximately 85 per cent of the students believing that they had varying amounts of influence on school policy. Although a high proportion of this high school sample have served in student government, the degree of perceived influence is surprising; only about 14 per cent of the sample have a sense of powerlessness. Similarly, we find a skewed distribution of perceived normlessness with most of the students perceiving fair treatment. In short, this elite sample of high school seniors are, by and large, *not* alienated and definitely perceive the students' influence on educational policy as significant.

However, when students compare their influence with other groups, a different perspective is portrayed. How much control and/or influence students have over school policies as compared with other relevant groups is shown in Table 1; students were asked the extent of influence or control each group has —too little, about right, too much. The five groups in Table 1 are ranked according to their mean scores on the extent of influence or control over school policies. Board of Education and Principal/Superintendent are considered to have the most control with teachers and parents ranked considerably lower. Students are ranked last with 63 per cent perceiving they have too little control, while 34 per cent stated their control was just about right. Thus, in terms of influencing or controlling school policy, students perceive themselves as having little influence, comparatively speaking.

3. Student Activism.   Political activism in the school context comprises the next measure of the school-based political socialization experience. The contemporary phenomena of disruptions through such forms as mass protests and legal assemblies have allowed students to actively participate in voicing their grievances. Although the avenues for lawful protests are limited in high schools, there is evidence that protest activity in high schools is increasing.[30] In operationalizing student activism, we are primarily concerned with participation in organized activities (official and unofficial), which are either protest-oriented or informational. Such activities include protesting school

TABLE 1

The Extent of Control Over School Policies
(N = 1437)

	Too Little (1)	Just About Right (2)	Too Much (3)	Total Percent	$\overline{X}$
Board of Education	2.6	40.0	57.4	100	2.5
Principal & Superintendent	3.2	51.1	45.7	100	2.4
Teachers	21.3	64.9	13.8	100	1.9
Parents	31.9	55.1	13.0	100	1.8
Students	63.0	34.2	2.8	100	1.3

regulations, informational assemblies on American involvement in Cambodia, environmental pollution, racial discrimination and poverty. In order to measure the extent of participation in activist movements, students were asked four questions concerning the extent of their participation on a 1 to 3 scale.

The distribution shows approximately 23 per cent of the students were fairly active in organizing protest movements (11.6 per cent responded they had been active with regard to all four questions), while 55 per cent of the students have attended protest assemblies to try to change school regulations, and 22 per cent have not been active in any of the organized protest assemblies. Out of the total sample, 78 per cent of the students were at schools where protest assemblies had occurred in the last three years; a reasonably significant proportion. The only issue that did not generate organized demonstrations was when American troops moved into Cambodia; only 20 per cent of the students were at schools where demonstrations had occurred. This markedly differs from the universities where extensive protest movements were organized when American troops entered Cambodia.

4. Formal Civics Curricula. Our final indicator of the political socialization experience is students' attitudes toward the formal civics curriculum. In analyzing student rating of civics curricula, there are two important areas which should be analyzed. The overall focus of the curriculum is an aspect which students evaluate constantly; the whole question of "relevance" has a lot to do with the content keeping abreast of the times. The other area of importance to students is the ability of the civics curricula to stimulate and develop students' political knowledge. In an attempt to measure student ratings of common criticisms of civics and government courses to provide and stimulate student political knowledge, students were asked to rate five common criticisms of civics on a four point accuracy/inaccuracy scale.

The profile shows the extent of variation in curriculum rating among high school seniors. The bulk (approximately 61 per cent) of the students hold "mixed" attitudes toward their civics and government courses, 14 per cent are very critical of the construction of civics education and the remainder (23 per cent) are favorably disposed toward their civics and government courses. This suggests that the attitudes of most students are a mixture of criticism and support, with distinct minorities vigorously supporting and criticizing the curriculum.[31]

5. Political Beliefs. A stratification approach to the study of political ideology is especially fruitful because it reveals how different strata view the mechanisms for distributing rewards in a society. In this case we are dealing with different political strata. Every system of stratification develops an ideology to legitimize or justify its presence or persistence. Since an ideology explains and vindicates the unequal distribution of rewards in a society, it follows that those who are the most favored recipients of the rewards support the ideology. The predominant ideology in America is "pluralism," where the struggle for power is largely confined to competing elites. There are, however, two other contending models of power distribution, which, purportedly, explain power distributions; that is, the elitist model which states that power is concentrated in the hands of a small elite, and the democratic model, which contends that there are *no* elites; the masses rule. These three contending models (elitism, pluralism and democracy), are the dominant schools of thought in America.[32]

There are four different questions that were asked of the high school students concerning the three models of power distribution (elitism, pluralism and democracy). Each question taps a different dimension of the power distributions.

Approximately 50 per cent of the student sample agreed, with varying degrees of strength, with the pluralist model, nearly 30 per cent agreed with the elitist model and about 20 per cent responded to the democratic model. In other words, the distribution is slightly skewed toward the elitist model. Although pluralism is selected more frequently as the dominant model of political control, the percentage does not represent overwhelming consensus.

THE RELATIONSHIP BETWEEN SOURCES OF EDUCATIONAL DISCONTENT

The interrelationships between the major sources of educational discontent is unclear. Recent research indicates that the major sources of student dissent (activism, alienation and political beliefs) are theoretically and empirically independent. Current research also suggests that there is a relationship between student power and academic interest. In order to test these propositions, and analyze the interlocking relationships between alienation, activism, formal civics curricula and political beliefs, zero-order product-moment correlation coefficients were used to test for the robustness of the relationships. Table 2 shows the results.

Table 2 shows that the two dimensions of alienation, powerlessness and normlessness, are significantly correlated ($r_{34} = .29$), and hold constant when activism and political beliefs are controlled for ($r_{34.15} = .28$), but the strength of the relationship does not clearly show whether student alienation is one or two factored. However, when educational discontent is controlled for, the relationship becomes insignificant ($r = .13$) which supports Finifter's contention that alienation is two factored.

Student dissent is generally stereotyped into two distinct typologies—activism and alienation. To what extent these typologies are mutually exclusive, or

TABLE 2

Correlation Matrix Between Political Beliefs, Student Activitism, Student Alienation and Curricular Attitudes

	X_1	X_2	X_3	X_4	X_5
Political Beliefs (X_1)	1.00	.17[a]	.20[a]	.20[a]	.13
Civics Curricula (X_2)		1.00	.31[a]	.20[a]	.01
Powerlessness (X_3)			1.00	.29[a]	.07
Normlessness (X_4)				1.00	.18[a]
Activism (X_5)					1.00

[a] Significant at the .001 level.

interrelated, can be shown by correlating the two variables. The relationship between alienation and activism ($r_{35} = .07$, $r_{45} = .18$) supports those who argue that the two forms of dissent are relatively independent of each other. The correlations are suprisingly similar to the findings reported by Deinst in her study of alienation and activism.[33] Therefore, Keniston's typology not only applies to society but also applies to specific contexts such as high school elites who have stayed with the system.

How much of student dissent is influenced by political beliefs is not clear. The confusion between political ideology and protest activity has been pointed out. The findings of this sample suggest that activism and political ideology are empirically independent ($r_{15} = .13$); levels of protest participation do not significantly increase as one moves toward the belief in political elitism. Similarly, there is only marginal support that alienation and political beliefs are significantly related ($r_{13} = .20$, $r_{14} = .20$). Obviously, students' attitudes toward the wider political system are different from their focus on the high school system.

Incongruities between the formal civics curriculum and student participation in educational policies were discussed earlier in this study. The civics curriculum is said to have little effect on political attitudes, but to be closely linked with feelings of internal control. Although we found no relationship between evaluation of civics courses and activism ($r_{13} = .13$), we did find a significant correlation between alienation and the evaluation of civics courses on both dimensions ($r_{23} = .31$, $r_{24} = .20$), although the relationship between powerlessness and civics rating is considerably stronger than between normlessness and civics rating, which is only marginally significant. Thus, students who have a sense of educational power also tend to rate civics courses highly. This supports a body of literature which shows a strong relationship between educational control and academic interest.

In supporting what now has become a recurrent research finding, we find the relationship between political beliefs and curricula assessment borders on insignificance ($r_{12} = .17$). In other words, there is only a marginal relationship between political beliefs and the way students rate civics courses. Students who believe in the elitist model do not necessarily judge civics courses as irrelevant.

Sources of Educational Discontent

Thus far, we have only considered the profiles and the interrelationships of the proposed sources of educational discontent. We now move on to measuring the relative contribution of each source in predicting educational discontent. Assuming interval measures for each of the six scaled variables and assuming a certain independence of each independent variable, we now can use the regression model to measure the contributions to educational discontent.

Figure 1 shows the relative contribution of each independent variable. Forty

FIGURE 1

Sources of Educational Discontent[a]

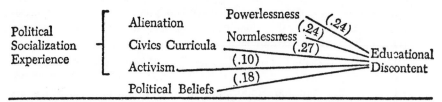

[a] Values given in parentheses are standardized regression coefficients.

per cent of students' dissatisfaction with high school education is explained by the four sources. By far the most important source is alienation (both dimensions) which accounts for 28 per cent of the variance; both powerlessness and normlessness contributing (betas = .24) equal amounts. Criticism of civics education is also another very important source (beta = .27) of educational discontent. However, political beliefs (beta = .18) and student activism (beta = .10) are only marginally significant predictors of educational discontent.

CONCLUSIONS

The level of student dissatisfaction in high schools is substantial; over 50 per cent of the students agree, partially or totally, with the radical critique of education. This represents a significant level of educational discontent. In reviewing the sources of educational discontent in high schools we found that 75 per cent of the students were at schools where protest had taken place, but only a small precentage (11 per cent) considered themselves as activists. The profiles on student alienation showed a definite skewed distribution with nearly 80 per cent of the sample perceiving they had varying degrees of influence on educational policy. In comparison to other influential groups, however, students perceive themselves as having limited influence on policy. Student rating on civics courses was varied with most students having "mixed" feelings concerning the effectiveness of civics courses. And finally, about half the students were in essential agreement with the pluralist theory of power distribution in America; the remainder of the students aligned themselves with either the elitist model or the democratic model.

In predicting educational discontent in high schools, the four variables discussed above explain 40 per cent of the variation in educational dissatisfaction. By far the most important source was alienation, which accounted for 28 per cent of the variance; both student powerlessness and student normlessness contributing equal amounts. Student rating of civics courses was also an important source of educational discontent. However, political beliefs and student activism were not important predictors of educational dissatisfaction. Thus, the findings tend to support the contention that students (especially elite students) of the 1970's are indeed entering a new phase of student dissent—with aspects of the school-based political socialization experience as an important source of educational discontent.[34]

If students' focus has shifted from optimism to pessimism, then a responsive model must confront the issue of alienation. This is especially true in the domain of political socialization where the governance of the high school should reinforce the formal civics curriculum. In order to check the increasing level of educational discontent and to make schools more responsive to students' needs, alternative models must facilitate student participation in educational policies and enforce equitable school rules. The latter point has particular relevance to racial minorities who have serious doubts about the commitment of the educational system to equal treatment.

Whether responsive models can actually reverse the tide of educational discontent is another question. It may well be that in reaction to the optimism of the 1960's, a general mood of pessimism has set in which has nothing to do with responsive models. However, our findings do not support this. Alienation, as a major source of educational discontent, is fairly specific to the particular school environment. This being the case, responsive models can play a significant role in decreasing the level of educational discontent in high schools.

NOTES

1. One radical view holds that schools are repressive, non-productive, and inhuman. Militant radicals propose to "activate" high school students to overthrow the system. Purdue Opinion Panel, *High Schools in 1970: A Study of the Student-School Relations,* 88 (Lafayette: Purdue University, 1970), p. 1.

2. A recent study by the National Association of Secondary School Principals states that 60 per cent of high school principals report some form of active protests in their schools. National Association of Secondary School Principals, "Report on High School Disruption." Unpublished manuscript (Washington, D.C., 1969).

3. For an interesting analysis of the inward looking generation, see: Jeffrey K. Hadden, "The Private Generation," *Psychology Today,* 3 (Oct., 1969), pp. 32–35, 68–69.

4. For discussions concerning the major agents of political socialization see Richard E. Dawson and Kenneth Prewitt, *Political Socialization* (Boston: Little, Brown & Co., 1969); Jack Dennis, ed., *Socialization to Politics* (New York: Wiley, 1973); Michael P. Riccards, *The Making of the American Citizenry* (New York: Chandler Publishing Company, 1973); Herbert Hirsch, *Poverty and Politicization* (New York: The Free Press, 1971).

5. See, for example, Dianne B. Gertler and Linda Parker, *Patterns of Course Offerings and Enrollments in Public Secondary Schools,* 1970–71, U. S. Department of Health, Education and Welfare, U.S. Office of Education DHEW Publication No. (OE)73-11400.

6. Dawson and Prewitt, *Political Socialization,* p. 147.

7. Frederick M. Wirt and Michael W. Kirst, *The Political Web of American Schools* (Boston: Little, Brown & Co., 1972), p. 29. See also, the report of the APSA Committee on Pre-Collegiate Education, "Political Education in the Public Schools: The Challenge for Political Science," *P.S.,* 4 (Summer, 1971), pp. 437–447.

8. Frederick R. Smith, "The Curriculum," in Byron G. Massialas and Frederick R. Smith, eds., *New Challenges in the Social Studies* (Belmont, Calif: Wadsworth Publishing Co., 1965).

9. Kenneth P. Langton and M. Kent Jennings, "Political Socialization and the High School Civics Curriculum in the United States," *American Political Science Review,* 62 (Sept., 1968), pp. 852–868; Richard M. Merelman, *Political Socialization and Educational Climates: A Study of Three School Districts* (New York: Holt, Rinehart & Winston, 1971); David Ziblatt, "High School Extra-Curricular Activities and Political Socialization," *Annals of the American Academy of Political and Social Science,* 361 (Sept., 1965), pp. 20–31.

10. Merelman, *Political Socialization;* Ziblatt, "High School Extra-Curricular Activities."

11. Merelman, *Political Socialization,* Chaps. 3 and 4.

12. *Ibid.,* p. 133.

13. For a list of this research see the report of the American Political Science Association Committee on Pre-Collegiate Education, "Political Education in the Public Schools," p. 445.

14. Simon Wittes, *People and Power: A Study of Crisis in Secondary Schools* (Ann Arbor, Mich.: University of Michigan, 1970).

15. J. Coleman, *et al., Equality of Educational Opportunity* (Washington, D.C.: U.S. Government Printing Office, 1967).

16. Allen Westin and Deann Murphy, "Civic Education in a Crisis Age: An Alternative to Revolution and Repression" (mimeographed, Sept., 1970), pp. 2–3, cited in report of the APSA Committee on Pre-Collegiate Education, "Political Education in the Public Schools," p. 446.

17. Richard M. Merelman, "The Adolescence of Political Socialization," *Sociology of Education,* 45 (Spring, 1972), p. 160. Also see Willis Hawley, "Political Education and School Organization," *Theory Into Practice,* 10 (Dec., 1971), pp. 328–335.

18. J. H. Block, N. Haan and M. B. Smith, "Activism and Apathy in Contemporary Adolescents," in J. F. Adams, ed., *Contributions to the Understanding of Adolescence* (Boston: Allyn & Bacon, 1968).

19. Steven H. Lewis and Robert E. Krant, "Correlates of Student Political Activism and Ideology," *Journal of Social Issues,* 28 (April, 1972), pp. 131–149.

20. James W. Clarke and Joseph Egan, "Social and Political Dimensions of Campus Protest Activity," *Journal of Politics,* 34 (May, 1972), pp. 500–523.

21. The 1,811 students came to Washington in six groups over a six week period to attend a program organized by a private, non-profit organization called the Presidential Classroom for Young Americans. Each group stayed a week and consisted of approximately 325 high school seniors from all 50 states. Participants were essentially self-selected and were chosen to attend by procedures peculiar to each high school. However, the Presidential Classroom organization does attempt to strike a geographical balance (based on Congressional districts) in accepting applicants. During their one-week stay in Washington, the students attend a daily series of lectures and seminars with various government officials representing different agencies and branches of the national government. The questions about the future used in this study were obtained from larger paper and pencil questionnaire administered to the students in classroom size groups by their instructors under the supervision of the second author. The sample is approximately equally divided by sex (55 percent), from public schools (80 percent), predominantly white (92 percent), college bound (96 percent), and academically successful (91 percent indicated their grades were "above average or excellent"). Approximately 93 percent of the sample were involved in student government or councils. The sample showed definite interests in social and political studies with 74 percent having taken at least one course in civics and government (at the ninth grade), and 20 percent having taken one or two additional American government courses. In terms of U.S. Census categories, 69 percent of the students' fathers held white-collar positions, 19 percent blue-collar positions, 6 percent farm related occupations, 3 percent service related positions, and 1 percent were retired. Sixty-six percent of the students' fathers had educational training beyond a high school diploma and 18 percent held advanced degrees. Ninety percent of the sample indicated they received no "special training" before coming to Washington.

22. For a recent treatment of elite recruitment and a bibliography on elite analysis see Kenneth Prewitt and Alan Stone, *The Ruling Elite: Elite Theory, Power and American Democracy* (New York: Harper and Row, 1973).

23. David Marsh, "Political Socialization: The Implicit Assumptions Questions," *British Journal of Political Science,* 1 (Oct., 1971), p. 464.

24. Brent Rutherford, "Time Variance Estimation: Comparing Scalograms and Psychometric Models by Monte Carlo Simulation of Respondent Behavior," paper delivered at the Annual Meeting of the American Political Science Association, 1971.

25. Purdue Opinion Panel, *High Schools in 1970,* p. 3.

26. The questions used in the instrument are available upon request from the authors.

27. Richard Schacht, *Alienation* (Garden City, N.Y.: Doubleday, 1970).

28. Ada Finifter, "Dimensions of Political Alienation," *American Political Science Review,* 44 (June, 1970), pp. 389–410.

29. Finifter, "Dimensions of Political Alienation," p. 395.

30. "Report on High School Disruption."

31. For a further discussion on the evaluation of civics courses using the same data see Richard C. Remy, "High School Seniors' Attitudes Toward Their Civics and Government Instruction," *Social Education,* 36 (Oct., 1972), pp. 590–597.

32. See William H. Form and Joan Rytina, "Ideological Beliefs on the Distribution of Power in the United States," *American Sociological Review,* 34 (Feb., 1969), pp. 19–30.

33. E. R. Deinst, "Psychological and Activist Political Alienation Related to Faculty-Student Interaction." Unpublished Ph.D. diss. (Berkeley: University of California, 1971).

34. A word of caution is in order. This is an elite sample of high school students which limits the scope of inference; whether indeed high school elites do reflect high school students is a question beyond the scope of this study. Also, this *ex post facto* study of a closed system limits an analysis of exogenous factors impinging on the interaction between the endogenous variables. Whether, for example, alienation is a result of the high school or other experiences is impossible to measure in this study.

Chapter Four

Graduate Education: Socialization to Occupational Roles

In their efforts to understand human behavior, psychologists, and to a greater extent psychiatrists, have stressed the importance of childhood experiences and socialization as determinants of adult personality. Consequently, socialization has often been thought of as a process that occurs only during childhood. In its extreme form this view regards the socialization experiences of the first six or seven years of life as the major determinants of adult personality.

But extreme positions have a way of generating their critics. There is a wealth of experiences from everyday life to suggest that adults do have socialization experiences that alter their personality and behavior. Almost everyone knows of persons about whom it is said, "My, but two years in the Army certainly changed him," or "He's a different person since he changed jobs," or "One year at Radcliffe and she thinks she's too good for us." Similarly, the fact that adult experiences can affect aspirations and life style preferences is pointedly reflected in the words of a post-World War I song about returning American soldiers: "How you gonna keep 'em down on the farm, after they've seen Paree?"

The fact that socialization is a lifelong process has been emphasized by sociologists as an antidote to the extreme "childhood socialization" perspective. Throughout their lives persons are exposed to and affected by the socializing influence of occupational groups, friendship groups and a host of voluntary associations. Consequently, the work of sociologists in this area has placed heavy emphasis on adult socialization.[1]

In their current work on adult socialization sociologists have been dealing primarily with two major topics: first, the nature of the socialization process per se and, second, the characteristics of a variety of formal organizations engaged in the socialization of adults. Since our interests here, graduate and professional schools, are examples of organizations engaged in socialization, the remainder of this discussion deals primarily with this second topic.

Graduate and professional education includes much more than what is usually described as "advanced or specialized education and training." Not only are specific kinds of specialized knowledge and skills transmitted, but, equally important, a more indirect, unintentional learning takes place through informal contact with teachers and peers. Besides learning a range of values and attitudes appropriate to their future occupational roles, graduate and professional school students also undergo a process of socialization whereby a new self-image is created. Quite apart from didactic forms of instruction, the novice begins to think of himself as a professional; the medical student comes to think of himself as a doctor; and the graduate student gradually develops a conception of himself as a future professor. This occurs not simply because the student has acquired the skill and knowledge of the profession but because of socialization to an occupational subculture and a professional role. It is this subtle process of occupational socialization to which sociologists have directed their attention.

Numerous descriptive studies have been conducted on the socialization process in medical schools,[2] nursing schools,[3] law schools,[4] and a variety of university graduate departments.[5] The main analytic concern of the sociologist remains: What conditions maximize socialization to specialized professional roles?

One of these conditions is the degree of isolation from other socializing influences attained by the socializing agency. This isolation of would-be professionals is found in its extreme form in those organizations preparing men for the priesthood and the military. In these cases the novice or recruit is physically separated from "outside" social contacts or at least there is an attempt to keep these contacts to a minimum. During the training period the life of the professional aspirant is highly regimented so as to leave little time for outside influences which might compete with the profession for his loyalty. Similarly, the occasion for exposure to potentially conflicting values, ideologies, and perspectives is minimized. While graduate and professional schools do not begin to approach this degree of total control over the lives of their recruits, it may be helpful to think about the extent to which isolation is part of the training system. Variation in isolation may account for variation in the effectiveness of socialization and the kinds of problems faced by the socializing agency. In the university setting medical and nursing schools represent examples of *relative* isolation. That is, compared to law school students or those in graduate arts and science programs, the residential arrangements and clinical aspects of training make for greater immersion in the medical subculture.

Another factor related to the effectiveness of socialization is the extent to which the professional school or graduate department maintains control over the selection and entry of new recruits. Socialization may be facilitated by the ability of the socializing agency to pre-select students on the basis of characteristics believed to be indicative of a high potential for success in the academic aspects of their student careers and ease of socialization to the professional role. Typically, professional schools such as law, dentistry, and medicine have greater autonomy than do graduate departments, although there may be a great deal of variation among the latter. The degree of autonomy possessed by a school or department may reflect its power position in the larger society. For example, cries of "doctor shortage" are largely ignored by medical schools but cries of "teacher shortage" may quickly result in efforts to produce more teachers through expanded facilities, lower entrance requirements, and the like.

In addition to identifying a variety of structural features of graduate education, two important determinants of the effectiveness of socialization in graduate school are discussed in the first article of this chapter by Rosen and Bates. One of these factors is the degree of consensus or agreement on the goals of socialization and the means for achieving them among those who operate the school or department. The second factor is the degree of compatibility between the goals of students and those of their teachers. High consensus and compatibility would be expected to contribute to maximum socialization.

The second selection in this chapter, by Pavalko and Holley, is a case study of socialization in graduate school. Focusing on graduate teaching assistants in a large university, the study attempts to identify the effects of a variety of experiences and conditions on the development of a professional self-concept.

NOTES

1. Orville G. Brim, Jr., and Stanton Wheeler, editors, *Socialization After Childhood,* New York: Wiley, 1966.

2. Robert K. Merton, George Reader, and Patricia L. Kendall, *The Student Physician,* Cambridge, Harvard University Press, 1957; Howard S. Becker, *et al., Boys in White,* Chicago: University of Chicago Press, 1961.

3. Ida Harper Simpson, "Patterns of Socialization into Professions," *Sociological Inquiry,* 37 (Winter, 1967), pp. 47–54; Fred Davis, editor, *The Nursing Profession,* New York: Wiley, 1966.

4. Dan C. Lortie, "Laymen to Lawmen: Law School, Careers and Professional Socialization," *Harvard Educational Review,* 29 (Fall, 1959), pp. 352–369.

5. Howard S. Becker and James Carper, "The Elements of Identification With an Occupation," *American Sociological Review,* 21 (June, 1956), pp. 341–347; Charles R. Wright, "Changes in the Occupational Commitment of Graduate Sociology Students: A Research Note," *Sociological Inquiry,* 37 (Winter, 1967), pp. 55–62.

10.   BERNARD C. ROSEN and ALAN P. BATES

The Structure of Socialization in Graduate School

Organizations preparing young adults for entry into specialized occupations are among the most important of the broad class of organizations centrally engaged in adult socialization. The present paper focuses on the structure of socialization in one subcategory of this class: an agency specifically devoted to training young adults to perform professional roles—the American graduate school. In this type of organization the twin foci of the social structure are the necessarily complementary roles of socializing agent and neophyte. Both are recruited into the system on the basis of their possession of certain qualities, skills, and aspirations. Both enter the system voluntarily and may leave when they desire. It is not expected in most cases that the neophyte will remain in the organization after his training is completed.[1] While the number of persons in graduate schools is relatively small, the fact that these centers train very advanced specialists makes their services enormously important to complex industrial societies, which makes it all the more surprising that there have been

Reprinted from *Sociological Inquiry,* 37 (Winter, 1967), pp. 71–84, by permission of the authors. This is a revision of a paper read at the 1966 meeting of the American Sociological Association. This paper was prepared while the senior author held a research grant from the National Institute of Mental Health.

very few empirical studies, and only slightly more analysis, of the socialization process in this type of training organization.[2]

In the following analysis particular attention will be paid to the influence of certain social structural factors typically ignored in most psychologically oriented discussions of the socialization process. Psychological theories of learning as they are applied to socialization are useful insofar as they help us to understand how connections between cues and responses develop. But they tell us nothing about who is being taught and by whom, or what is being learned and for what purpose. For learning theories in themselves do not describe the content of a cue, nor explain why certain responses are rewarded, or for that matter, what is regarded as a reward.[3]

It has long been apparent that the content of socialization and the conditions for learning often vary greatly between societies, or even between subgroups within a society. We know also that the criteria for selecting socializing agents and neophytes, the basic assumptions made about their nature, and the way they are expected to perform their roles will vary with the organization in which socialization occurs. Thus, the degree to which value is placed upon certain socialization outcomes, the areas in which they are expected, and what constitutes acceptable performance in these areas are matters which reflect the patterning of expectations and norms in a given milieu. In short, the situation in which most learning, and all socialization, occurs is a social one. Its definition will vary with the norms and values of the group in which the learning takes place.

Over time, through prolonged interaction these values and norms (and the reciprocal expectations with which they are associated) produce relatively enduring stable relationships between members of a social system. These relationships constitute a social structure whose most salient features are the division of labor, the expression of affect and the flow of communication, the nature and distribution of power and authority, and the degree of consensus and conflict. An adequate understanding of the socialization process in an organization engaged in training disciplinary specialists is not possible, we submit, without taking these dimensions of social interaction into account.

Participants in a socialization system bring with them, or develop over time, a model of how interaction should be structured. Both the agent and the neophyte have some notion as to how labor should be divided and authority distributed, to whom one should turn for information and under what conditions it may be expected, and what constitutes appropriate goals for the socialization agency and its clients. These expectations are expressed in the norms and values built around particular sets of role prescriptions and practices designed to equip the neophyte with the knowledge and skills required for adequate performance in the position he is expected to fill.

To the degree that they form a more or less coherent whole, these expectations constitute a normatively-oriented model of how the socialization process should operate. As such it is an "ideal" and not a "real" type. In any normative system, behavioral departures from the norms must be expected, of course. Such empirical deviations from the model will necessarily have implications for its usefulness. But they may also contribute to our understanding of the socialization process, particularly its failures. For discrepancies between the "ideal" and the "real" often reveal strains in the system. These strains may arise from structural as well as psychological factors, and their consequences can be dysfunctional for the system as well as for the individual. The nature of these strains will become apparent as we set the model into motion, so to speak, by examining a specific case: the American graduate school at the departmental level. To the "ideal" model we shall put this question: "How should the socialization system be structured so as to be optimally effective?" And of the "real" system, we shall ask: "What occurs in fact? Why? What are some of its consequences?"

The discussion which follows is based on long continued participant observation and reading in the area rather than formal research. Our effort to sketch the "ideal" structure of the socialization process must necessarily be tentative, as is the description of instances in which the system actually does not work in the manner expected. We know that what is said will fit some graduate schools and training in some disciplines better than others. Moreover, limitations of space clearly preclude the analysis of all but a small part of the complex process of socialization in graduate schools. Exhaustiveness is not our goal. Our main concern is to illustrate the ways social structure affects socialization and to do so in terms which might stimulate thinking and research in this area at a time when students of socialization are extending their interests to cover the entire human life span.

THE CENTRAL ROLES: AGENT AND NEOPHYTE

In large, complex organizations roles tend to proliferate with Parkinsonian speed and inevitability. Universities are no exception. Administrative and various service personnel increase in number as universities continue to grow in size and complexity. Yet despite the growth of subsidiary roles, the central roles of the socialization structure remain the same: the agent as teacher and the neophyte as student.

The Role of the Agent.   A well-functioning socialization system such as is envisaged in our ideal model expects the agent to convey all essential information to the neophyte accurately and completely. For this to occur the agent must possess some part of the knowledge or skill which is to be transmitted to the neophyte. Collectively, the group of agents is expected to have *all* of the knowledge or skills needed to complete the training of neophytes in a manner required by the goals of the organization. Every agent should also possess the skills necessary for the effective transmission of socialization content and be motivated to engage in instructional activities.

The agent is more than a transmitter of knowledge. He also serves as a role model, embodying, representing and dramatizing, so to speak, the goal toward which the neophyte is moving. Thus, it becomes critical that his portrayal of the role be accurate and sufficiently complete so as not to confuse or mislead the neophyte in any essential respect.

Does this model-derived description of the agent's role accord with reality? In some ways it does. Probably most agents have adequate levels of competence in their areas of specialization. However, given the variations and vicissitudes which accompany graduate staff building these days, the *summation* of competencies in a given department may not provide good coverage of a discipline from the standpoint of the neophyte professional. Gaping holes in critical areas are sometimes found even in relatively large departments.

Most certainly the expectation that all agents have good pedagogical skills is often unfulfilled. The teaching performance of many graduate professors seems based on an assumption that each has a handful of protégés and ample time to reveal in a slow apprenticeship what scholarship means, within the framework of a loose-knit organization which encourages intellectual companionship between agent and neophyte. The conditions which once made this assumption viable have changed radically, and the assumption has become in large part a myth. Today graduate professors (who, like academics generally, have no specific training in pedagogy) cling to the myth as they try to cope with the diverse demands made upon them. Serious discussions of the problem are seldom encountered, except that there is virtual unanimity that it should not be turned over to the schools of education!

In those fields where the neophyte is planning an academic career, the *visible* role enactment of the agent ordinarily falls far short of the completeness which his function as a role model makes desirable. Most graduate students know far less about the professional lives of their mentors than they think they do. This is mainly because professors not only have diverse tasks but these duties are located in different organizational compartments of the university. Agent and neophyte meet in one compartment, but the latter cannot follow the former into all the arenas where he works. No doubt the failure of neophytes to achieve a realistic grasp of all parts of the agent's role accounts to some extent for the difficulties sometimes experienced by new faculty members just out of graduate school—difficulties which may be amusing to older hands but troublesome to the newcomers.

The Role of the Neophyte.   The main task of the neophyte is to learn enough of the content of a discipline so that he can achieve his personal goal of being certified as competent in his field of study and then begin a career. To this task he is expected to bring at the outset strong and appropriate motivation and background preparation, and other qualities and characteristics defined as essential by agents and certified by them to be present in his case.[4]

In relation to the agent's role, the neophyte's is passive in one significant respect: the agent is the giver of knowledge, the neophyte is the receiver. Nevertheless, the neophyte is supposed to be active in the pursuit of knowledge, and great stress is laid on his developing critical and innovating intellectual habits.

When this abbreviated, model-oriented description of the neophyte's role is juxtaposed with reality, certain disjunctions appear. In many though not all disciplines it is very difficult to devise efficient selection procedures which will admit only those students who ought to be admitted and exclude those who should not. The art of diagnostic testing is woefully imprecise in this area, so that in some cases neophytes inadequately endowed or prepared do pass through the screening process. Nor is a major in the field necessarily a good guide to future performance. In some disciplines undergraduate training is so affected by its predominantly "service" functions in the undergraduate college that the possession of a major means little or nothing as a predictor of graduate success. Even motivation for entering graduate training may be misplaced in instances where the student has a highly inaccurate knowledge of the sort of field he contemplates entering. Beyond such considerations, admissions into graduate departments may be affected in a given year by the need for more or fewer persons to fill graduate assistantships. The outcome of such factors is wastage of the time and other resources of both agents and neophytes.

Another potential source of strain is the fact that the neophyte is faced with learning not one but two interlocking roles, both of which involve relationships with other members of the socialization system. In order to be certified as a disciplinary specialist he must produce during socialization acceptable performance as a client of the socialization agency. He must also learn to play the role of neophyte. In other words, before becoming a professional the neophyte must learn to be a student, and this includes much more than the acquisition of the professional knowledge or skills essential for his career plans. He enters a society of graduate students complete with its distinctive subculture. He must learn its norms, find a place in its competitive structure, give to and receive support from peers, and learn the prevailing folklore of how to cope with the agents in whose hands his fate lies for several years. As compared with the faculty this is a world that is open-ended; new persons enter each year, and others leave. And it is a threat-oriented society. But its traditions give answers of a sort to enduring problems, and he must come to terms with it.[5]

Most graduate professors are probably aware that there is a student role which the neophyte must learn, and even that there is a definite society of graduate students. But fewer are well acquainted with this role and society or realize the extent of its threat orientation or its potential for developing counter-norms which can oppose and undermine the official means and ends of the socializing agency. After all, agents are a source of the danger which the neophytes feel, and obstacles to full communication between the two roles prevent vital information from being given and received.

It must be conceded that, given the basic structure of the socialization system, this state of affairs cannot altogether be avoided. The more important question is whether or not there are *unnecessary* grounds in the socialization process for the fear, hostility and threat felt by students and sometimes given expression in informal social organization. Our subsequent comments will have some bearing on this question, and we shall shortly also deal with the apparent "passive-active" paradox referred to above. As a final comment on the student role and student organization in the graduate school, we may raise the question of whether students do not often (as part of the role) learn to manipulate agents in ways helpful to their progress through the program, but having nothing to do with their substantive training.

In sum, we have a system in which the two major, complimentary roles are bound together in a relationship which is important to the agent, crucial to the neophyte, and which continues over a period of years. Yet to the players of either role, major parts of the other role remain unknown (though highly significant to the relationship). And on both sides the extent of this ignorance is seldom realized.

THE STRUCTURAL DIMENSIONS OF ROLE INTERACTION

While the central roles of agent and neophyte define the major axes along which labor is divided, a mere description of the activities associated with these roles presents an essentially segmentalized picture of the socialization process. It is only through interaction that relationships develop between role incumbents and the process acquires its structural characteristics. Some characteristics of a social structure are the nature of role prescriptions, the sequential aspects of socialization, the distribution of authority, the sanction system, and the degree of consensus and conflict over goals.

Role Prescriptions: Ambiguity and Stringency. The agent in our model is expected to communicate role prescriptions to the neophyte in such a way as to adequately represent the socialization content. Another way of putting this is to state that the agent's demands should be efficiently related to the goals of socialization. These demands should be consistent, clear and complementary as they proceed from each agent, from all agents, and throughout the socialization sequence. They should closely reflect the relative importance of the various aspects of the socialization content and be perceived as such by the neophyte.

A comparison of this picture with the actual state of affairs brings some discrepancies to mind at once. Some requirements are perfectly clear and made explicit in graduate catalogues and departmental bulletins. Others are communicated to the neophyte in less formal ways through interaction with agents. In some areas, however, neither channel adequately communicates what needs to be known. One problem stems from the ambiguities inherent in the content being transmitted, at least in many fields. In some fields, to be sure, a clearly delimited subject matter is presented in systematically organized units. But in the humanities and social sciences such simplicity and clarity is missing. Knowledge in these fields, especially at its frontiers, has an ambiguous and problematic character ill suited to being organized into predigested chunks which can be fed to students. Neophytes often have great difficulty in determining just what they are supposed to be learning and how this is related to the goals of socialization as they understand them.

To some degree such ambiguities stem from the tradition of independent scholarship which remains in these fields, even though its implications for training may not be as suitable to the crowded departments of today as was once the case. The student is on his own to a very large degree. He is expected to read widely, to have informal conversations with his professors, and simply to reflect. Probably, no curriculum seriously attempts to present the entire field of knowledge in a discipline. A neophyte's program may easily leave lacunae which he is expected to fill on his own. A realization that this is the case may not occur until the student's training is very far along or until he has begun to prepare himself for the terminal examinations, when it may be too late.

The model further assumes that the agents, being thoroughly acquainted with the needs of the field served by the socialization agency, know how stringent their requirements must be to meet the necessary standards of quality. Role requirements should be realistic in that they can be met by all neophytes with the requisite potential for entrance into the occupational field. At the same time they must be sufficiently stringent to eliminate recruits who lack the ability or motivation to complete their training.

How closely requirements in graduate schools approach optimum stringency is a matter on which no doubt there is considerable variation in fact and even more variation in opinion. Probably few students with the requisite potential fail to obtain their degrees because too much is demanded of them. What seems much more likely to happen is that some poorly qualified students win through, because not enough has been demanded of them. Perhaps it would be more accurate to say that enough is asked of students, but a careful followup is not always made to see if these demands have been met. In some cases too little information to enable accurate judgments about student performance is accumulated and made available for ready evaluation. When this state of affairs is coupled with a "sink or swim" attitude toward neophytes, the result is that poorly endowed students may remain in the program for long periods of time. A familiar phenomenon is the student who has plodded through the formal requirements and to the dismay of his mentors has arrived at the door of the degree. In such cases, he may be reluctantly pushed through while the socializing agents wonder how he happened to get so far.

Sometimes stringency is introduced into the social structure in a disguised form. Consider the requirement that the student demonstrate a working knowledge of one or more foreign languages. The knowledge acquired is often so superficial as to be useless, a fact which is widely known but not always acknowledged. A kind of uncomfortable pretense is maintained by agents that this requirement has utility, while all concerned realize that the students are not fooled. In effect the language requirement is often an aspect of the stringency of agents' demands, making the degree more difficult to obtain, but otherwise largely functionless. When this is its primary purpose, the requirement is difficult to defend. For surely the stringency of demands should be associated with content which makes sense in terms of socialization goals.

Sequential Aspects of Socialization. As applied to any particular neophyte, socialization moves forward through time to a definite terminus: the certification of his competence to perform a professional role. From the standpoint of the socializing agency, the process is cyclical, repeated continuously as new individuals move into the system to replace those who have left. Normally there are neophytes present in many stages of the socialization process.[6]

The socialization sequence in a formal organization is marked by formal gateways through which each neophyte must pass. In the graduate school these include course completion, establishment of supervisory committees, approval of programs, passing of foreign language requirements and terminal examinations, approval of dissertation subject, and completion of dissertation. Many of these gateways are arranged sequentially. When utilized in the manner indicated by our model, they perform a very useful function. They permit agents to review the neophyte's progress and either signal to him that he is making headway or facilitate his elimination from the program, thus minimizing waste for both agent and neophyte. The more important checkpoints are fraught with emotion for neophytes because of their importance for his future.

Movement of the neophyte through the socialization system is also accompanied by more informal, but nonetheless significant changes. His status among his peers normally rises till he becomes a wise old hand, expecting and receiving some deference from younger students. His relationship to at least some of the agents gradually escapes the purely formal requirements of their mutual obligations and takes on a personal character. He begins to feel less like a student and more like a professional as he approaches the end of his training and the assumption of a fully professional role and status.

All of this time-ordered experience is either contained in the formal requirements of the system or in the informal expectation of agents who are in control of the process. How well does it accord with the typical facts? Perhaps the key question is: How effectively do the various changes and checkpoints relate to the goals of socialization? On the whole the system of gateways, used as intended and viewed independently of other factors, is adequate. If in operation it does not always perform its functions efficiently, this is mainly because of the intervention of considerations not inherent in the nature of the gateways. As we have observed earlier, it sometimes happens that marginal students win their way through to the end partly because agents have examined their work in too remote and segmented a fashion, or because each evidence of ability has not been seen in the total context of the training program. Or again, agents may differ considerably in the nature and stringency of their demands, so that quite different standards are applied to the work of the neophyte. Or, as in the case of the language requirements, questions may be raised about the content of what is being tested. But this is less a criticism of the nature of the gateway, than of the training that precedes it and of the uses to which it is put.

Finally, in some departments neophytes are allowed to dawdle for long periods of time without being required to face up to the various checkpoints which are naturally threatening to them. Many observers feel that training for graduate degrees takes a longer time than is necessary, and there is little doubt that the laissez-faire attitude toward neophytes so characteristic of many departments permits and encourages students to resort to functionless evasions and delays.

The Structure of Authority.   As a recognized representative of the organization in which the training function is being performed, the agent possesses power over the neophyte. This power is legitimated by the socializing agency and by client organizations which will absorb the neophyte upon the completion of his training. The authority of the agent is not shared with his neophytes. It is supposed to be exercised at every stage of the socialization process, beginning with the admission of neophytes into the system and including control over the outcome of the process.

Since the neophyte enters the socialization system voluntarily, he must accept the conditions it imposes. Throughout the process of socialization the neophyte is expected to acknowledge the authority of the socializing agent and subject himself to it in all matters relevant to the socialization process. He does this in return for a promise that the agency will certify his competence upon completion of training.

How well does this model correspond to empirical reality? Rather well if one is concerned only with legitimate power. Everywhere the explicit definition of the relation between professor and student which assigns the neophyte a distinctly subordinate position is apparently accepted as legitimate. One does not yet hear of graduate students engaged in rebellions against faculty domination—except as leaders of undergraduate groups.

But it is misleading to assume that neophytes are as powerless to influence the content and direction of the socialization process as the norms would suggest. The relationship which develops between agent and neophyte is in fact reciprocal, not unidirectional.[7] Students may influence the behavior of professors in a number of ways: for example, through claims based upon affectional ties which develop out of interaction over time, by attaching themselves to some member of the faculty who acts as an ally and intercessor between the student and other agents, or by performing so well that their services are attractive to the agent. It is not uncommon for professors to compete for very able students; where there is competition, the object of that competition will inevitably acquire some power to control the situation.

It is not so much in the description of the actual authority structure as in the assumption about its consequences that the model is faulty. Thus, it is assumed that the socialization process will function most effectively when the agent has the power to control the neophytes' behavior, to influence or even dictate relevant alternatives. The neophyte is seen as essentially too uninformed to help establish standards or make certain decisions relevant to his training. Perhaps unintentionally, this encourages dependence. Yet graduate training places great importance on the development of highly critical and innovative attitudes *toward the subject matter.* The student is urged to be independent in scholarly endeavor. Training an individual to be independent in an authoritarian social structure has a potentially paradoxical quality which is not always recognized by the agent. In effect, professors say to students, "Become an independent thinker; be critical, innovate, and question the established body of knowledge; but remember, we will be the sole arbiters of what you must do and how well you go about it."

Professors probably see little inconsistency in this injunction, since presumably they are able to discriminate between their authority over the student in the socialization structure and their scholarly competence as disciplinary specialists. Students, however, may and often do fail to see this distinction. In such cases students are likely to see professorial authority as monolithic, capricious, and applicable in all cases. The result is to make more difficult the achievement of one of the primary purposes of graduate training: the development of independent scholars. Confusion as to the proper limits of professorial authority and competence sometimes operates to strengthen early training in getting by and playing it safe.

Sanctions. Every socialization agency employs a system of rewards and punishments to reinforce effective role performance and extinguish or prohibit poor or inadequate behavior. In a well functioning agency, such as the one posited by our model, rewards and punishments are functionally related to the objectives of the training; they are known to all agents and neophytes and are presumed to be applied uniformly, rationally and justly. Emotional factors of various kinds and intensities inevitably develop in the relationship between agent and neophyte, but they are not expected to affect the agent's use of sanctions. Sanctions should not be applied capriciously or vindictively even though the dependent position of the neophyte and the punishment which the agent must occasionally administer will often generate some tension and even hostility. In the type of socialization organization described here, sanctions chiefly take the form of grades, though verbal approbation or disapproval, much sought after fellowships or grants can also be effective in eliciting and reinforcing appropriate responses from the neophyte.

Actual deviations from the model are especially difficult to document in operating systems. But it is at least possible to question whether grades or other sanctions are applied with high degrees of uniformity, rationality and impartiality in the typical graduate training organizations. There can be no question, however, that many neophytes in the system do question precisely this. In many disciplines this may result from the highly informal nature of graduate instruction and the great professional autonomy of the professor, which conspires with still other factors in the situation to confuse the student as to the performance criteria used by a single socializing agent or by the group of agents.

The fact that he is being evaluated by a group further accentuates his anxiety. In graduate school the neophyte faces a comparatively small number of mentors who are in communication with one another and who collectively hold his fate in their hands. This is structurally different from undergraduate work, where his professors were more numerous, located in many different fields, and seldom in a position to take collective action. In undergraduate work the student's record is accumulated slowly, a few credits or grades at a time, in a rather impersonal process. Graduate school professors are believed to talk to one another about the student, to evaluate his work collectively, and they are in a position to eliminate him from the program at many different points. The net effect is to heighten the sense of threat felt by the student. In some cases this situation results in a retreat into passivity, in other instances in attempts to establish a sycophantic relationship with one professor—a strategy which is not always discouraged.

Goals: Consensus and Conflict. The "ultimate" goal of socializing structures such as the one under discussion is to provide for the continuation, and possibly the development, of an occupation and the body of knowledge or professional skills with which it is associated. This may mean not only the replacement of personnel leaving the occupation but also the expansion of the field.

A more proximate goal, itself a means to the ultimate end, is the training of a succession of individuals who come to possess the skill and knowledge, attitudes, values and motives requisite for full membership in the field being served. A related but more short-run goal is the training of neophytes for acceptable performance in the socializing agency itself. As we have already noted, the neophyte must not only learn the content of his field, he must also learn to play the role of student in the socialization structure. Among other ends which operate as means to the achievement of major goals are the provision of competent socializing agents and the recruitment of a supply of neophytes who meet the requirements for entrance into training.

For the socialization process to function optimally, our model assumes that the goals of the organization are clearly defined, known to all socializing agents and neophytes, accepted by them as valid, and mutually compatible. Organization goals are also expected to be compatible with the personal objectives sought by both agents and neophytes as members of the organization. The norms which guide the interaction between agent and neophyte in the pursuit of common goals should be explicit, mutually compatible, and unreservedly internalized by everyone in the system. A well-functioning socialization structure must prevent the development of counter-norms which operate against the goals of the larger social system.

In actual practice the socialization organization seldom, if ever, achieves complete consensus on the goals. Even where a relatively high degree of consensus exists on the nature of the goals, disagreement may arise over the means for attaining them.

Consider the case of graduate training in the social sciences. Most agents probably regard the training of well-grounded and methodologically sophisticated neophytes as a major objective of the socialization process. When it comes to the means of achieving this goal, however, there may be much less agreement. Agents in some fields have very different commitments to the several branches of their discipline. In other cases, agents may change the direction and orientation of their instruction as they reflect the winds of doctrine which sweep across rapidly changing new sciences. Often there is no consensus on the content of instruction. As a consequence the graduate curricula may be more a compromise of different viewpoints than reflections of solid consensus.

Greater agreement on ends than means may well confuse the neophyte about the relationship between the means they encounter in their daily work and the ends toward which they are told to aspire. To the extent that this is true the neophyte is tempted to come to terms with each agent in an idiosyncratic manner rather than trying to grasp clearly the organization of the training program as a whole. "Use plenty of statistical references with Professor A," or "Be sure to make belittling remarks about fact-grubbing with Professor B."

A longer-term source of difficulty in achieving organizational goals relates to the implicit assumption that the goals of the graduate school are compatible with the personal objectives of the individuals in it. The truth is that graduate instruction is usually only one of the professional tasks of the graduate professor. He is also likely to be engaged in undergraduate teaching, in research, and in the administrative tasks of an increasingly bureaucratic educational enterprise. The sheer competition of these other tasks for the agent's time, and especially the fact that the greatest rewards of the agent are likely to follow from research and publication, often mean that teaching gets shortchanged. Exceptions may occur in cases where the neophytes are protégés, ego-extensions of the agent, or tools used to explore research areas of mutual interest. In terms of personal rewards, it is understandable that some professors seek to do as little teaching as possible and that others would like to eliminate it altogether. But this state of affairs is surely dysfunctional when viewed from the standpoint of the objectives of the graduate schools as socializing agencies.

NOTES

1. This type of socialization agency is similar to Wheeler's "Type IV collective interpersonal socialization setting." His analyses differ from ours in that he focuses upon the "organization itself and not on the direct interchange between agent and recruit." See Stanton Wheeler, "The Structure of Formally Organized Socialization Settings," in Orville G. Brim and Stanton Wheeler, *Socialization After Childhood* (New York: Wiley, 1966), p. 109. By our definition it would be impossible to analyze the structure of socialization without considering interaction between agent and neophyte.

2. Some exceptions are David Gottlieb, "Processes of Socialization in American Graduate Schools," *Social Forces,* 40 (December, 1961), pp. 124–31; Gosta Carlsson and Bengt Gesser, "Universities as Selecting and Socializing Agents: Some Recent Swedish Data," *Acta Sociologica,* 9 (Fasc. 1–2, 1965), pp. 25–39; Louise E. Merz, "The Graduate School as a Socializing Agency: A Pilot Study of Sociological Aspects of Graduate Training in the Physical Sciences," unpublished Ph.D. dissertation, Cornell University, 1961; Walter L. Wallace, "Institutional and Life-Cycle Socialization of College Freshmen," *American Journal of Sociology,* 70 (November, 1964), pp. 303–18. Dan C. Lortie, "From Laymen to Lawmen: Law Schools, Careers and Professional Socialization," *Harvard Educational Review,* 29 (Fall, 1959), pp. 352–69.

3. This position is discussed more fully in Bernard C. Rosen, *Adolescence and Religion* (Cambridge: Schenkman Publishing Co., 1965), Chapters 5 and 6.

4. See Bernard C. Rosen, "Some Structural Sources of Achievement Motivation and Values: Family and Society," mimeo paper to Social Science Research Council Committee on Socialization and Social Structure, Puerto Rico, 1965.

5. He may also perform another role—that of teaching assistant. There are possibilities for inter-role strain here as the neophyte moves from a position of authority (over undergraduates) to one of equality (with fellow-graduates) and subordination (to faculty).

6. Wheeler sees this as a potentially trouble-producing aspect of this type of socialization organization. "There is the likelihood that the former recruits will train the new ones using the defeating pattern." Brim and Wheeler, *op. cit.,* p. 62.

7. Cf. Howard S. Becker, Blanche Geer, Everett C. Hughes, and Anselm L. Strauss, *Boys in White: Student Culture in Medical School* (Chicago: University of Chicago Press, 1961).

11.   RONALD M. PAVALKO and   JOHN W. HOLLEY

Determinants of a Professional Self-Concept among Graduate Students

The effort of social scientists to understand the nature of occupational subcultures and their impact on individuals has given rise to a distinct tradition of research on "professional socialization." In particular, this tradition has focused on independent variables that facilitate the development of a "professional self-concept."

This study is concerned with the socialization of graduate teaching assistants (hereafter referred to as TA's). While most of the research in this area has dealt with socialization to relatively homogeneous professional roles, the academic profession is a relatively heterogeneous mixture of scientific and scholarly disciplines. Thus, one goal of this study is to see whether or not the conclusions of previous research are borne out in the more amorphous context of graduate school.

Reprinted from *Social Science Quarterly,* 55 (September, 1974), pp. 462–477, by permission of the authors and the Southwestern Social Science Association.

This study was partially supported by a grant (OEG-0-71-3244-520) from the U.S. Office of Education to the Graduate Training Program in the Sociology of Education, Department of Sociology, Florida State University. This is a revision of a paper presented at the annual meeting of the Pacific Sociological Association, Portland, Oregon, 1972.

PREVIOUS RESEARCH

One of the main conclusions that has emerged from previous research is that the development of a professional self-concept is facilitated by opportunities to enact the professional role while still in training. In Huntington's pioneering study of medical students[1] the last two years of training during which the student has extensive opportunities to play the professional role are seen as critically important for the development of a professional self-concept. Similarly, in Kadushin's study of music students[2] actual professional musical performances facilitate the development of a professional self-concept.

The sheer amount of exposure to professional education has also emerged as an important variable in explaining the development of a professional self-concept. In Huntington's study, the proportion of students reporting that they felt more like doctors than students increased dramatically from the earlier to the later years of training.[3] Kadushin's study of music students also indicated that "standing in school, as measured by a student's official class, and meaningful contact with the professional world of music, as indicated by professional performing, contribute about equally to the development of a professional self-concept as a musician. . . . "[4]

In addition to role-enactment and amount of exposure to professional school, subjective feelings of "success" are also related to professional self-concept. Huntington identifies "difficulty in adequately meeting patients' problems" as an important variable. Forty-five per cent of the first year students who had little or no difficulty in handling patients' problems reported feeling more like doctors than students, while only 25 per cent of those who had a fair or considerable amount of difficulty felt like doctors.[5]

The kind of future career anticipated by students is also related to the development of a professional self-concept. Among Kadushin's music students the professional self-concept of those who planned to become teachers rather than performers was affected less by professional performing experience.[6] The implication is that there is some kind of anticipatory socialization operating. Potential socialization experiences that do not involve activities similar to those the individual expects to perform later may be downgraded in importance and not enter into the process of acquiring a professional self-concept.

HYPOTHESES GUIDING THE PRESENT STUDY

In the present study, professional role-enactment, exposure to graduate school, perceived success, and career expectations are expected to be related to professional self-concept. However, the graduate school socialization context permits an examination of two independent variables not dealt with in previous studies.

Autonomy in the enactment of the professional role has not been dealt with largely because of its absence in the socialization contexts that have been studied. Because of the structure of medical education and a concern for patient safety, medical students are granted very little autonomy in their dealings with patients. Rather, they are relatively closely supervised by qualified MD's.

The controversy over the extent to which medical students develop a professional self-concept generated by Becker's study of the University of Kansas Medical School[7] revolves largely around this issue of autonomy. Becker concluded that medical students did not acquire a professional self-concept during the course of their medical education. He states that they "do not take on the professional role, largely because the system they operate in does not allow them to do so. They are not doctors, and the recurring experiences of being denied responsibility make it perfectly clear to them that they are not."[8]

Thus, autonomy has not been dealt with in studies of medical (and law)[9] students because it does not exist in these socialization contexts. On the other hand, the music students studied by Kadushin always have complete autonomy when engaging in professional performances, a condition that does not permit examination of the effect of variations in autonomy on self-concept.

In studying graduate TA's it is possible to conceptually and empirically separate the effects of role-enactment and the effects of autonomy on the development of a professional self-concept. Two TA's in charge of the same kind of course in two different departments may differ considerably in the kind and amount of autonomy they are given. One may be required to keep strictly to a departmental syllabus, while the other may be free to seek out and organize his own material. The department may choose the text, or this may be left up to the individual, etc. In this study, autonomy is the major independent variable. We will be primarily concerned with assessing its effects on self-concept.

Previous experience is the second "new" variable examined here. While medical and law schools simply do not get students who have previously worked as doctors or lawyers, it is not uncommon for persons to practice the academic profession for some time and then return to school to complete work on a graduate degree. There are, in fact, many students in graduate programs who have held responsible professional positions in the past. It seems reasonable that such persons will bring with them a moderately well-developed professional self-concept, and that the socialization experiences of graduate school and the teaching assistantship in particular will operate differently on them than on students who have not had such experiences. Thus, we expect the existence of a "conditional relationship" such that persons with previous professional experience will be less influenced by the various socializing factors that have been found to be important than will those who lack such previous experience.

DATA AND METHODS

The population for this study consists of all graduate teaching assistants at Florida State University during the late spring of the 1969–70 academic year. The population was identified by department chairmen and through official payroll records. Data were collected by means of a mailed questionnaire. A follow-up "reminder" letter was sent to those teaching assistants who had not responded within ten days of the first mailing. Of the original population of 516, some 364 questionnaires (70.5 per cent) were returned.

Restricting the study to TA's is clearly a limitation in that not all graduate students become TA's. Many work as research assistants and others are supported by fellowships that carry no work obligations. Consequently, our study cannot claim to deal with the totality of potential socializing experiences of graduate students. The graduate education process is simply more diversified and varied than that of professional schools where student cohorts have the same kinds of experiences at the same times. However, since our main theoretical concern is with the interplay of autonomy in a particular role and other socializing variables, TA's seem to be the most appropriate sub-population to deal with. The structural possibility of autonomy is certainly greater than for the research assistant or fellowship student and there is greater proximity to the professional role of "teacher" than there is for the research assistant compared to the role of "researcher."

The dependent variable of this study is professional self-concept. As dealt with by most psychologists, self-concept usually has connotations of self-esteem or self-evaluation. Our use and measurement of the concept is more specific to a particular research tradition and does not carry such broad evaluative connotations. The measurement technique chosen was modeled after that used by the Bureau of Applied Social Research of Columbia University in the study that resulted in the publication of *The Student Physician.* Obviously, the wording of the item had to be changed to fit this different research context. The only additional change made was to follow the lead of Kadushin's study and convert a dichotomous scale to a six-category graphic equal-appearing intervals scale.[10] In presenting the data in tabular form, the two lowest, two middle, and two highest categories of the scale were combined to produce the categories low, medium, and high, respectively, in Table 1.

Autonomy is operationalized with seven items measuring extent of faculty supervision, freedom in the selection of text materials, latitude in the determination of course content, selection of evaluation techniques, control over grades assigned students, access to office supplies, and the adequacy of office facilities provided.

Extent of professional role-enactment is operationalized by an item measuring the extent to which duties are routine and menial as opposed to complex (e.g., grading objective tests as opposed to teaching senior level courses), an item asking the extent to which tasks are perceived as being similar to faculty work activities, and an item on length of service as a TA.

Exposure to graduate school is measured in two ways. The first is simply the number of quarters in graduate school. Since there is some indication[11] that passing through such transitions as doctoral comprehensive examinations results in somewhat abrupt changes in role identification, exposure is also measured in terms of the extent to which the student has progressed through the various formal hurdles and requirements on the road to a graduate degree. In order to capture both the quantitative and qualitative aspects of exposure, an index was constructed from these two items. Because of the frequently irregular and non-standardized nature of progress through graduate school, greater weight was given to stages of graduate education where marked discrepancies occurred.

Success as a teaching assistant was measured with an equal-appearing intervals item with division into six response segments. These were dichotomized in the analysis and are presented as low and high in Table 1.

Career expectations were measured by two items, one of which asked the student to select one of four career descriptions as best matching his plans. The other item asked those planning academic careers to indicate their preference for different types of institutions ranging from junior colleges to research oriented universities.

Previous experience was measured by asking students whether they had ever held a teaching position at any level (elementary school through university). While most of those with previous experience indicated that it had been at the high school or junior college level, this variable was dichotomized into those with no previous experience and those with some, regardless of level.

FINDINGS

In examining the data our strategy will be to first look at zero-order relationships between the independent variables and the dependent variable of self-concept (Table 1). Next, the relationship between autonomy and self-concept

TABLE 1

Relationship Between Professional Self-Concept in the Teaching Assistant Role Context and Selected Variables (In Percent)

Variables	Self-Concept in TA Role Context					Gamma
	Low	Medium	High	Total	(N)	
Measures of Autonomy						
Extent of Faculty Supervision of Teaching Activities						—.000
Considerable supervision	12.9	31.0	56.0	99.9	(116)	
Minimal supervision	13.8	29.8	56.4	100.0	(225)	
Autonomy in Selection of Text Materials						.062
All materials specified in syllabus	17.2	25.8	57.0	100.0	(93)	
Text standardized—outside readings up to assistant	9.5	24.6	65.9	100.0	(126)	
Entire matter left up to assistant	10.7	32.1	57.1	99.9	(56)	
Autonomy in Selection of Course Content						.307
Departmental syllabus must be followed	23.7	28.7	47.5	99.9	(160)	
Some content is prescribed, rest optional	12.2	32.2	55.6	100.0	(90)	
Entire matter up to assistant	3.2	29.8	67.0	100.0	(94)	
Selection of Tests and Evaluation Techniques						.249
Entirely left up to Department	30.0	40.0	30.0	100.0	(20)	
Partially departmental decision, partially left up to the assistant	20.4	26.9	52.8	100.0	(108)	
Entirely left up to the assistant	9.6	30.8	59.6	100.0	(208)	
Control over Grades Given Undergraduate Students						.334
None	52.4	23.8	23.8	100.0	(21)	
Partial	13.9	39.2	46.8	99.9	(79)	
Complete control	12.0	28.1	59.8	100.0	(249)	
Access to Secretarial Supplies such as mimeograph paper and stencils						.087
Never available	15.8	36.8	47.4	100.0	(19)	

TABLE 1 (continued)

Irregularly available	13.0	37.0	50.0	100.0	(46)	
Always available when needed	15.6	28.0	56.4	100.0	(289)	—.157
Type of Office Facilities Provided						
None provided	9.5	25.4	65.1	100.0	(63)	
Desk in large room with other assistants	16.7	29.8	53.5	100.0	(198)	
Private or semi-private office	16.4	35.1	48.5	100.0	(97)	.454
Measures of Extent of Role-Enactment						
Type of Work Assignment as Teaching Asst.						
Grading tests, keeping records, etc.	33.3	47.6	19.0	99.9	(42)	
Conduct lab or discussion section	20.0	36.2	43.8	100.0	(80)	
Teach introductory course	12.4	28.8	58.8	100.0	(170)	
Teach upper division course	6.6	14.8	78.7	100.1	(61)	.313
Perceived Similarity of Own Work to Faculty Work Activities						
Low 1	29.9	29.0	41.9	99.8	(31)	
2	22.9	33.3	43.8	100.0	(48)	
3	23.3	37.2	39.5	100.0	(43)	
4	20.7	36.2	43.1	100.0	(58)	
5	8.8	29.7	61.5	100.0	(91)	
High 6	6.0	22.9	71.1	100.0	(83)	.397
Number of Quarters Served as Teaching Asst.						
1 – 6 quarters	18.9	38.3	42.9	100.1	(175)	
7 – 12 quarters	11.3	21.4	67.3	100.0	(159)	.339
Exposure to Graduate School						
Number of Quarters in Graduate School						
1 – 6 quarters	18.2	44.6	37.2	100.0	(121)	
7 – 12 quarters	18.2	25.0	56.8	100.0	(132)	
13 quarters or more	9.2	21.1	69.7	100.0	(109)	

TABLE 1 (continued)

Relationship Between Professional Self-Concept in the Teaching Assistant Role Context and Selected Variables (In Percent)

Variables	Self-Concept in TA Role Context				(N)	Gamma
	Low	Medium	High	Total		
Stage in Graduate Education						
Just began graduate work	22.2	45.6	32.2	100.0	(90)	.334
Masters complete or nearly so	14.1	32.8	53.1	100.0	(64)	
Engaged in post-Masters work	15.7	25.2	59.1	100.0	(115)	
Ph.D. Candidate (Comprehensives passed)	11.0	17.1	72.0	100.1	(82)	
Index of exposure to graduate school						
Minimal exposure	18.1	41.6	40.4	100.0	(166)	.380
Maximal exposure	13.3	20.9	65.8	100.0	(196)	
Success						
Perceived success as a Teaching Asst.						
Low	21.1	40.6	38.3	100.0	(133)	.401
High	12.4	23.9	63.7	100.0	(226)	
Career Orientation						
Desired Work Context						
Practitioner	29.6	35.2	35.2	100.0	(54)	
Non-academic research	22.2	24.4	53.3	99.9	(45)	
Teaching	10.5	28.7	60.8	100.0	(209)	
Academic research	14.6	39.6	45.8	100.0	(48)	
Previous Experience						
Prior Teaching Experience at any level						
None	17.9	32.1	50.0	100.0	(196)	.170
Some	12.7	28.3	59.0	100.0	(166)	

will be examined with controls to identify interaction effects (Tables 2–5) and, finally, Coleman's measure of effect parameters will be used to measure the relative effects of the independent variables on self-concept (Tables 6–8).

Only three of the seven measures of autonomy (in the selection of course content, in the selection and construction of tests and evaluation techniques, and in the control exercised over grade assignment) are directly related to self-concept. Given the lack of relationship between the other four measures of autonomy and self-concept, and in order to render presentation of the data more manageable, only the three measures related to self-concept will be dealt with in the remainder of this analysis.

Turning to role-enactment, the complexity of work performed is directly related to the strength of professional self-concept, and the more the work is perceived to be like that of the faculty, the more professional is the self-concept. Amount of time as a teaching assistant is also positively related to self-concept.

Both measures of exposure are related to self-concept. The same is true for the index of exposure which yields an association with the dependent variable that is slightly stronger than the analogous relationships involving either of its components.

Perceived success is also directly related to self-concept, but career expectations are not. However, in the case of career expectations, 60 per cent chose teaching over the other three alternatives, while only 13 per cent chose academic research. This distribution is sharply at variance with what was expected, given the nature of the reward structure of academia. Since this variable bears no zero-order relationship to the dependent variable and, given the small amount of variation in responses, career orientation is dropped from the remaining analysis.

Turning to the last independent variable, a weak but positive association exists between previous experience and self-concept.

We examine next the relationships between autonomy and self-concept with other variables controlled.[12] Beginning with autonomy in the selection of course content (Table 2) we find that the introduction of complexity of work markedly decreases but does not eliminate the relationship. Length of time has essentially no effect, while similarity to faculty work reveals a somewhat stronger relationship among those who perceive their work as similar to that of the faculty. Control for exposure does not produce any striking changes, but the relationship is slightly stronger among those with longer exposure. Control for perceived success makes no appreciable change in the relationship.

Except for the lower level of association and two pronounced reversals, the pattern for the relationship of autonomy in test selection to self-concept largely follows that of the previous autonomy measure. The first two role-enactment controls had no effects of any consequence, but when length of time is con-

TABLE 2

Gamma Values for Relationship between Autonomy Measures and Self-Concept with a Variety of Control Variables Held Constant

Control Variable		Autonomy Measures		
		Selection of Course Content	Construction & Selection of Tests	Assignment of Grades
Role-Enactment				
Complexity of work	Mostly clerical	.162	.125	.184
	Complex	.195	.295	.131
	Zero-order	.307	.249	.334
Similarity to faculty work	Not similar	.169	.234	.142
	Similar	.331	.301	.443
	Zero-order	.307	.249	.334
Length of time as TA	Short	.352	.365	.453
	Long	.327	.086	.135
	Zero-order	.307	.249	.334
Other Measures				
Index of Exposure to Graduate School	Brief	.218	.182	.276
	Long	.360	.264	.340
	Zero-order	.307	.249	.334
Perceived Success as TA	Unsuccessful	.246	.104	.151
	Successful	.300	.312	.411
	Zero-order	.307	.249	.334
Previous Teaching Experience	None	.162	.092	.207
	Some	.449	.421	.481
	Zero-order	.307	.249	.334

trolled, autonomy in student evaluation is strongly related to self-concept only among those who have been TA's a relatively short period of time.

The last measure of autonomy (grade assignment) is most strongly related to self-concept. When controls were introduced few striking changes occurred. In no case was the relationship reduced so drastically that it might be said to have been "explained away" by the marginal relationships involving the control variable.

An unusual pattern emerges with control for length of time as a T.A. For, all three autonomy measures the primary relationship holds only among those who have been TA's a relatively short time. Examination of the marginals reveals that there is essentially no relationship between the length of time one has been a TA and the amount of autonomy one is granted. Perhaps one takes only other TA's in one's department as a reference group and, since the relationship between autonomy and seniority is somewhat random, downgrades the importance of autonomy as a form of recognition, thereby nullifying its effect on self-concept.

Length of exposure to graduate school and perceived success produce similar effects when applied to the relationship between autonomy and self-concept. In both cases the primary relationship is stronger among those who perceive themselves as more successful and among those who have had a longer period of exposure.

The effects of previous teaching experience proved to be something of a surprise. The relationship between autonomy and self-concept decreases sharply among those with no previous experience, while for those with at least some previous experience the relationship is quite strong. This is clearly at variance with the expectation that the relationship would go in the opposite direction. Perhaps experience as a teacher sensitizes one to the importance of autonomy. If this is the case, it could be argued that the current socialization context carries more weight in determining self-concept than the accumulated effects of past experience which, additionally, make the withholding of autonomy more degrading than for the new teacher who has no basis for expecting a high degree of autonomy.

Turning to role-enactment we find much less consistency than was the case with autonomy (Table 3). In no case can it be said that the control variables "explain" or drastically weaken the primary relationship.

The relationship between complexity of work and self-concept held more strongly among those with greater exposure while the reverse was true for the relationships involving similarity to faculty work and length of service. Of the three relationships, the most pronounced was that involving complexity of

TABLE 3

Gamma Values For Relationships Between Role-Enactment Measures and Self-Concept with a Variety of Control Variables held Constant

| Control Variable | | Role-Enactment Measures | | |
		Complexity of Work	Similarity of Faculty Work	Lenth of Time as TA
Exposure to Graduate School	Brief	.341	.413	.403
	Long	.556	.304	.262
	Zero-order	.459	.356	.397
Perceived Success as TA	Unsuccessful	.277	.448	.267
	Successful	.552	.227	.411
	Zero-order	.459	.356	.397
Previous Teaching Experience	None	.293	.315	.580
	Some	.633	.406	.135
	Zero-order	.459	.356	.397

work, the variable with the strongest primary relationship with self-concept.

Among those who perceived themselves as highly successful, the relationship between complexity of work and self-concept was stronger than among those with less positive perceptions of their performance. Surprisingly, the relationship between similarity to faculty work and self-concept was stronger for those who perceived themselves as less successful. No obvious explanation for this finding is apparent but we can speculate that if there is a tendency to cast about for justifications of a highly professional self-concept, it is possible that those who count themselves unsuccessful seize upon the fact of their relatively important teaching assignments as evidence of the esteem of the faculty as a way of maintaining a professional self-concept.

Experience as a teacher produces some unusual results. Complexity of work and similarity to faculty work are related to self-concept more strongly among those with more previous experience. This is reversed for length of service which is related to self-concept only among those with no previous experience.

In the interest of parsimony, only the controlled relationships of the index of exposure to the dependent variable will be examined (Table 4). When complexity of work is controlled, the relationship of exposure to self-concept is most pronounced among those whose work involves actual teaching rather than merely clerical work and the like. When perceived success is controlled,

TABLE 4

Gamma Values for Relationship between Exposure to Graduate School and Perceived Success, and the Dependent Variable with a Variety of Control Variables Held Constant

Control Variable		Exposure to Graduate School	Perceived Success as TA
Complexity of Work	Mostly clerical	.246	.203
	Complex and Professional	.468	.477
	Zero-order	.380	.401
Perceived Success as TA	Unsuccessful	.226	—
	Successful	.442	—
	Zero-order	.380	—
Previous Teaching Experience	None	.482	.421
	Some	.203	.361
	Zero-order	.380	.401
Index of Exposure to Graduate School	Brief	—	.283
	Long	—	.462
	Zero-order	—	.401

the relationship is stronger among those who perceive themselves as quite successful in their teaching. Only among those without any previous experience is exposure appreciably related to self-concept. For those who have already been through a lengthy period of socialization as teachers, the amount of time spent in graduate school may be relatively insignificant and thus have no important effect on self-concept.

When the relationship between perceived success and self-concept is subjected to the same controls used to examine the relationship of self-concept to exposure, the pattern is essentially the same as that just discussed for exposure.

Given the kinds of conditional relationships revealed in the foregoing analysis, it is essential to attempt to assess the simultaneous effects of several variables on the dependent variable. To do this we have selected Coleman's[13] measure of "effect parameters" which estimates the amount of variation in a

TABLE 5

**Gamma Values for Relationship between Autonomy and Self-Concept
with Complexity of Work Tasks (Role Enactment),
Extent of Exposure to Graduate School Context (GS)
and Perceived Success as a Teaching Assistant Controlled**

| | Autonomy Measures | | |
| | Control of Grades | Test Selection and Evaluation | Selection of Course Content |
Control Variables			
Routine work tasks			
Short exposure GS	.221	.203	.611
Long exposure GS	—.116	—.059	—.152
Complex work tasks			
Short exposure GS	—.085	.202	.079
Long exposure GS	.210	.345	.390
Routine work tasks			
Unsuccessful as Teach. Asst.	—.172	.043	.300
Successful as Teach. Asst.	.122	.008	.175
Complex work tasks			
Unsuccessful as Teach. Asst.	—.080	.082	.206
Successful as Teach. Asst.	.258	.472	.208
Short exposure GS			
Unsuccessful as Teach. Asst.	.007	—.082	.277
Successful as Teach. Asst.	.396	.354	.284
Long exposure GS			
Unsuccessful as Teach. Asst.	.196	.226	.326
Successful as Teach. Asst.	.303	.168	.361

dichotomous dependent variable that is attributable to each of three dichotomous variables when the other two are controlled.

As an intermediate step it was necessary to generate the appropriate contin-
gency tables from which the effect parameters are calculated. Three tables (one
for each of the autonomy measures) were constructed with self-concept as the
dependent variable while simultaneously controlling for two of the three variables of role-enactment (complexity of work), exposure to the graduate school
context (index), and perceived success. Rather than present all three contin-
gency tables, the gamma values from each are presented in Table 5.

The effects of autonomy in the control of grades are not as strong as those
of the other variables in the table. Comparisons for the other variables indicate
percentage increases for high values for role-enactment, exposure, and perceived success. This pattern is essentially repeated for autonomy in the selection of tests and evaluation techniques and for autonomy in the selection of
course content.

The effect parameters are presented in Tables 6, 7, and 8, each of which
contains a different measure of autonomy and the various possible combinations of role-enactment, exposure, and perceived success. The effect parameters for each combination are summed to obtain the total proportion of
variation in the table explained by the three variables in the model taken
together.

The only condition under which autonomy in control of grades explains any
appreciable amount of variation (10 per cent) is when role-enactment is absent
from the model (Table 6). This conclusion holds, though less strongly, for all
three autonomy measures. On the other hand, the three-variable combination
that excludes role-enactment explains more variation in the dependent variable
than either of the combinations that include it. A little over one-half of the total
variation in self-concept is explained by autonomy in control of grades, exposure, and perceived success, while the autonomy, role-enactment, exposure

TABLE 6

The Effects of Autonomy in Control of Students' Grades and Three Other Variables in Combinations of Threes, on Professional Self-Concept (Calculated from Table 5)

Predictor Variables				
Autonomy (Control of Grades)	Role-Enactment (Complexity of Work)	Exposure to Graduate School Context	Perceived Success as TA	Total
.004	.247	.170		.421
—.014	.242		.162	.390
.109		.212	.180	.501

TABLE 7

The Effects of Autonomy in Selection of Tests and Three Other Variables, in Combinations of Threes, on Professional Self-Concept (Calculated from Table 5)

| | | Predictor Variables | | |
Autonomy (Selection of Tests)	Role-Enactment (Complexity of Work)	Exposure to Graduate School Context	Perceived Success as TA	Total
.041	.232	.206		.478
.018	.204		.188	.410
.051		.199	.206	.455

combination explains only 42 per cent of the variation. This same pattern holds for autonomy in selection of course content (Table 8), but not for autonomy in the selection of tests (Table 7).

Autonomy in the selection of tests, though explaining less variation in the absence of role-enactment than the other two autonomy measures, was least drastically reduced in its effects when role-enactment entered the model (Table 7). With role-enactment in the model, autonomy in test selection explained more variation than either of the other autonomy measures, although the absolute amount of variation explained remains small. The three-variable combination including test selection autonomy that explains more variation than the other two is that of autonomy, role-enactment, and exposure, explaining about 48 per cent of the variation.

Autonomy in the selection of course content (Table 8) explains about 9 per cent of the variation in the dependent variable when role-enactment is not in the model. When role-enactment is substituted for either exposure or perceived success, the amount of variation explained drops to about 1 per cent. More of

TABLE 8

The Effects of Autonomy in Selection of Course Content and Three Other Variables, in Combination of Threes, on Professional Self-Concept (Calculated from Table 5)

| | | Predictor Variables | | |
Autonomy (Course Content)	Role-Enactment (Complexity of Work)	Exposure to Graduate School Context	Perceived Success as TA	Total
.014	.286	.119		.419
.013	.285		.194	.491
.093		.249	.218	.560

the total variation in self-concept (56 per cent) is explained by the combination of autonomy in course content selection, exposure, and perceived success than by any other combination of three variables examined.

Examining all three of the tables of effect parameters, role-enactment explains the most variation—an average of 25 per cent through all three tables. Exposure is next (19.4 per cent), with perceived success at 19.1 per cent. Autonomy finishes a rather poor last place with an average explained variation of 3.7 per cent.

CONCLUSIONS

Our findings support the conclusions of previous research regarding the effects of opportunities to enact the professional role, amount of exposure to the socialization context, and perceived success in professional tasks on the development of a professional self-concept. While autonomy does not have a strong independent effect on self-concept, its interaction with role-enactment, exposure, and perceived success suggests that it can be an important (positive or negative) part of the professionalization process and should be incorporated into our conception of that process.

Our findings contain several policy implications if we assume that maximum development of a professional self-concept is a desired end product of the graduate education process.

To begin with, greater awareness and self-consciousness about the socialization process and the function of the teaching assistantship in it may be called for. Our finding that there is no relationship between autonomy and length of time as a TA suggests that this is not the case. It also suggests that the handling of this important socialization experience may result in a variety of frustrations, feelings of failure, and confusion regarding where one stands in the eyes of one's mentors. A system of progressively responsible and autonomous assignments, in phase with where the student is in his progress toward the completion of his degree requirements, would maximize the attainment of socialization outcomes.

In times of financial austerity, which the 1970's have thus far proved to be in academia, it may be tempting for graduate departments to view the teaching assistantship as a way of increasing their teaching productivity with minimal costs. To do so may be very short-sighted insofar as it slows down or disrupts the development of professional orientations among graduate students. While this study did not directly explore the link between the handling of the teaching assistantship and "student discontent," it is possible that the frequent complaints and disaffection of graduate students may be related to the way the teaching assistantship is handled. Being granted autonomy at too early a stage in one's graduate education or being asked to do tasks that are "beneath" the student about to receive his PhD may both be disorienting and work against the acquisition of a professional self-concept.

The professional is expected to be autonomous, that is, to be capable of coping with the responsibilities that go with his position. Yet, the opportunities to exercise autonomy in the course of the graduate training process are few. The teaching assistantship constitutes such an opportunity and under the conditions identified in this study can contribute to the development of a professional self-concept.

NOTES

1. Mary Jean Huntington. "The Development of a Professional Self-Image." in Robert K. Merton, George Reader, and Patricia L. Kendall, *The Student Physician* (Cambridge: Harvard University Press, 1957), pp. 179–187.

2. Charles Kadushin, "The Professional Self-Concept of Music Students," *American Journal of Sociology,* 75 (Nov., 1969), pp. 389–404.

3. Huntington, *op. cit.,* p. 180.

4. Kadushin, *op. cit.,* pp. 398–399.

5. Huntington, *op. cit.,* p. 186.

6. Kadushin, *op. cit.,* p. 398.

7. Howard S. Becker, Blanche Geer, Everett C. Hughes, and Anselm Strauss, *Boys in White* (Chicago: University of Chicago Press, 1961).

8. *Ibid.,* p. 420.

9. Dan Lortie, "Laymen to Lawmen: Law School, Careers, and Professional Socialization," *Harvard Educational Review,* 29 (Fall, 1959), pp. 363–367.

10. The following item was used to measure professional self-concept: In the context of your work as a teaching assistant, how have you tended to think of yourself recently?

Primarily as a student.

Primarily as a member of my discipline or profession (biologist, historian, social welfare worker, physicist, educational theorist, etc.).

11. D. T. Hall, "Identity Changes During the Transition from Student to Professor," *School Review,* 76 (Dec., 1968), pp. 445–469.

12. It was initially expected that field of study would be an important variable to take into account. When TA's were classified into natural sciences, social sciences, humanities, and professional (business, education, etc.), field of study was essentially unrelated to either self-concept or autonomy. Hence, this variable was dropped from the analysis.

13. James S. Coleman, *Introduction to Mathematical Sociology* (New York: The Free Press, 1964).

Part III

The School as a Social Institution

Chapter Five

Schools and the Larger Society

All too often education is discussed as though schools operated in a vacuum, that is, as though they were totally independent of and unaffected by other segments of the society. In part, this view of education may be a consequence of emphasizing the innovative, creative, and change-producing role of education in modern society. But seeing education as an "active" or "independent" social institution is only one possible "model of education" which the analyst might develop. An equally plausible model or perspective might be one that regarded education as a "re-active" or "dependent" social institution. This latter perspective emphasizes a high degree of interdependence between education and other social institutions, particularly political and economic institutions. Thus, increased demands for technologists to staff an increasingly complex industrial economy are responded to or reacted to by the educational institution with an attempt to meet those demands. While the creative-innovative role of education is not denied, the fact that education may be shaped by the general society and specific segments within it must not be overlooked.[1]

The articles in this chapter tend to emphasize or highlight this "re-active" model of education. That is, they are oriented around the general theme that social forces and institutions *external* to education are important determinants of the scope, form, and function of the educational institution.

In the first article of this chapter Herriott and Hodgkins present an analysis of the effect of the environment in which schools exist on selected high school characteristics. Focusing on the "modernity" of the environment, they first identify regions in the United States that vary in modernity and then examine the way in which modernity is related to the educational level of teachers and the post-high school educational attainment of students.

"Accountability" has become an issue of major proportions at every level of the educational system. Increasingly school boards, legislators, publics, etc., are demanding that schools be held "accountable" for both their utilization of resources and the quality and quantity of their products. In the second article, Hills discusses the value system of the educational system and the societal function that schools perform and argues that these are incompatible with both the goals and techniques of accountability.

There is probably no educational issue in recent years that has received more public attention than the "busing" of students to achieve racial desegregation of the public schools. One response of white parents to busing has been to withdraw their children from public schools and enroll them in (white) private schools, thereby undermining the goal of desegregation. It is this "white flight" that is the focus of the third article of this chapter. Giles, Gatlin, and Cataldo examine the relationship of several characteristics of busing (distances involved, racial composition of schools, etc.) to parental compliance with or rejection of busing. They also suggest several strategies for minimizing the effect of busing on "white flight" from the public schools.

Juvenile delinquency has long been recognized as a serious problem in American society. However, only recently have social scientists begun to examine the connection between delinquency and attitudes toward school, academic performance, peer groups, and other schooling experiences. In the last article of this chapter Frease reviews some of the research on this topic and presents data from a study that attempts to unravel the linkages between delinquency and a variety of school characteristics and experiences.

NOTES

1. For further discussion of this issue see Burton R. Clark, *Educating the Expert Society,* San Francisco: Chandler Publishing Company, 1962, Chapter 1, and A. H. Halsey, Jean Floud, and C. Arnold Anderson, *Education, Economy, and Society,* New York: The Free Press, 1962, pp. 1–12.

12.   ROBERT E. HERRIOTT
and BENJAMIN J. HODGKINS

Social Context and the School:
An Open-System Analysis of Social
and Educational Change

~ Formal education is an integral part of modern societies, yet we know very little about its relationship to the process of modernization. The term "modernization" has generally been equated with social changes in specialization, industrialization, urbanization or economic development,[1] but a full understanding of it requires going beyond the more observable manifestations of the change process to a consideration of the primary basis on which societies modernize. Such a basis seems to involve: (1) the introduction of new technology; and (2) the social acceptance of the consequences of that technology in both technological and nontechnological areas of social life.[2]

The introduction of a new technology is often very rapid and can be identified historically as stemming from either innovation or cross-cultural diffusion. The general acceptance of the consequences of that technology, however, is often quite gradual. Lerner (1958:45) has captured the essence of the nontechnological aspects of modernization when he speaks of the challenge to all societies who seek modernization regarding ". . . the infusion of a rationalist and positivist spirit." In effect, given increasing technological knowledge, there must be an increasing willingness on the part of a significant and influential segment of a society's membership to restructure social life in order to maximize the potential benefits to be derived from that technology. With these "pre-requisites" the developmental change has, as noted by Levy, been toward an *ideal modern state of society wherein the structure and organization of social behavior are maximally adapted to the use of the most advanced technological knowledge for the ultimate material benefits to be derived from its efficient utilization.*[3]

Reprinted from *Rural Sociology,* 34 (June, 1969), pp. 149–166, by permission of the authors and the Rural Sociological Society.

Revision of a paper presented at the annual meeting of the American Sociological Association at Boston, 1968. The research reported herein was supported in part by the U.S. Office of Education through Grant No. OEG–2–6–062972–2095. The theoretical framework and empirical analyses presented in this article have been developed more fully in Robert E. Herriott and Benjamin J. Hodgkins, *The Environment of Schooling: Formal Education as an Open Social System* (Englewood Cliffs, N.J.: Prentice-Hall, Inc., 1973).

Societies, as well as various social aspects within them, vary in terms of their resiliency to pressures for social change; therefore it seems reasonable to assume that the degree of modernization both among and within societies also varies.[4] Within a particular society, modernization may be viewed not only as a continuous process, but as an uneven one since it is dependent on the variable nature of social and cultural characteristics which facilitate or impede changes in that society.[5]

The following discussion explores the relationship of the school as a social organization to the social context in which it is located. After discussing the function of formal education in modern societies, we will introduce an explanatory model of the American public school as an open social system. Two hypotheses generated by this theoretical framework are then tested using data from a large national sample of public senior high schools, and implications are drawn regarding the relationship of modernization, as a form of social change, to formal education within contemporary America.

THEORETICAL CONSIDERATIONS

Formal Education in Modern Societies

The importance of education in modern societies is readily acknowledged in most literature dealing with social change and development. Educational variables are also frequently used in cross-cultural studies as indicators of the degree of development of a society (e.g., Shannon, 1959; Cattell et al., 1952; Schnore, 1961). The effect of modern development on the role of formal education, however, has for the most part been considered primarily in a speculative manner. Its existence has usually been assumed from the demonstrated fact that as societies become more modern, literacy rates and the educational level of the population rise. The "why" and "how" of this covariation too often remains unspecified. It is our view that the underlying feature of this relationship between modernization and education is the *dependence* of technological development on the social institution of formal education; a dependence important not only in terms of the transmission of technical knowledge,[6] but also in terms of the development of an instrumental orientation amenable to the implementation of that knowledge (Gerth and Mills, 1946:426–434).

In modern societies, the only formal and systematic attempt to instill this instrumental orientation occurs in formal education. Couched in terms of achievement based on universal standards of performance, and affectively neutral evaluation in specific role contexts, mass formal education generally places the neophyte in a social milieu quite unlike his limited family experiences, but not unlike the social context in which he will spend his adult life.[7] By "adjusting" to the school milieu over a period of years, the student internalizes the instrumental orientation to social relationships necessary for successful performance as an adult in a rapidly modernizing society.[8] Thus, the institutional role of education can be viewed in terms of the social needs of modern industrialized society as they are reflected in the technical requirements and values associated with modern life.[9]

Although several bases undoubtedly exist for examining the dynamics of this process, the insights of Max Weber on education as a bureaucracy seem particularly relevant. Weber suggests that "a rational and bureaucratic (modern) structure" of education best corresponds to the "ideal" means for imparting specialized training (Gerth and Mills, 1946:426). Thus, as a society becomes more modern, the formal education system tends to become increasingly rational and bureaucratic in nature.

If one views formal education within a modern society in this manner (as being rationally constituted to fulfill an institutional role), it is relevant to ask how the inputs, structural characteristics, and outputs of formal education vary with the degree of modernization. To the extent that inputs and structural characteristics approach the bureaucratic ideal, the outputs of the educational system may be expected to approximate the needs of modern society, thereby resulting in an "effective" formal educational system. With regard to inputs, for example, both the number and type of students in societies at early stages of modernization generally are not determined rationally in terms of modern social needs. The formal educational system of such societies tends, in Weber's terms, to emphasize a "pedagogy of cultivation" for the elite and not the specialized training and orientation necessary for modern life (Gerth and Mills, 1946). Many ex-colonial African states are examples of this phenomenon (see Ashby, 1964). In such cases the effectiveness of the formal system is low.

Such a view of the relationship between the degree of modernization and the effectiveness of education has generally been used to compare societies, but it can also be applied within a modern society. There is research, for example, which suggests that the process of modernization varies *within* American society in a manner similar to the variations more frequently noted among societies (Allen and Bentz, 1965; Anderson and Bowman, 1955; Gillin, 1955). If this is indeed the case, it seems reasonable to expect similar variation in the effectiveness of the formal education system in terms of its development toward an ideally rational bureaucratic form.

The School as a Social System

Historically, the study of the school *as a social organization* has been a neglected area of empirical research (Gross, 1956:64; Bidwell, 1965:972). Although many reasons exist for this oversight, of particular importance has been the tendency of past analysts of the school to utilize conceptual models derived from economic or social psychological assumptions (e.g., Burkhead, 1967; Barker and Gump, 1964). In such instances the results have been somewhat disappointing from a sociological perspective, because the fundamentally social nature of the school as a formal organization has been overlooked.

To overcome this limitation, we have chosen to consider the relationship of modernization and education utilizing a general systems approach which focuses on education at the organizational level. At this level, the institutional role of education may be identified as the extrinsic *genotypic* function of the organization, the "purpose" of the organization vis-à-vis the larger society.[10] For systems theory generally, and organizational analysis in particular, the concept of "purpose" is a complex, but highly relevant one. By purpose we do not imply an ultimate goal or end, nor do we mean the conscious intent of the organization's membership. Rather, organizational purpose vis-à-vis the larger society refers to the state of organizational behavior consistent with its social institutional role. Thus, if we acknowledge the economic institution's social role as primarily that of distributing goods and services, the "purpose" of business organizations may be defined accordingly. So also, if the primary social purpose of the institution of education in modern society is that of transmitting technical skills and an appropriate orientation for their implementation in adult life, the school as a social organization can be viewed analytically as a purposive organization consistent with that institutional role.

A second characteristic of importance to our systems approach is the perception of the school as an *open* social system. As described by Buckley (1967), Allport (1960), and von Bertalanffy (1962), an open system is a set of elements: (1) in mutual interaction, (2) characterized by an input and output in energy, (3) existing in a homeostatic state wherein its input and output will not appreciably affect its form, (4) manifesting an increasing complexity over time, and (5) displaying a high degree of interaction with its environment. It is this final characteristic that is of particular importance in the discussion and analysis to follow, where we shall attempt to articulate the effects of interaction with the environment on the structure and functioning of educational organizations.

The Environment of American Public Schools

To understand the dependence of the American public schools, as a social organization, on its environment, it is helpful to consider sociocultural changes in American society attendant to the modernization process. These changes can best be viewed in terms of changes in ideology and values.[11] Briefly, the most modern sectors of American society may be characterized ideally as manifesting a universalistic value orientation, wherein instrumental performance on the part of the individual is valued and status granted based on achievement. Beliefs about the worth of individual performance in terms of abilities, effort, and rewards are extolled in terms of their contribution to the larger society.[12] In contrast, less modern sectors of American society tend to have traditional values and ideology, characterized as expressing a particularistic value orientation, in that individuals, objects, or situations are appraised in a unique and relative sense rather than in terms of universal achievement. In these sectors ideology is focused on the sacredness of past events and the desirability of traditional behavior.[13]

If the above assumptions hold, the criteria sensitizing the organization to feedback from its environment will vary from one sociocultural context to another. The effect of this on the public school can be anticipated in somewhat the following manner: In the more modern sectors of American society, universal values and ideology will lead to an emphasis on the larger sociocultural needs of society. Such an emphasis will be reflected in the concern for the school regarding its production and adaptation relative to the standards of the larger society. Conversely, the more traditional sectors of society will be more attuned to particularistic values and ideas associated with their local environments. In such settings, school-community relations and the internal stability of the organization will be of paramount concern in the school to the probable detriment of meeting the standards of the larger society.

Further insight into the effects of differing sociocultural contexts on the school as an open system can be gained by considering the different adaptation of schools within different sociocultural contexts. We would expect schools in the more modern sectors of American society to have more complex structures consistent with a more highly specialized division of labor among their membership. In contrast, schools in more traditional areas would be less specialized, and would evidence a greater permeability from their local sociocultural environment.

There are, of course, many additional ways in which variability in the sociocultural context of schools could influence their organizational structure and functioning. The preceding discussion is illustrative rather than exhaustive. We would now like to present a brief empirical test of selected aspects of our general reasoning.

METHODOLOGICAL CONSIDERATIONS

Research Design

During the past several years we have conducted a study exploring the general thesis noted above that the more modern the sociocultural context in which American public schools are located, the more modern their structure, inputs, and outputs (Herriott and Hodgkins, 1969). In this paper we wish to report some specimen results of the larger inquiry dealing with three context variables, one input variable, and one output variable, and focusing on public senior high schools. The two hypotheses we will test are as follows:

I.   *The more modern the sociocultural context of American public senior high schools, the more specialized their inputs.*

II.   *The more modern the sociocultural context of American public senior high schools, the more effective their outputs.*

The three sociocultural contexts we will consider are each major social dimensions within American society: (1) region, (2) metropolitan area, and (3) school neighborhood. Elsewhere we have developed at length a discussion of how each dimension can be subdivided into social settings of differing degrees of modernity (Herriott and Hodgkins, 1969:ch. 9). For the sake of brevity we shall simply assert that a region composed of the U.S. Census divisions of New England, Middle Atlantic, East North Central, Pacific, and Mountain can be characterized as being more modern than one composed of the West North Central, West South Central, East South Central, and South Atlantic. We shall further assert that the central cities of the Standard Metropolitan Statistical Areas (SMSAs) of the Bureau of the Census are more modern than are the rings of SMSAs, which are more modern than non-SMSA settings. Finally, we shall assert that school neighborhoods which are largely white-collar in their adult composition are more modern than those predominantly blue-collar or farm.

Our measure of the specialization of organizational input for senior high schools focuses on the specialized training of the schools' faculties. It is measured by the proportion of full-time faculty members who hold at least a Master's degree. The measure of effectiveness of organizational output focuses on the production of students seeking further formal education consistent with the requirements of the larger society. It is represented by the proportion of previous tenth graders who, after the twelfth grade, go directly on to some form of further schooling. Such a measure of output takes into account not only graduates who go on, but also adjusts for the former tenth graders who have dropped out.

A sample of three- and four-year public senior high schools was obtained from data collected by the U.S. Bureau of the Census during the 1965–66 school year as one phase of the Equality of Educational Opportunity (EEO) survey of the U.S. Office of Education.[14] To accomplish one of the minor objectives of the EEO survey, the October 1965 educational supplement of the monthly Current Population Survey (CPS) of the Bureau of the Census was expanded to learn the enrollment status of the 28,000 persons age 6–19 in the CPS national sample of households.[15]

In addition to learning the enrollment status of these individuals, the CPS also learned the identity of the elementary or secondary school then being attended by the enrollees and last attended by the nonenrollees. In this way, the 10,500 public and private elementary and secondary schools most recently attended by these 28,000 persons were identified.

A precoded questionnaire was then mailed to the chief administrative officer of each school. It requested information about the school relevant to an exploration of educational opportunity (e.g., type of control, number of students in attendance, percentage of students who are Negro, percentage who are Catholic, etc.). Completed questionnaires were returned by 7771 (73 per cent) of the schools, of which 6,333 were public and 1,212 Roman Catholic.[16] The test of the current two hypotheses involves only 1,124 *public* three- and four-year senior high schools, drawn from this sample.

Test of Specimen Hypotheses

To test Hypothesis I, the mean proportion of teachers holding at least a Master's degree was computed within each of 12 sociocultural context categories defined jointly by the two regional, three metropolitanizational, and two social class categories noted earlier.[17] As predicted by the hypothesis, the largest proportion of such teachers (52.6 per cent) is found in the most modern context (that characterized as being of high social class, in the central city, and in the more modern region); and the smallest proportion (29.8 per cent) is found in the least modern sociocultural context (that characterized as being of low social class, in nonmetropolitan areas, and in the less modern region) (Table 1). In addition, for all six possible social class context comparisons (holding constant both region and metropolitanization), the high social class

TABLE 1

Mean percent of senior high school teachers with at least a Master's degree by sociocultural context

| | Sociocultural Context | | | Number |
Region	Metropoli-tanization	Social Class	Mean Percent	of Schools
More Modern				
	Central City	High	52.6	109
		Low	43.3	98
	Ring	High	47.9	233
		Low	38.1	142
	Nonmetropolitan	High	37.4	59
		Low	32.4	65
Less Modern				
	Central City	High	44.7	45
		Low	34.8	32
	Ring	High	40.9	89
		Low	33.6	50
	Nonmetropolitan	High	34.9	74
		Low	29.8	128
	All Contexts		40.6	1124

category has a larger percentage of teachers with at least a Master's degree than does the low social class category. For all four possible metropolitaniza-tion context comparisons (holding constant both region and social class), the central city has a higher proportion of teachers with at least a Master's degree than does the ring, which in turn has a higher proportion than do the nonmet-ropolitan areas. Further, for all six possible regional comparisons (holding constant both metropolitanization and social class), the more modern region has a higher proportion of such teachers than does the less modern region (Table 1).

In order to summarize independent main effects of each of these three sociocultural context variables on the organizational input of schools, a least-squares regression analysis was performed with dummy main effects and in-teraction terms pivoted on the least modern sociocultural contexts (see Table 2 for all operational definitions).[18] The results of this analysis are presented in Table 3, and serve to clarify what was suggested in Table 1. Each sociocul-tural context makes a significant independent contribution to the explanation of variation in organization input, whereas none of the interaction terms is significant (Table 3). Thus Hypothesis I receives clear support.

To test Hypothesis II, the mean proportion of former tenth-grade students going directly on to any form of further formal schooling was computed within

TABLE 2

Definition of dummy sociocultural context main effects and interaction terms

	Original Variable		Dummy Variable	
Variable	Category	Symbol	Value	Interpretation
Main Effects				
Region	NE, MA, ENC, M, P	R_1	1	Modern
	SA, ESC, WSC, WNC	–	0	Not Modern
Social Class	35–100% White-collar	S_1	1	High Social Class
	0–34% White-collar	–	0	Not High Social Class
Metropolitanization	Central City	–	0	Not Ring
	Ring	M_1	1	Ring
	Non-SMSA	–	0	Not Ring
Metropolitanization	Central City	M_2	1	Central City
	Ring	–	0	Not Central City
	Non-SMSA	–	0	Not Central City
Interaction Terms				
Region–Ring	$R_1 = 0, M_1 = 0$	–	0	
	$R_1 = 0, M_1 = 1$	R_1M_1	1	
	$R_1 = 1, M_1 = 1$	–	0	
	$R_1 = 1, M_1 = 0$	R_1M_1	1	
Region–Central City	$R_1 = 0, M_2 = 0$	–	0	
	$R_1 = 0, M_2 = 1$	R_1M_2	1	
	$R_1 = 1, M_2 = 1$	–	0	
	$R_1 = 1, M_2 = 0$	R_1M_2	1	
Region–Social Class	$R_1 = 0, S_1 = 0$	–	0	
	$R_1 = 0, S_1 = 1$	R_1S_1	1	
	$R_1 = 1, S_1 = 1$	–	0	
	$R_1 = 1, S_1 = 0$	R_1S_1	1	
Ring–Social Class	$M_1 = 0, S_1 = 0$	–	0	
	$M_1 = 0, S_1 = 1$	M_1S_1	1	
	$M_1 = 1, S_1 = 1$	–	0	
	$M_1 = 1, S_1 = 0$	M_1S_1	1	
Central City–Social Class	$M_2 = 0, S_1 = 0$	–	0	
	$M_2 = 0, S_1 = 1$	M_2S_1	1	
	$M_2 = 1, S_1 = 1$	–	0	
	$M_2 = 1, S_1 = 0$	M_2S_1	1	

Unstandardized regression equation:

$$\hat{Y} = a + r_1R_1 + s_1S_1 + m_1M_1 + m_2M_2 + (r_1m_1)(R_1M_1) + (r_1m_2)(R_1M_2) + (r_1s_1)(R_1S_1) + (m_1s_1)(M_1S_1) + (m_2s_1)(M_2S_1).$$

where:

$\hat{Y}_i$ = predicted mean on the dependent variable for the *i*th cell.

a = predicted mean for the pivotal (least modern) cell.

r_1, s_1, m_1, and m_2 = unstandardized regression coefficients for the main effects.

$(r_1m_1), (r_1m_2) \ldots (m_2s_1)$ = unstandardized regression coefficients for the interaction terms.

TABLE 3

Eighth-order unstandardized regression coefficients for the relationship of sociocultural context and percent of senior high school teachers with at least a Master's degree

Sociocultural Context Variable[a]	Coefficients (N = 1124)
Main Effects	
Modern Region (R_1)	7.0*
Ring (M_1)	6.5*
Central City (M_2)	10.3*
High Social Class (S_1)	9.1*
Interaction Terms	
R_1M_1	−1.6
R_1M_2	−2.7
R_1S_1	−0.4
M_1S_1	−1.8
M_2S_1	−2.0
Predicted Mean for Least Modern Cell	29.9
F-Ratio	14.8*
Multiple R	.33

[a] See Table 2 for the operational definition of each variable.
* $p < .05$.

TABLE 4

Mean percentage of senior high school tenth-grade entrants later going directly on to any post-secondary education, by sociocultural context

Region	Sociocultural Context Metropoli-tanization	Social Class	Mean Percent	Number of Schools
More Modern				
	Central City	High	62.1	94
		Low	41.6	90
	Ring	High	64.4	221
		Low	50.6	135
	Nonmetropolitan	High	51.6	56
		Low	50.0	60
Less Modern				
	Central City	High	59.6	42
		Low	38.5	27
	Ring	High	57.7	82
		Low	43.2	42
	Nonmetropolitan	High	56.7	62
		Low	47.1	98
	All Contexts		54.3	1009

each of the 12 sociocultural contexts. Although the mean of 62.1 per cent for the most modern of these contexts is clearly greater than that of 47.1 per cent for the least modern, the results are not as systematic as in the case of organizational input (Table 4). Nevertheless, for all six possible social class context comparisons (holding constant both region and metropolitanization), the high social class category has a larger percentage of students going on to further schooling than does the low social class category. For five of six regional comparisons (holding constant both metropolitanization and social class), the more modern region has a higher proportion of such students than does the less modern region. However, the pattern varies greatly across the four possible metropolitanizational context comparisons (holding constant both region and social class). For the high social class schools of the less modern region, the predicted relationship is observed, but for the low social class schools of the same region just the opposite occurs. For schools in both high and low social class contexts of the more modern region, the ring has the highest proportion of students going on, followed by the central city, and then by nonmetropolitan areas. With respect to the organizational output of schools, there is clearly an interaction between metropolitanizational context and the other two sociocultural contexts.

TABLE 5

Eighth-order unstandardized regression coefficients for the relationship of sociocultural context and percent of senior high school tenth-grade entrants later going directly on to any post-secondary education

Sociocultural Context Variable[a]	Coefficients (N = 1009)
Main Effects	
Modern Region (R_1)	5.2*
Ring (M_1)	2.6*
Central City (M_2)	−0.9
High Social Class (S_1)	18.1*
Interactions	
R_1M_1	−4.1*
R_1M_2	−1.9
R_1S_1	1.6
M_1S_1	−4.4*
M_2S_1	−7.8*
Predicted Mean for Least Modern Cell	47.9
F-Ratio	24.8*
Multiple R	.43

[a] See Table 2 for the operational definition of each variable.
* $p < .05$.

In order to summarize the independent main and interactional effects of each of the three sociocultural contexts on the organizational output of schools, we performed a least-squares regression analysis again. These results, presented in Table 5, clarify what was suggested in Table 4. Although the independent main effects of regional and social class context are each significant, the effect of the metropolitanizational context is primarily through its interaction with the other two contexts (Table 5). Nevertheless, considerable support for Hypothesis II is apparent. Also noteworthy is the rather strong interaction effect of the central city in combination with low social class (M_2S_1). The suppressing effect of the urban ghetto on education output can be clearly seen.

SUMMARY

Specimen hypotheses were proposed regarding the relationship of the sociocultural context of schools to organizational inputs and outputs. Specifically, it was hypothesized that the more modern the sociocultural context in terms of region, metropolitanization, and social class: (a) the more specialized the inputs, and (b) the more effective the output. Results of an analysis of 1,124 public three- and four-year senior high schools supported our input hypothesis. The output hypothesis was supported for region and social class contexts. However, it was not supported for metropolitanization. Subsequent analysis revealed that although the region and social class context effects upon school output were direct, the effect of metropolitanization was primarily through its interaction with social class.

DISCUSSION

This study has reported some specimen results of an analysis of the relationship between the school as a social organization and the sociocultural context in which it exists. The larger study of which this is a part provides many additional examples of the relationship of the sociocultural contexts of schools to their organizational structure and functioning. Although the empirical portion of all of our analyses utilizes data collected for other purposes and possesses the usual shortcomings of such secondary analysis, we believe the results have implications for theoretical, methodological and substantive concerns.

On the theoretical level, we have endeavored to set forth a model of the school in society that incorporates two major concepts not generally considered simultaneously by those interested in the sociological study of education and social change. These are "modernization" and "open social system." We feel that our efforts to integrate these two concepts have been worthwhile for they have helped us to focus on some important aspects of the effects of social change on the school in contemporary American society. We expect we have just begun to scrape the surface in this endeavor. An elaboration and extension of our consideration of the American public school as an open social system within sociocultural contexts of varying modernity can be carried out, and can shed additional light on the relationship of modernization to education.

With respect to methodology, we believe we have avoided two major limitations of past sociological research on the school as a formal organization: the tendency to overgeneralize from case studies of a few schools, and the use of students as the unit of analysis when the primary focus is on the school. By combining, within a large sample of schools, the span of survey research and the parsimony of multivariate regression statistics, we were able to examine systematically relationships between variables conceptualized, measured, and analyzed *at the level of the school itself.* This approach also appears to warrant elaboration and extension.

Although the general theoretical and methodological innovations of our endeavor seem to us important, perhaps the most crucial result of our total effort is the support this research offers for the hypothesis that the sociocultural context has a systematic influence on the school. By identifying an important characteristic of a school's environment (the extent to which that environment has been influenced by the modernization process), inputs and outputs have been shown to vary systematically from one sociocultural context to another. Our total findings suggest that the issue of environmental effects on the school is not whether the social context influences the organization, but rather what *aspects* of the sociocultural context have an influence on the school and in what *manner* that influence is expressed.

There are many substantive implications from our findings for both basic and applied concerns. For example, our total research effort suggests that the question of "inequality of educational opportunity" probably needs to be reconsidered with greater emphasis on the organization—community relationship—past research has tended to focus primarily on the individual's potential for educational attainment. If the logic of our model holds, significant changes in the structure and functioning of the American public school are greatly dependent on the sociocultural context in which the school exists. The pouring of extraordinary money, teacher talent, curricula, etc., into public schools in "depressed areas" undoubtedly has a useful short-run effect; but if our interpretations are correct, it will prove inadequate in the long run without significant changes in the values and ideology of the sociocultural context in which the school exists as an open social system.

Perhaps even more important are implications related to the old argument of the school's role as an agent of change within the larger American society. This issue must be recast when the school is viewed as an open social system, for within such a framework there is a high degree of reciprocity between school and environment. However, this reciprocity is severely constrained by the ideology and values dominant in the sociocultural context in which the school is controlled. We would argue that the community probably permits the school to be a change agent only to the extent that it wants to be so changed. The widely cited lack of success of the school as an agent of change in the urban ghetto speaks clearly to the school's dependence as an organization on sociocultural factors currently beyond its control.

If our reasoning and interpretations are valid, the reform of public schools in the less modern areas of America through local initiative is likely to be a very slow and sporadic process. On the other hand, future efforts to reform public schools in the less modern sections of American society from a central (primarily federal) level are likely to be greatly resisted and eventually evaded by the more traditional sociocultural context in which such schools are located. On the basis of reasoning and data in addition to that presented above, we expect that the greatest change in the structure and functioning of the American public school in less modern areas will come not from local, state, or federal initiative focused directly upon the schools, but rather from external forces that can modify the sociocultural context in which these schools exist. We suspect that until the local environment which supports, maintains, and controls the American public school can be changed, little widespread change can be made in the structure of the school itself.

NOTES

1. These terms are frequently used interchangeably with the term modernization, and usually reflect the author's predilection for one of the four emphases as being most important in distinguishing amounts or types of social change. For interesting variations that reflect this divergent emphasis, see Levy (1966); Bendix (1959); Theodorson (1953); Smelser (1964); Moore (1963); Hauser and Schnore (1965); Nash (1964); or Hauser (1963).

2. This is not to suggest that other factors, such as nationalism, may not have contributed to modernization, but rather to note that without technology and the acceptance of its consequences, modernization as we know it today simply could not

have occurred. Technology and its acceptance, then, are viewed here as necessary (but probably not sufficient) conditions for modernization, and therefore can be considered as the primary basis for its occurrence. See Levy (1966); and Lerner (1958).

3. In large measure, the view of modernity as an ideal, and accordingly, the process of modernization as a continuum, is discussed by several authors. Levy (1966) and Nash (1964) relate it most closely to technology, however. For a different view of the relativity of modernization and its meaning for measurement, see Ginsburg (1961: 1–5).

4. The idea that variation in modernization occurs cross-culturally is readily accepted—even variation among the more developed countries. Variation of modernization *within* one society, however, is a much less commonly accepted idea. Yet its tenability has been argued by several authorities in the area: see Hoselitz (1963); Lerner (1958); Levy (1966).

5. Exemplary of the continuous and uneven process of modernization in contemporary American society is the differential development of some aspects of urban life leading to "problems" for city administrators. Thus, archaic political and administrative procedures create a great impediment to the resolution of welfare problems brought about by the rapid urbanization of the American population. See, for example, Hauser (1965).

6. For a most interesting discussion of this relationship, see Keyfitz (1963).

7. For an excellent discussion of the distinction between family and school as socializing agencies, see Dreeben (1968: esp. chs. 2, 3).

8. Interestingly enough, examples of the successful end product of this experience are not seen as particularly desirable by many contemporary writers. We refer here to the negative connotations surrounding the "white-collar man," the "organization man," or the "bureaucrat." And yet, as many students of the problem have argued, this type of personality configuration seems necessary in order to operate within the modern complex bureaucratic milieu.

9. Durkheim has expressed essentially the same view in defining education's role in society, although the meaning of his definition has never been systematically explored for modern society. Durkheim defines this role as ". . . to arouse and to develop in the child a certain number of physical, intellectual and moral states which are demanded of him by both the political society as a whole and the special milieu for which he is specifically destined" (Durkheim, 1950: 71).

10. Following Katz and Kahn (1966: 62), we are distinguishing here between *intrinsic* functions necessary for the maintenance of the organization, and *extrinsic* functions which are performed by the organization as a part of a larger social system. *Genotypic* in this instance refers to the primary function as determined by the organizations' institutional role.

11. We are using ideology and values in the Parsonian sense, i.e., an *ideology* is a ". . . system of beliefs held in common by members of a collectivity," with some level of commitment as an aspect of group membership; *values* are ". . . of a shared symbolic system which serves as . . . criterion of standard(s) of selection among the alternatives of orientation which are intrinsically open in a situation. . . ." See Parsons (1951: 349, 12).

12. These generalizations are derived essentially from Parsons' discussion (1951: 132–191) of the "Universalistic-Achievement pattern."

13. An excellent discussion of traditional society is set forth in Hoselitz (1963: 11–31).

14. For the larger study of which this was a minor part, see Coleman et al. (1966).

15. For the results of this research, see Nam et al. (1966: sec. B–F). This report has been summarized in Coleman et al. (1966: ch. 6).

16. Neither the target sample nor the resulting one is in any sense a random probability sample of American schools. However, the sample is large (approximately six percent of all American schools). An extensive analysis of non-response has been conducted, and suggests that whatever bias may exist within the sample has led to an underestimate of relationships rather than to an overestimate. See Herriott and Hodgkins (1969: Appendix A).

17. The operational definition of sociocultural context categories is as follows:

1. Region: (a) more modern—New England (NE), Middle Atlantic (MA), East North Central (ENC), Pacific (P), Mountain (M); (b) less modern—South Atlantic (SA), East South Central (ESC), West South Central (WSC), and West North Central (WNC).

2. Metropolitan: (a) Central city of SMSA; (b) Ring of SMSA; (c) Non-SMSA.

3. Social class: (a) High—35—100% white-collar fathers as estimated by the school principal; (b) Low—0—35% white-collar fathers. (The split was made at the median across all 7,771 schools in the larger study.)

18. For a technical discussion of this procedure, see Suits (1957); Davies (1961); Melichar (1965); Johnston (1963). For social science applications, see for example, Orcutt *et al.* (1961: 216–231); Morgan *et al.* (1962); or Wilson (1963: 217–235).

REFERENCES

Allen, Francis R., and W. Kenneth Bentz. "Toward the measurement of sociocultural change." *Social Forces,* 43 (May, 1965): 522–532.

Allport, Gordon W. "The open system in personality theory." *Journal of Abnormal and Social Psychology,* 61 (November, 1960): 301–311.

Anderson, C. Arnold, and Mary Jane Bowman. "Educational distributions and attainment norms in the United States." Pp. 931–942 in *Proceedings, World Population Conference, 1954.* New York: United Nations, 1955.

Ashby, Eric. *African Universities and Western Culture.* Cambridge: Harvard University Press, 1964.

Barker, Roger G., and Paul V. Gump. *Big School, Small School: High School Size and Student Behavior.* Stanford: Stanford University Press, 1964.

Bendix, Reinhard. "Industrialization, ideologies, and social structure." *American Sociological Review,* 24 (October, 1959): 613–623.

Bertalanffy, Ludwig von. *Modern Theories of Development.* New York: Harper and Row, 1962.

Bidwell, Charles E. "The school as a formal organization." Pp. 972–1022 in James G. March (ed.), *Handbook of Organizations.* Chicago: Rand McNally, 1965.

Buckley, Walter. *Sociology and Modern Systems Theory.* Englewood Cliffs, N.J.: Prentice-Hall, 1967.

Burkhead, Jesse. *Input and Output in Large-City High Schools.* Syracuse: Syracuse University Press, 1967.

Cattell, R. B., H. Breul, and H. Parker Hartman. "An attempt at more refined definition of the cultural dimensions of syntality in modern nations." *American Sociological Review,* 17 (August, 1952): 408–421.

Coleman, James S., *et al. Equality of Educational Opportunity.* Washington, D.C.: U.S. Government Printing Office, 1966.

Davies, M. "Multiple linear regression analyses with adjustment for class differences." *Journal of the American Statistical Association,* 56 (September, 1961): 729–735.

Dreeben, Robert. *On What Is Learned in Schools.* Reading, Mass.: Addison-Wesley, 1968.

Durkheim, Emile. *Education and Sociology* (trans. by Sherwood D. Fox). Glencoe, Ill.: The Free Press, 1950.

Gerth, H., and C. Wright Mills (trans. and eds). *From Max Weber: Essays in Sociology.* New York: Oxford University Press, 1946.

Gillin, John. "National and regional cultural values in the United States." *Social Forces,* 34 (December, 1955): 107–113.

Ginsburg, Norton. *Atlas of Economic Development.* Chicago: University of Chicago Press, Department of Geography, Research Paper No. 68, 1961.

Gross, Neal. "Sociology of education." Pp. 62–70 in Hans L. Zetterberg (ed.), *Sociology in the United States of America: A Trend Report.* Paris: UNESCO, 1956.

Hauser, Philip M. "The social, economic and technological problems of rapid urbanization." Pp. 199–217 in Bert F. Hoselitz and Wilbert E. Moore (eds.), *Industrialization and Society.* New YOrk: UNESCO, 1963.

————. "Urbanization: an overview." Pp. 26–31 in Philip M. Hauser and Leo F. Schnore (eds.), *The Study of Urbanization.* New York: Wiley, 1965.

Hauser, Philip M., and Leo F. Schnore (eds.). *The Study of Urbanization.* New York: Wiley, 1965.

Herriott, Robert E., and Benjamin J. Hodgkins. *Sociocultural Context and the American School: An Open-Systems Analysis of Educational Opportunity.* Washington, D.C.: U.S. Department of Health, Education, and Welfare, USOE Final Report No. 602972, January, 1969.

Hoselitz, Bert F. "Main concepts in the analysis of the social implication of technical change." Pp. 11–31 in Bert F. Hoselitz and Wilbert E. Moore (eds.), *Industrialization and Society,* New York: UNESCO, 1963.

Johnston, J. *Econometric Methods.* New York: McGraw-Hill, 1963.

Katz, Daniel, and Robert Kahn. *The Social Psychology of Organizations.* New York: Wiley, 1966.

Keyfitz, Nathan. "The impact of technological change on demographic patterns." Pp. 218–236 in Bert F. Hoselitz and Wilbert E. Moore (eds.), *Industrialization and Society.* New York: UNESCO, 1963.

Lerner, Daniel. *The Passing of Traditional Society: Modernizing the Middle East.* Glencoe, Ill.: The Free Press, 1958.

Levy, Marion J., Jr. *Modernization and the Structure of Societies,* Volume I. Princeton: Princeton University Press, 1966.

Melichar, Emanuel. "Least-squares analysis of economic survey data." Paper presented at the annual meeting of the American Statistical Association, Philadelphia, 1965.

Moore, Wilbert E. "Industrialization and social change." Pp. 299–372 in Bert F. Hoselitz and Wilbert E. Moore (eds.), *Industrialization and Society.* New York: UNESCO, 1963.

Morgan, James N., Martin H. David, Wilbur J. Cohen, and Harvey E. Brazer. *Income and Welfare in the United States.* New York: McGraw-Hill, 1962.

Nam, Charles B., A. Lewis Rhodes, and Robert E. Herriott. *Inequalities in Educational Opportunities: A Demographic Analysis of Educational Differences in the Population.* Tallahassee: Florida State University, 1966.

Nash, Manning. "Social prerequisites to economic growth in Latin America and Southeast Asia." *Economic Development and Culture Change,* 12 (April, 1964): 225–242.

Orcutt, Guy H., Martin Greenberger, John Korbel, and Alice M. Rivlin. *Microanalysis of Socioeconomic Systems: A Simulation Study.* New York: Harper & Brothers, 1961.

Parsons, Talcott. *The Social System.* Glencoe, Ill.: The Free Press, 1951.

Schnore, Leo F. "The statistical measurement of urbanization and economic development." *Land Economics* 37 (August, 1961): 229–245.

Shannon, Lyle W. "Socio-economic development and political status." *Social Problems,* 7 (Fall, 1959): 157–169.

Smelser, Neil J. "Toward a theory of modernization." Pp. 258–274 in Amitai and Eva Etzioni (eds.), *Social Change.* New York: Basic Books, 1964.

Suits, Daniel B. "Use of dummy variables in regression equations." *Journal of the American Statistical Association* 52 (December, 1957): 548–551.

Theodorson, George A. "Acceptance of industrialization and its attendant consequences for the social patterns of non-western societies." *American Sociological Review,* 18 (October, 1953): 477–484.

Wilson, Alan B. "Social stratification and academic achievement." Pp. 217–235 in A. Harry Passow (ed.), *Education in Depressed Areas.* New York: Columbia University, Bureau of Publications, Teachers College, 1963.

13.   JEAN HILLS

On Accountability in Education

For reasons too complex and obscure to analyze here, the problem of accountability has acquired a heightened salience on the current North American scene.[1] If one may regard the mass media as reliable sources of evidence, then it is apparent that there is increasing expression of, and support for,[2] the view that business and industry should be held accountable for its impact on the environment; that governmental bodies—both bureaucratic and representative —should be held accountable for serving the interests of constituencies and for

Reprinted from *Educational Administration Quarterly,* 10 (Winter, 1974), pp. 1–17, by permission of the author and the *Educational Administration Quarterly.*

the use of public funds; that universities should be held accountable for satisfying the interests of students, and that public schools should be held accountable for the results they get, for satisfying the interests of constituents, and for the use of public funds.

How one might account for this heightened emphasis on accountability is a fascinating question, and, since it is not to be assumed that the more fundamental causes are what the proponents of accountability say they are, one well worth investigating. Our interest here, however, lies not in that direction, but rather in making a convincing case for the proposition that, *given the nature of the educational enterprise, and of the advocated approaches to the enhancement of accountability, those approaches will not only fail to achieve the ends they are designed to achieve, but also will result in severe damage to the capacity of the school to fulfill its societal functions.* A somewhat different, and only partly facetious, way of putting this is to say that there are some probable consequences of the implementation of accountability proposals for which we might wish to hold their authors accountable.

At the most general level, our argument has two parts, namely, (1) that *what* proponents of accountability wish to achieve is incompatible with the value system and function of the school, and (2) that *how* they propose to achieve those ends will deprive the school of inputs that are essential to the performance of its function. Our elaboration of these points will proceed as follows. First, we shall identify what we conceive to be the broad outlines of the value system of the public school. Following that, we shall consider the function of the school in the societal system and some obligations imposed by that function. Next, we shall examine the educational process from the point of view of some of the inputs essential for its success. On those bases, then, we shall consider, first, the ends sought by proponents of accountability and the nature of the incompatibility between those ends and the value system and functionally-related obligations of the school, and second, the means by which proponents of accountability propose to achieve their ends, and the manner in which the utilization of those means would interfere with the flow of essential inputs.

THE VALUE SYSTEM OF THE PUBLIC SCHOOL

The value system of the school, like that of any organization, is a specified subsystem, or specialized application, of the more general societal value system. That is to say, the value system of the school is derived from the societal value system through a process involving the "spelling out" or specification of the implications of the general value principles for the conduct of education. For our purposes,

The values which come to be constitutive of the structure of a societal system are . . . the conceptions of the desirable type of society held by the members of the society of reference and applied to the particular society of which they are members. The same applies to other types of social systems. (Parsons, 1968: 136)

The value pattern characteristic of American society, and with some subtle variations, Canadian society as well, involves an orientation to the environments of the system as objects to be mastered, by active shaping and control, in the interest of the attainment of goals that are transcendental in relation to the society itself, i.e., higher, religiously sanctioned ideals (Parsons, 1960). Since the environments of a social system include not only the physical environment, but also cultural systems, other social systems, the psychological systems or personalities of members, and the members as organisms, active mastery of the environments means shaping and controlling all of these. The specification of this pattern to any particular context defines, among other things, ". . . a particular mode of rationality or approach to implementation. The most familiar of these is economic rationality" (Parsons and Platt 1968: 138). Here, specification of the value pattern to the context of economic production—which concerns the relation between the system and the physical environment—yields an obligation to maximize production at minimum cost. Applied to the university, where attention is focused on relations with the cultural environment, the result is an orientation toward mastery over the cognitive problems of the empirical world, i.e., *cognitive rationality.* This entails a mandate to contribute to the advancement, transmission, and application of knowledge. Rationality in this context means adherence to the values of scientific inquiry—conceptual clarity, logical consistency, and empirical validity (Parsons and Platt, 1968).

We suggest that the focal concern of the public school is not relations with the physical, cultural or social environments, but with the environment constituted by the psychological systems, or personalities, of the students entrusted to its care. The relation does have a cultural aspect, however, and seen in those terms, the schools' charge is to transmit to students the cognitive, expressive, evaluative, and other components of the cultural system that are essential prerequisites of future role performance. The same charge, phrased in psychological terms, may be characterized as developing in students the motivational and technical capacities required for participation in the societal system. Emphasizing this latter phraseology, it seems appropriate to speak of the value pattern of the school as *"development rationality."*

Developmental rationality, as we conceive it, involves an orientation to the mastery of the psychological environment—the personalities of students—in the sense of modifying them in the direction of functional significance for the societal system.[3] "This involves a process analogous to the 'mastery' of the physical environment by technology and the 'conquest' of disease by modern medicine and public health measures at the somatic level" (Parsons, 1971: 119). Rationality in any concept entails the utilization of systematic knowledge of the empirical world as a means to the realization of ends. In the medical field it consists in the utilization of knowledge to bring about the restoration of health, and to prevent deviations from that state. It is often said that one of the outstanding differences between education and medicine is that the objectives of the latter field are so much more clear than are those of the former. No doubt there is a good bit of truth in that assertion, but perhaps we have not identified the most useful analogy. The pediatric branch of medicine would seem more appropriate. In that field the concern might be said to be to bring about, and correct deviations from, the normal pattern of physical growth and development.

Viewed in this light, we think the goal of the school to be no less clear. It is to bring about, and to correct deviations from, normal patterns of educational development. Although *what* constitutes normal educational development is far less clearly and consensually defined than what constitutes normal physical development, it seems apparent to us that educational activity is governed by relatively clear, and widely shared, though seldom articulated, conceptions of the desirable *patterns* of intellectual, social, emotional, and moral characteristics that students should exhibit at given age grade levels. The crucial point here seems to be that the desirable type of educational development is seen as one which exhibits an appropriate balance of components. It is seen, not as a process of advancement on a number of independent dimensions—such that intellectual development proceeds as rapidly as possible without reference to character development—but as a process of balanced or patterned advancement on a number of *interdependent* dimensions. Value implementation for the school consists in developing the "well-proportioned" student, not the socially retarded genius, and certainly not the converse. This seems to be the significance of such phrases as "the whole child" and "meeting the needs" of students.

THE FUNCTION OF THE SCHOOL IN THE SOCIETAL SYSTEM

Our interest in this section is not in the question of what the function of the school *ought* to be, but in what it may be said to *actually* be in a scientifically verifiable sense. The approach to the question in these terms may be sufficiently unfamiliar to warrant the inclusion of a brief illustration from a non-educational context. The wide familiarity with the business firm makes it a particularly appropriate subject for that purpose. However, anything approaching an adequate understanding of the structure and internal and external functioning of the business firm necessitates at least a minimum level of understanding of the economy as a functional subsystem of the society. Certain of the firm's properties derive from its status as a system characterized by the primacy of its orientation to the attainment of a specific collective goal.[4] Others, which distinguish it from other types of collectivities, e.g., hospitals, schools, governmental bureaucracies, etc., derive from its status as a unit, or subsystem, of the economy.[5] Hence, it behooves one who proposes to reform the firm to know something not only about the firm as such, but also about the firm as an element, or component, of the economy, and the functionally related obligations imposed by that status.

Concretely, the principal product of the business firm is "goods" or commodities for consumption. On a more general level, from the point of view of the societal system, however, economic production may be said to be a process of value implementation, or fulfillment of value commitments.

> . . . it is the use of factors of production [resources] to increase the utility [want satisfaction capacity] of the goods and services available in the economy as a system and, through its outputs, for "consumption." (Parsons, 1968: 139)

Production is a "combinatorial," "value-added" process. The utility of both resources and products is measured in terms of monetary price and it is a *condition of the survival* of the firm that it combine resources in such a way that all the monetary costs of production are covered by the proceeds of sales. Only when the monetary price of the product exceeds the monetary cost of the resources utilized can the firm be said to have made a contribution which *adds* value in the sense of enhancing the utility of available resources. To put the matter very simply, the standard of successful contribution to economic function is *solvency.* A variety of enterprises are subsidized on grounds other than economic, e.g., national interest, but in the general case the economic producer is expected, in the long run, to meet that standard.

Turning now to the public school, it may, like the business firm, be characterized as a system oriented to the attainment of relatively specific collective goals. It is ". . . an agency through which individual personalities are trained to be motivationally and technically adequate to the performance of adult roles" (Parsons, 1964: 130). The technical level product of the school then, that which parallels commodities in the economic case, may be identified as "change in the character, knowledge and skill levels of *individual* pupils:" (Parsons, 1960: 76). Just as understanding the business firm requires a knowledge of its place in the economy, however, an understanding of the school requires a knowledge of its place in the pattern-maintenance subsystem of the society. The patterning, or organizing, elements of a society are the patterns of normative culture, especially, but not only, values, that are institutionalized in its norms, collectivities, and roles. It is a condition of the stability and/or orderly change of the society that the integrity of the value pattern, and of the members' motivational commitments to its implementation, be maintained. Clearly, a critical aspect of the maintenance of the pattern is the development of motivational commitments in each on-coming generation.

Like economic production, education may be seen as a process of value implementation. The relevant value standard, however, is not utility, as measured in monetary terms, but *integrity.* That is to say, the product output of the school may be seen as a contribution to the maintenance and/or enhancement of the integrity of the system of cultural patterns which constitute the normative order of the societal system. The basis of that order lies in the fact that units of social systems, whether individuals in roles or collectivities of them, constitute subsystems structured by integrated, or "pattern consistent," patterns of values. Such patterns permeate the functioning of the unit or subsystem—its adaptation, goal attainment, integration, and pattern-maintenance activities. Thus the obvious way for an individual or collective unit to contribute to the maintenance of the integrity of the system value pattern is to implement the value commitments ascribed to it, or undertaken, as a member of the system. If all member units implement their value commitments, then the pattern is, by definition, maintained. Hence, the standard of successful contribution to the pattern-maintenance function is *pattern-consistency,* consistency of action with commitments.

The parallel of money as a measure of utility, and as a generalized facility for securing control of the requisite factors of production, in the pattern-maintenance context is *generalized commitments* (Parsons, 1968). Although space will not allow its extensive treatment here, we may briefly elucidate the concept as follows. If money is thought of as the generalized symbolic medium, for measuring the value, and securing control, of objects having intrinsic value in the sense of utility, then generalized commitments may be seen as the generalized symbolic medium for measuring the value, and securing control, of objects having intrinsic value in the sense of maintaining or enhancing the integrity of the system value pattern. As indicated above, "objects" having such value are the performances of individuals and collectivities which do in fact implement the relevant values. Thus, generalized commitments are symbolic "messages" with which actors secure control of value implementive action or the resource factors required for its "production." A more general definition is

> Commitments constitute a generalized medium for the activation of obligations which are presumptively *morally binding* by virtue of values which ego and alter share. (Parsons, 1968: 143)
>
> Its messages are essentially assertions of commitment to the relevant value pattern which may take the form of elements implicit in acts

pointing toward implementation, such as promises, which we often explicitly call commitments, to undertake specified obligations. (Parsons,
1968: 148)

The fact that they are *generalized,* however, means that they do not specify
in advance the particular implementive obligations undertaken. (Money does
not specify the particular goods for which it can be exchanged.) Now, the
recipient of money

> ... gains the *expectation* that he can "request," by virtue of his hold-
> ing money, access to goods and services of a given value. There is an
> institutionalized obligation on those receiving such requests—if they are
> "in business"—to comply. (Parsons, 1968: 470)

Failure of that expectation to be fulfilled undermines confidence in the monetary medium and threatens the stability of the market system. Similarly, the
recipient of generalized commitments gains the *expectation* that he can request
specific "real" commitments, i.e., performances actually implementing the
relevant values in specified situations. Here too, the failure of the expectation
to be fulfilled undermines confidence, but in this case in the *integrity* of the
committed unit. The consequence is that trust in its future commitments, and
possibly those already in force, will be lessened. Thus the capacity to activate
obligations which are presumptively morally binding by virtue of shared values
grounded in *"moral authority."* Moral authority is acquired through a
"reputation for integrity of commitment, individual or collective" (Parsons,
1968: 148). In short, given an initial stock of generalized commitments based
on the presumption of shared values, the unit may "spend" those commitments
to secure access to the resources required for actual value implementation.[6]
Continued access to such resources, however, depends on success in the utilization of those resources in implementive action. Failure to "come through" with
successful implementive action jeopardizes continued access to resources.

The point to be emphasized here is that the school, like other pattern-
maintenance organizations, finds itself in special circumstances. It does not
have independent control of financial resources growing out of its own operation, and its capacity to impose binding decisions on environing systems
through the promulgation of decisions is limited. Unlike the university—also
a pattern-maintenance organization—it has limited prestige, and hence, limited capacity to secure support through persuasion, or the exercise of influence.
This means that a crucial role is played by generalized commitments, and the
need of the school to maintain its "solvency" with respect to such commitments. Since the school has limited scope of authority to impose binding
decisions—though not nearly as severely limited as the church—it must rely
heavily on the willingness of participants to assume *moral* responsibility for

the implementation of educational values. Since schools do not support themselves out of the proceeds of production, they must depend heavily on the commitments of occupationally involved personnel to provide services, i.e., on "orientations to service." Finally, since it has relatively low prestige, and hence low capacity to exert influence, it must rely heavily on common commitments to the implementation of the values institutionalized within the school. The maintenance of "solvency" with respect to these essential inputs makes it critical that the school maintain the integrity of its commitment to developmental rationality. It must not deviate too far from the valued conception of the appropriate pattern of development for given age-grade levels. If "sex-education" is admissible at all, it must be in a form, and at a level, consistent with the capacity of students to "handle it" wisely.

As a collectivity oriented to the fulfillment of relatively specific expectations, analytically speaking, the school is a structural component of the polity of the society. That is to say, it is a member of the category of *structural components* the societal system differentiated with respect to the attainment of collective goals. As such, it is expected not only to contribute to the maintenance and/or enhancement of the integrity of the societal value pattern, but also to effectively mobilize its collective resources in the maintenance of goal states in relation to its environments, particularly its clients and those having an immediate interest in education. This expectation of collective effectiveness, however, is qualified appropriately in terms of the nature of the school's primary function. Perhaps a further comparison with the business firm will clarify the point. The business firm is subject to the standard of effectiveness, but skewed in a direction appropriate to its function by the value of economic rationality and by *solvency* as a standard of successful contribution to the enhancement of the utility of resources. A goal-state for the firm consists in maintaining a satisfactory relation with consumers of its products, *but the criterion of solvency limits that obligation to those cases in which all costs of production can be covered by the proceeds of sales.* The school also is subject to the value standard of effectiveness, skewed in its case in a direction appropriate to its function by the value principle of integrity, and by *pattern-consistency* as the standard of successful contribution to the maintenance of integrity of the societal value pattern. *That standard limits the obligation to those cases in which the goal can be attained without serious cost to the integrity of the school's commitment to the guiding value pattern.* School personnel have a moral responsibility to resist strenuously any demand which is perceived as a threat to the realization of the "proper" pattern of development.

Schools do respond to opportunities and threats posed by changes in environing systems—recall the post-Sputnik phenomenon—and they do attend to efficiency norms—far too closely in the view of some teachers. And they do utilize technological developments, where they can be "fitted in." But all these considerations are tempered by a heavy emphasis on the maintenance of the integrity of the school's value commitments. In contrast to the firm, the school is an inwardly oriented organization; its obligations to mount effective collective action in the interest of attaining goal states vis-à-vis its social or non-social environment are curtailed by its status as an element in the pattern-maintenance subsystem of the society.

CRITICAL INPUTS TO THE EDUCATIONAL PROCESS

Some of the critical inputs to the educational process were considered briefly in the preceding section. In this section, we wish to examine these inputs, as well as others, particularly from the point of view of their bearing on the teacher-student relation and the attainment of developmental goals. Perhaps the first point to be made in this connection is that the attainment of developmental goals in education *must be a joint endeavor.* An absolutely essential input to the process is the student's participatory contribution. In this respect, education bears a marked resemblance to medicine, law, and the therapeutic professions. In all these fields, the probability of success when the client does not want the endeavor to succeed, when he engages in active or passive resistance, or even simply remains indifferent, is extremely low. In those instances in which the student fails, for whatever reason, to fulfill his obligation to enter actively into what can only be a joint endeavor, the school has no alternative (short of intensive therapeutic procedures) but to fall back on lower-order goals, e.g., custody and protection. The critical input, then, is the assumption of responsibility on the part of the student, within the limits of his capacity, for the implementation of educational values.

This input of value commitments can be broken down into several components. One is a generalized commitment to common values, i.e., an affirmation of the value base of the educational enterprise. This is parallel to the generalized commitment to health which provides the basis for the doctor-patient relationship.[7] That initial commitment, however, must be specified to the level of commitment to the implementation of those values in a specific, concrete, social context. That is, like the patient with a commitment to health, and an illness, the student with a commitment to education cannot "go it alone," he must adopt membership status in a collective system in which those values are institutionalized. Ideally, in accepting membership, he makes a commitment to participate in the implementation of the common values by performing a variety of more specific acts extending over time, including commitment to accept the teacher's authority and advice. That commitment, of course, must be reciprocated by the teacher's commitment to supervise the student's educational development. The initial commitment to solidarity then, is the primary lever by which the teacher exercises continuing control over the student's behavior. The continuation of that commitment, however, depends on the "assembled" commitments of teacher and student, as well as other students, having greater value implementive impact than they would otherwise have had. Finally the more specific commitments on both sides of the relation are made meaningful by the more general commitment, also on both sides, to the valuation of education.

In addition, the student becomes bound, to a degree, by obligations of loyalty to the teacher (and more generally, to the school), and may be legitimately expected to provide support for endeavors toward value implementation. The relationship is very different from the ordinary commercial transaction where the recipient owes no loyalty whatever to the commodity-providing agent or agency. On the other side, the teacher is similarly bound by obligations of loyalty to the student, and by expectations to provide support for endeavors to implement values. The principle of *caveat emptor* does not apply in the classroom. The teacher has an obligation to further the educational well-being of students, which goes well beyond simply purveying "educational commodities."

ENDS SOUGHT BY PROPONENTS OF ACCOUNTABILITY

Perhaps the most satisfactory way to characterize the ends sought by proponents of accountability is to say that they seek a greater degree of *social control* over public elementary and secondary education. More specifically, they wish to strengthen the mechanisms by which conformity with normative standards, or expectations, may be secured, obviously with a view to securing greater conformity with certain standards. Given that, the question then becomes, "What are the normative standards with which greater conformity is sought?"

By our analysis there are four such standards. One of these, reflected in the emphasis on accountability, conformity and control, is societal *solidarity* or *integration*. Another, which catches up several subordinate norms, is utility, or maximizing the utility (want satisfaction capacity) of societal resources. The wants to be satisfied, of course, are those of consumers. Hence, the standard of utility implies the norm of consumer sovereignty. Another subordinate norm here is *economic rationality,* or, maximizing production at minimum cost. Directly related of course is the norm of *efficiency.* Still another is *collective effectiveness* in the attainment of collective goals. The subordinate norm here may be termed, "political rationality," i.e., maximizing goal decentralization, goal-attainment at minimum cost in terms of political support. The fourth, which applies across the other three, is *technological rationality.* Another which applies within the organization, parallel to the application of efficiency, is *effectiveness* in reaching and implementing collectively binding decisions.

Every normative standard listed above is legitimated to varying degrees, by the societal value system, and hence, legitimately applicable, in some measure, to all manner of social units. But what is especially noteworthy about the list is that it contains no reference whatever to the primary normative standard in terms of which the school's contribution is assessed—that of maintaining and enhancing the integrity of the societal value pattern. As we have emphasized, that standard requires, above all, that the school maintain the integrity of *its* commitment to its own value pattern; that, as a condition of the maintenance of its "solvency" in terms of value commitments it must attend primarily to the consistency of its actions with its commitments, and only secondarily to their economic, political, and integrative implications.

On the assumption that the values institutionalized in the school are widely, though not uniformly shared, some probable consequences of a pronounced shift of emphasis in the directions advocated by proponents of accountability are (1) a loss of inputs of "moral responsibility" for the implementations of educational values from both students and occupationally involved personnel —teachers, administrators, counselors, etc.; (2) a loss of inputs of commitments to provide educational services from teachers, i.e., a diminution of the "service motivation," or "dedicatory ethic" of teachers (Lortie, 1969), and; (3) a loss of inputs of commitment to the common values institutionalized in the school from all parties concerned, teachers, administrators, students, parents, etc. Quite apart from the question of the degree to which values are shared, a pronounced shift of the kind under consideration would certainly undermine developmental rationality as the value pattern which provides the basis for orienting and evaluating action in the school. This, in turn, opens the door to the wholesale introduction of technological rationality and the consequent development of the intellectual, social, emotional, and moral aspects of personalities independently of one another. Moreover, the continuity of educational programs would very likely be no greater than that of women's fashions and automobile styles.

In our judgment, none of these "doomsday" prophecies is very likely to come to pass. Long before that stage is reached equilibrating process will have been set in motion to restore a more appropriate balance. Still, there are a number of areas in which the price paid while the "pendulum swings" could be sizeable.

MEANS PROPOSED BY PROPONENTS OF ACCOUNTABILITY

By what means do proponents of accountability propose to achieve greater conformity with the normative standards outlined above? Although this may not be an exhaustive list, the principal mechanisms they wish to employ are (1) the discipline of the market, ". . . by which, it is said, untrustworthy sellers will lose out to their competitors" (Parsons, 1970:12–13). Or, to put it positively ". . . participating units will act responsibly by following the dictates of their own self-interest, as measured in terms of monetary gain or loss" (Parsons, 1969:118); (2) the power of the courts to enforce such legal institutions as "contract" which supplements the discipline of the market; (3) ". . . the accountability of the elected official . . ." to his constituents with the punishment of electoral defeat for betrayal of trust, and; (4) the administrative enforcement of policies determined by trustworthy elected officials.

The discipline of the market provides the rationale for such proposals as "performance-contracting" and "voucher plans," and while there is little explicit mention of the courts, they are necessarily involved in the enforcement of contractual obligations. The vulnerability of elected officials underlies proposals for the decentralization of large urban school districts, and, of course, the effectiveness of that mechanism depends on the effective exercise of administrative authority and sanctions to enforce policies.

What effects might we anticipate as consequences of the application of these measures? There are several: (1) The emphasis—through market mechanisms —on monetary payment for education in proportion to value received (however that might be assessed) could reduce the student from his status as a member of the school, rightfully entitled to its services, to that of a customer. The possible loss of students' rights, however, is far less likely than the loss of the students' commitment to provide a participatory contribution which is entailed by membership. In effect, it relieves the student of any responsibility for the implementation of educational values. Moreover, it could undermine the solidarity of the teacher-student relation—insofar as, and wherever, it exists. The loss of solidarity, in turn, would deprive the teacher of influence with which to persuade the student to accept his tutelage. That, in its own turn, could deprive the system of the commitment to common values which is the basis for the obligation to promote the educational interests of the student. The customer has no obligation of loyalty to the firm, and the firm no responsibility to the customer beyond ordinary honesty.

The loss of commitment to common values on the part of students could be critical, for it would deprive the teacher and the school of the generalized facility for specifying more particular educational obligations. Critics overlook the fact that the attainment of developmental goals is contingent on the attainment of a prior goal—the socialization of the client in the role of student. As we noted above, failure to secure some level of commitment from the student to the values institutionalized in the school, and to his obligation to enter actively and cooperatively into what can only be a joint endeavor, precludes the possibility of attaining developmental goals.

Paradoxically, one of the most likely, and most unfortunate, outcomes of the extensive implementation of accountability-enhancing proposals, is a serious loss in the area about which the proponents of these proposals express so much concern—social control. This is a consequence of what we take to be the fact that in those areas in which persons with superior competence and authority perform technical operations on human individuals, there is no satisfactory substitute for the assumption of fiduciary responsibility by the superior as a means of assuring, to some reasonable degree, that superiority will be used in ways that are compatible with both the societal interest and the interest of the client. All mechanisms of social control—the discipline of the market, legal controls, public and administrative authority, and public opinion—either fall short of protecting those interests, or are altogether inappropriate.

Satisfactory levels of control require the institutionalization of fiduciary responsibility, and such responsibility must rest on a sharing of values and the expectation that superior competence and authority will be used to implement those values within the limits of organizational and personal capacity (Parsons, 1970: 12). The most general context in which fiduciary responsibility is firmly institutionalized is the modern professions. In that setting the relevant controls operate on two levels. First, the individual practitioner undergoes an extended period of socialization in which he acquires the relevant value commitments and the cultural competencies to implement them. It is the possession of these factors which legitimates the authority of the professional, and provides the basis for the assumption of a special level of responsibility for the implementation of societal values. Second, given the special level of competence of the professional, it is essential that the professional association be, to some degree, self-regulating, taking responsibility for determining and enforcing standards of technical competence and integrity of commitment to serving individual and societal interests. That is, the association must assume a major responsibility for social control.

In our view, then, by far the most appropriate and promising approach to social control in education is through its more complete professionalization. We do not suggest that the level of competence of teachers is such that only they are capable of determining whether or not service has been rendered competently, or whether or not the interest of the client and the society have been served in a particular case. But we do suggest that the developmental trend over the history of the public schools has been in the direction of the professionalization of teaching. Even now, there is little room to doubt that experienced teachers possess a level of competence that cannot be matched by either their administrative superiors or "lay" persons. Moreover, we contend that seeking to enhance accountability in the ways, and on a scale, currently being proposed would undermine the basis for a professional level of commitment to, and responsibility for the implementation of educational values.

The overwhelming emphasis on external controls and close supervision, rather than legitimating the considerable degree of technical authority and autonomy the "professional" teacher now exercises, and hence the responsibility assumed for the implementation of values, can only diminish present levels of authority with a consequent reduction of responsibility and commitments. If educators have been lax in accepting responsibility and little committed in the past, we should be prepared for them to be far more so under the proposed schemes. There appear to be certain limits to its development, but indications are that schools are moving slowly toward an approximation of the collegial type of internal organization characteristic of the university. The realization of proposals for the enhancement of accountability as currently envisaged would, in all probability, effectively halt that movement and reduce teachers to the level of a class of "employees" to be hired and fired at the discretion of the administrator and/or trustees. That, in turn, is almost sure to tip the scales in the direction of a trade union orientation among teachers rather than a professional one. What that means, essentially, is the rejection by teachers of the level of fiduciary responsibility they now bear, and of the ethical obligations that such responsibility entails.

On the other side of the coin, it is equally important that we emphasize the obligations of teachers, both individually and collectively. Above all, trust in the integrity of their commitment to utilize their competence and authority in the collective interest must be *earned*. It cannot be bought, it cannot be coerced. It can only be won by demonstrating in action the integrity of commitment to shared values. (Which brings us back to the reason why pattern-consistency, not solvency or effective satisfaction of interests, is the standard of success in education.) Unfortunately, the teacher's worst enemy seems at times to be his own association. Whatever the reality of the situation, the image the associations convey publicly is too often one of greater concern for member benefits than for the enhancement of client and societal interests.

NOTES

1. The same concerns are expressed somewhat less frequently, and with somewhat less intensity, in Canada.

2. Unfortunately, there is little reliable evidence concerning either the breadth or depth of this support.

3. What constitutes functional significance is itself a function of the societal value

system. Thus, in our society, some of the functionally significant capacities are, capacity for autonomous, responsible behavior, capacity to achieve, capacity to control impulse and effect, and capacity to accept and exercise authority. (Parsons and Platt, 1970)

4. That is, its status as a structural element of the polity.

5. Still others, which distinguish it from a firm in the U.S.S.R., for example, derive from the societal value pattern.

6. E.g., command of influence within a solidary association, power within an organized collectivity, and money in an occupational role.

7. The analysis which follows is based on Parsons' analysis of the doctor-patient relationship. See Talcott Parsons, *Politics, and Social Structure* (New York: Free Press, 1969). Postscripts to Chapter 15, pp. 430–438.

REFERENCES

Jackson, Phillip W., *Life in Classrooms* (New York: Holt, Rinehart and Winston, 1968).

Lortie, Dan C., "The Teacher's Shame: Anger and the Normative Commitments of Classroom Teachers," *The School Review* (Summer, 1967).

Lortie, Dan C., "The Balance of Control and Autonomy in Elementary School Teaching," in Amitai Etzioni (ed.), *The Semi-Professions and Their Organizations* (New York: The Free Press, 1969).

Parsons, Talcott, *Structure and Process in Modern Societies* (New York: The Free Press, 1964).

———, *Social Structure and Personality* (New York: The Free Press, 1964).

———, "On the Concept of Value Commitments," *Sociological Inquiry* 38:2 (Spring, 1968), pp. 135–159.

———, and Gerald M. Platt, *The American Academic Profession: A Pilot Study* (Cambridge, Mass., 1968).

———, "Research with Human Subjects and the Professional Complex," in Paul A. Freund (ed.), *Experimentation with Human Subjects* (New York: George Braziller 1969), pp. 116–150.

———, "How Are Clients Integrated into Service Organizations," in W. R. Rosengren and M. Lefton (eds.), *Organizations and Clients* (Columbus, Ohio: Charles Merrill, 1970), pp. 1–16.

———, "Comparative Studies and Evolutionary Change," in Ivan Vallier (ed.) *Comparative Methods in Sociology* (Berkeley: University of California Press, 1971), pp. 97–139.

14.   MICHEAL W. GILES, DOUGLAS S. GATLIN and EVERETT F. CATALDO

The Impact of Busing on White Flight

Racial segregation of the public schools persisted in the South long after the Supreme Court ordered desegregation "with all deliberate speed."[1] By the late 1960's, the major remaining hindrance to desegregation was the prevailing pattern of residential segregation.[2] Since blacks and whites tended to live in separate neighborhoods, redrawing school attendance boundaries produced only token desegregation in many districts. This impasse to desegregation was surmounted, however, when the courts began to require that children be assigned and transported to schools outside their own residential areas.[3] Dramatic advances in school desegregation occurred with the advent of busing. From 1968 to 1972, the percentage of black students attending majority white schools in the South jumped from 18.4 per cent to an estimated 44.4 per cent, and the South now seems to lead the nation in school desegregation.[4]

But a new phenomenon, "white flight," has replaced residential segregation as a stumbling block in the path of further progress toward school desegregation. Some three hundred private elementary and secondary schools were founded in 1970 alone, and it is estimated that between 300,000 and 500,000 white children in the South are currently attending private academies.[5] "White flight" from the public schools has manifold consequences. It is said to be largely responsible for an erosion of community support for public education in some districts. Also, public school officials in districts throughout the South have had to revise their desegregation plans repeatedly in order to maintain racial balances in the face of declining white enrollments. In some districts, a mass movement of whites to private schools has left the public schools almost entirely to black children.[6] White flight has been less extensive in other districts but, in varying degrees throughout the South, it has brought about a resegregation of the schools and has thwarted the educational and social goals that desegregation is intended to achieve.

Reprinted from the *Social Science Quarterly*, 55 (September, 1974), pp. 493–501, by permission of the authors and the Southwestern Social Science Association.

The research reported herein was conducted under a grant from the National Science Foundation, Division of Research Applied to National Needs, GI-34955. The opinions expressed, however, are those of the authors and should not be construed as representing the opinions or policy of any agency of the United States government.

"White flight" is the cumulative outcome of individual decisions by white parents to transfer their children from public to private schools.[7] While evidence from polls shows that whites almost uniformly oppose the idea of busing for the purpose of desegregation, no studies have yet revealed the impact of busing upon parental decision to abandon the public schools.[8] Such is the purpose of this study.

It is important to note that a school district's desegregation plan does not impose the same busing conditions on all students in the district. Some are bused, some are not. Among children scheduled for busing, some will have experienced it previously while others face it for the first time. Busing distances from home to school may vary considerably within the boundaries of a single district. And both for those bused and not bused, wide variations may occur in the racial balance of the public schools to which they are assigned. Our goal, then, is to show how these conditions of busing are related to parents' decisions to keep their children in the public schools or to transfer them to private schools.

Answers to the question of how busing influences parents' decisions to reject the public schools are vital to policy-makers charged with the responsibility for planning school desegregation. To the extent that parents' decisions are related to identifiable conditions of busing, policymakers may be able to alter their desegregation plans so as to minimize those conditions and thereby minimize white flight.[9] Of course, it is possible that the logistics of busing have little relationship to whites' abandonment of the public schools. If so, policymakers can face the public clamor over busing without fear that it increases white flight and seek other answers to the problem of desegregation.

Data for the study are drawn from a survey of parents of elementary and secondary school children in eight Florida county-wide school districts that have implemented desegregation. Only white respondents to the survey are examined in the present study. The 8 districts were selected from among the 67 in the state to assure variation in urbanization, total enrollment and the per cent Negro of the school-age population.[10] Various sources were used to identify white rejecters—parents with a child enrolled in a public school in the district in 1971–72 but enrolled in a local private school in 1972–73.[11] Interviews were completed during the winter and spring of 1973 with 1,386 white rejecters. For comparison purposes, a sample of 2,112 white compliers— parents with a child enrolled in the public schools in both 1971–72 and 1972–73—were also interviewed. The survey included items on the conditions of busing in the public schools attended by the children of all respondents in 1971–72.[12] Rejecters were further questioned about the busing conditions in the public school to which their children were assigned (but did not attend) in 1972–73. Compliers were asked parallel questions about busing for the public school their children were attending at the time of the interview. Thus, we may compare compliers and rejecters with respect to the conditions of public school busing across two school years.

FINDINGS

Are rejecters' children more likely than compliers' to have been scheduled for busing to their assigned school in 1972–73? Rejecters were asked how their children would have reached the assigned public school had they attended it, and compliers were asked how their children get to school. About 55 per cent of the rejecters' children would have been bused to public schools while 52.9 per cent of the compliers' children were bused. However, the relationship of parents' compliance/rejection decisions to the prospect of a bus ride is not statistically significant (see Table 1, Item 1).[13] A majority of both compliers and rejecters were scheduled to be bused to public schools, though a large minority of rejecters (43 per cent) were not. At best, the prospect of a bus ride to a public school may contribute ever so slightly to rejection decisions; clearly, however, busing is neither a necessary nor a sufficient condition of that decision.

Many children in the eight districts were bused to school in 1971–72 and were scheduled to be bused again in 1972–73. Parents familiar with busing may perceive it as less of an inconvenience than parents of children not previously bused. Moreover, the fact that many parents kept their children in public school in 1971–72 while experiencing busing suggests that busing *per se* may not be an important consideration in their decisions to comply or reject. On the other hand, parents of children newly designated to be bused may anticipate an unfamiliar and perhaps disturbing change in the pattern of their daily lives. Thus, we would expect compliers more often than rejecters to have experienced busing in the preceding year. The data confirm this hypothesis. For 43 per cent of the rejecters, the bus trip to public school in 1972–73 constituted a change from the previous year, but this was the case for only 26 per cent of the compliers (Table 1, Item 2). Thus, the onset of busing appears to contribute moderately to parents' decisions to reject.

A majority of the children in the eight districts were scheduled to be bused in 1972–73, but the distances that they were to be transported varied from two to fifteen miles and even farther. The inconvenience often associated with busing—early morning departures and the time spent in transit—increases with the distance traveled. Among those scheduled for busing, we would expect that rejecters' children were likely to be bused longer distances than compliers' children. The data are consistent with our expectations. Rejecters' children were slightly more likely to have faced the prospect of a bus ride of

TABLE 1

Compliance/Rejection by Selected Variables and Attributes in Percents (Ns in parentheses)

Variable/Attribute	Compliers	Rejecters	Q	P
1. Children were/would have been bused to school	52.9 (1102)	54.8 (727)	.0378	n.s.
2. Children were not bused to school in 1971–72 but were scheduled for busing in 1972–73	26.2 (287)	43.3 (314)	.3637	.01
3. Children were/would have been bused:				
One-way distance of less than 10 miles	70.7 (774)	61.4 (408)		
One-way distance of 10 miles or more	29.3 (320)	38.6 (256)	.2056	.01
4. Children were scheduled for busing in 1972–73 and in 1971–72 (Bus-Bus):				
One-way distance of less than 10 miles	75.6 (607)	71.9 (281)		
One-way distance of 10 miles or more	24.4 (196)	28.1 (110)	.0960	n.s.
5. Children were scheduled for busing in 1972–73 but not in 1971–72 (Not Bus–Bus):				
One-way distance of less than 10 miles	56.5 (160)	46.3 (126)		
One-way distance of 10 miles or more	43.5 (123)	53.7 (146)	.2023	.05
6. Children bused one-way distance of less than 10 miles:				
Bus-Bus	79.1 (607)	69.0 (281)		
Not Bus–Bus	20.9 (160)	31.0 (126)	.2596	.01
7. Children bused one-way distance of 10 miles or more:				
Bus-Bus	61.4 (196)	43.0 (110)		
Not Bus–Bus	38.6 (123)	57.0 (146)	.3580	.01
8. Children were scheduled for busing a greater distance in 1972–73 than in 1971–72	22.8 (184)	33.0 (136)	.2505	.01
9. Assignment to a school with 50 percent or more black enrollment	15.0 (317)	15.1 (209)	.0027	n.s.

TABLE 1 (continued)

10. Assignment to school with less than 50 percent black enrollment:				
Children scheduled for busing in 1971–72 and in 1972–73	71.3 (645)	57.0 (319)		
Children scheduled for busing in 1972–73 but not in 1971–72	28.7 (260)	43.0 (241)	.3042	.01
11. Assignment to school with 50 percent or more black enrollment:				
Children scheduled for busing in 1971–72 and in 1972–73	87.3 (158)	69.9 (72)		
Children scheduled for busing in 1972–73 but not in 1971–72	12.7 (23)	30.1 (31)	.4947	.01
12. Children scheduled for busing in 1972–73 but not in 1971–72; assigned to school with less than 50 percent black enrollment:				
One-way distance (1972–73) of less than 10 miles	54.6 (142)	44.4 (107)		
One-way distance (1972–73) of 10 miles or more	45.4 (118)	55.6 (134)	.2023	.05
13. Children scheduled for busing in 1972–73 but not in 1971–72; assigned to school with 50 percent or more black enrollment:				
One-way distance (1972–73) of less than 10 miles	78.3 (18)	61.3 (19)		
One-way distance (1972–73) of 10 miles or more	21.7 (5)	38.7 (12)	.3891	n.s.
14. Children were scheduled for busing in 1972–73 and in 1971–72; assigned to school with less than 50 percent black enrollment:				
Scheduled for busing a greater distance in 1972–73 than in 1971–72	76.5 (495)	72.3 (243)		
Scheduled for busing less or the same distance in 1972–73 as in 1971–72	23.5 (152)	27.7 (93)	.1097	n.s.
15. Children were scheduled for busing in 1972–73 and in 1971–72; assigned to school with 50 percent or more black enrollment:				
Scheduled for busing greater distance in 1972–73 than in 1971–72	80.0 (128)	43.4 (33)		
Scheduled for busing less or the same distance in 1972–73 as in 1971–72	20.0 (32)	56.6 (43)	.6781	.01

ten or more miles, and slightly less likely to have been bused under ten miles, than the children of compliers (Table 1, Item 3). Busing distances, therefore, appear to be related to rejection decisions.

The relationship between busing distance and compliance/rejection, however, is not simple or direct. Items 4 and 5 in Table 1 present analyses of the distance bused controlling for past experience with busing. Among parents whose children had been bused in the previous year and who were again scheduled to be bused, the relationship between the distance bused and compliance/rejection is not significant. Only among respondents who had not experienced busing in the previous year does the mileage to the assigned school for 1972–73 tend to be greater for rejecters than for compliers. This finding suggests that the decision to reject may result not so much from the onset of busing alone as from the onset of busing combined with a long bus ride. However, controlling for distance bused, the relationship between past experience with busing and the decision to reject remains much the same (Items 6 and 7 in Table 1). Rejecters were more likely than compliers to be experiencing the onset of busing in 1972–73 whether the distance bused was less than ten miles or ten miles or more. Thus, both the onset of busing and distance, when combined with the onset of busing, are related to the decision to reject.

The importance of distance may lie not so much in the number of miles traveled as in an increase in mileage from one year to the next. For those in the "Bus-Bus" group, the distance bused in 1971–72 did not provoke rejection, and we would not expect these respondents to become rejecters if scheduled for a bus trip of the same distance in 1972–73. Only if bus mileage for 1972–73 is greater than the mileage for 1971–72, should distance become operative in the rejection decisions of the "Bus-Bus" group. Among the latter, then, we would expect to find that rejecters' children were more likely than compliers' to have been subjected to an increase in busing distance to the assigned school from one year to the next. The data bear out this expectation (Item 8 in Table 1); in the "Bus-Bus" group, rejecters were more likely to face an increased busing distance than were compliers.

A common generalization in the field of race relations holds that prejudice and discrimination among whites increases in the presence of increasing numbers of blacks.[14] Consistent with this generalization, the concept of a racial tipping point has had considerable vogue in discussions of "white flight" from the public schools.[15] According to the tipping point argument, large-scale withdrawals of whites can be expected when blacks become a majority or near majority in the public schools—further increasing the per cent black in the schools and starting a new round of white withdrawals. From this argument, we would expect rejecters' children to be more likely than compliers' to be assigned to majority black schools.

The acceptance of the tipping point argument by school planners and recent federal pressures have left few majority black schools in our eight counties.

Only 15 per cent of our white respondents' children were assigned to such schools and they were evenly distributed between compliers and rejecters (Item 9). Assignment to a majority black school, thus, appears unrelated to the decision to reject.

While majority black has no simple effect on the decision to reject the public schools, it does appear to influence that decision indirectly. The relationships between the onset of busing and the decision to reject (Items 10 and 11), and increased distance bused and the decision to reject among children in the "Bus-Bus" group (Items 14 and 15), appear to be enhanced when the assigned school has a majority black enrollment. Indeed, an increase in busing distance is unrelated to rejection where the assigned school has a minority black enrollment (Item 14). Thus, an increase in busing distance only appears to influence the decision to reject when combined with a majority black enrollment. Per cent black appears to have the same influence on the relationship between distance bused and compliance/rejection, among the "Not Bus-Bus" group (Item 13). This relationship appears stronger when the assigned school is majority black, but the small number of respondents experiencing the onset of busing to a majority black school results in a statistically non-significant relationship.[16] While little may be said from these results taken singly, the overall pattern suggests that assignment to a majority black school in conjunction with certain busing conditions does influence the decision to reject.

SUMMARY

The decisions of many Florida parents to comply with public school desegregation or to transfer their children from public to private school appear related to the conditions of busing affecting their children. Nevertheless, a large percentage of our rejecter sample had not experienced busing last year and were not scheduled to be bused this year. Thus, while busing conditions are related to many parents' rejection decisions, many white children are withdrawn from the public schools for reasons seemingly unrelated to busing.[17]

The relationships between busing and rejection found in this study are as follows:

1. Rejecters' children were more likely than compliers' to have been scheduled for a change to busing in 1972–73.

2. Among respondents who were not bused in 1971–72 but were bused in 1972–73, rejecters' children were more likely than compliers' to be bused more than ten miles.

3. Majority black in the assigned school had no direct effect on rejection; however, the relationships delineated in 1 and 2 *supra* appeared strengthened when the assigned school was also majority black.

4. Among respondents who were bused in both 1971–72 and 1972–73 and assigned to a majority black school in 1972–73, rejecters' children were more likely than compliers' to have experienced an increase in busing distance.

Our analyses suggest that any application whatever of busing to white parents will result in some measure of "white flight." But this could only be avoided by applying busing exclusively to blacks—an alternative that has received considerable and justified criticism. Beyond indicating the inevitability of some loss in white students as a function of busing, our findings imply that additional "white flight" could be minimized by policy-makers through the careful design of busing plans. At least three guidelines for reducing the incidence of rejection emerge from our analyses. First, since distance is related to rejection only among those persons whose children are experiencing the onset of busing, the first bus trip should be kept as short as possible. Apparently, so long as the assigned school does not have a majority black enrollment, the distance can be increased in the subsequent years of busing without penalty. Second, the findings of this study suggest that the onset of busing should not be accompanied by assignment to a majority black school. Third, the combination of the onset of busing, a bus trip of more than ten miles and assignment to a majority black school should also be avoided. Of course, certain local contingencies may prevent policy-makers from following such guidelines—e.g., the geographical dispersion of schools in their districts, the concentration of blacks and whites in far-flung neighborhoods, traffic conditions and the like. But within such constraints, desegregation plans may be subject to revision in some of the ways suggested by our analyses, thus reducing the extent of "white flight" due to busing and alleviating the threat of re-segregation of the public schools.

NOTES

1. The slow enforcement of school desegregation is well-documented. See, for example Benjamin Muse, *Ten Years of Prelude* (New York: Viking Press, 1964); J. W. Peltason, *58 Lonely Men* (New York: Harcourt, Brace and World, 1961).

2. Karl E. Taeuber and Alma F. Taeuber, *Negroes in Cities* (Chicago: Aldine Publishing Co., 1965).

3. The use of busing was approved by the U.S. Supreme Court in *Swann* v. *Charlotte-Mecklenburg,* 402 U.S. 1.

4. Harrell R. Rodgers, "On Integrating the Public Schools; A Legal and Empirical Assessment" (University of Missouri—St. Louis, Mimeo, 1973), Table 1.

5. The Associated Press, "Trend to Private Schools in South Reported Slowing," *The New York Times* (Sept. 2, 1972), p. 13; Kitty Terjen, "The Segregation Academy Movement," in *The South and Her Children* (Atlanta: Southern Regional Council, 1971), pp. 69–79.

6. John Beckler, "Has School Integration in the South Gone as Far as It Can Go?" *School Management,* 15 (Oct., 1971), p. 2.

7. "White flight" may also occur through other means but the present study only focuses on flight to the private schools. In the school districts included in the present study and in much of the South, where county school districts abound, this is the most feasible means of flight.

8. Renée Woloshin, "Public Opinion and School Desegregation," *Equal Opportunity Review* (Aug., 1973), pp. 1–3.

9. Several system-wide approaches to desegregation are available to policy-makers, e.g. target area busing, pairing and clustering, or some combination thereof. Whatever the overall approach, the same conditions of busing will be operative to some extent. Therefore, we are not concerned with alternative types of plans but rather with conditions of busing that will be found in any of the current approaches.

10. The eight county school districts were Escambia, Dade, Duval, Jefferson, Lee, Leon, Manatee, and Palm Beach.

11. In several districts, lists of the parents of children transferred to a private school were supplied by the public school official. In districts where official sources were non-existent or incomplete, private schools were approached directly for the parents' names of children entering in the 1972–73 school year from local public schools. Most private schools were cooperative. Compliers were randomly selected from public school attendance records in seven districts. In the eighth, lack of cooperation from public school officials necessitated a random sampling of households in the district with screening at the door for interview eligibility. All interviews were conducted in the home of the parents or guardians by trained professional interviewers. Where both parents were in the home, the interviewer's decision to question the mother or father was made on a random basis.

12. The questionnaire focused on only one child in each family.

13. The measure of association used in the present analysis is Yule's Q. A test of the significance of Q is presented in James A. Davis, *Elementary Survey Analysis* (Englewood Cliffs, N.J.: Prentice-Hall, 1971), pp. 56–58, and that procedure is adopted to evaluate the Q's presented. Q is preferable for our analysis because of its insensitivity to multiplication or division of row or column frequencies by a constant. Rejecters make up a very small percentage of the population of parents of school age children. We therefore over-sampled this group to facilitate analysis. The value of Q is unaffected by this over-sampling (which is equivalent to multiplying the cell frequencies for the rejecters).

The nature of the sampling also accounts for percentaging on the dependent rather than the independent variable.

14. Hubert Blalock, Jr., *Toward a Theory of Minority Group Relations* (New York: Wiley, 1967), pp. 143–189.

15. Carl F. Hansen, *Danger in Washington* (West Nyack, N.Y.: Parker Publishing, 1968); Eleanor P. Wolf, "The Tipping Point in Racially Changing Neighborhoods," *Journal of American Institute of Planners,* 29 (Aug., 1963), pp. 212–217; Nilo Kopanen, "The Myth of a 'Tipping Point,'" *Integrated Education,* 4 (Aug.–Sept., 1966), pp. 10–14; U.S. Commission on Civil Rights, *Racial Isolation in the Public Schools* (Washington, D.C.: Government Printing Office, 1967), p. 10.

16. The cell frequencies in Item 13 are small but the expected value in each exceeds 5, which is the rule of thumb for the use of Q. See Davis, *Elementary Survey Analysis,* pp. 50–51.

17. The authors are currently evaluating the impact of non-busing variables on the compliance/rejection decision.

15.   DEAN E. FREASE

Schools and Delinquency: Some Intervening Processes

The idea is widely held that delinquency is a group phenomenon flowing from and perhaps demanded by a specific set of social norms and values. However, sociologists do not always agree in their explanation of the particular cultural, social or psychological conditions giving rise to these norms and values.

The purpose of this paper is to investigate some of the empirical implications of theoretical formulations which have attempted to provide answers to two basic questions related to delinquency and its association with educational experience: (1) Do there appear to be linkages between school behavior and delinquency? (2) If there are these linkages, what are the structural and social-psychological conditions in the school setting that seem to foster the growth of the delinquent subculture?

THE PERCEPTION OF HIGH SCHOOL AND ACADEMIC PERFORMANCE

In a certain sense, it should not be particularly surprising to discover the relationship between academic pipeline and affective attachment to school. High school in America becomes meaningful only as it relates to college attendance. College-bound youngsters receive subtle cues indicating the wisdom of their plans for higher education. Because the normative structure of the secondary education system in the United States is geared to producing students going on for more schooling, those adhering most closely to the norms receive the greatest rewards, and, conversely, those not wholly buying into the normative structure receive fewer rewards or even oblique sanctions (for one of the most complete statements on the nexus between deviance and education, see Polk and Schafer, 1972).

Largely as a result of this restricted status conferral, it may be that a dislike for school, in general, develops. If we, in fact, discover that a dislike for school is associated with low academic performance, might it not be that the grades

Reprinted from the *Pacific Sociological Review*, 16 (October, 1973), pp. 426–448, by permission of the author and Sage Publications, Inc.

received (later in school) are simply an extension, reflection, and culmination of an alienation process started at some point in the temporal past?

RESEARCH DESIGN

The data for the current study were gathered as part of a wider investigation known as the Marion County Youth Study, a grantee of the National Institute of Mental Health, charged with investigating the phenomenon of "maturational reform."

Data for the present study were drawn from the 1,227 male sophomores who had been followed up over time by the Marion County (Oregon) Youth Study under the direction of Kenneth Polk. Upon reaching senior year, a 25 per cent random sample of this cohort was approached again.

Since the study was concerned chiefly with troublesome youth behavior, the decision was made to interview all the delinquents and all the school dropouts, in addition to the 309 randomly selected youngsters. When the random and the nonrandom samples were combined, there were 570 selected potential respondents, 528 or 93 per cent of whom were actually interviewed.[1]

THE ISSUE OF ACADEMIC PERFORMANCE AND AFFECTIVE ATTACHMENT

Several writers (Kelly and Balch, 1971; Polk and Halferty, 1966; Stinchcombe, 1964) have pointed toward the importance of the phenomenon of low academic abilities to at least a partial understanding of youth deviance. The educational institution has been designed specifically to add significant amounts of both knowledge and intellectual flexibility to the mental workings of those progressing through the system.

What, in fact, happens is something quite different for many youngsters. Havighurst *et al.* (1962) report on findings from Chicago that show a close relationship between socioeconomic status with school ability and achievement. Those school districts which rank in the top third, according to the socioeconomic status of the residents, have schools in which the range of pupil achievement is from the expected grade level to one year above this level. With one exception, the districts ranking in the lowest one-third on socioeconomic status have students who are all approximately one year below grade level.

In a study of the "streaming" system in an English school, Hargreaves (1968) points to a set of differences that develop between groups selected by ability and achievement. For example, a sharp increase appears in absence rates as they went from the higher ability stream to the lower ability stream. Second, *the degree of satisfaction* with life at school falls as they went from the high to the low stream. When asked the question of whether or not the boys would like to leave school before age fifteen (the statutory leaving age), it was found that boys in the high stream responded negatively at a much higher rate than the other streams. In general, Hargreaves reports data from which the most obvious conclusion is that the higher the stream, the greater the degree of commitment to school. Furthermore, he states, "The higher the stream the greater is the tendency for high status to be associated with attitudes, values, and behavior expected by the school; in low streams, high status is negatively associated with conformity to school expectations" (Hargreaves, 1968: 67).

With regard to academic performance of the low-stream boys, the English and American experiences are quite similar. The boys in the lower streams seem to have become progressively retarded by the fourth year, and their interactions with both teachers and high-stream boys were increasingly hostile. Indeed, Hargreaves (1968: 104) states:

> In short, the allocation of teachers to upper or lower streams on the basis of teacher competence reinforces the dominant trends of the new group; the pupils in higher forms increase in achievement and improve their relationships with teachers whom they like, and the pupils in lower streams become increasingly retarded and their relationships with teachers deteriorate to the point of mutual toleration at best and mutual hostility at worst.

Why is this? What facts appear to be at work that enhance the possibilities of low performance?

EXPLANATIONS OF LOW ACADEMIC PERFORMANCE

(1) Class. Perhaps one of the most commonly found explanations has to do with social class origins. Patricia Sexton (1966) and others (Reiss and Rhodes, 1959; Hollingshead, 1949: 172; Havighurst et al., 1962: 38) present a mass of data correlated with income levels that argue the point for income as the important independent variable in performance. Sexton's data show that achievement test scores for the major income groups, without exception, rise with family income levels.

It is clear that school subjects are cumulative and, as such, within a few years the child from a low-income background is retarded, perhaps permanently, in basic skills, such as reading, which are a prerequisite for success in later grade levels.

With regard to IQ scores, the Sexton data show that the scores increase with income level. By virtually any measure of academic achievement or allocation of community resources, those children from the lower-income groups are on the low end.

Sexton concludes that the nub of the problem is not the low-income groups being inherently inferior, but that the problem results from an unequal distribution of educational effort. The poor are given the worst facilities, the worst teachers, fewer scholarships, inadequate attention to their academic problems and are subject to invidious distinctions made by class-biased tests.

(2) Poor schools and teaching. The HARYOU organization in Harlem conducted a study in which it was concluded that there was massive failure of Central Harlem students to perform up to grade level. The report states that there are two competing explanations for this failure. One stresses the shortcomings and disinterest on the part of the schools; the other stresses the deprived economic and cultural background of the pupils (Sykes and Matza, 1964).

The argument that the schools are the culprit says, basically, that the schools have lost faith in the ability of their pupils to learn. Thus, HARYOU states, "it must be concluded that the major reason why an increasing number of Central Harlem pupils fall below their grade level is that substandard performance is expected of them" (Sykes and Matza 1964: 237).

Administrators are acutely aware of the studies that show Central Harlem students entering school, in the main, unprepared for what awaits them. These studies show an inability to focus attention on the subject at hand for a sustained period of time and a lack of "reading readiness," among other things. Largely as a result of lowered expectations and, hence, lowered goals set by the school officials, the students do indeed function at a diminished plateau. Additionally, rewards are given for the lowered performance, thus further reinforcing that behavior, and the result is a steadily increasing gap between the norm of that grade and what is actually accomplished.

(3) Teacher expectations. An experimental study conducted by Rosenthal and Jacobson (1968), which may be destined to become a classic in the area of the effect of teacher expectations on classroom performance, brings into sharp focus the issue of the self-fulfilling prophecy.

Within each of the eighteen classrooms, an average of twenty per cent of the children, randomly selected, were reported to their teachers as having unusual potential for academic growth. Prior to this, nonverbal IQ tests had been administered to obtain a measure of intellectual ability before the introduction of the experimental stimulus. The difference, then, between the experimentals and the controls was simply a function of the eye of the beholder.

All the children in the school were retested with the same IQ form after one semester, after a full academic year, and after two full academic years. After the first year of the experiment, the expected "bloomers" showed a significantly greater IQ gain than did the controls. The controls had 19 per cent of their number gaining 20 IQ points or more, while the experimentals displayed 47 per cent of their members with a 20-point or greater gain.

When the children's classroom behavior was rated by their teachers, the expected "bloomers" were painted as possessing more positive qualities than the controls. An interesting sidelight developed when children who were not expected to develop intellectually did so. They seemed either to show accompanying undesirable behavior or at least were perceived by their teachers as showing such undesirable behavior. It appears that there are unexpected hazards to unpredicted intellectual growth.

Perhaps a more frequently heard explanation of low academic achievement is that it is merely a reflection of home and community pathology. As a result, the schools are forced to deal with a relatively large number of youngsters from homes in the "culturally deprived" areas. These children bring with them specific handicaps which dull the educational efforts of the schools. According to some researchers, these handicaps are:

(1) a tendency to be withdrawn and uncommunicative;
(2) a hostile reaction to authority figures;
(3) difficulty in developing a consonance of conduct;
(4) a dearth of educational experiences prior to entering school, and
(5) low motivation to do well in school (Sykes and Matza, 1964: 197).

This argument implies that the school is working up to its capacity, but that the home and community thwart its efforts. Regardless of what form educational innovation may take, it is doomed to failure until the cultural milieu of the child is somehow modified first.

(4) Tracking. Recently, attention has been turned to the notion that the type of track or style of academic program in which a youngster becomes involved has important ramifications for his behavior.

Often in sociological discourses, it is useful, for analytical purposes, to cast the concept under discussion into as extreme a form as possible. We are then able to examine the concept in its "pure" form, unencumbered by extraneous factors. This is what Weber was talking about when he discussed his notion of the ideal type. He is quite insistent on making clear that such an ideal type must be at least in the realm of probability and not merely possible. That is, there must be found somewhere at least a close empirical approximation to the abstracted referent.

In casting about for a relatively pure form of academic track, it became clear that the English experience more closely resembled the ideal type of Weber than the American system of tracking.

In the Hargreaves (1968: 182) study cited earlier, the author declares, "Perhaps the main consequence of this study has been to affirm the fundamental importance of the social system of the school, and especially the structure of peer groups in relation to the educative process." He makes clear in his work that, once in the academic setting, the youngster is exposed to a variety of forces and circumstances which have important consequences for his behavior. Where streaming is widely and rigidly employed, each group, through accretion, develops its own system of status hierarchies, values, and norms by which the social situation is structured and defined for each adolescent.

One striking finding from this study is that the streaming system under analysis did not reflect selection by social class. That is, middle-class boys were not found disproportionately in the upper stream and lower-class boys in the lower stream. This finding from England, of course, effectively destroys the argument that the observed stream differences were simply a function of early class selection.

A point repeatedly made was the amount of status deprivation undergone by low-stream boys. The low-stream boys, in the main, were not allowed to take a set of examinations which would clearly place them in a better position to run the occupational race upon leaving school. Those who were not allowed to take the exams quite accurately perceived their occupational goals as relatively lower, since many skilled occupations are unavailable to those not taking these exams.

One of the principal reasons for the low academic performance among the low-stream boys is the fact that they are unlikely to be motivated toward high grades under a situation of little payoff. They perceive little congruence between working hard academically and receiving a tangible reward for their labors.

Further evidence of low academic ability under a streaming program comes from a study by Douglas (1964). He observed that, at each IQ level, the subjects in the upper streams increased their scores between the ages of eight and eleven, whereas those in the lower streams showed a progressive decline in their IQs. Thus, one possible interpretation, and one being given growing credence, is that the streaming system is self-validating, in that it created, to a certain degree, the differences which were then used to justify its existence by school officials.

THE CURRENT DATA

Cloward and Ohlin contend that social relationships among youth who lack legitimate access to success goals eventuate in a shared sense of injustice regarding their position, vis-à-vis the position of advantage held by others. The withdrawal of sentiments supporting the dominant normative structure may be the result.

Once the affective attachments have been severed, these youngsters are then free to adopt an illegitimate normative system (Cloward and Ohlin, 1960). Delinquents who experienced low opportunity in the legitimate structure were distinguished from nondelinquents by their lack of attachment to legitimate norms and institutions and subsequently attached themselves to illegitimate norms and institutions.

A common source of alienation from the norms of a social group is failure, or the anticipation of failure, in achieving the group goals by approved means. Whether or not persons who experience failure will become alienated from the structure will depend upon how they account for their failure.

> It is our view that the most significant step in the withdrawal of sentiments supporting the legitimacy of conventional norms is the attribution of the cause of failure to the social order rather than to oneself, for the way in which a person explains his failure largely determines what he will do about it (Cloward and Ohlin, 1960: 111).

Other writers have suggested the importance of the youngster's reaction to failure or anticipated failure. Sykes and Matza, for example, maintain that techniques of neutralization are developed by youngsters as devices for minimizing the pains of failure (Sykes and Matza, 1957). Thus, the alienation process is seen as related to the youngster's reaction to anticipated or actual failure. Furthermore, we may now hypothesize that:

(1) as a result of anticipated academic failure, youngsters will display a lack of affective attachment to the school system and will indeed fail;
(2) as a result of anticipated failure, the non-college-bound will be more likely than the college-bound boys to display academic failure and the subsequent lack of affective attachment to the legitimate institution of the school.

By way of introducing the data, let us first present the zero-order table displaying the relationship between academic performance and affective attachment to school (see Table 1).

The above hypotheses were tested by way of the subject's grade point average and by gathering his response to a question designed to measure affective attachment to school. High academic performance here was taken to mean a 2.00 grade point average or above. Affective attachment to the legitimate institution of the school was measured by the simple question, "I like school" with responses of "yes," "no," or "don't know" available.

It became immediately clear that there was a strong relationship between these two variables. Seventy-seven per cent of those high on academic performance also measured positive on affective attachment to the schools (see Table 1).

TABLE 1

Affective Attachment to Schools by Academic Performance (in percentages)

	Affective Attachment to Schools	
Academic Performance	Positive	Negative
High	77	51
Low	23	49
Total	100 (229)	100 (35)

$Q = .52 \quad X^2 = 10.97 \quad P < .001$

NOTE: An additional 45 cases fell into residual categories.

While the zero-order table yields a strong association, what might be the result if partialling were conducted by college plans?

From the point of view of the non-college-bound student, the administration of the high school milieu may be understood as a series of "status degradation ceremonies" (Garfinkel, 1956: 421–422) which have crucial implications for the emergence of deviant behavior in the school.

In the world outside the classroom, most institutions succeed in legitimizing their norms to the point that authority instead of coercion is the main driving force impelling conformity to the rules and regulations. But for many non-college-bound students, this phenomenon does not take place. These students are less likely to impute legitimacy to the bases of social control in the school than is typical of persons in other spheres of the society. Having been denounced and degraded in a number of subtle and not so subtle ways, the non-college-bound may in turn renounce the legitimacy of the invidious definitions to which they were subjected. Hence, pressure toward deviance is created. Table 2 displays the data. Previously we presented data (Table 1)

TABLE 2

College Plans by Affective Attachment to Schools by Academic Performance (in percentages)

	Affective Attachment			
	College-Bound		Non-College-Bound	
Academic Performance	Positive	Negative	Positive	Negative
High (2.00+)	91	85	44	32
Low (1.99 or less)	9	15	56	68
Total	100 (161)	100 (13)	100 (68)	100 (22)

which showed a positive association between affective attachment and academic performance. This relationship is brought into even closer focus by the current data. That is, when we partial on college plans, we find the differences becoming more extreme, with 32 per cent of the non-college-bound students who have negative attachment to school also being high on academic performance. At the other end of the continuum, we find 91 per cent of the college-bound who have a positive attachment to school also being high on academic performance.

In an effort to gauge the extent of the differences between the college-bound and the non-college-bound, four Kendall's Q values were computed from Table 2. The first measured the departure from independence of the college track on grade point average when the youngsters in the two pipelines had positive affect toward school (see Table 3). The table indicates high association between college track and grades, holding affect constant. Even though a youngster may have positive affect toward the school, and if he is in the college track, he is more likely to be high on grades than if he is in the non-college track. Grades, in other words, are not a simple function of liking school. A 47 per cent gap is seen for youngsters whose only difference under consideration is curriculum placement.

Second, we examined the reciprocal argument—namely, what effect might the college track have on the grades of youngsters with *negative* affect toward the school (see Table 4). The difference between the college-bound and non-college-bound is greater than in the previous table (see Table 3). The combination of being in the non-college track and having a negative view of school appears to produce a marked dampening effect on academic performance. For those not going to college, 32 per cent appear in the negative affect–high academic performance cell, a difference of 53 per cent from the college-bound.

TABLE 3

College Plans by Positive Affect to the Schools and Grade Point Average (in percentages)

Academic Performance	Positive Affect	
	College-Bound	Non-College Bound
High	91	44
Low	9	56
Total	100 (161)	100 (68)

$Q = .86$ $X^2 = 63.79$ $P < .001$

For those going to college, 85 per cent have high grade point averages in spite of the fact they possess negative affect toward the schools. It appears their distaste for school is overridden by their awareness that good grades are crucial for college admittance. Relevance for this group may not be the issue. Rather, they may couch the question of whether or not to pursue high grades in much less abstract terms. They perceive the situation as one in which high grades are necessary for college attendance. Those in the non-college group, on the other hand, see little payoff in the struggle for high grades. They are not going on to college, and particularly for the group which holds the school in low esteem, low grades can be the result. A Q of .84 lends strength to this view.

The following two tables (Tables 5 and 6) are presented to further illustrate the point previously made. Within each track, there is not much grade variation. The low Qs reflect this small departure from independence. Those going to college, in general, receive high grades, and those not going, in general, receive low grades, regardless of affect toward school.

We have presented data in support of the position that curriculum placement is a crucial variable in determining several things. First, affective attachment to school was seen to be strongly related to curriculum placement. Second, we saw a slightly stronger relationship between affective attachment to school and academic performance. Finally, we observed the relationship between affective attachment and academic performance under the influence of partialling by curriculum placement. Under the effects of partialling on curriculum placement, academic performance was shown to vary widely. Thus, the data presented supported the argument that a linkage among variables was initiated by curriculum placement and eventuated in low academic performance through the intervening variable of affective attachment to school.

TABLE 4

College Plans by Negative Affect to the Schools and Grade Point Average (in percentages)

Academic Performance	Negative Affect	
	College-Bound	Non-College-Bound
High	85	32
Low	15	68
Total	100 (13)	100 (22)

$Q = .84 \quad x^2 = 7.84 \quad P < .01$

TABLE 5

Affective Attachment to the Schools by Grade Point Average for College-Bound Students (in percentages)

| | Affective Attachment | |
Academic Performance	Positive	Negative
High	91	85
Low	9	15
Total	100 (161)	100 (13)

$Q = .28 \quad x^2 = 1.16 \quad$ not significant

TABLE 6

Affective Attachment to the Schools by Grade Point Average for Non-College-Bound Students (in percentages)

| | Affective Attachment | |
Academic Performance	Positive	Negative
High	44	32
Low	56	68
Total	100 (68)	100 (22)

$Q = .25 \quad x^2 = .99 \quad$ not significant

ACADEMIC SELF-ESTEEM AND ROLE THEORY

It is logically consistent to expect that teachers play a crucial role in our self-definition as students. While the Rosenthal and Jacobson (1968) study cited earlier did not deal directly with the issue of self-perception, its implications for self-image research appear unmistakable. It will be recalled that children selected at random from eighteen classrooms were reported to their teachers as having great potential for learning. Eight months later, these same children showed significantly greater gains in IQ than did the control group.

Because of the negative evaluation given by a significant other, and because of "objective" evidence of his academic failure, the student takes on a spoiled self-identity. He accepts a conception of himself as a failure. But much of the impact of academic failure appears to be along another dimension of self-image

—the tendency for the student to internalize the social rejection implicit in his status and suffer the pains of both a lowered self-esteem and self-rejection. These attacks on the offender's self-image can be taken as a vital condition giving rise to the rebellious student value system. Self-esteem is restored by participating in a system that enables the student to reject his rejecters rather than himself (Simmel, 1948: 41; Faris, 1946).

Just as the critics of the frustration-aggression theory in race relations have pointed out, frustration does not invariably lead to aggression, so spoiled self-identity does not invariably lead to delinquent acts in direct cause and effect relationships. Rather, in many cases, damaged self-esteem leads to a wide variety of behavior on the part of the youngsters who may or may not receive further stigmatization by school officials.

Whether or not the student product of a rejecting and irrelevant school system becomes delinquent depends on several variables. Because the overwhelming majority of delinquent acts are committed in the proximity of others, it would appear that one of the crucial conditions necessary for the translation of ideology into behavior is the presence of social support.

In addition, the notion of anticipatory socialization becomes relevant. This concept involves the preparatory responses that frequently precede an actual change in group membership such as the movement from non-gang to gang membership. We would expect to find the youth not yet gang members, but contemplating membership, possessing attitudes similar to actual members.

Role theory, then, would explain delinquency among high school students in terms of the teachers' roles and expectations and the resultant befouled self-identity. The pain of low self-evaluation is handled by rejecting the rejecters and forming groups that assign status on a base quite different from academic success.

THE PERCEPTION OF SELF AS STUDENT

The theory of the origin and maintenance of self has not often been applied to the school situation, and this lack has been felt by some contemporary researchers (Brookover et al., 1964).

Research by Brookover and Gottlieb points out that, when IQ is controlled, there is a significant and positive correlation between self-concept and academic performance. An additional check of symbolic interactionism revealed that the self-concept is positively correlated with the perceived evaluations that significant others hold of the student (Brookover et al., 1964: 276–279). It is highly plausible to argue that the significance of these conclusions is that the student's perceptions of his academic abilities largely determine his behavior within the school setting.

In the current study, we developed an index of academic self-concept. The index was constructed from a series of questions asking the student respondents to rate their own scholarly abilities.

The first dimension selected for inclusion in the index requested the respondent to place himself on a continuum anchored by the bipolar adjectives of studious–non-studious. The second question asked for agreement or disagreement to the statement, "I will be remembered at school as being a good student." The third question asked for agreement or disagreement to the statement, "I seem to be a little less capable than the other guys at school." Finally, we asked the respondent to place himself on a continuum of smart–dumb.

TABLE 7

Grade Point Average by Index of Self as a Capable Student (in percentages)

Index of Self-Conception as a Capable Student	Grade Point Average	
	High (2.00+)	Low (1.99 or less)
High	81	43
Low	19	57
Total	100 (199)	100 (72)

$Q = .47$ $x^2 = 36.60$ $P < .001$

NOTE: An additional 38 cases fell into residual categories.

Conforming to the expectations developed from the Meadian school of social psychology, we found the index of self-conception as a capable student to be strongly and positively related to academic performance. The difference of 38 per cent between those high on academic performance and those low on academic performance represented the strongest relationship thus far discovered.

SELF-CONCEPTION AND DELINQUENT FRIENDS

In Albert Cohen's terms, these students suffering from a spoiled self-identity as scholars should be in the market for a solution to an important problem of adjustment. Clearly, the youngsters have failed to win the acclaim and praise implied in the awarding of grades. They have not only failed to achieve grades, but, even more importantly, they have received a negative evaluation from a person very important to their future, the teacher.

For our present concern, the index of self-concept as a student is operationally defined in the same terms used previously. The dependent variable of number of delinquent friends, however, has not been introduced in the prior discussion. The question we used asks the respondent to "agree strongly," "agree somewhat," "disagree somewhat," or "disagree strongly" with the statement, "My friends could have gotten in lots of trouble with the police for some of the stuff they pull." Thus, the number of persons whom the respondent considered to be friends and who also could have been in trouble with the police were our basic data for Table 8.

TABLE 8

Index of Self-Conception as a Student by Perception of Friends as Delinquency-Prone (in percentages)

Friends Perceived as Delinquent-Prone	High	Low
Yes	37	61
No	63	39
Total	100 (198)	100 (82)

$Q = .46$ $X^2 = 13.72$ $P < .001$

NOTE: An additional 29 cases fell into residual cases.

The findings lend support to the notion that youngsters with low self-identification as students tend to group with youngsters they see as being involved in a delinquent life style. The relationship is strong, and in the direction predicted from the foregoing analysis.

In unfolding his concept of "differential identification," Glaser (1965) makes explicit how he will be using the term by stating, "the choice of another, from whose perspective we view our own behavior." Cast in this general frame, he readjusts Sutherland's (1955: 78) "differential association" scheme in role-theory terms, drawing in great measure from Mead (1934). Glaser (1956: 440) says that "a person pursues criminal behavior to the extent that he identifies himself with real or imaginary persons from whose perspective his criminal behavior seems acceptable."

At any given point on the time spectrum, Glaser argues, prior identifications, in combination with present circumstances, bring forth the choice of individuals with whom we identify ourselves. Identifications which have been pleasing tend to persist; those that have not tend to vanish. That reshuffling of the hedonism principle bears on why delinquents avoid delinquent acts in situations where they play satisfying conventional roles in which a delinquent act would threaten their integration into the legitimate normative system.

THE CURRENT DATA

We are positing that one operationally adequate measure of the intensity of identification is involvement with persons identified as "friends." Furthermore, the intensity variable can be placed on a continuum anchored at either end by people identified as strangers and those seen as friends. Individuals seen as acquaintances would be between these bipolar adjectives. Thus, differential identification would lead us to expect a positive relationship between degree of identification with delinquent friends and degree of delinquency.

Thus, we are hypothesizing, delinquency involvement of an individual will be positively correlated with the delinquency involvement reported for his friends. These data are reported in Table 9. As the data reveal, there is a clear-cut association between friends vis-à-vis delinquency status.

TABLE 9

**Delinquency Status of Respondent by Delinquency
Status of Friends (in percentages)**

Delinquent Status of "Friends"	Delinquent	Nondelinquent
Delinquent	76	49
Nondelinquent	24	51
Total	100 (291)	100 (898)

$Q = .33$ $X^2 = 62.02$ $P < .001$

NOTE: An additional 38 cases fell into residual categories.

A second hypothesis derived from the same item states that the delinquency involvement of an individual will be positively correlated with the delinquency involvement of an acquaintance, but that this association will be to a lesser degree than with friends. An "acquaintance" by definition is one with whom a person less closely identifies than a "friend."

A comparison of the results of Table 9 with Table 10 is necessary to test this hypothesis. The difference observed between the respondents and their acquaintances (6 per cent) in Table 10 is considerably less than the difference between the respondents and their friends (27 per cent). Apparently the differential identification mechanism is effectively shielding the non-delinquents from intimate kinds of contacts with delinquent youngsters. These data have suggested that the greater the degree of identification between individuals, the greater will be the degree of uniformity of their actions.

TABLE 10

**Delinquency Status of Respondent by Delinquency
Status of Acquaintance (in percentages)**

Delinquency Status of Acquaintance	Delinquent	Nondelinquent
Delinquent	74	68 .
Nondelinquent	26	32
Total	100 (284)	100 (896)

$Q = .16$ $X^2 = 58.49$ $P < .001$

NOTE: An additional 47 cases fell into residual categories.

SUMMARY

It would seem that the foregoing analysis and empiric results contain clear implications for the functioning of the school system. The findings pointed out some very basic differences between those in the college track and those in the non-college track. Coupled with these differences was the discovery of a self-conception quite consistent with the teacher's evaluation in the form of grade point average.

It would seem that the mechanism requires scrutiny. To declare in resolute tones "abolish the tracking system" is not enough simply because with or without a tracking structure, some youngsters will be going to college, and others will not, and invidious distinctions may be drawn on another even more arbitrary dimension. After we learn more about interactional styles, it may be possible to combine a search for skillful teachers with training techniques designed to allow students greater intellectual development.

In general, the study has supported the explanation that youngsters not going to college, but in a school situation that supports college attendance, face a major adjustment problem to which delinquent behavior appears to be a response. On the other hand, it appears as though none of the separate etiological processes discussed is capable of explaining adequately the dialectic whereby those experiencing "unjust" deprivation become delinquent. Obviously, it has not been possible to test all the implications of these theories, but the findings nevertheless suggest that an eclectic position is necessary if the explanation is to apply to the broad spectrum of juvenile delinquency.

The linkages appearing to receive empirical support were: non-college-bound youngsters tended to be low on affect to school $\longrightarrow$ boys low on affect toward the schools tended to be low on academic performance $\longrightarrow$ youngsters low on academic performance tended to be low on an index of self-perception as a student $\longrightarrow$ students low on the index of self-perception as a student tended to have a high number of delinquent friends $\longrightarrow$ those with a higher number of delinquent friends would themselves tend to have high delinquency rates.

Thus, we have attempted to integrate seemingly disparate theories of human behavior, drawn from several intellectual traditions, into a unitary perspective on youth crime.

NOTES

1. A rather crucial decision that should be made explicit was made at this point regarding a data analysis technique employed. To gain a clearer understanding of the dynamics of delinquency, we decided to use all the available delinquents rather than simply those who appeared in the random sample. The latter population consisted of a 25 per cent sample selected randomly from those youngsters completing a questionnaire at time 1.

One of the important functions of any statistical method is to provide a technique whereby two or more quantities may be meaningfully compared. In the situation just described, it would be quite inappropriate to attempt to compare a 25 per cent random sample with a complete census of delinquents. Hence, the need arose for a norming or standardizing tool to make the two directly comparable. To allow this comparability, we simply multiplied the two non-delinquent cells by 4 (4 because of the original 25 per cent sample which would thereby norm to a base of 100). This done, we recognized that the statistical inferences and assumptions underlying the various tests of significance were no longer applicable because of the lack of a true n. Nevertheless, X^2 tests appear with several of the normed tables. They should be regarded as decision helpmates and nothing more. That is, the X^2 should, in this instance, be regarded only as a measure of statistical stability. Tables 1–8 include only the randomly selected sample, while Tables 9 and 10 are normed tables.

In addition to the information contained in the interview schedule, grades and juvenile court records were obtained for each respondent.

REFERENCES

Brookover, Wilbur B. and David Gottlieb. *Sociology of Education.* New York: American, 1964.
Brookover, Wilbur B., Shailer Thomas, and Ann Paterson. "Self-concept of ability and school achievement." *Sociology of Education,* 37 (Spring, 1964), pp. 271–279.
California Youth Authority. *Community Treatment Project Report No. 7,* August, 1966.
Chicago Board of Education. *The Public Schools of Chicago: A Survey for the Board of Education of the City of Chicago,* 1964.

Cloward, Richard A. and Lloyd E. Ohlin. *Delinquency and Opportunity: A Theory of Delinquent Gangs.* New York: Free Press, 1960.

Coser, A. and B. Rosenberg (eds.). *Sociological Theory: A Book of Readings.* New York: Macmillan, 1965.

Coser, Lewis. *The Functions of Social Conflict.* New York: Free Press, 1956.

Douglas, J.W.B. *The Home and The School.* London: MacGibbon & Kee, 1964.

Faris, Ellsworth. "Some results of frustration." *Sociology and Social Research*, 31 (November/December, 1946), pp. 87–92.

Garfinkel, Harold. "Conditions of successful degradation ceremonies." *Amer. J. of Sociology,* 61 (March, 1956), pp. 420–424.

Glaser, Daniel. "Criminal theories and behavioral images." *Amer. J. of Sociology* 61 (March, 1956), pp. 433–444.

Hargreaves, David H. *Social Relations in a Secondary School.* New York: Humanities, 1968.

Havighurst, Robert J., Paul H. Bowman, Gordon P. Liddle, Charles V. Matthews, and James V. Pierce. *Growing Up in River City.* New York: Wiley, 1962.

Hollingshead, A. B. *Elmtown's Youth.* New York: John Wiley, 1949.

Kelley, Delos H. and Robert W. Balch. "Social origins and school failure." *Pacific Soc. Rev.* 14 (October, 1971), pp. 413–430.

_____. "The imagination in Wundt's treatment of myth and religion." *Psych. Bull.* 3 (1906), pp. 393–399.

_____. *Mind, Self, and Society.* Chicago: Univ. of Chicago Press, 1934.

_____. "The relations of psychology and philology." *Psych. Bull.* 1 (n.d.), pp. 375–391.

Polk, Kenneth and David S. Halferty. "Adolesence, commitment, and delinquency." *J. of Research in Crime and Delinquency* 3 (July, 1966), pp. 82–96.

Polk, Kenneth and Walter E. Schafer. *Schools and Delinquency.* Englewood Cliffs, N.J.: Prentice-Hall, 1972.

Reiss, Albert J., Jr. and Albert L. Rhodes. "A sociopsychological study of adolescent conformity and deviation." U.S. Office of Education Cooperative Research Project 507, 1959.

_____. "The distribution of juvenile delinquency in the social class structure." *Amer. Soc. Rev.* 26 (October, 1961), pp. 720–732.

Rosenthal, Robert and Lenore Jacobson. *Pygmalion in the Classroom.* New York: Holt, Rinehart & Winston, 1968.

Sexton, Patricia. *Education and Income: Inequalities in Our Public Schools.* New York: Compass, 1966.

_____. *The American School: A Sociological Analysis.* Englewood Cliffs, N.J.: Prentice Hall, 1967.

Simmel, E. (ed.). *Anti-Semitism: A Social Disease.* New York: International Universities Press, 1948.

Simmel, George. *Conflict* (K. H. Wolff, trans.). New York: Free Press, 1955.

Stinchcombe, Arthur L. *Rebellion in a High School.* Chicago, Ill.: Quadrangle, 1964.

Sutherland, Edwin H. *Principles of Criminology.* Philadelphia: J. B. Lippincott, 1955.

_____, and Donald R. Cressey. *Principles of Criminology.* Philadelphia: J. B. Lippincott, 1960.

_____. *Principles of Criminology.* Philadelphia: J. B. Lippincott, 1966.

Sykes, Gresham and David Matza. "Techniques of neutralization: a theory of delinquency." *Amer. Soc. Rev.,* 22 (December, 1957), pp. 664–670.

_____. *Youth in the Ghetto: A Study of the Consequences of Powerlessness.* New York: Harlem Youth Opportunities Unlimited, 1964.

Chapter Six

Schools as Formal Organizations

In popular usage, the term "bureaucracy" or "bureaucrat" generally has rather negative connotations. These terms have become epithets used to refer to disliked and dislikeable features of large organizations such as "red tape," impersonality and the apparent senselessness of having to fill out six copies of some lengthy form. As used by sociologists, "bureaucracy" (and its synonyms "formal organization" and "complex organization") is a neutral term. That is, it is not intended to convey any kind of evaluation or criticism of the activity, organization, or persons under consideration.

While bureaucracies are not new—they existed in ancient Egypt and Rome, for example—the *extent* to which they have flourished in modern urban-industrial societies represents a qualitative change in social organization. In both the public and private spheres the need for coordinating large numbers of persons performing highly specialized and interrelated tasks has led to the increasing bureaucratization of human activity. Work activities, leisure time activities, religious worship, consumer behavior, legal processes, formal education, etc., all involve essentially bureaucratic forms of social organization and interaction.

Even though our concern here is with schools as bureaucracies, bureaucratic organizations are so pervasive and cover such a wide variety and range of human activities that it is necessary to identify some features or characteristics that are common to all.

The German sociologist Max Weber was one of the first scholars to attempt a systematic and comprehensive analysis of the structural characteristics of bureaucracies. Paraphrasing Weber, the following list can serve as a definition of bureaucracy.[1]

1. A bureaucracy is a structure of *offices,* and there is an explicit definition of official activities considered to inhere in specific offices.
2. *Authority* inheres in the office rather than the person, and areas of authority and competence tend to be formally specified.
3. There is a high degree of *specialization* of functions, tasks, and duties.
4. The functioning of the organization is governed by *rules of procedure* which emphasize the categorizing and routinizing of activities and problems.
5. Procedure in bureaucratic organizations tends to be *formal and impersonal,* especially in dealings between superordinate and subordinate offices. Communications are recorded and the forms of communication are highly stereotyped and ritualized. The intrusion of "personal" elements into organizational activities tends to be discouraged.
6. Bureaucratic organizations are *hierarchical and stratified.* Every office is a link in the chain of authority. As a general rule, communications (e.g., requests, orders, information) pass through all offices intermediate to the communicants.

Though by no means exhaustive of Weber's discussion of the characteristics of bureaucracy, the foregoing can serve as a working definition or theoretical model of bureaucracy.

The conduct of formal education in American society has for a long time been carried on by bureaucratic organizations, that is, by an organization of social roles explicitly created to accomplish some particular goal or objective. In this sense, the roles of teacher, student, principal, etc., have been created and are related to each other in a manner that is assumed to accomplish the goal of transmitting specific knowledge and skill as well as a set of moral precepts to the student.

In looking at schools as bureaucratic organizations it is important to keep in mind that there is a great deal of variation in the scale and complexity of schools in the United States. Surely the rural elementary school is vastly different from the urban multiversity. But these differences are a matter of degree. Despite differences in locale, level and size, all schools exhibit the characteristics of bureaucracy to some degree.

Weber's model of bureaucracy has stimulated numerous investigations of all kinds of organizations. Hospitals, the military, churches, business organizations, governmental agencies, factories and schools have all been examined as bureaucratic organizations. The first article of this chapter by Miller presents an analysis of schools focusing on key aspects of Weber's model of bureaucracy and illustrates the way in which these characteristics become part of the perceptions and assumptions of school personnel.

The "free school" movement in the United States is, in several respects, a reaction to and against the bureaucratization of schooling. Generally child-centered and developmental in their approach to education, free schools emphasize creativity, innovativeness and exploration. The planned out, tightly scheduled curriculum is anathema in the free school.

In the second article of this chapter Cooper presents a case study of the origins, problems and eventual fate of seven such free schools. Viewing the process as a "social movement," he identifies various stages through which these schools move and attempts to isolate conditions that account for their continuation or failure to continue.

In most large cities centralized school systems have become overwhelming bureaucracies which allow for few if any inputs from outside groups, particularly parents. Large, centralized school systems may make system-wide decisions and establish standardized rules and procedures which overlook or ignore the unique problems of particular schools or neighborhoods. Largely in response to public demands for special attention to particular problems, some large school systems have attempted to "decentralize" their decision making and administrative apparatus by increasing participation in decision making from within the local community. In the third article, Usdan describes New York City's experiences in decentralization, identifies problems and conflicts experienced there and examines the implications of New York City's experiences for decentralization and community control in other cities.

The last article of this chapter examines universities as bureaucratic organizations. Gross first identifies various perspectives on organizations and deals with their applicability to universities. Focusing on the goals of universities, the article then presents data from a large sample of faculty and administrators on different perceptions of the goals of universities and the relation of power to those goals.

NOTES

1. Hans H. Gerth and C. Wright Mills, *From Max Weber: Essays in Sociology,* New York: Oxford University Press, 1958, Chapter VIII.

16.   JON P. MILLER

Social-Psychological Implications of Weber's Model of Bureaucracy: Relations Among Expertise, Control, Authority and Legitimacy

Weber's ideal-typical model of bureaucracy has been useful in directing attention toward the societal dimension of bureaucracy, dealing with the role of "bureaucratization" in modern legal social structures (cf. Bendix, 1945, 1947; Blau, 1956; Etzioni, 1961a). More research has focused on the organizational dimension of Weber's model, having to do with the objective structural characteristics of complex organizations. (cf. Udy, 1959; Hall, 1963; Hall *et al.,* 1967; Blau, 1955, 1957, 1960; Blau and Scott, 1962).

Weber's analysis also suggests a number of straightforward hypotheses concerning the characteristics and behavior of individuals within organizations. Yet with few exceptions social-psychological research in organizations has proceeded explicitly from more recent theoretical formulations.[1] The purpose here is to make explicit some of the social-psychological implications of Weber's ideal-typical model, focusing particularly on the distributions of the variables expertise, control, authority and legitimacy, and then to test these ideas among the individual members of five schools in a public school system.

RECONSTRUCTION OF WEBER'S MODEL

Weber discusses two basic problems confronted by most "rational" organized collective activity. They are (1) to ensure that individuals officially designated to exercise control actually direct an organization's activities, and (2) to ensure that decisions are made on the basis of the best possible informa-

Reprinted from *Social Forces,* 49 (September, 1970), pp. 91–102, "Social-Psychological Implications of Weber's Model of Bureaucracy: Relations among Expertise, Control, Authority, and Legitimacy," by Jon P. Miller. Copyright © The University of North Carolina Press. By permission of the author and the University of North Carolina Press.

This research was supported by Grant GS-691 from the National Science Foundation. I am indebted to Robert Hagedorn and Sanford Labovitz for their assistance throughout the development of the study, and to William Rushing and Bruce Mayhew, Jr., for their critical appraisal. Thanks are also due the members of the organization who responded to the questionnaire. An earlier version was read at the annual meeting of the Pacific Sociological Association, April, 1969.

tion. Two strategic consequences follow. First, organizations (especially as they increase in size) rely increasingly on formalization of organizational structure and specification of organizational rules (i.e., they become more "bureaucratized"). Second, organizations attempt to achieve rational allocations of expertise, control and authority among the individual members of the organization, in such a way that the members will "legitimate" the organizational arrangements.[2] Thus, at the same time that Weber specified the structural arrangements of such variables as expertise, control and authority and their relationship to legitimacy in organizations, he also specified how they would be distributed as attributes among the members of an organization. They will be distributed among individuals in accordance with the organization's policies and abstract rules, and they will be closely related to each other.[3]

With this in mind, the distributions among individuals of the following organizational variables will be explicated and explored in more detail: (1) *expertise,* including two dimensions (Weber, 1947:339)—(a) formal training in the skills essential to the organization, and (b) the knowledge of facts and documentary material a member possesses about how his organization carries out its activities (referred to here as "organizational knowledge"); (2) *control* (or "power") which Weber (1947:152) defined as ". . . the probability that one actor will be in position to carry out his will despite resistance, regardless of the basis on which this probability rests"; (3) *authority,* defined as ". . . the legitimate exercise of imperative control . . . the probability that a command with a specific content will be obeyed by a given group of persons" (Weber, 1947:152–153); and (4) *legitimacy,* or the probability that attitudes will exist that validate or confirm the positions exercising authority (Weber, 1947:326–327).[4]

According to Weber, persons with superior training should be able to gain superior knowledge of the operation of an organization. Although it is possible for an individual to possess intimate knowledge of how an organization operates without having a large amount of prior training in the skills essential to the organization (Weber, 1947:339; Bendix, 1962:452), in general the correlation between the two types of expertise should be high. Both training and organizational knowledge should also be positively related to the amount of influence an individual is able to exercise, since, ideally, control in a bureaucracy is exercised by experts (Weber, 1947:337–339).

Although expertise and the ability to control are inextricably linked in the ideal type, sheer power, whatever its source, is not sufficient to ensure the continuous, efficient functioning of an organization (Weber, 1947). Decisions must be made in accordance with organizational rules. In order to establish this condition, organizations formalize the system of control in a hierarchical distribution of "legitimate authority." Persons with expertise, then, should be able to exercise legitimate control because their influence and importance are codified in a formal system of offices which possess authority. In other words, authority adheres to an organizational position which demands expertise for its incumbent,[5] and it follows that official position will be closely related to each of the two types of expertise.

A further implication in Weber's model is that there will be a high correlation between official and actual patterns of control. People occupying positions of authority will issue "commands" with specific, regulated content (Bendix, 1962:429; Weber, 1947:152). The range of their discretion will be circumscribed, but the probability is high that their commands will be obeyed by those who officially are under their influence, since they have the "right" to exercise control over the organization's activities. When this condition exists, the possession of official authority should be consistent with the ability to exercise actual control.[6] In other words, the higher a person's official position in an organization, the greater his control over how the organization functions should be.

Ultimately, the type and degree of obedience to commands which occurs (or fails to occur) in an organization is related to whether the system of authority is seen as legitimate, valid or desirable by the members of the organization (Weber, 1947:124). This legitimacy is based in turn on a belief in the "legality" of the bureaucratic order and results in a ". . . readiness to conform with rules which are formally correct and [which] have been imposed by accepted procedure" (Weber, 1947:131). This disinterested obedience presupposes that members of the organization confirm the expertise of those in control and validate their legal right to issue commands (Weber, 1947:328). Officials' right to control is based on the criteria of their appointment and the legality of the positions they occupy (Weber, 1947:143–144, 325–327), and these as we have seen are based on the amount of training and knowledge they have. In the ideal-typical case then, the perceived expertise or competence of those with authority and control should reflect the degree to which the hierarchy of authority and the system of control are legitimated by the members of the organization.[7] Thus, the degree of professional competence which actual and official control figures are perceived to have (referred to here as "professional prestige") can be used as an indirect indicator of the degree of legitimacy they enjoy.

To formalize, in the ideal-typical case there should be a close correlation between the amount of control a person exercises and the professional prestige he is accorded by others in the organization. Concurrently, the members of the system who occupy positions of authority will be recognized as competent and therefore will be seen as having the right to exercise control. As a consequence of this, they will be accorded high professional prestige.

Finally, if as in the ideal-typical case professional prestige is accorded on the basis of recognition of differing actual amounts of expertise, then both professional training and organizational knowledge should be correlated with the amount of prestige individuals enjoy.

In short, what Weber's model suggests is that persons with superior expertise will be elevated into positions in the official hierarchy of control; they will be vested with the "right" to issue commands and can expect to be obeyed as long as their positions, the legal correctness of their commands and their own competence are legitimated by other members of the organization. What this means empirically is that expertise, control, authority and legitimacy can be treated as an interacting system of variables, with variation in one having clear implications for the others.

CONTRASTING VIEWS

Some functionally oriented case studies and theoretical statements have dealt, at least indirectly, with the individual dimension of Weber's model (cf. Merton, 1957; Selznick, 1948; Blau, 1955; Gouldner, 1954; for a critique of this approach see Wolin, 1969). Many of these statements appear to conflict with the basic proposition presented here. For example, a persistent observation of such studies is a lack of correspondence or a "conflict" between official authority and actual control; for different reasons in different organizations individuals who are not designated to control are seen as exercising undue influence over organizational functioning. Because of such observations, Weber is criticized for overemphasizing the "formal" and "rational" elements of bureaucracy while neglecting the confusing effect of "nonrational," "informal," and "dysfunctional" contingencies which may intrude to break down the unity of authority and control.

The intention is not to imply that such observations are incorrect,[8] yet they do fail clearly to specify the conditions under which a breakdown in authority or legitimacy will occur.[9] Being descriptive in method, such studies are not easily replicable, and for this reason the findings are not empirically comparable or "additive." It follows that they cannot direct our attention to the particular conditions which prevent (or bring about) a close correspondence between authority and control in organizations.

On the organizational level of analysis, there is evidence which suggests that *structural* elements of the ideal type are not as closely related as Weber implied that they would be. Udy (1959) found that bureaucratic elements of the ideal-typical model did not generally occur in the same organizations as rational elements of the model.[10] Additionally, Hall (1963) has offered evidence that organizations may be more or less "bureaucratized" along six different variable dimensions and that these six dimensions will be differentially stressed by different organizations. These findings question the utility of Weber's model, since they question the interconnections among the elements of the ideal type.

Because the latter two studies involved the testing of hypotheses derived from Weber's model, they represent important theoretical contributions to this area of study. However, by focusing on organizations as units of analysis, they leave the bureaucratically demanded characteristics of individuals in organizations unanalyzed. It is no doubt true that organizations place different amounts of stress on various organizational elements and display different configurations of organizational elements. Yet the same organizations which deemphasize authority and control may still achieve a correspondence between the two in the sense that, to the extent that they are stressed, they are identified with the same individuals. For this reason it remains to be determined how the variables (or characteristics) specified by the ideal type are related when they do occur together and when individuals are taken as the unit of analysis.

METHODS

Questionnaires were given to teaching and nonteaching personnel of five public schools in a small northwestern university town.[11] Seventy-five of 82 members surveyed completed the instrument, for an overall response rate of 91.5 per cent. The assumptions are justified that there are differentiations in expertise in the school system, that some individuals do exercise more control than others, that there are differentials in authority, and that individuals do differ in the degree to which they are accorded prestige by the other members of the system. The task then, is to determine how accurately Weber's model allows us to predict relationships among these variables. Structured and sociometric questions were used as indicators of the variables expertise, control, authority and legitimacy.

Professional training was measured by two sets of ordinal categories: (1) academic degree held (a distinction was made between those with graduate degrees and those without graduate degrees), and (2) the total number of years of schooling completed (four years college, one year graduate school, and two or more years graduate school).

Organizational knowledge was measured indirectly by a sociometric question (first used by Jacobson and Seashore, 1951) which yielded ordinal data about the number of times a person was mentioned by others in the system as a source of information (in this as in other sociometric questions the personnel were instructed to respond in terms of the total school system). Four ordinal categories resulted ("*0*," "*1*," "*2* or *3*" and "*4* or more" choices).

Authority was measured by responses to the question: "What is the formal title of your position?" and "What kind of work do you do in this position? (Please indicate the major duties or tasks involved.)." Responses to these questions yielded an ordered dichotomy, with 8 people classified as exercising official supervisory authority, and the remaining 67 classed as not exercising official supervisory authority.

The operational measure of *control* was derived from responses to the following sociometric question: "Please give the names and positions of the five people in your organization who you feel have the most to say about how the organization is run." The distribution of responses to this question is markedly skewed (59 members were not perceived as exercising control; of the remaining 16 members, 6 received 1 choice each, 1 each received scores of 2 and 4, and the other 8 scores ranged from 6 choices to a high score of 68 choices). For purposes of correlation, two ordinal categories were used, corresponding to scores of "*O*" and "*1* or more" choices. It should be apparent that this measure of control is symptomatic, not direct; it is not possible to determine whether the perceptions of the members of the system accurately reflect the distribution of control in the system. Note also that the measure reflects control over decisions affecting the organization as whole, and not control over situation-specific, momentary decisions. A measure reflecting the latter would probably produce a different impression of the distribution of control in the school system (for a discussion of the differences between generalized and specific power, see Lehman, 1969).

Each individual was assigned an ordinal *professional prestige* score according to the number of times he was mentioned in response to the following sociometric question: "Of all the people you work with, please list the five whose opinion of your work you respect most highly." Scores on this variable were also skewed and were collapsed in the ordered categories "*O* or *1*," "*2* or *3*," and "*4* or more" choices.[12]

The ordinal measures outlined above were intercorrelated by means of *gamma* coefficients (Goodman and Kruskal, 1954). It should be noted that the use of a measure of association in a case such as the present one adds little to the substantive interpretation of the findings beyond what is possible with visual inspection of the data. The *gammas* reported are intended only to summarize the data and to provide a comparative ranking of the degrees to which various pairs of variables are associated.

FINDINGS

With the exceptions of the correlations between organizational knowledge and the two measures of professional training (*gamma* = .15 and .19), the correlations reported in Table 1 are generally high.

TABLE 1

Intercorrelations (Gamma) of Five Organizational Variables Among Seventy-Five Members of a Public School System

Organizational Variables	Number Years Schooling	Organizational Knowledge	Control	Position	Prestige
1. Academic training					
A. Degree held	.98	.15	.81	.84	.63
B. Number years schooling		.19	.85	.87	.67
2. Organizational knowledge			.58	.76	.62
3. Control				1.00	.97
4. Position					.96
5. Prestige					—

The relationship between authority and control is especially important because it reflects the organization's degree of success in solving what has been referred to as a basic task of bureaucracy, *viz.*, achieving a correspondence between formal, rational prescriptions and actual behavior. The *gamma* coefficient of 1.0 reported in Table 1 indicates that position occupied is clearly predictive of the amount of control a person is perceived as exercising. However, because a *gamma* value of 1.0 can be misleading, the relevant data are presented in Table 2. As the data indicate, knowing that a person occupies a position of authority is sufficient for predicting that he will be perceived as exercising control over the activities of the system, since none of those possessing official authority are seen as lacking control. On the other hand, authority is not necessary for predicting control, since 8 of the 67 people in the system who do not possess authority are seen as exercising some control.[13] (These 8 "unofficial control figures" received on the average 1.5 choices, compared with 30.4 choices for administrators.)

Consistent with Weber's argument, both authority and control command prestige in the school system (*gamma* = .97 and .96), and similarly, control

TABLE 2

Cross-Tabulations of Position Occupied and Amount of Control Exercised by Seventy-Five Members of a Public School System

Position Occupied	Control Exercised		
	No Control	Some Control	Total
Exercises no authority	59	8	67
Exercises authority	0	8	8
Total	59	16	75

and authority are also related to professional training. As Table 1 shows, control is related to both indicators of professional training (*gamma* = .81 and .85). Additionally, both indicators of training are clearly related to position occupied (*gamma* = .84 and .87).[14]

The results presented so far are consistent with Weber's reasoning that persons with superior training will achieve positions of authority and be able to exercise control, and that consistent with their expertise, their positions and the degree of control they exercise will be legitimated by the members of the organization.

Table 1 shows that "organizational knowledge" (the second dimension of expertise) is also related to the position a person occupies (*gamma* = .76) and to the amount of control he exercises (*gamma* = .58), although the correlations here (particularly the latter) are not as high as those reported above. The likelihood that persons seen as exercising control will be named as sources of information is considerably greater than that they will not be so named. The correlation is far from complete, however, since some persons with control were not recognized as sources of information, while some persons without control were so recognized, indicating that the possession of organizational knowledge is neither necessary nor sufficient for predicting the ability to exercise control.

In short, the relationships among expertise, control and authority are more pronounced when professional training is taken as the indicator of expertise than when organizational knowledge is taken as the indicator. In either case, those with authority and control in the school system do generally have superior expertise.

The question of whether expertise commands prestige in the school system can also be answered in the affirmative. The correlations between prestige and degree held, years of schooling and organizational knowledge are, respectively, .63, .67, and .62. These figures suggest that expertise tends to command prestige, regardless of the basis of the expertise. However, no one of these measures of expertise is as closely related to prestige as are authority and control. A comparison of correlations in Table 1 reveals the additional fact that whereas organizational knowledge is as highly correlated as professional training is with prestige, it is not as highly correlated as professional training is with control and authority. A clue for explaining this may lie in the correlation between the two separate dimensions of expertise.

It was expected that professional training and organizational knowledge, though conceptually distinct, would be empirically related. Contrary to this prediction, the correlation between years of schooling and organizational knowledge is only .19 and the correlation between degree held and organizational knowledge is only .15. These correlations are insufficient for accurate prediction, but they are interpretable. Examination of the data in Table 3 reveals that those without graduate degrees are more likely to lack organizational knowledge than they are to possess it, while for those with graduate degrees the likelihood of having organizational knowledge is about equal to the probability of not having it. A similar pattern appears when years of schooling are used as the measure of training. It is possible that the lack of training serves as a barrier to gaining organizational knowledge. However, the possession of professional training does not in itself assure that a person will have access to organizational knowledge. Among those with superior amounts of professional training, the possession or lack of possession of organizational knowledge must be explained by factors which have not yet been explored.

DISCUSSION

Weber's prediction that there will be a correspondence between official bureaucratic authority and actual control is substantiated in the school system. Persons with authority are able to exercise control and apparently for reasons suggested by Weber, competence and legitimacy. There is no evidence of any mechanism which systematically prevents administrators from exercising effective control over the activities of the system. Some of the possible reasons for this findings should be explored.

Conflict over the issues of competence and legitimacy may be avoided in this educational organization because of legal prerequisites specifying that authority can only be achieved by those with adequate professional training. Administrators are not likely to be ignorant of the skills required to direct the activities of the organization. Typically also, administrators will have the same type of training and the same basic goals as the other members of the system.

TABLE 3

Cross-Tabulations of Organizational Knowledge and Academic Training for Seventy-Five Members of a Public School System

Organizational Knowledge (Number of Times Contacted for Information)	Academic Training						
	Degree Held			Years of Schooling			
	B.A.	M.A.	Total	16	17	18 or More	Total
0	9	6	15	5	6	7	18
1	15	9	24	10	6	8	24
2 or 3	11	9*	20	2	11	8	21
4 or more	4	5	9	1	3	5	9
Total	39	29	68†	18	26	28	72†

*This category includes one person who reported having a Ph.D.
†These totals are less than 75 because of people who did not respond to the questions measuring academic training and organizational knowledge

Both teachers and administrators are professional educators, and the fact that administrators have extensive training in skills important to education could enhance their ability to exercise effective control while enjoying the professional respect of the other members of the system. Where these conditions are absent (that is, where administrators are not "professionally" trained) the correspondence between authority and control may not be as close (cf. Etzioni, 1964:83ff.).

A related fact is that organizational knowledge (knowledge not derived from professional training) is not apparently "exploited" as a means of usurping the control of those with official authority. Although 8 people without official authority were seen as exercising some control, the amount of this perceived control does not compare with the control attributed to the administrators,[15] nor do these unofficial control figures have substantially more organizational knowledge than other nonadministrators (they received on the average 1.6 contacts for information, compared to 1.3 contacts for all nonadministrators and 5.6 contacts for the administrators). Examination of the sociometric data also indicates that while those with unofficial control received more than the average number of choices in terms of work contacts, friendship and prestige,[16] they did not receive these choices from persons with official authority. The control they are seen as exercising does not apparently derive from exploitation of any special closeness to administrators. Nor do they form an unofficial control "clique" since they generally did not exchange choices among themselves on the various sociometric criteria.

If administrators were seen as illegitimate or derelict, then teachers could of course restrict information and refuse cooperation as a weapon or as a defense against them (cf. Becker, 1961). Again this is not as likely in an educational ("normative") organization as it might be in other types of organizations (such as "coercive" or "utilitarian" organizations) where the possibility of monopolizing critical information is greater.[17] In other words, it is likely that organizational knowledge will be used as a source of control when some people can take advantage of information which others lack and when they have some reason for doing so. This will be especially likely if those in positions of authority lack the information they need to control the organization effectively or if some statuses in the organization require or provide access to critical information to which others (including officials) do not have access.[18] In the absence of these conditions, organizational knowledge may be more closely related to legitimate authority and prestige than it is to control, per se.[19] From the point of view of legitimate control then, organizational knowledge will have positive or negative effects depending on the type of organization and the level of training and awareness of administrators.

In the present case the expertise which the members have in common probably decreases the likelihood that any limited group will be able to use information illegitimately as a means of monopolizing control over others in the organization.[20] As a case in point, in this organization unofficial control is more closely related to professional training and prestige than it is to organizational knowledge. The 8 unofficial control figures are more qualified than other nonadministrators in terms of the professional training they have, and they command more respect than their official peers in the organization.[21] The unofficial control they are seen as exercising cannot be characterized as divisive or disruptive, since it is not apparently so defined by other members of the system. In the absence of evidence to the contrary, it is reasonable to conclude that their control is consistent with their qualifications and with the respect they enjoy among those who officially are their peers in the organization. While this verifies Weber's speculation about the importance of expertise as a source of control in an organization (since superior expertise in terms of professional training is related to the ability to exercise control even when it is not coupled with official authority), it also underlines the importance of how each person is evaluated by others in the organization (since the prestige of the unofficial control figures indicates that the personnel "legitimate" their control). This suggests a modification of Weber's model, since it indicates that organizations may be able to accommodate the exercise of some unofficial control without displaying disruption or conflict. It could be that control will not be the exclusive possession of those with official authority when persons who are qualified and respected are available to share the exercise of organizational power. In this case the exercise of unofficial control would not reflect a "breakdown" of formal authority, but rather a complement to it. In such a context, control need not be treated as a "zero-sum" concept (cf. Dahrendorf, 1959) or as a scarce commodity which provokes conflict in an organization, since it can be distributed among different official statuses depending on such variables as authority, professional competence and professional prestige. One hypothesis suggested by this is that in normative organizations unofficial control (to the extent that it occurs) will be exercised by individuals who are intermediate between administrators and other personnel in terms of professional training and professional prestige.[22]

Also contrary to Weber is the suggestion that a lack of impersonality may contribute to an organization's functioning. The quality of being well-liked, for example, may contribute to the ability to exercise organizational control. Both official and unofficial control figures received more than the average number of friendship choices (6.3 and 3.5 choices, respectively, compared to 2.3 choices for all nonadministrators). Additionally, both authority and control are statistically related to the number of friendship choices received (the correlations are .68 and .64 respectively). This reinforces the suggestion that unofficial control need not represent a breakdown in morale or formal control mechanisms.

Interpersonal relations can also help explain the role of organizational knowledge in the school system. Friendship is related to organizational knowledge (*gamma* = .68); with the exception of authority, no other variable is as highly related to organizational knowledge. Additionally, both friendship and organizational knowledge are related to professional prestige (the correlations are .72 and .62, respectively), but neither friendship nor organizational knowledge is closely related to the two indicators of professional training (correlations between organizational knowledge and training are reported in Table 1; friendship is related .27 to years of schooling and .29 to degree held). What this suggests is that homogeneity of training among the members of an organization may mean that professional training will not distinguish between those who have organizational knowledge and those who do not. Because most of the members of the school system have more than the minimum amount of training required, they apparently look to other sources for information and form friendships according to other criteria. Speculatively, it could be that the members contact their friends for information which is not provided by professional training, that is, that people are named as friends more often because they are perceived to have valuable organizational information. This would help explain the relationships between friendship and prestige, and between prestige and organizational knowledge, since it may be that friendship and prestige are rewards given for providing valuable information (cf. Homans, 1961; Blau, 1955:137ff., 1964).[23] In any case the distribution of organizational knowledge cannot be explained as an *impersonal* exchange of intelligence in accordance with abstract rules of the organization, nor as a weapon to be used against the official authority structure. Factors other than those suggested by Weber must be taken into account. Exchange theory seems well suited for this type of organizational question.

In short, although Weber insisted that one source of the superior efficiency of modern bureaucratic organization is its ability to "depersonalize" itself by excluding personal feelings entirely from its operation (Bendix, 1962:425–427; Weber, 1947:340), this is one element of the ideal type which apparently is not inevitable, at least in small organizations of the type studied here. Alternatives to impersonality exist, since this system at least has achieved what appears to be a harmonious relationship between authority and control (including unofficial control) in the presence of some "personalism."[24] Evidence such as this indicates that the system does not operate in a spirit of "bureaucratic impersonality." To the contrary, it could be that the patterns of friendship and cohesiveness among the members contribute to its operation. In other words, to say that personal concerns may interfere with the operation of an organization does not mean that all interpersonal relations on the job will become impersonal in nature. In fact there is evidence that extreme impersonality may detract from the operation of an organization. (cf. Merton, 1957; Blau, 1955:75ff.)

If impersonality is not intrinsic to all formal organization, and if it can be disadvantageous as well, then the ideal-typical model must be modified accordingly. The conditions under which impersonality will develop must be specified, as well as the consequences it will have when it does occur. In particular, the variable size must be considered, since it appears clearly related to the degree of impersonality in organizations (cf. Rushing, 1966; Hall *et al.,* 1967). The small size of the school system probably contributes to the close connections among expertise, control, authority and legitimacy. Future research should also take into consideration the type of technology employed, since, as Perrow (1967) has pointed out, technology (even in schools) is an important determinant of organizational structure and behavior (see also Harvey, 1968).

SUMMARY

The close relationships among expertise, control, authority and legitimacy reported here generally substantiate Weber's characterization of bureaucratic organization. In exploring the implications of the findings, however, it is suggested that several modifications of Weber's model are in order. In particular the size, type, degree of impersonality and technology of the organization must be taken into account. What is particularly brought into question is Weber's reasoning concerning the roles of organizational knowledge and impersonality in organizations. Organizational knowledge does not play a crucial role in the distribution of control, and the lack of impersonality apparently contributed to the close relationships among organizational variables. Ironically, this suggests that social-psychological propositions derived from Weber's model may be more applicable to small, cohesive organizations than to large, impersonal ones. In larger organizations of different types, different results might be expected, so that different conclusions about the utility of the ideal-typical model would be reached. This of course remains to be seen.

NOTES

1. Notably, exchange theory (Blau, 1955:137–142, 1964; Homans, 1961), human relations theory (Homans, 1961; Whyte, 1961), and psychological theory (Homans, 1961; Argyris, 1957).

2. Put another way, since the assumption is made that organized collective activity requires a predictable and recognized decision-making process, it follows that organizations will face the task of ensuring that control and authority will be exercised by the same individuals. Whether this result is achieved through coercive power, through manipulation, through charismatic leadership, through formalization of the structure

or through consensus will in turn be determined by the organization's technology, its size, its major activity, its goals, its clientele, etc. In the Weberian model, the correspondence between authority and control will be achieved by means of the rational utilization and allocation of expertise and by legitimacy.

3. By a strict interpretation of Weber, it can be argued that a close relationship among these variables is the defining characteristic of bureaucracy. Stated this way, the basic proposition is tautological. It is more fruitful to treat the statement as a complex hypothesis and attempt to determine the conditions under which it is in fact confirmed. The present formulation of Weber's model may be unconvincing to sociologists who are accustomed to treating his analysis as a distinctly "structural" one. This is not the place to determine what Weber "really" meant in his analysis; the point is that the present analysis proceeds from a useful interpretation of Weber. A similar conceptual scheme has been applied to small group analysis by Hopkins (1964; see Zetterberg's discussion, 1965:90–92).

4. Also relevant here is Weber's (1947:124) discussion of the "validity" of a social order: the recognition that maxims are binding on the actor or constitute a desirable model for him to follow.

5. Although authority is nominally defined in terms of the exercise of imperative control, individuals do not possess authority; rather they have the right to issue commands because of their occupancy of a position which is defined in terms of the authority which goes along with it. In Weber's (1947:328) words, "In the case of legal authority, obedience is owed to the legally established impersonal order. It extends to the persons exercising the authority of office under it only by virtue of the formal legality of their commands and only within the scope of authority of the office."

6. As Weber recognized, persons who do not occupy positions of authority or who do not possess the requisite technical and organizational knowledge can sometimes "illegitimately" monopolize information which is essential to the organization. By doing this they can achieve a degree of influence over organizational functioning which is not in keeping with their official position. Whenever such a situation occurs, we can expect that it will affect the relationship between official authority and actual control, since those with the right to control will not in every instance be seen as "legitimate" by other members of the organization.

7. As Weber used it, the term "legitimacy" can be applied to the organizational structure, to the system of rules, to specific decisions and to individuals. Weber implied that these different types of legitimacy would occur together. This is an assumption which should be subjected to an independent test.

8. This disparity is noted in most case studies of organizations, including those not clearly functional in orientation (see Karsh and Siegman, 1964; Bensman and Gerver, 1963; McCleery, 1960; for general statements on such discrepancies resulting from "staff-line" conflicts, see Dalton, 1950; Etzioni, 1964:75ff.).

9. Also generally unrecognized is the possibility that whatever relationship between authority and control exists in a given organization has evolved quite naturally through the organization's career. Any observed departure from a correspondence between authority and control is usually interpreted as a "deviant" breakdown in formal control mechanisms. It may be that some organizations are moving toward a correspondence between the two, or that formal control mechanisms are simply not salient for much of the organization's operation.

10. Since Udy's findings were based on a sample of organizations engaged in the production of material goods in nonindustrial societies, his research does not alone constitute an adequate test of Weber's model, as it is not clear if the model was intended to apply to organizations in non-industrial settings. Conversely, Udy's findings may not be applicable to organizations in modern industrial societies.

11. Because its members chose not to participate, the public high school was excluded from the study. It could be that excluding these personnel produces an incomplete picture of the distributions of expertise, control, authority and legitimacy in the system, although the connections among these variables among those who responded will be accurately reflected. Secretarial and janitorial personnel were also excluded while nurses, counselors, librarians, etc., were included. The findings which are offered should be read with these qualifications in mind, since the structural context of the school system is less than complete.

12. Of the 75 members included in the study, 30 received "*0 or 1*" choice, 30 received "*2 or 3*" choices, and the remaining 15 received "*4 or more*" choices.

13. In response to the question measuring control, the 75 members of the school system exercised a total of 255 choices; of these, 243 (95.3 per cent) were directed toward those in positions of authority, while only 12 choices (4.7 per cent) were directed toward those not in positions of authority. Scores for principals range from 6 to 20 choices each (representing from 82 per cent to 100 per cent of the total number of choices each could receive from the members of his own school). The other 3 administrators received 68, 45 and 52 choices each (representing 91 per cent, 61 per cent, and 70 per cent of the possible number of choices each could receive). For a discussion of this and other clarifying information see Miller (1968:60–63).

14. Seven out of 8 of those with authority report having graduate degrees, whereas the majority of those without authority report having only bachelor's degrees. Similarly, 7 out of 8 of those with authority report 18 or more years of schooling, whereas only one-third of the non-administrators fall into this category.

15. See note 13.

16. "Work contacts" refers to the total number of times each person was named in response to the communications checklist, one item of which was used to measure organizational knowledge. "Friendship" refers to the number of times a person was named in response to the question "Who are your close friends in the organization?"

17. The distinction between "normative," "coercive" and "utilitarian" organizations is discussed in detail by Etzioni (1961b).

18. For descriptions of such situations see Karsh and Siegman (1964) and McCleery (1960).

19. The correlation between organizational knowledge and control in Table 1 (.58) could be a spurious product of high correlations between position and control (1.00) and between position and organizational knowledge (.76). There is some evidence of this: 5 of the 8 persons with authority received 4 or more information contacts, while none of the "unofficial control figures" received 4 or more contacts. This indicates that the scores of those with official control contribute more heavily than those of unofficial control figures to the relationship between organizational knowledge and control.

20. The fact that the school system is located in a university town no doubt contributes to the fact that most of the members have advanced academic training. The evidence in this school system contrasts with Etzioni's (1964:87–88) statement that professionals in school systems have on the average "well below five years of professional training."

21. Seven of 8 people with unofficial control (88 per cent) report graduate degrees, while among all nonadministrators only 23 of the 62 who reported degrees (37 per cent) have graduate degrees. Unofficial control figures received on the average 4.9 prestige choices, compared to 1.8 for all nonadministrators and 19.8 for administrators.

22. It is probably true in normative organizations that relatively little exercise of control or power is required, since the organizational strategy is to permit a wide range of autonomy for the personnel. Therefore the distribution of control is probably not as salient as in other types of organization.

23. This argument of course leaves the source of organizational knowledge unexplained. An alternative argument is that organizational knowledge is related to friendship because those with access to information have such access because they come into intimate contact with more people. In this case friendship would be the determinant of organizational knowledge. In the absence of information about the *content* of organizational knowledge it cannot definitely be determined which of these arguments is correct (whether organizational knowledge is likely to be the product or the source of friendship and prestige).

24. The method by which this has been accomplished is acceptable to the members of the organization, if we judge by the fact that the vast majority of them are satisfied with various aspects of their jobs and are convinced that their activities are understood and judged important by their supervisors as well as by their co-workers. For a more complete discussion of the level of job satisfaction and perceived work importance, see Miller (1968:75–76).

REFERENCES

Argyris, C. "The Individual and Organization: Some Problems of Mutual Adjustment." *Administrative Science Quarterly,* 2(June, 1957), pp. 1–24.

Becker, H. S. "The Teacher in the Authority System of the Public School." Pp. 243–251 in Amatai Etzioni (ed.), *Complex Organizations: A Sociological Reader.* New York: Holt, Rinehart & Winston, 1961.

Bendix, R. "Bureaucracy and the Problem of Power." *Public Administration Review,* 5(Summer, 1945), pp. 194–209.

———. "Bureaucracy: The Problem and its Setting." *American Sociological Review,* 12(October, 1947), pp. 493–507.

———. *Max Weber: An Intellectual Portrait.* New York: Doubleday, 1962.

Bensman, J., and I. Gerver. "Crime and Punishment in the Factory." *American Sociological Review,* 28(August, 1963), pp. 588–599.

Blau, P. M. *The Dynamics of Bureaucracy.* Chicago: University of Chicago Press, 1955.

———. *Bureaucracy in Modern Society.* New York: Random House, 1956.

———. "Formal Organizations: Dimensions of Analysis." *American Journal of Sociology,* 63(July, 1957), pp. 401–414.

———. "Structural Effects." *American Sociological Review,* 25(April, 1960), pp. 178–193.

———. *Exchange and Power in Social Life.* New York: Wiley, 1964.

Blau, P. M., and R. Scott. *Formal Organizations.* San Francisco: Chandler, 1962.

Dahrendorf, R. *Class and Class Conflict in Industrial Society.* Stanford: Stanford University Press, 1959.

Dalton, M. "Conflicts Between Staff and Line Managerial Officers." *American Sociological Review,* 15(June, 1950), pp. 342–351.

Etzioni, A. "Organization and Society." Pp. 257–340 in Amitai Etzioni (ed.), *Complex Organizations: A Sociological Reader.* New York: Holt, Rinehart & Winston, 1961a.

———. *A Comparative Analysis of Complex Organizations.* New York: Free Press, 1961b.

———. *Modern Organizations.* Englewood Cliffs, N.J.: Prentice-Hall. 1964.

Goodman, L. A., and W. H. Kruskal. "Measures of Association for Cross-Classifications." *Journal of the American Statistical Association,* 49(December, 1954), pp. 732–764.

Gouldner, A. W. *Patterns of Industrial Bureaucracy.* Glencoe: Free Press, 1954.

Hall, R. H. "The Concept of Bureaucracy: An Empirical Assessment." *American Journal of Sociology,* 69(July, 1963), pp. 32–40.

Hall, R. H., N. J. Johnson, and J. E. Haas. "Organizational Size, Complexity and Formalization." *American Sociological Review,* 32(December, 1967), pp. 903–912.

Harvey, E. "Technology and the Structure of Organizations." *American Sociological Review,* 33(April, 1968), pp. 247–259.

Homans, G. C. *Social Behavior: Its Elementary Forms.* New York: Harcourt, Brace & World, 1961.

Hopkins, T. K. *The Exercise of Influence in Small Groups.* Totowa: Bedminster Press, 1964.

Jacobson, E., and S. E. Seashore. "Communication Practices in Complex Organizations." *Journal of Social Issues,* 7(March, 1951), pp. 28–40.

Karsh, B., and J. Siegman. "Functions of Ignorance in Introducing Automation." *Social Problems,* 12(Fall, 1964), pp. 141–150.

Lehman, E. W. "Toward a Macrosociology of Power." *American Sociological Review,* 34(August, 1969), pp. 453–465.

McCleery, R. "Communications Patterns as Bases of Authority and Power." *Social Science Research Pamphlet,* 15(March, 1960), pp. 49–77.

Merton, R. K. "Bureaucratic Structure and Personality." Pp. 195–206 in Robert K. Merton, *Social Theory and Social Structure.* New York: Free Press, 1957.

Miller, J. P. "Relations among Patterns of Expertise, Authority, Control and Legitimacy in Weber's Model of Bureaucracy." Unpublished Ph.D. dissertation, Washington State University, 1968.

Perrow, C. "A Framework for the Comparative Analysis of Complex Organizations." *American Sociological Review,* 32(April, 1967), pp. 194–209.

Rushing, W. A. "Organizational Rules and Surveillance: Propositions in Comparative Organizational Analysis." *Administrative Science Quarterly,* 10(March, 1966), pp. 423–443.

Selznick, P. "Foundations of the Theory of Organization." *American Sociological Review,* 13(February, 1948), pp. 25–35.

Udy, S. H., Jr. " 'Bureaucracy' and 'Rationality' in Weber's Organizational Theory: An Empirical Study." *American Sociological Review,* 24(December, 1959), pp. 791–795.

Weber, M. *The Theory of Social and Economic Organization.* New York: Oxford University Press, 1947.

Whyte, W. F. *Men at Work.* Homewood, Illinois: Dorsey Press, 1961.

Wolin, S. S. "A Critique of Organizational Theories." Pp. 133–149 in Amitai Etzioni (ed.), *A Sociological Reader on Complex Organizations.* New York: Holt, Rinehart & Winston, 1969.

Zetterberg, H. L. *On Theory and Verification in Sociology.* Totowa: Bedminster Press, 1965.

17.   BRUCE S. COOPER

Organizational Survival: A Comparative Case of Seven American "Free Schools"

It is curious that so few schools with so few students[1] could attract so much scholarly attention. Perhaps one explanation for this interest is that these radical alternative schools appear to defy our sense of logic about how organizations function: they seem to challenge our view that without defined structure, goals and procedures, organizations cannot survive. They stimulate renewed speculation and theorizing about how small organizations begin, develop and function. In this article we shall present a new way of looking at school organization, refined through efforts to understand why some free schools have grown and flourished while others have floundered and closed.

Our inquiry took us initially to some one hundred free schools in the United States; from this sample we selected seven private alternative programs for intensive investigation. Four had failed; three were still functioning. Of the seven, three were for elementary school children, three for high schoolers, and one for junior high pupils (see Table 1 for a summary description of sample schools).[2]

In many respects the seven sample programs were typical of these new-wave schools: they were *small,* averaging about thirty students; they *charged tuition,* about $500 a year; and they practiced a form of *open, libertarian education* associated with the "free school movement (for an excellent discussion of the philosophy of free schools, see Graubard, 1972: chs. 3, 4).

RESEARCH DESIGN

Comparative case histories of seven programs were compiled through interviews, observations, and examinations of documents. These accounts were *in depth, inclusive* of relevant groups inside and outside the schools, and *longitudinal* from school inception to the time they closed or data collection ceased in June, 1972.

Reprinted in abridged form from *Education and Urban Society,* 5 (August, 1973), pp. 487–508, by permission of the author and Sage Publications, Inc.

TABLE 1

Summary of Seven Sample School Characteristics, as of June 1972

School Name	Type	Aver. Size Per Year	Location	Staff Per Yr.	Years Open	Yearly Tuition
Defunct:						
Group	Elementary	20	Inner-city	4	None	$500
Walden Pond	Secondary	25	Small city	4	1 only	$500
Cooperative	Jr. high	13	Inner-city	2	3 only	$600
Family	Elementary	40	Inner-city	5	2 only	$600
Continuing:						
Green Earth	Elementary	20	Small city	3	3+	$500
Collegetown Community	High school	55	Small city	9	3+	$500
County Community	High school	45	Suburban	4	3+	$600
Overall average		31		4.4	2.1	$542.86

It became apparent that existing organizational theory was too narrow in focus and too static in approach. "It is useless to try to explain change," Theodor Lowi asserts, "with the precise variables and patterns with which we explain persistence." The solution is to concentrate upon the "process of *forming* groups rather than that of *formed* groups, and then to look at phenomena of change rather than at phenomena of maintenance" (see Lowi, 1971: 34–35, italics added). To broaden our focus and capture the fluidity of free school development, we extended our theoretic considerations to include not only formed organizations but "social movements" and "small groups" as well. Our contention is that free schools start as *movements,* become defined *groups,* then *organizations,* and finally, if they survive, *institutions.*

Let us spell out these four phases briefly:

(1) Activities surrounding the formation of a free school most closely resemble *social movement behavior,* as described by analysts like Herbert Blumer. Earliest behaviors "take the form of groping and un-coordinated efforts," he begins:

They have only a general direction, toward which they move in a slow, halting, yet persistent fashion. As movements they are unorganized, with neither established leadership nor recognized membership, and little guidance and control (Blumer, 1951: 202).

Perhaps we are splitting hairs, but while traditional (e.g., Weberian) organizational theory would see early free school efforts as chaotic organizational behavior, we are comforted somehow understanding them as organized chaos!

(2) Once school boundaries are established and membership defined, these programs function as *small groups* with an emergent status system, often charismatic in nature, and with some level of shared expectations. Furthermore, Herbert Thelen (1954: 229) explains,

> There is a sense of shared purpose among members. The members can state some "reasons" for their being a group, and the reasons include a concept of something being striven for, some advantage to be gained through mutual effort [for an extensive examination of theories of small groups, see Shaw, 1971].

At the culmination of the "group" phase of growth, these schools turn their attention from mostly interpersonal concerns to more instrumental emphases —directly toward opening the school.

(3) The *organizational phase* begins with differentiation of roles—as between older people functioning as "staff" and younger ones called "pupils." Often support is lent by "parents" in raising funds, constructing materials, recruiting members, and so on (for an overview of roles in schools, see Bidwell, 1964).

Though there is routinization of procedures and impersonalization of communication, these developments during the third phase must be seen in light of the "movement" and "group" stages that precede it. Some schools seem to survive with little bureaucratic structure due perhaps to size and close interpersonal relations established during the "group" phase; others collapse even with a division of labor, hierarchical structure, and regularized functions.

(4) And if the school survives the passage of several generations of members and succession of leaders, it could reach the final stage of growth, which we have called the *institutional* phase.[3]

Underlying these four stages of development is a set of assumptions about how collectivities change. We assert that *just as human beings individually pass through life stages, so do human groups.* Many of men's and women's lifelong problems seem to appear and repeat themselves in collective life.[4] Psychotherapist Erik H. Erikson describes "eight ages of man (for social scientist's use of Erikson's eight stages, see Torbet, 1972). Following Birth, the individual sequentially seeks to develop, according to Erikson, the components of "mental vitality": "Trust," "Autonomy," "Initiative," "Industry," "Identity," "Intimacy," "Generativity" and "Integrity" (for a full discussion of the eight stages of human growth, see Erikson, 1959, 1950a: ch. 7, 1950b: 91–207). These psycho-social aspects of human life are useful in analyzing the activities and dynamics of collective life as well.

Movements are born,[5] often in a context of broader societal difficulties.[6] Based on varying levels of *Trust,* members join together in hopes of changing their life chances.[7] In young children, the development of "basic trust" is the foundation for future ego growth, Erikson (1950b: 96–107) explains (see Figure 1).

As participants in a collective enterprise realize that they share a sense of commonality and trust with their associates, movement chaos subsides and *group* behavior begins. A primary activity for all new groups is the establishment of boundaries differentiating those inside from those outside (for discussion of the formation and transformation of activist groups in society, see Zald and Ash, 1966). Group *Autonomy* is analogous to efforts by young children to define their own being in relation to their families. As Erikson (1950b: 114) explains, "The stage of autonomy, of course, deserves particular attention, for in it is played out the first emancipation, namely, from the mother." Once Autonomy has been established—for groups as well as children—these entities can begin to assert themselves, a dynamic Erikson has called *Initiative.* For groups, Initiative involves the delineation of roles and the assignation of tasks. For children, Initiative means that they learn to "move around more freely," perfect their "sense of language," and "comprehend possible future roles" (Erikson, 1950b: 116–117).

In turn, Initiative prepares individuals as they mature for more organized

FIGURE 1

The Psycho-Organizational Paradigm

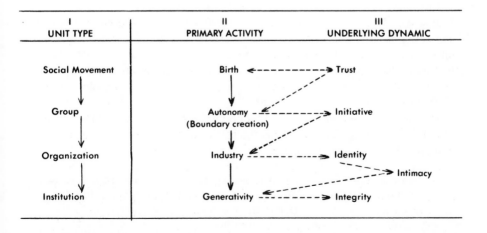

activities which we have called *Industry;* fledgling *organizations* likewise are characterized by high levels of industriousness as their goals are enacted. "This is socially a most decisive stage," Erikson (1950b: 126) declares:

> Since industry involves doing things beside and with others, a first sense of division of labor and of differential opportunity—that is, a sense of the *technological ethos* of a culture—develops at this time. . . . This is the lasting basis for co-operative participation in productive adult life.

For a new organization like these free schools, the ordering of roles and functions enables the program to be carried out.

Continued interaction leads to a developing sense of member *Identity,* that feeling of allegiance to the efforts of the organization. Similarly young people strive to understand themselves in relation to others and to the tasks of adulthood ahead. "The growing and developing youths," explains Erikson (1950a: 261)

> faced with this physiological revolution within them, and with tangible adult tasks ahead of them, are now primarily concerned with what they feel they are, and with the question of how to connect the roles and skills cultivated earlier with the occupational prototypes of the day.

Free schools too confront the problems of balancing the internal needs of the organization with the demands of the society around them. Taxes and rent must be paid, parents satisfied and the city and county inspectors ameliorated, while at the same time freedom and individuality of staff and students must be considered. Collective Identity means somehow holding on to the uniqueness of the program while accommodating the practical demands of the society.

Just as the next dynamic *Intimacy* prepares the adult for parenthood and lasting social commitments, so too in organizations does Intimacy become, according to Erikson (1950b: 137), "the guardian of that elusive and yet all-pervasive power of cultural and personal style which binds into a 'way of life' the affiliations of competition and co-operation. Only through the warmth and influence of the socialization process can the *institution* regenerate itself and continue to exist."

As though to adumbrate the Psycho-Organizational Paradigm, Erikson (1950b: 139; italics added) explains the role of institutions in the processes of *generativity:*

> As to the institutions which reinforce generativity and safeguard it, one can only say that all institutions by their very nature codify the ethics of generative succession. *Generativity is itself a driving power in human organizations.* And the stages of childhood and adulthood are a system of generation and regeneration to which institutions such as shared

households and divided labor strive to give continuity. Thus the basic strengths enumerated here and the essentials of an organized human community have evolved together as an attempt to establish a set of proven methods and a fund of traditional reassurances which enables each generation to meet the needs of the next in relative independence from personal differences and changing conditions.

Thus through activities of generativity, an institution passes on its message while at the same time reassuring individual members of their role in the collectivity.

Finally, in old age, a person can look back over the past, finding a sense of pride and integrity in his/her accomplishments. Institutions face a similar situation: without a positive feeling about its past, the institution will be unable to convey a sense of meaning "faithful to the image-bearers of the past" (Erikson, 1950b: 139) and will lose the loyalty of new generations of participants. Splinter groups may emerge, often resembling *social movements* in their zeal and behaviors—and the cycle of collective life will begin again.

RESULTS: THE SCHOOLS AND THE PARADIGM

The case histories of the sample schools present a range of survival problems which illustrate the Psycho-Organizational Paradigm. Application required that we transform these psycho-social concepts into operational measures of school unit behavior, a task too involved to present here. Rather we shall allude to ways of finding proxy measures for such vague concepts as "Autonomy" and "Identity" as we present brief sketches of the four defunct and three surviving free schools.

(a) Group School illustrates the particular difficulties involved with opening a free school (for a discussion of how other free schools started, see Graubard, 1972: 46–64; Cooper, 1972, 1971: 36–48; Kozol, 1972: 1–6; Rasberry and Greenway, 1972, 1970: 11–24). Though a group of would-be teachers calling themselves the "teachers' collective" met for over six months, they were unable to recruit enough interested parents and the school never opened. About 25 different families came to one or more meetings, but there was little on which to build the necessary trust and little developed. As one teacher explained:

> We really didn't know many families in the neighborhood. When parents came to meetings, they didn't know us and they didn't know one another. It was rough. We had hoped that our "teacher collective" could negotiate with the parents for the kind of program we all would like. But the parents never really formed a group.[8]

A parent explained:

> We found out about the school from the newspaper. The other parents were not former acquaintances and the staff were not together. First they said for us to make decisions and the next meeting we learn that they'd already decided. It was a mess. We never had the same group show up two weeks in a row; so we were afraid to make decisions for those not around. In June and July, it seemed that everyone was going on vacation.[9]

Records of meetings indicate a high member turnover; minutes show that because the group never stabilized, tasks could not be carried out.

To rephrase in terms of the paradigm, Group School was "born" through the efforts of a group of staff who had no basis for local recruitment. Hence when families came, they came as lone individuals, without the intrastructure on which trust is based. Since the group never became autonomous and initiative was not possible, the school did not open.

(b) *Walden Pond School,* like Group School, was created by four "teachers" for high school students. At several preliminary meetings, both staff and student turnover was high. When summer came, the vacations interrupted plans for opening the school in September. Finally in July, one of the teachers, a 44-year-old tenured professor, supplied the initiative without group consent and prepared the school to open. He incorporated it, recruited among university families for students, and helped locate staff among some of his graduate students.

When the school opened, the level of trust was low, for many of the ideological concerns had never been discussed. Though the school was functioning as an organization, it had many of the characteristics of small groups. It fought constantly over the thrust of the program: half the students and staff wanted an academic community; the rest wanted a program that was unstructured and nonacademic. These groups, one staff member explained, "became known as the Jack-off's and the Heavies. Neither could agree and when we tried something, it always seemed to fail."[10]

By Christmas the professor quit. "The kids didn't want to do anything interesting," he began. "Besides, I'm too old to hold kids' hands while they experience their adolescent problems."[11] Trying to replace him illustrated the primitive nature of the school's organization. His leadership had been based on his age and rank: there were no mechanisms for legitimizing his successor; and no one was able to become the acknowledged leader. The structure remained entirely flat, with a parent handling the only specialized function, that of "treasurer." But she had no contact with the school itself, handling the tuition collection and payment of bills and salaries by mail.

In July, member identification was low and the level of industry nonexistent.

When staff decided to leave, there were no groups to carry on and the school closed.

(c) Cooperative School was created by three families for their junior high youngsters. Trust was based on long-standing friendship developed over years of working together to improve local public schools. They hired a teacher, located a site, and opened with seven students. The initiative grew out of their former joint activities. Though staff came and went—on an average of three a year for three years—the nuclear family group remained intact, supplying the support structure to find new staff, new facilities (one a year), and new families. The school never grew to more than 13 children, nor more than three staff members at any one time.

Organizationally, Coop School remained simple and personal. The families functioned as an ad hoc "board." The changing staff handled the daily program. Because it remained small—though it tried constantly to find new families—the need for more structure among staff or families was minimal. The major threat to the survival of the program came from the city in which it was located. After neighbors complained, the state's attorney's police raided the school, arresting the adults for "contributing to the delinquency of minors" and the children for being truant.[12] The case was later dropped, though they were harassed year after year for code violations. Finally after three years, the families decided to close the school, rather than start for a fourth time the process of staff recruitment and site location.

(d) Family School by all indicators should have succeeded. It was formed by a highly cohesive group of theatrical families who needed play and babysitting facilities for their preschool children. Trust was based on their shared interests. They located the play group in the theater, taking turns with supervision. As the children grew older, the school program was extended upward to nursery, kindergarten and finally primary school. After the first year, the parents formed a board and hired two teachers, one of whom was the wife of the board president. After four years, the school was divided into a preschool and primary unit with a single board and with about 40 children in each. For the fifth year, the board purchased a storefront and even sent their staff to a summer workshop in "open" education.

Thus levels of industry had accomplished much toward stabilizing the program; group identity was high and there were even signs that with the succession of leaders and members, the school was on its way toward institutionalization. But in September of the fifth year, at a board meeting, the board president—a white radical—wanted to admit some twelve black children and not the twenty whites from the waiting list. A battle ensued, in which he was voted down. The next day, he personally enrolled the children, increasing the size of the school to nearly 70. The storefront became overcrowded and children got hurt. Families withdrew. Finally, as a compromise, the school split into five smaller groups—most of which closed before the year was out. Thus rapid growth overwhelmed the ability of the school to absorb new members.

(e) Green Earth School was also formed by a group of parents, all affiliated with a local university, for their elementary school youngsters. Their intention was to open a British infant school; they agreed on a philosophy and hired a mature teacher to carry it out. But newly recruited families and the teacher herself wanted a looser program than the founders. At a showdown in January of the first year, the founding group was outvoted and it left, reducing the size of the school from 26 to 16 students. From that point on, the school had a highly cohesive group of families and has withstood a number of staff changes without major problems.

In terms of the paradigm, Green Earth School was founded by a close group of friends; trust and initiative grew from their already existing relationship. But the admittance of new families and staff with a different educational philosophy renewed the "movement" behavior as the participants attempted to iron out differences. With the showdown and the loss of the minority group, the school became a "staff run" program. For three years, the staff has operated the school, leadership revolving around the "head teacher" with a structured board handling business matters. The division of responsibility has resulted in a high level of industry among members and a strong sense of member identity. With the succession of participants, the processes of intimacy have begun, leading to the beginning of generative succession.

(f) Collegetown Community School was created by the merging of four "alternative" programs for secondary school students. Interested in forming a full-time high school, the new "group" built a sense of autonomy upon the trust already existing in each of the smaller programs. Everyone was already committed to and experienced in some form of "alternative" education. Three of the former units, however, were more "radical" than the fourth, led by a former priest and a 36-year-old public school teacher.

Like Walden Pond School, this school opened without basic philosophical differences being ironed out. The older teacher supplied much of the early initiative without group support and without means for legitimating her leadership. As another staff member explained,

> We purposely left things loose. Anyone who wanted to do things, could. Harriet [the older staff member] liked doing all the busy work and she was really efficient. But once the school really got going, she got tired of doing everything. The other seven staff didn't get up tight when things went haywire. The other staff and the kids were really together.[13]

Halfway through the second semester, Harriet left the school, taking along her own two children and about eight others who were upset by the direction the school had taken.

As an organization, Collegetown Community School evolved toward a strict division of responsibilities: (1) the staff and students had almost total autonomy, with staff as a group hiring new staff; (2) the parents formed a separate corporation called Friends of CCS to finance the school's program and the $55,000 building purchased in the third year. Organizational identity was high, so high, in fact, that new students complained about difficulty "breaking in" to the social structure of the school. Data clearly indicate that the core group of students and staff rarely left (graduated or took new jobs). Thus the processes of socialization (intimacy) were constricted by the cliqueishness of the participants. Consequently, the school was unable for a while to retain new members—a central concern of the budget-minded parents of Friends of CCS. In the fourth year, however, several of the older students (19- and 20-year-olds) left, making way for new leaders. The basic activities of generativity are under way and survival as an institution seems assured.

(g) County Community School was founded by a civil liberties lawyer through his contacts in eight conservative suburban communities. His leadership style was markedly different than founders of the other six sample schools: (1) He located a director, an older, experienced free-school coordinator from another city; (2) he offered this man $16,000 a year; (3) he put up funds for a school building; and (4) he stayed out of the daily operation since he had no children of high school age. Initial trust from member families came from the lawyer's "liberal" image in the suburban area; he supplied the initiative, and parents seemed willing to remain passive during much of the school's existence.

Once the school opened, the director handled all in-school programs, relying on the lawyer to garner support from the parents. The director sat on the board, becoming the only source of information about what was going on in school. As the 45 students and some parents became more disenchanted with the high-handed tactics of the director, they insisted on having representation on the board. Slowly it became apparent that the director was incapable of leading the students; finally late in the second year, he resigned. The lawyer found two candidates for the post in an administrative training program in a nearby university; one took the job.

The school settled into a period of high member industry: parent and student identity rose as the program met member needs. Signs are that the school will survive as the processes of intimacy and generativity continue.

CONCLUSIONS

These short sketches indicate the wide range of developmental problems free schools faced. From these data, we can draw six tentative conclusions.

(1) The problem of "Trust among strangers" is minimized by preexisting

acquaintanceship among members. In the case of these seven schools, the relationship among members was based on a common neighborhood (place) or common membership in other organizations (interests). Data indicate that only 8.6 per cent of free school members resided *outside* the neighborhood or "community" where the school was located. Furthermore, only 21 per cent of the families did not at least know a few other member families when they joined (see Tables 2 and 3). Group School was the exception, with 33 per cent of "interested" families indicating that they knew "no other members" when they attended their first meeting. Walden Pond, Green Earth, and Collegetown Community Schools drew heavily from university-related families in Collegetown; County Community School recruited from a network of "liberal" Democratic families in an essentially "conservative" Republican suburban ring. And Coop School, more than any other, was made up of a small number of close friends.

(2) The time necessary for school Autonomy to emerge (boundary delimitation) is often shortened by unilateral actions of "leaders." Though individual initiative had short-run utility, it may later have been dysfunctional, since schools were opened before differences were worked out and before new members understood the goals of the school's program. Walden Pond, Green Earth, Collegetown Community, and County Community Schools all encountered problems later in their history—a delay of anywhere from four months to seventeen months—because a member in a sense "short-circuited" the group processes of resolving goal differences (see Table 4). Family School's goal disagreement lay dormant for four years, though the problems of "integrating"

TABLE 2

Number and Percentage of Families Residing Outside School "Community"

	Total Families	Number Residing Outside "Community"	Percentage
Group School	15	2	13.3
Walden Pond School	19	1	5.2
Family School	111	11	9.9
Cooperative School	23	4	17.4
Collegetown Community School	81	3	3.6
Green Earth School	41	1	2.0
County Community School	85	0	0.0
Total	375	22	8.6

fee-charging schools with poor and often black children is an inherent problem to all radical schools.

(3) Schools have little ability to contain tensions and pitched ideological battles, endangering member identification and intimacy. Walden Pond and Family Schools, for example, were badly fragmented over issues like "structure" and "integration." Schools, therefore, with lower disparity among member goals (and stronger outside support) will stand a better chance of survival.

(4) During the organizational phase, levels of industry may result in a division of labor between those working in the school and those providing outside support. A clear division may avoid the entanglement of authority and emotions, permitting the program to retain its "free" nature while the business of maintaining the schools is handled dispassionately by those less involved on a daily basis. Collegetown Community School and County Community School seemed most successful in this division; Walden Pond failed because there were no outside structures to support it.

(5) The succession of leadership will be less damaging if there are formed

TABLE 3

Initial Family Acquaintance Structure Among Sample School Recruits

Percentage of Families	Group	Walden Pond	Family	Cooperative	Collegetown Community	Green Earth	County Community	Total %
1. Knew over half before joining	(0) 0	(4) 21.1	(12) 10.81	(15) 65.22	(12) 14.82	(8) 19.51	(6) 7.05	19.61
2. Knew over one-fourth	(0) 0	(2) 10.5	(11) 9.90	(2) 8.69	(17) 20.98	(6) 14.64	(5) 5.88	10.03
3. Knew at least five families	(1) 6.7	(5) 26.4	(24) 21.62	(1) 4.36	(11) 13.58	(6) 14.64	(17) 20.0	15.31
4. Knew two other families	(2) 13.33	(2) 10.5	(21) 18.92	(2) 8.69	(12) 14.82	(4) 9.75	(15) 17.64	13.79
5. Knew only one other family	(7) 46.7	(2) 10.5	(19) 17.12	(2) 8.69	(14) 17.28	(8) 19.51	(24) 28.24	21.11
6. Knew no other members	(5) 33.3	(2) 10.5	(17) 15.32	(0) 0	(11) 13.58	(4) 9.75	(14) 16.48	13.72
7. "Did not know." or "no answer."	(0) 0	(2) 10.5	(7) 6.31	(1) 4.35	(4) 4.94	(5) 12.19	(4) 4.71	6.93
n=	(15)	(19)	(111)	(23)	(81)	(41)	(85)	(375)

TABLE 4

School Problems, Leadership, and Outcomes in Sample Schools

School	"Leader"	Nature of Goal Conflict	Outcome	Time After Opening
Walden Pond	"professor"	Structure v. nonstructure	Professor left	After 4 mos.
Green Earth	A university mother	"Free school" v. British "infant" school	All founders left	After 5 mos.
Family	Board president	Number of black students	School split into 5 "affinity groups"	4 years
Collegetown Community	"Harriet"	Structure and style	Harriet and some students left	17 mos.

groups of members (boards of parents, for example) who can assume leadership in the interim. Failure to fill positions will lead to chaos and organizational regression. Walden Pond and Coop Schools closed because the burden of staff turnover was too great; County Community School, on the other hand made a smooth transition because of the efforts of the board president.

(6) The processes of generativity can occur when organizations have means for acquiring and socializing new members into a stable social unit. County and Collegetown Community Schools, of the seven sample programs, appear to have successfully begun the process of "generative succession" and have good chances of surviving as alternative schools.

These six conclusions are only a small number of possible organizational insights made possible by our studying social collectivities with the same precision with which we treat individual human development. If we are to understand more about social life in complex societies, further research into the creation and development of organizations is necessary.

NOTES

1. Recent estimates based on a national survey indicate that about 400 private "free schools" enroll about 14,000 students nationally. See Cooper (1971).

2. All names, places, and organizations are pseudonyms to protect the confidentiality of data sources.

3. Amitai Etzioni (1964: 3) writes that the term "institution is used in two senses in the literature: it refers to a particular kind of organization *and* to a normative principle that culturally defines behavior such as marriage or property." The literature on social institutions is extensive. See, for example, Eisenstadt (1965: 3–68), Parsons and Smelser (1956), Shils (1961) and Durkheim (1960).

4. The notion that ontogeny recapitulates phylogeny seems applicable here. If each individual from conception relives the history of race, so too might not human collectivities reenact a "birth," "growth" and "maturity" process with many of the same characteristics? For a treatment of history as an analogous process, see Brown (1959). See Freud (1939: 129ff: 1950; see also Rieff, 1954: 430).

5. One analyst has attempted to define the creation of human groups statistically, using the concepts of mass and propinquity which he calls "entitativity." See Campbell (1958).

6. Numerous social scientists have attempted to explain the causes of social movements using such concepts as "structural strain" (Smelser, 1963), "culture drift" (Blumer, 1951: 200ff.) and "the intolerable gap" (Davies, 1962: 8).

7. Davies (1962: 8) has a theory about why major social upheavals occur. Using a J-curve, he posits that "revolutions" occur when social setbacks follow a period of relative improvement. "The crucial factor is the vague or specific fear that ground gained over a long period of time will be quickly lost." See also Heberle (1951).

8. Field notes, May 21, 1972.

9. Field notes, May 13, 1972.

10. Field notes, April 5, 1972.

11. Field notes, April 8, 1972.

12. During the "bust," one volunteer staff member had the wit to turn on a tape recorder. A copy of the tape is in the possession of this writer and provides an interesting drama complete with poetry reading to the police, guitar playing, and some general hysteria.

13. Field notes, June 7, 1972.

REFERENCES

Bidwell, C. E., "The school as a formal organization," pp. 972–975 in J. G. March (ed.), *The Handbook of Organizations.* Chicago: Rand McNally, 1964.

Blumer, H., "Social movements," in A. M. Lee (ed.), *New Outline of the Principles of Sociology.* New York: Barnes & Noble, 1951.

Brown, N. O., *Life Against Death: The Psychoanalytical Meaning of History.* Middletown, Conn.: Wesleyan Univ. Press, 1959.

Campbell, D. T., "Common fate, similarity, and other indices of the status of aggregates of persons as social entities." *Behavioral Sci.,* 2 (1958), pp. 14–25.

Cooper, B. S., "Two Schools," pp. 207–227 in D. A. Erickson and J. D. Donovan (eds.), *The Three R's of Nonpublic Education in Louisiana: Race, Religion, and Region.* Washington, D.C.: President's Commission on School Finance, 1972.

———, *Free and Freedom Schools: A National Survey of Alternative Programs.* Washington, D.C.: President's Commission on School Finance, 1971.

Davies, J. C., "Toward a theory of revolution," *Amer. Soc. Rev.,* 27 (1962).

Durkheim, E., *The Division of Labor.* New York: Free Press, 1960.

Eisenstadt, S., "The study of processes of institutionalization, institutional change, and comparative institutions." Pp. 3–68 in S. Eisenstadt (ed.), *Essays on Comparative Institutions.* New York: Wiley, 1965.

Erikson, E. H. (1959) "Identity and the life cycle." Psych. Issues 1, 1, 1959.

————, *Childhood and Society.* New York: Norton, 1950a.

————, *Identity: Youth and Crisis.* New York: Norton, 1950b.

Etzioni, A., *Modern Organizations.* Englewood Cliffs, N.J.: Prentice-Hall, 1964.

Freud, S., *The Question of Lay Analysis: An Introduction to Psychoanalysis.* New York: W. W. Norton, 1950.

————, *Moses and Monotheism.* New York: Alfred A. Knopf, 1939.

Graubard, A., *Free the Children: Radical Reform and the Free School Movement.* New York: Pantheon Books, 1972.

Heberle, R., *Social Movements.* New York: Appleton-Century-Crofts, 1951.

Kozol, J., *Free Schools.* New York: Houghton Mifflin, 1972.

Lowi, T., *The Politics of Disorder.* New York: Basic Books, 1971.

Parsons, T., and N. J. Smelser, *Economy and Society: A Study in the Integration of Economic and Social Theory.* New York: Free Press, 1956.

Rasberry, S., and R. Greenway, *Starting Your Own High School.* New York: Random House, 1972.

————, *Rasberry Exercises: How to Start Your Own School . . . and Make a Book.* Albion, Calif.: Freestone, 1970.

Rieff, P., "The authority of the past: sickness and society in Freud's thought," *Social Research,* 21 (1954).

Shaw, M. E., *Group Dynamics: The Psychology of Small Group Behavior.* New York: McGraw-Hill, 1971.

Shils, E. A., "Centre and periphery," in *The Logic of Personal Knowledge: Essays Presented to Michael Polanyi on his 70th Birthday.* New York: Free Press, 1961.

Smelser, N. J., *Theory of Collective Behavior.* New York: Free Press, 1963.

Thelen, H. A., *Dynamics of Groups at Work.* Chicago: Univ. of Chicago Press, 1954.

Torbert, W., "Personal and organizational challenges in postbureaucratic life." Paper prepared for the Eastern Psychological Association symposium on youth, April 29, 1972, Boston.

Zald, M. N., and R. Ash, "Social movement organizations: growth, decay, and change," *Social Forces* 44 (1966), pp. 327–341.

18.   MICHAEL D. USDAN

Citizen Participation: Learning From New York City's Mistakes

The New York City educational situation has never been easy to describe. The size and inherent diversity of a system that has some 900 schools, 1,100,000 students, 57,000 teachers, and 3,700 administrators militate against neat generalizations or tidy analyses. The complexity of a school system with a $1.4 billion budget (more than is spent by 26 states to run their entire governmental operation) and more students than all but nine states in the country should require little elaboration. The diversity found in a city as massive and heterogeneous as New York must always be borne in mind. There are few, if any, monolithic power structures to identify as the determiners of policy. Pluralistic decision making is characteristic of New York City. An analysis of the three most visible and significant efforts to strengthen citizen participation in educational decision making, for example, reflects New York City's diversity. These three decentralization experiments, namely, Ocean Hill-Brownsville, I.S. 201, and Two Bridges, have had somewhat different histories despite a somewhat common genesis. The Ocean Hill-Brownsville situation, as we all know, exploded, while the other two situations, remained *relatively* quiescent. Thus even when discussing a specific issue like decentralization, one should exercise the utmost care in articulating judgments that may not be equally applicable throughout an almost indescribably vast and diverse city.

With these significant limitations and the unique complexity of New York City kept firmly in mind, let me attempt to discuss some of the implications for the rest of the country of the New York City experiments in decentralization. Controversial educational issues in New York, as well as issues in other major public policy realms, appear to generate great interest and to elicit much response throughout the country. Many believe, for example, that the contract breakthrough of New York City's United Federation of Teachers in the very early 1960s triggered the burgeoning teacher militancy of recent years. Whether the issue is desegregation, compensatory education or teacher strikes, what happens in New York City is important nationwide news. In addition to its size and obvious economic and cultural prominence, New York's visibility is doubtless maximized by its being the home base of so many of the country's major communications media. Numerous key outlets of the various

Reprinted from *The Urban Review,* 4 (September, 1969), pp. 9–12. By permission of the author and The Academic Press.

news media, papers like the New York *Times,* and important journals are based in New York. Indeed, some observers from other sections of the country refer somewhat critically to New York's dominance of the communications media as a reflection of the powerful "eastern syndrome" which allegedly characterizes American life. In any event, there can be little question but that an issue in New York as significant as the conflict over school decentralization and community control will reverberate throughout the nation and profoundly affect other cities confronted with similar problems.

Although the issues in New York may be more complex and dramatic because of the city's size, countless other urban centers are facing analogous problems as their black populations and student enrollments increase. In essence, the problems of the poor and alienated, whose ranks are so inordinately composed of blacks, are similar in substance, if not in scale, in city after city throughout the nation. These problems, particularly as they have reflected the various thrusts of the civil rights movement, are national in scope and significance and predate by years the more recent demands for decentralization and community control of public education in the cities. The disenchantment of so many blacks with current educational systems is predicated upon years of festering frustration as the promises of equal educational opportunity for their children implicit in the Brown decision of 1954, abortive desegregation plans and platitudinous speeches by public officials have remained unfulfilled. Growing numbers of ghettoized blacks are thus no longer committed to reform of the existing educational structure. They are not only questioning, but are actively and vigorously opposing, its very legitimacy.[1]

The bitter disappointment with the failure of efforts that have been made thus far to desegregate schools or to provide adequate compensatory education has precipitated dramatic changes in the educational demands of numerous blacks. In many cities it is now believed that meaningful reform is impossible to achieve within the existing system and that only community control will provide adequate educational opportunities for black youngsters. Increasingly, efforts to alter existing educational structures are being made by black leaders who are implacably hostile to the white school establishment. These leaders derive their support from community groups which, rightly or wrongly, have lost all confidence in the white leadership's desire to educate their children. These community groups and their vocal spokesmen now reject mere palliatives such as administrative reform and demand a fundamental "redistribution of power in the school system through decentralization and increased community control."[2] In New York City this increasingly strident movement to achieve a "redistribution of power" is symbolized by the drive to permit local communities to elect boards of education with decision-making prerogatives with regard to budget and personnel. It is the issue of personnel that was the immediate cause of the recent conflict.

Some contend that New York is so different from the rest of the country that its conflicts have little relevance to other cities. These skeptics about the national importance of the current controversy over citizen participation in New York City should be reminded of evidence that indicates that protest strategies used in one city are quickly disseminated and often used in other cities. The school boycotts protesting de facto segregation in 1963 and 1964, for example, quickly spread from city to city as the dynamics of the civil rights movement permeated the country with the important goal of desegregating urban schools.

Why, it might be asked, has the issue erupted first and so dramatically in New York City, where the school system has at least attempted to project a *relatively* progressive image in its attempts to mitigate de facto segregation and provide meaningful compensatory education opportunities? Perhaps part of the answer can be derived from the fact that revolutions are more apt to occur the closer people are to achieving their goals. The nation is in the midst of a racial revolution and the drive for school decentralization and community control of education in the cities cannot be detached from this fact of contemporary American life. In other words, what is now happening in New York is not a local aberration but is symptomatic of a national drive for citizen participation that will not be restricted geographically to a single city or region of the country. For example, a group called the Five States Organizing Committee for Community Control has issued strong pronouncements espousing community control of city school systems.[3] Also, legislation proposing community control and independent city school districts was introduced last year not only in New York, but in Massachusetts, Michigan and Kentucky.[4]

Cities throughout America must seek to avoid the volatile and tragic confrontation that erupted in Ocean Hill-Brownsville between community groups and the teachers' union. This confrontation, which was exacerbated by charges and countercharges of white racism and black anti-Semitism, is threatening to destroy the very political and social fabric of the nation's most populous city. A multitude of mistakes were made by all parties involved in the New York confrontation. If other cities do not learn from these mistakes—with statesmanship being exercised by all parties—they may well face the same kind of destructive community-teacher conflict.

In most of our large cities, teacher organizations are becoming more militant and powerful at just the same time that the demands for decentralization and community control escalate. Teacher organizations having grasped power relatively recently are understandably reluctant to jeopardize hard-won benefits and prerogatives. The job security and vested interests of members are of primary importance to teacher groups which have achieved their political leverage through collective bargaining procedures. Efforts to achieve decentralization and community control often are viewed as threats to the organizational power of teacher groups. After all, it is largely the ability to shut down a school system through a strike supported by an overwhelming percentage of a district's teachers that provides a teachers' organization with its political muscle. Many teacher groups fear that decentralization and community control will fragment their political strength by compelling them to negotiate different contracts with different governing boards. The ultimate strength of any large organization, they contend, is in a membership committed to unified action on issues that affect all members of the group. This teacher unity, buttressed by the sanction of the ultimate strike weapon, will be dissipated, it is feared, if city school districts are "balkanized." Some leaders of teacher organizations thus see the decentralization issue as a matter of life and death for their groups and professional ideologies.

One observer has analyzed the strong teacher response to decentralization in New York as follows:

> One reason for the high intensity of the emotions on the part of the teachers in the New York battle against community control is that, in effect, decentralization denies all the assumptions about education that have been held for more than a generation. Theories of teacher selection, qualification, tenure, methods, and curriculum—indeed, the entire professional ideology, is being challenged.
>
> This challenge comes just at a time when the long struggle for teacher recognition seemed to be won. Over the last ten years teachers have acquired, through their unions and increasingly militant teacher associations, substantial influence in educational policy making. Now, suddenly they are faced with a threat of the disintegration of the very system they were coming to control.
>
> They will not yield without a bitter fight, for they were only able to achieve their power taking education out of municipal politics. They see decentralization as a hammer about to smash the protective glass of professional standards which were originally developed as a means of improving the quality of teachers and to allow the system to take in minorities kept out through political interference. Now it is the same "professionalized" system which appears to be functioning to keep other minorities out.[5]

The very sanctity of the basic concepts of job security and seniority is at stake from the perspective of some non-teacher employee groups. As a result, the struggle in New York City has escalated to include other public employee groups which foresee potential threats to their rights, if teacher employment and assignment is determined not by a negotiated central contract but by community groups. In New York, for example, the state AFL-CIO and New York City's powerful Central Labor Council gave strong support to the United Federation of Teachers in the union's struggle to have the governing board of

Ocean Hill-Brownsville reinstate dismissed teachers. Similar developments are predictable elsewhere, particularly in industrialized states where organized labor is politically potent. John Doar, the former president of the New York City Board of Education, reportedly made the following statement on the seemingly intractable New York City conflict:

> Union concepts of security and seniority were formulated in the period of struggle between company and union. Now the struggle is between the Negroes and the unions. . . . It is our position that a basic conflict exists between labor union concepts and civil rights concepts. Something has to give. . . .[6]

A. H. Raskin, assistant editor of the editorial page of the New York *Times,* summarizes cogently the burgeoning conflict between organized public employees and disadvantaged minorities that exists in New York and that has erupted, or will erupt, in many other communities as well:

> What emerges from the name-calling and back-biting and the political posturing on every side of the municipal labor scene is the certainty of still more strife. The city's public service system is a repository of money and power, the two things the ghetto wants most. Payroll costs take nearly $3.5 billion of New York's $6 billion expense budget. But the undereducated, underequipped people of the slums find their access to that pot of gold blocked by a wall of rules built up over the years to shield those already inside the civil service. The point of these rules, of course, is to ban the spoils system and enshrine merit as the sole test in appointments and promotions. To the job-hungry on the outside wanting in, however, the whole qualifications structure is part of a conspiracy by their white overlords to hold them in colonial subjugation and shut them out of either participation or control of the agencies that have most to do with their daily lives. The white civil servant becomes "the enemy," and the better union protectionism makes his job, the more intense the ghetto's resentment.[7]

In a sense the struggle over the schools may be the first stage of a larger struggle concerning involvement in governmental institutions. In a society that is growing more complex, most public as well as private agencies have become much larger and increasingly bureaucratized. Citizens in a purportedly democratic society have a growing sense of detachment from the governmental institutions that are supposed to respond to their desires and needs. Professional educators, like others in public employ, have become insulated and isolated from the people they purport to serve. A new reform movement to make big government more responsive to citizens seems to be emerging. The detachment of citizens from massive governmental structures is compounded by racial animosities in the cities. We thus find in New York City and elsewhere that new political alignments are taking place. The "good government" forces that in the past supported the civil service reform movement now often support decentralization as a means of buttressing grass roots participatory democracy through community control of the schools. This pro-decentralization coalition of reformers and community groups finds itself opposed by powerfully organized and entrenched public employees who see any change in governmental structure as a threat to their job security.[8] In education, as well as in other policy areas, the basic question may well be: Who will control governmental institutions, the public or the professional?

Assuming that other urban school systems also are confronted with a situation in which their communities and professional staffs are headed on a collision course, what lessons can be learned to avert or at least mitigate some of the harmful byproducts of the New York City's decentralization crisis?

First of all, it is important for educational leaders to recognize that the civil rights movement, the antipoverty program, the growing foundation and university involvement in city problems, the newly created Urban Coalition and other developments of recent years have triggered an irreversible response in the urban ghettos. This response is basically the desire of the poor and particularly the black poor to participate in decisions affecting their lives. The very perceptible political backlash of recent years will not thwart these demands to influence public policy in pivotal areas like education, welfare, housing and employment. The ferment in education is a central component of an even larger societal revolution in which rapid change is inevitable. In New York, for example, civil rights leader Milton Galamison, who just a few years ago was viewed by critics as a militant "outsider" (he was arrested several times for precipitating school boycotts and sit-ins), was appointed by Mayor Lindsay to serve on the Board of Education and was one of its more vocal and influential members until it was reconstituted, with new members, as a result of the recent decentralization legislation.

The bitter conflict over decentralization which permeated New York City need not be replicated in other cities. Philadelphia, Boston, Chicago, Washington and Detroit have launched decentralization experiments without the intense furor that engulfed New York. Political and educational leaders simply failed to plan decentralization adequately in New York. Once community expectations had been aroused, a more specific plan delineating the responsibilities of the experimental governing boards should have been developed and a timetable for implementation adopted. The vacillation of the city's political and educational leadership aggravated the black community's suspicions concerning the school system's commitment to decentralization and improved education. There was an appalling lack of communication, for example, between the New York City Board of Education and the fledgling governing board of Ocean Hill-Brownsville. There were no general guidelines or procedures to follow. Not surprisingly, chaos and confusion ensued. Then, too, there was no basis for day-to-day working relationships between the central board and its staff and their Ocean Hill-Brownsville counterparts. The responsibilities and prerogatives of the new decentralized boards were never delineated explicitly. The unit administrator and the governing board could never be certain of their legal authority on personnel and other issues. The 1968 conflict over teacher transfers had been presaged by the dispute in 1967 over whether the central Board of Education or the governing board had the authority to appoint principals in the district. Much of the intense bitterness might have been averted if from the project's infancy there had been clearer demarcations of responsibility between the Board of Education and the governing board.

There were no attempts to hammer out compromises cooperatively. No efforts were made to involve headquarters staff members from the regular system as the Ocean Hill-Brownsville district came into existence. New York City's powerful central educational bureaucracy, which was to side with the teachers' union in the subsequent showdown, was suspicious of the decentralization experiment from the outset. The fact that no attempt was made either by the Board of Education or the governing board to link the new district with the established ongoing system may have guaranteed that overt conflict would occur.

Some observers contend that meaningful experiments which threaten the status quo are very vulnerable to concentrated and focused opposition when they occur in only one or two places in a vast enterprise. Many critics of the powerful New York City bureaucracy believe that the city's school establishment was able to sabotage decentralization because of the piecemeal approach employed. It may be that educational changes of any magnitude will have to be implemented on an all-or-nothing basis in large cities if they are to succeed against the entrenched and influential establishment.[9] Although the prospect of massive and immediate change in a city the size of New York must be viewed with apprehension because of the meager planning competence in contemporary education, in smaller, less complex, cities the "blitz" strategy may work if some lessons are learned from the somber mistakes made by so many of the parties in New York. For example, advocates of community control in other states should recognize the factors that helped to defeat strong decentralization legislation in New York in 1969. In other major industrialized states supporters of decentralization would do well not to underestimate the backlash that was generated by the controversial tactics of the adherents of community control. The political muscle of the entrenched educational establishment, when closely linked with the goals of organized labor, is difficult to surmount as advocates of decentralization found to their chagrin during the course of the 1969 legislative session in New York.

NOTES

1. For an interesting rationale of the need to restructure fundamentally existing educational institutions see Charles V. Hamilton, "Race and Education: A Search for Legitimacy," in *Harvard Educational Review,* Fall, 1968.

2. Marilyn Gittell, "Urban School Reform in the 1970s," *Education and Urban Society* (November, 1968), p. 11. In this article, Professor Gittell distinguishes between two kinds of urban educational reform. One kind of reform, more traditional in nature, is found in a city like Philadelphia where there is a strong movement for change within the system being led by the superintendent of schools and the president of the board of education. The second type of reform, which is far more prevalent, emanates from non-school leaders who struggle for change from the grass roots level with their community supporters.

3. Five State Organizing Committee for Community Control to the Office of Metropolitan Sub-systems, *Position Statement* (Jan. 25, 1968).

4. Marilyn Gittell, *op. cit.,* p. 12.

5. Wallace Roberts, "The Battle for Urban Schools," *Saturday Review* (November 16, 1968), p. 117.

6. A. H. Raskin, "Why New York Is 'Strike City'," *The New York Times Magazine* (December 22, 1968).

7. *Ibid.,* p. 29.

8. See Stephen Zeluck, "The UFT Strike: Will It Destroy the AFT?" *Phi Delta Kappan* (January, 1969), for one teacher union leader's criticism of the UFT strategy in New York City. Mr. Zeluck deplores the union-community cleavage and the resulting destruction of the UFT's "widely recognized patina of progressiveness." Teacher union and black community symbiosis, he maintains, is essential for the reform of urban education, and the AFT's very survival is predicated upon a "bold and comprehensive alliance with the civil rights movement."

9. For analyses of the entrenched power of the school bureaucracy in New York City see Marilyn Gittell, *Participants and Participation: A Study of School Policy in New York City.* New York: Frederick A. Praeger, 1967; and David Rogers, 110 *Livingston Street.* New York: Random House, 1968.

19.   EDWARD GROSS

Universities as Organization:
A Research Approach

Universities are usually not viewed as formal organizations. The extant literature in the field (Riesman, 1958; Knapp and Goodrich, 1952; Knapp and
Greenbaum, 1953; Barton, 1961a; Corson, 1960; Capen, 1953; Woodburne,
1958) tends to see them in one or both of two major ways: (1) as institutions,
that is, as being concerned with performing something essential for the society,
such as educating the youth, passing on the cultural heritage, providing lines
of upward mobility and the like; (2) as communities, that is, as providing
"homes" or "atmospheres" in which persons may set their own goals, such as
self-fulfillment, the pursuit of truth, the dialogue at the two ends of the log,[1]
and other traditional ivory-tower values. It is those who follow this latter view
who feel disturbed at the "intrusion" of government money into the presumably sacred confines of the university, sacred referring here to the value of
"disinterested pursuit of the truth."

However, neither of these two approaches seems to have told us much about
the university, though they often reveal how professors and administrators in
the university feel. Apart from the sheer paucity of research, our view is that
a part of the reason is that much of what goes on in universities is not "caught"
by either model, though they each explain some things. Perhaps, it was our
judgment, light might be shed on universities by seeing them as organizations.
In so doing, we do not mean to imply that this model should supplant the
others, for a single-minded view of universities as "bureaucracies" (Cf. Stroup,
1966) is as onesided as viewing them only as institutions or only as communities. This paper is an attempt to test the usefulness of an organizational model
in accounting for structural variables in universities.

Reprinted in abridged form from *American Sociological Review,* 33 (August, 1968), pp. 518–
544, by permission of the author and the American Sociological Association.

This research was supported in part by a grant from the U.S. Office of Education. The larger
study, of which this paper is a small part, was carried out by the author and Paul V. Grambsch,
Dean of the School of Business Administration, University of Minnesota.

NATURE OF THE ORGANIZATIONAL MODEL[2]

As Parsons (1960, Chap. 1 and 1961, pp. 38–41) has noted, the distinctive feature of organizations that marks them off from other kinds of social systems is that the problem of goal attainment has primacy over all other problems. It is not the presence of a goal (or goals) as such, since all social systems will have, from time to time, goals of various kinds, but rather that the system's adequacy is judged in terms of its relative success in attaining or moving toward the goal, or its state of "readiness" to move toward or orient itself toward such a goal (Cf. Georgopoulos and Tannenbaum, 1957; Price, 1968). The polar concept is that of "community," illustrated by such systems as a group of friends, a set of colleague peers, a gang or a nuclear family. Such a group may develop goals (attacking another gang, having a baby) but even if it fails in the attainment of those goals, the group does not necessarily break up. It does break up when hostilities or cleavages mean that persons are no longer at home in one another's presence. On the other hand, in organizations, any failure in goal attainment (however much the members may enjoy one another's company) throws the whole system into jeopardy. Of course the use of a systems approach hardly implies any lesser centrality of organizational goals, for it is through goal attainment (or the claim that such is its intent) that the organization translates its inputs into outputs, or at least legitimizes its right to operate and to call on the society for its inputs.

In spite of the central importance of "goal" in organizations, it is surprising how little attention has been given to developing a clear definition of what is meant by "goal" (Simon, 1964). Etzioni (1964:6) defines an organizational goal as "a desired state of affairs which the organization attempts to realize." But this definition immediately raises the question, pointed to by many, of *whose* state of affairs it is that is desired. Theoretically, there could be as many desired states for the organization as there are persons in it, if not more. What appear to be goals from the point of view of the top administrators may not be goals at all from the point of view of those further down.

But even before one can talk about different perceptions of organizational goals, it is essential to distinguish private from organizational goals. A private goal consists of a future state that the individual desires for himself. Such a notion comes close to the psychologist's conception of a motive. This meaning may be distinguished from what a particular person desires *for the organization as a whole* (Cartwright and Zander, 1953:308–311). The latter comes closer to the notion of an organizational goal, although it still consists of something that the particular person wishes and may not at all correspond to the organization's goals. Further, it still leaves open the question of how one is to determine an organization's goals when there are differences of opinion. In a small organization there may not be much difficulty, for there the top man's personal goals for the organization *are* the organization's goals. It is this simplification which made it possible for classical economics to develop the theory of the firm (as a "person") without being concerned much about developing a precise definition of organizational goal which was any different than the goal of the entrepreneur. The firms that the classical economists were talking about were in the main small ones which had essentially no greater problem to solve than decide what price to sell its product at and how many units to produce for the market. Once organizations grow large, one must be concerned with the possibility that there will be many persons in a position to influence the goals of the organization (Cf. Cyert and March, 1963, Chap. 3). In the case of ideological organizations, where personal values coincide, there may be a close correspondence between private goals for the organization and group goals. Yet in general one cannot assume that private and group goals will coincide. In fact in the typical case it is safe to say that they will not. It is consequently necessary to offer a person an inducement to participate (March and Simon, 1958, Chap. 4), so that he attains his personal goal through the group goal of the organization. That is, when the organization attains its group goal, means are provided for taking care of the personal goals of the persons in it so that they will then be motivated to participate. They must be motivated to participate to the extent that they will give up their personal goals (for the moment) for the organization as a whole should these differ from organizational goals. Nevertheless in order to avoid any reification of the concept, it is necessary to emphasize that goals will always exist in the minds of certain persons. That is to say, although an organizational goal is not the same thing as a personal goal nor necessarily the same as the goal that a particular person desires for an organization (as distinct from what he desires for himself), it certainly would seem that one kind of evidence on the nature of organization goals would consist of the statements of particular persons attesting what they thought the organization's goals were.

Thompson and McEwan (1958) and Parsons (1960:17) have attempted to define goals in terms of system linkages. Both have seen a goal as involving some type of output to a larger society. In this sense organizations are always subsystems of larger systems, the goal of one subsystem being a means or input of a different subsystem. In the simplest case the production of automobile batteries is a goal to the firm that manufactures them but will be a means or input to an automobile manufacturing firm. Such an approach has the great value of emphasizing the need to relate organizations to one another and to the surrounding society.[3] Furthermore, when goals are defined in this manner, it becomes clear that those within organizations have only a limited amount of freedom to set the goals of the organization. They will be constrained by what outsiders can be persuaded to accept. On the other hand such an emphasis may tend to underestimate the contribution that rational decision-makers within organizations make in choosing the goals or organizations rather than being limited to the demands of the market.[4] A more serious limitation of the output approach follows from the fact that organizations have a great many outputs, both intended and unintended, many of which will be no different than functions or consequences. It becomes a problem to single out certain kinds of outputs as *the* goals of the organization. The importance of by-products in industrial organizations should alert the investigator to the danger here.

In spite of the strictures we have suggested on the definitions offered thus far, there is no doubt that they all touch on the elements of a definition of goals. Goals will exist in someone's mind and they will involve the relationship between an organization and the situation in which it is implicated.

An important contribution has been made by Etzioni (1964:16–19) in a work in which he criticizes the goal approach to the study of organizations as being too limited. To define an organization solely in terms of its goal and therefore to judge its effectiveness in terms of its degree of success in obtaining that goal is to doom the investigator to disappointment. The "metaphysical pathos" to which Gouldner (1961) has called attention—namely the pessimism of those who see men doomed forever to disappointment in their organizational hopes —Etzioni sees as being due to expecting too much. Few organizations succeed in attaining their goals to the degree that those in them will wish they could be attained. One typically must settle for a good deal less and the leaders of organizations, their hopes high, would seem to be always expecting more than they will ever receive. Rather than seeing these limited results as a consequence of man's inherent limitations or as the basis for a sad romantic lament on man's smallness in the face of his large goals, Etzioni takes the view that the definition itself may be at fault. He compares organizations to electric lights and other types of mechanical equipment which may have very low efficiencies. Much of the energy may be lost in heat. Nevertheless no one expresses great concern but rather compares one mechanical gadget to another and discovers that one may be twice as efficient as another even though it is only 10 per cent efficient, compared to the other which is 5 per cent efficient.

THE PROBLEM OF SUPPORT AND MAINTENANCE

Etzioni's analogy calls attention to a basic fact about organizations of all kinds: no organization can spend all of its energies on goal attainment. At least some of these energies, and perhaps a great deal, must be spent on activities which cannot easily (if at all) be shown to be contributing to goal attainment.

One of the first to point this out was Bales (1958) in his studies of task-oriented small groups under laboratory conditions. He found that two major sets of processes were in operation in these groups. The groups, on being assigned a particular task or goal, would typically begin by giving their attention to the most efficient way of moving towards that goal, which consisted of solutions to various problems which he posed to them. Very early, however, it was discovered that other kinds of activities began to make their appearance. When someone would make a proposal that a given approach be tried, others had to agree, disagree or take no stand, and this activity began to divide the group on the basis of their estimates of the most worthwhile procedures. The consequence of such cleavage was the development of feelings toward one another or toward the solutions proposed, irritation at not having one's own views taken properly into account, as well as ordinary fatigue. It became necessary, Bales found, for the group to stop its goal-directed activity and give some attention to repairing the social damage that was being done as the group attempted to move towards the solution of the problem. A kind of "maintenance" activity was necessary, with certain persons assuming the role of "maintenance engineers," as it were, in giving attention to what Bales came to speak of as "social-emotional" needs. Such needs might be taken care of in a phase manner or in other ways. It has of course been the experience of persons who have worked with conference groups and other kinds of task-oriented groups that some time must always be given to such maintenance activities. For example, all have noticed the tendency of many meetings to begin with informal chit-chat and to end with laughter or other kinds of activities which are related to solidarity or to satisfaction of various kinds of personal needs.

The paradox may be stated as follows: an organization must do more than give attention to goal attainment in order to attain its goals. A useful approach is that suggested by the Parsonian functional imperatives (Parsons, 1961). Whether one is prepared to agree that these and no other imperatives exist, they do represent an attempt, based on Bales' work as a matter of fact, to state a set of conditions necessary for system survival. As such they apply directly to organizations. It is noteworthy that only one of the system imperatives is goal attainment. The names given to the other imperatives are, as is now widely known, adaption, integration, pattern maintenance and tension management. The import of these categories is that a good part of any system's energies must be given over to activities that do not contribute in any direct sense to goal attainment but rather are concerned essentially with maintaining the system itself.[5]

However, it does not carry one far to seek to dispose of such energies as "used up" in a manner analogous to wasted smoke coming out the stack of a steam engine, for such a view is the very one Etzioni is criticizing. It is true that some of the energy of participants is given over to support or maintenance activities. But it is also the case that such activities may, in the minds of participants, still constitute organizational goals in every sense of the term. An example is the problem of what to do with profit or money as a goal of a business. On the one hand, it is hard to imagine a discussion of the goals of a business which could go on for very long without the importance of making money being brought up as, obviously, "why we are in business." However, as Parsons (1960) has pointed out, an organization cannot legitimize its existence in society simply by making money: it must do something for the society, i.e., produce some kind of output which can be exchanged for money (or which can be used as a claim for tax or philanthropic money). In one sense, one could insist that "money" is the means used to buy the inputs necessary to produce the output. On the other hand, one could insist that the output (or product) is the means used to get the money, which is what the enterprise is about to begin with. In our view, Etzioni (1958:309) probably offers the best solution to this dilemma when he defines economic organizations as "those whose primary aim is to produce goods and services, to exchange them, or to organize and manipulate monetary process."

We would generalize his solution to all organizations: money is only one kind of support or maintenance activity. Any support or maintenance activity can be a goal of an organization. For the university, take the case of one activity which we designated (in our research) as a possible organization goal as follows: "Ensure the continued confidence and hence support of those who contribute substantially (other than students and recipients of services) to the finances and other material resource needs of the university." Such a goal may be ranked moderately high in a great many universities, and there may be considerable agreement that it deserves this ranking. Persons may decide that this goal is a moderately important one by statements which they hear, by statements made in the catalogue or other publications of the university, by the activities of certain members of the administration and perhaps by the general concern of the faculty and others to so behave in public situations as to "represent the university" in an honorable manner. Persons who engage in behavior which secures unfavorable public attention may be criticized by their colleagues as threatening the likelihood of attaining this goal. We cannot see any useful purpose served by insisting that this goal is, after all, a *means* which enables the university to then pursue its "output" goals. This is, of course, true but it is no less a goal for all that. Deliberate attention is given to it for the entire university, and the university must move toward it in the same way as it moves toward its goal of giving direct service or teaching students. The same will be true of such possible goals as "making sure that the university is run democratically," "protecting the faculty's right to academic freedom" and even "maintaining the character of the university." Indeed, the claim could be that some obvious goals are only means themselves. For instance, only by producing students with certain skills (a goal) can the university continue to "maintain its character." The latter might be considered the more basic goal.

We think that the reason for possible confusion here is that it is often assumed that only a goal which is reflected in some visible or operationally definable output deserves the name "goal." It is of course true, as Downs (1967) points out, that ideological elements often get so intimately intertwined with organizational goal statements as to make such statements relatively dubious or even useless as operational guides in the definition of organizational procedures. Hence, it is more dependable to look for specific outputs that can be pointed to as evidence of what the organization is really doing, whatever it says it is doing. However, there remain goal activities which are still goals, even though it is difficult to assign or point to outputs. Their goal character is attested by the simple fact that participants talk about them as intentions for the future of the organization, and they go ahead and try to realize those intentions. Whether they succeed often requires, for test, further verbal statements, or perhaps rather vague products, such as "the image of the organization."

In our conceptual work, we speak of goals which admit of clear outputs as "output goals." For the university, these involve the usual goals of teaching, research and community service (further subdivided, as shown below). Those which do not involve clear outputs turn out to be what we speak of as "support goals." These involve a variety of activities designed to help the organization survive in its environment, those activities which ensure that the university is run in desired ways, those designed to ensure motivated participation and those designed to ensure the university's position in the population of universities. Further, we found it useful to list a large number of goals, assuming that all of them would be present at a given university but in differing degrees. The extent of emphasis on given goals would be our measure of the importance of that goal at a university.

DEFINING A UNIVERSITY'S GOALS

A serious problem in studying any organization's goals is that of devising a way of describing them that will avoid the usual tendency of participants to "gloss" their own organization's goals (the confounding of ideological elements, as mentioned above), as well as get some measure of degree of emphasis (rather than the common assumption that something either is or is not an organization goal). For the case of the university, we wanted, furthermore, a measure which was not dependent on specific measurable outputs (which, as

TABLE 1

Sample Goal Question

One of the great issues in American education has to do with the proper aims or goals of the university. The question is: What are we trying to accomplish? Are we trying to prepare people for jobs, to broaden them intellectually, or what? Below we have listed a large number of the more commonly claimed aims, intentions or goals of a university. We would like you to react to each of these in two different ways:

     (1) How important *is* each aim at this university?
     (2) How important *should* the aim be at this university?

	of absolutely top importance	of great importance	of medium importance	of little importance	of no importance	don't know or can't say
Example: to serve as substitute parents Is	☐	☐	☒	☐	☐	☐
Should Be	☐	☐	☐	☐	☒	☐

A person who had marked the alternatives in the manner shown above would be expressing his perception that the aim, intention or goal, "to serve as substitute parents," *is* of medium importance at his university but that he believes it should be of no importance as an aim, intention, or goal of his university. NOTE: "of absolutely top importance" should only be checked if the aim is *so* important that, if it were to be removed, the university would be shaken to its very roots and its character changed in a fundamental way.

noted previously, are only available for some goals). Our solution was the use of the model indicated by the sample question in Table 1.

The special features of this approach are: (1) it does not ask the subject to volunteer a goal statement himself. Hence it is possible to measure degree of consensus on a particular goal statement. Asking the subject to compose a verbal statement invites the "ideological confounding" referred to above. (2) It keeps separate the subject's *perception* of what is from his *feelings* about what should be. It asks the respondents to serve as informants as it were, and tell the investigators how they see the university separately from the question of how they would like it to be. These are not entirely separate, of course, but it was our feeling that degree of consensus would constitute a partial control on such biases. We decided to include a goal only if the standard deviation of the scored perception was less than 1. For over half of the goals we finally used, the standard deviation is actually 0.80 or less. A given respondent may be cut off from opportunities to observe the actual importance of a goal. But not everyone is, and it is a fair assumption that the average is a reasonable estimate of what the goal really is. One can, of course, quote Samuel Johnson's famous remark that an average of the opinions of gossips is still gossip, but we do not believe we are in the presence of gossip. We do not ask for opinions, but for perceptions. In effect, we ask Professor X or Dean Y at the University of A to act as our eyes. We say: "We cannot come to the University of A to check on how you actually spend your time. So we ask you to look for us and give us a report on what you have seen." The procedure can, perhaps, be compared to asking several astronomers each to look through a telescope and then each report what he has seen. We require consensus, not because we are sure that the average is near the truth, but because it is probably closer to the truth than any other estimate.

Finally, the "score" which a given goal received at a university provided us with a measure of the degree of emphasis it receives, whether the outputs are clearly visible or not. In any case, in the last analysis, outputs are not only measures of goals but of *success* in goal realization, a factor which confounds considerations of efficiency and effectiveness in goal measurement.

Through examination of literature on university goals by the investigators and members of the research staff, and through pre-testing among administrators and colleagues at the University of Minnesota, the 47 goal statements listed in Table 2 were secured. They are presented there in the order in which we conceptualized them. On the questionnaire, the descriptive summary statements were not, of course, present, and the goal statements were presented in a random order.

We make no special apology for the length of the list of goals. Indeed it is our belief that the study of organizations has suffered from an over-simple view of goals. Most organizations are characterized as having but one goal and many classifications that are available in the literature are based on such simplified views of organizations. We suggest that one of the reasons that such classifications have not been more helpful is that they describe very little about the organizations that they are meant to comprehend. A goal structure would seem to be more descriptive.

Organizations undoubtedly differ in the complexity of their goal structures, with universities being among the more complex. Yet every organization must grapple with adaptation, management, motivation and positional goals, in addition to its output goals. The university in the United States is probably unique in the number of *output* goals it has, but its support or maintenance goals may not be particularly complex. A manufacturing organization may have a much shorter list of output goals, but perhaps a longer list of support or maintenance goals, depending on any special management problems it may face, difficulties in securing supplies or various forms of competition. At the end, its list of goals might turn out to be quite as long as that faced by a university.

Finally, some might quarrel with the use of the word "goal" to describe support and maintenance activities. Of course, many maintenance and support activities are not organizational goals. By an organizational goal, as stated above, we understand a state of the organization as a whole toward which the organization is moving, as evidenced by statements persons make (intentions) and activities in which they engage. The most obvious organizational goals are,

TABLE 2

University Goals

(A) Output Goals

Output goals are those goals of the university which are reflected, immediately or in the future, in some product, service, skill or orientation which will affect (and is intended to affect) society.

1. *Student-Expressive:* Those goals which are reflected in the attempt to change the student's identity or character in some fundamental way.

1.1 Produce a student who, whatever else may be done to him, has had his intellect cultivated to the maximum.

1.2 Produce a well-rounded student, that is one whose physical, social, moral, intellectual and esthetic potentialities have all been cultivated.

1.3 Make sure the student is permanently affected (in mind and spirit) by the great ideas of the great minds of history.

1.4 Assist students to develop objectivity about themselves and their beliefs and hence examine those beliefs critically.

1.5 Develop the inner character of students so that they can make sound, correct moral choices.

2. *Student-Instrumental:* Those goals which are reflected in the student's being equipped to do something specific for the society into which he will be entering, or to operate in a specific way in that society.

2.1 Prepare students specifically for useful careers.

2.2 Provide the student with skills, attitudes, contacts, and experiences which maximize the likelihood of his occupying a high status in life and a position of leadership in society.

2.3 Train students in methods of scholarship and/or scientific research, and/or creative endeavor.

2.4 Make a good consumer of the student —a person who is elevated culturally, has good taste, and can make good consumption choices.

2.5 Produce a student who is able to perform his citizenship responsibilities effectively.

3. *Research:* Those goals which reflect the dedication to produce new knowledge or solve problems.

3.1 Carry on pure research.

3.2 Carry on applied research.

4. *Direct Service:* Those goals which reflect the provision of services directly to the population outside of the university in any continuing sense (that is, not faculty, full-time students, or its own staffs). These services are provided because the university, as an organization, is better equipped than any other organization to provide these services.

4.1 Provide special training for part-time adult students, through extension courses, special short courses, correspondence courses, etc.

4.2 Assist citizens directly through extension programs, advice, consultation, and the provision of useful or needed facilities and services other than teaching.

4.3 Provide cultural leadership for the community through university-sponsored programs in the arts, public lectures by distinguished persons, athletic events, and other performances, displays or celebrations which present the best of culture, popular or not.

4.4 Serve as a center for the dissemination of new ideas that will change the society, whether those ideas are in science, literature, the arts, or politics.

4.5 Serve as a center for the preservation of the cultural heritage.

(B) Adaptation Goals

Those goals which reflect the need for the organization to come to terms with the environment in which it is located. These revolve about the need to attract students and staff, to finance the enterprise, secure needed resources, and validate the activities of the university with those persons or agencies in a position to affect them.

1. Ensure the continued confidence and hence support of those who contribute substantially (other than students and recipients of services) to the finances and other material resource needs of the university.

2. Ensure the favorable appraisal of those who validate the quality of the programs we offer (validating groups include accrediting bodies, professional societies, scholarly peers at other universities, and respected persons in intellectual or artistic circles).

3. Educate to his utmost capacities every high school graduate who meets basic legal requirements for admission.

4. Accommodate only students of high potential in terms of the specific strengths and emphases of this university.

5. Orient ourselves to the satisfaction of the special needs and problems of the immediate geographical region.

6. Keep costs down as low as possible through more efficient utilization of time, and space, reduction of course duplication, etc.

7. Hold our staff in the face of inducements offered by other universities.

(C) Management Goals

Those goals which reflect decisions on who should run the university, the need to handle conflict, and the establishment of priorities on which output goals are to be given maximum attention.

TABLE 2 (continued)

1. Make sure that salaries, teaching assignments, perquisites and privileges always reflect the contribution that the person involved is making to his own profession or discipline.
2. Involve faculty in the government of the university.
3. Involve students in the government of the university.
4. Make sure the university is run democratically insofar as that is feasible.
5. Keep harmony between departments or divisions of the university when such departments or divisions do not see eye to eye on important matters.
6. Make sure that salaries, teaching assignments, perquisites and privileges always reflect the contribution that the person involved is making to the functioning of this university.
7. Emphasize undergraduate instruction even at the expense of the graduate program.
8. Encourage students to go into graduate work.
9. Make sure the university is run by those selected according to their ability to attain the goals of the university in the most efficient manner possible.
10. Make sure that on *all* important issues (not only curriculum), the will of the full-time faculty shall prevail.

(D) Motivation Goals

Those goals which seek to ensure a high level of satisfaction on the part of staff and students, and which emphasize loyalty to the university as a whole.

1. Protect the faculty's right to academic freedom.
2. Make this a place in which faculty have maximum opportunity to pursue their careers in a manner satisfactory to them by their own criteria.
3. Provide a full round of student activities.
4. Protect and facilitate the students' right to inquire into, investigate, and examine critically any idea or program that they might get interested in.
5. Protect and facilitate the students' right to advocate direct action of a political or social kind, and any attempts on their part to organize efforts to attain political or social goals.
6. Develop loyalty on the part of the faculty and staff to the university, rather than only to their own jobs or professional concerns.
7. Develop greater pride on the part of faculty, staff and students in their university and the things it stands for.

(E) Positional Goals

Goals which serve to help maintain the position of this university in terms of the kind of place it is in comparison to other universities, and in the face of attempts or trends which could change its position.

1. Maintain top quality in all programs we engage in.
2. Maintain top quality in these programs we feel to be especially important (other programs being, of course, up to acceptable standards).
3. Maintain a balanced level of quality across the whole range of programs we engage in.
4. Keep up-to-date and responsive.
5. Increase the prestige of the university or, if you believe it is already extremely high, ensure maintenance of that prestige.
6. Keep this place from becoming something different from what it is now; that is, preserve its peculiar emphases and point of view, its "character."

of course, what we have called "output goals," (making shoes, protecting society from criminals, healing the sick, and so forth), and it is those kinds of goals that the layman has in mind when he speaks of an organization's goals. Yet it is possible for *anything* to become an organizational goal, even such an activity as repairing broken plumbing provided it is conceived of as an organizational problem. For example, if repeated breakdowns occurred to the point where it became one of stated targets for the next year to seek funds to put in a new plumbing system, and if persons were then observed to be moving in the direction of saving money or diverting it to make this possible, then a new organizational goal would have been created. Goals may and do change over time, but *some* kind of adaptation, management, motivation and positional goals will always be present in every organization.

The data on goals were related to a variety of other measures, especially the power structure of universities, as well as materials on university characteristics secured from other documentary sources, as will be described below.

METHODS OF DATA COLLECTION

The original motivation for the research extended beyond the simple desire for reliable knowledge about universities as organizations. As educators ourselves, we were concerned by the oft-made claim that there is a widening gulf in values and interests between academic administrators and members of the faculty. The resentment of the faculty at what they feel is administrators' arrogance in thinking of themselves as the "spokesmen for the university," the general derogation of administration ("He became assistant to the provost and that was the last anyone ever heard of him," "I'm only an administrator temporarily since no one else wanted to do it," or, in the words of one, who, though Dean of Letters and Sciences at the University of Wisconsin at Milwaukee, is definitely not a "former sociologist": "Remember that Dean is a 4-letter word"), and the suspicion that administrators receive generally higher salaries than others are often matched by equally uncomplimentary sentiments from administrators. The latter accuse faculty of being little interested in students, of caring little for the university (inter-university mobility, or the "job offer" being regarded as disloyalty), and of the scarcity of persons willing to serve as "working members of the faculty" (that is, willing to serve on committees concerned with administrative matters). We were interested in how much substance there was to the claims that such fundamental differences existed, how much of it was based on value differences, and positional differences, and how much on differing conceptions of proper role, with the faculty often conceiving of themselves as the "central figures" and the administration as "support," while administrators often conceive of themselves, in the manner of the high school principal, as simply a special kind of member of the faculty.

Because of these interests, we deliberately decided to limit our attention to educational organizations highly likely to exhibit a range of conditions of such conflict and difference. One could find many schools, e.g., a small, church-controlled liberal arts school for men only, in which there may be almost complete consensus on organizational goals and values. Hence, we deliberately excluded all colleges which were dominated by some single point of view or a commitment to a uniform task which is of such a nature as to severely limit the goal variation that can exist. Not included in our original plans, therefore, were church-controlled schools, liberal arts colleges, teacher's colleges and technical training institutions.

Our population consisted of the non-denominational[6] universities in the United States. It is these universities, with their graduate and professional schools, that seemed certain to exhibit the kind of goal variation we were interested in. It is further in this kind of educational institutions that the "support functions" are claimed to have increased greatly and in which administrators are often accused of having attained positions of considerable power. The universities are also distinguished by the importance in them of the graduate school and, for our purposes, a graduate school is necessary to provide assurance that the goal of research will be well represented in the university.

The institutions were selected on the basis of the following criteria:

1. The Ph.D. degree must be granted in at least three of four fields (humanities, biological sciences, physical sciences, and social sciences).

2. Ph.D. degrees granted in the two least emphasized fields must come to 10 per cent or more of the total degrees conferred. This provision was designed to overcome any undue concentration in one field, and thus help insure the kind of diversity of goals that we were interested in.

3. There must be a liberal arts undergraduate school or college with three or more professional schools.

4. The institution must have conferred ten or more degrees during the years 1962–1963. This conservative rule enabled us to keep the number of universities studied to manageable size in view of the large number of new universities that have appeared in recent years.

We secured the data for making the above decisions from *American Colleges and Universities,* ninth edition, 1964 (appendix IV and VI).[7]

It turned out that there were 70 universities defined in this way, and we decided to include all but two of them. The two exceptions were the University of Minnesota and the University of Washington, since these were the home institutions of the investigators. They were excluded because of the involvement of the investigators in them and because the University of Minnesota was used for pretesting purposes. The list of universities turned out to be substantially equivalent to that used by Berelson (1960:280–281), with denominational, technical and starred universities excluded, except for the addition of a small number of universities which have attained university status since the time at which his list was drawn up.

The securing of accurate data on numbers of faculty and administrators at the 68 universities proved to be an exceedingly difficult task, owing to inadequacies of catalogue information (multiple listings, variations in inclusiveness, mixing in of part-time with full-time, problems of "clinical staff," members of institutes, laboratories, and other semi-autonomous portions of universities, overseas branches and so forth), description of duties, date of materials and other problems. We had to telephone university officers and friends at particular universities to secure many of these data. Finally, on the basis of the best information we were able to get, there were, in the spring of 1964 when our study began, the following numbers in the sixty-eight universities: 8,828 administrators and 67,560 faculty. Although the focus of the research was on administrators, we desired a sample of faculty to serve as a basis of comparison, particularly with reference to the question of whether administrators differed, as a group, from faculty, but also to examine differential career patterns, self-conceptions, and other variables not being reported on in this paper. Because of the desire to make rather detailed comparisons among administrators, we attempted to get all of the academic administrators. On the other hand, since we planned only very broad groupings among the faculty (e.g., social sciences, humanities, etc.), we felt that a 10 per cent sample would suffice. Hence, the total number surveyed consisted of 8,828 administrators plus 6,756 faculty members, for a total of 15,584.

The questionnaire was very long (300 questions, requiring a minimum of one and a half hours to fill out, and often—some of the respondents wrote—requiring three hours), and faced the usual problems of mailed questionnaires. A variety of devices was used to stimulate response: (1) the enlistment of the endorsement or assistance of accrediting bodies and professional societies; (2) an earlier study of Deans of Business Administration at 101 universities resulted in offers from approximately one-half of the deans to stimulate interest at their own universities; (3) the president of the University of Minnesota at the time (Meredith Wilson) wrote to all presidents of member universities of the American Association of Universities that fell in our sample (approximately one-half of them) asking for their assistance. In addition, it must be remembered that we were contacting a highly literate, questionnaire-sophisticated group, on a subject of direct, immediate interest to them—their own jobs. It is also a subject, as we have said, on which there are few data of any validity. We therefore offered the *quid pro quo* of a copy of the findings, if desired, or at least the general results which would later be published. (To our dismay we received well over 1,500 requests.) Offsetting such obvious interest is the clear fact that this group is continually the target of surveyors, to the point, we were told by several, that their secretaries had standard instructions to file all questionnaires unless otherwise advised ahead of time. Our final response rate for the entire questionnaire of usable replies was 50.9 per cent for administrators and 40.4 per cent for the faculty. A short form of the questionnaire, dealing only with careers, was sent out to non-respondents. It resulted in a total response rate for that portion of the questionnaire of approximately 76 per cent. A variety of tests was employed to test the likelihood of bias. They left us with confidence that the response group was not appreciably biased at least with reference to dimensions of interest to us. The main reason for the lower than desirable response rate (actually high by usual mail questionnaire standards) appears to be the length of the questionnaire.[8]

MAJOR FINDINGS

The following findings are limited only to the goal analysis, the relationship of goals to the power structure and the implications of those findings for the empirical characterization of universities in organizational terms.

In Table 3, an overall, composite ranking of the 47 goals at all 68 universities is presented. The scores there are based on unweighted means. However, subsequent analyses of the same goals making use of various weights (response rate, treating universities equally, use of single scores for entire university) produce no important shifts in goal position. As presented in Table 3, however, they do reflect the somewhat lower response rate of faculty; that is, they reflect somewhat more the perceptions and views of administrators. The column labelled "is" refers to the ranking of goals on the portion of the question (as illustrated in Table 1) that represented the answers to the "is" row (the respondent's report on his perception of how important the goal in fact is); the column labelled "should," in turn, refers to the ranking in terms of respondent's conception of how important he thought the goal *should* be.

As can be seen, the top goal at the 68 universities is perceived as being that of protecting academic freedom. Furthermore, not only do the respondents see it as in fact the top goal, but they believe that it should be the top goal. As will be shown below, this finding is of the first importance in our ability to characterize universities in organizational terms. It should further be noted that if we had elected to restrict our attention only to the usual output goals (teaching, research, service), we would never have made this discovery since we would not have thought of "protecting academic freedom" as a goal.

TABLE 3

Ranking of the Goals of American Universities

"Is"	Goal	"Should"
1	Acad Freedom	1
2	U Prestige	11
3	Top Qual Imp	7
4	Ensur Confidence	26
5	Keep up to Date	6
6	Train Scholarship	2
7	Pure Research	16
8	Top Qual All	4
9	Mntn Fav Apprsl	34
10	Ensure U Goals	9
11	Dissem Ideas	5
12	Applied Research	30
13	Stud Careers	32
14	Stud Intellect	3
15	Hold Our Staff	18
16	Comm Cult Ldshp	28
17	Stud Inquire	10
18	Encour Grad Wk	27
19	Preserve Heritage	20
20	Stud Good Citzn	14
21	Well Round Stud	17
22	Max Opprtunity	25
23	Stud Objectivity	8
24	Keep Costs Down	35
25	Fac U Govt	19
26	Reward Prof	21
27	Stud Activities	43
28	Stud Success	33
29	Run U Demo	22
30	Affect Stud Perm	15
31	Assist Citizens	36
32	Just Rewd Inst	13
33	Devlp Pride Univ	23
34	Sat Area Needs	42
35	Mntn Bal Qualty	31
36	Will of Fac	24
37	Special Training	38
38	Stud Character	12
39	Educ to Utmost	37
40	Accp Good Stud Only	39
41	Stud Pol Rights	40
42	Devlp Fac Lylty	29
43	Keep Harmony	41
44	Undrgrad Inst	44
45	Stud Univ Govt	46
46	Pres Character	47
47	Stud Taste	45

Paying attention, for the moment, only to the "is" list (that is, the goals as listed on the table), one can characterize the "top" and "bottom" goals by the simple device of ranging the actual average scores in a single distribution, marking the distribution off in standard deviation units (from the overall mean), and asking which goals fell in the top standard deviation (of 6) and which in the bottom.

The *top goals*, then, turn out to be:

1. protect the faculty's right to academic freedom
2. increase the prestige of the university
3. maintain top quality in those programs we feel to be especially important
4. insure the continued confidence and support of those who contribute substantially to the finances and other material resource needs of the university
5. keep up-to-date and responsive
6. train students in methods of scholarship and/or scientific research and/or creative endeavor
7. carry on pure research

At the other end, the *bottom goals* are seen to be:

44. emphasize undergraduate instruction even at the expense of the graduate program
45. involve students in the government of the university
46. keep this place from becoming something different from what it is now
47. make a good consumer of the student

What is most striking about the list of top goals is that practically all of them are what we have called support goals and only one of them in any way involves students. Even that one refers to training students for research or other creative endeavors which is, after all, closely associated with what the professors consider to be important and represents a possible output to them, or to the academic field. This squares with the goal of carrying on pure research, which is also rated very high. The singular scarcity of any emphasis on goals that have anything to do with students is all the more remarkable in view of the fact that of our total of 47 goals among which respondents could choose, 18 involved direct reference to students in some way. Thus there was ample opportunity, and a result so striking as this could hardly have been produced by chance or by a sampling bias.

Supporting this general finding is the fact that students are mentioned more frequently among the goals at the bottom. The goal fourth from very bottom involves undergraduate instruction. This is quite consistent then with the finding that pure research and preparing students for research or creative careers are emphasized as top goals in American universities.

No particular pattern among the support goals is evident among the top goals although three of them are positional (increasing prestige of the university, maintaining top quality in programs felt to be important, and keeping up-to-date and responsive). As a general finding one can say that American universities, taken collectively, emphasize only pure research as an output, but put it seventh to a variety of other goals which are more concerned with the position of one's own university and the programs that it offers and with efforts to maintain a high quality at the university. At the very top they put academic freedom as a goal. Such a goal appears to be of first importance in American universities and refers to the importance in them of autonomy from outside interference of any kind. One must remember also that these findings do not refer to what people think ought to be the case, but rather to their perceptions of the way things are. The administrators and faculty at American universities believe that actually, right now, universities *do* protect the faculty's right to academic freedom more than they do any one of 46 other possibilities.

What Persons Feel the Top and Bottom Goals Ought to Be

We utilized the same procedure in selecting a top and a bottom group—one standard deviation in the distribution of means at the top, and one standard deviation at the bottom. When we did so, we found the following to be those goals that persons felt *ought* to be at the top in the American university:

1. protect the faculty's right to academic freedom
2. train students in methods of scholarship and/or scientific research, and/or creative endeavor
3. produce a student who, whatever else may be done to him, has had his intellect cultivated to the maximum
4. maintain top quality in all programs we engage in
5. serve as a center for the dissemination of new ideas that would change the society, whether those ideas are in science, literature, the arts or politics
6. keep up-to-date and responsive
7. maintain top quality in those programs we feel to be especially important
8. assist students to develop objectivity about themselves and their beliefs and hence examine those beliefs critically

9. make sure the university is run by those selected according to their ability to attain the goals of the university in the most efficient manner possible

On the other hand, those goals felt to belong at the very bottom are:

45. make a good consumer of the student
46. involve students in the government of the university
47. keep this place from becoming something different from what it is now

When we examine this distribution, we see that although students come out a little better, the student goals are far from being prominent. Persons felt that the faculty's right to academic freedom not only was the most important goal (as shown above) but that it ought to be the most important goal. In this list, however, two student goals came in second and third places: one referred to the same goal as had occurred in the previous table (training students in research and related activities); in addition persons felt that the goal dealing with cultivating the student's mind deserved a high amount of emphasis (although it was not perceived as in fact given that emphasis). In other words, respondents' conception of the way things ought to be is different from the way they actually are. In their view more attention should be given to cultivating the student intellect than is in fact being given.

One other student goal also was present in this top group of nine, namely the goal dealing with assisting students to develop objectivity about themselves. This goal, which did not rank high among the goals actually being emphasized, was felt to be one which ought to be emphasized.

At the other end there was a feeling that involving students in the government of the university ought to be of very little importance. It would seem that those students seeking a greater share in decision-making power at the university will not receive much support from administrators and faculty. On the other hand, students might take some consolation from the fact that there is no particularly strong feeling that the faculty should be involved in the government of the university either. In general, then, students as a group are not felt to be particularly important, nor is there any strong feeling that the situation in that respect is different from what it ought to be (with one or two exceptions —training a student in research and cultivating his intellect, and assisting him to develop objectivity about himself). Nor is there evidence, either in what the goals are or what they should be, to suggest that it is an important goal of the university to prepare a student for a useful career, to assist him in upward mobility, to assist him to be a good consumer or to become a good citizen.[9]

Goal Congruence. In the case of seven goals, there is congruence between the actual position and the position that persons feel they ought to be in. Four goals are perceived to be important and our respondents feel they ought to be important. These are:

1. protect the faculty's right to academic freedom
2. maintain top quality in those programs we feel to be especially important
3. keep up-to-date and responsive
4. train students in methods of scholarship and/or scientific research and/or creative endeavor

The following three are at the bottom and our respondents feel that that is where they belong:

1. make a good consumer of the student
2. keep this place from becoming something different from what it is now
3. involve students in the government of the university

On the whole the above is rather impressive evidence that, at least at the top and bottom, there is a fairly strong sentiment that things are the way they ought to be. Four out of the seven top "is" goals and four out of the nine top "should" goals are congruent with one another. Practically all of the goals at the bottom are congruent with one another.

This generally happy[10] situation does not seem to prevail throughout the distribution. One way of examining the lack of general congruence is through "sins of goal commission" and "sins of goal omission." That is we can compare those goals which seem to be out of line with one another on the two scales. For example the goal "to develop loyalty on the part of faculty and staff to the university, rather than to their own jobs or professional concerns" is very low on the list of the way goals are perceived to actually be (being actually sixth from the bottom). On the other hand, when we look at the list of what persons think goals ought to be, we find that this goal is considerably higher up (19th from the bottom). Such goals, which persons feel ought to be given more attention than they are being given ("sins of goal omission") include in order of discrepancy of ranks:

1. produce a student who, whatever else is done to him, has had his intellect cultivated to the maximum
2. make sure that salaries, teaching assignments and perquisites always reflect the contribution that the person involved is making to the functioning of the university

3. assist students to develop objectivity about themselves and their beliefs and hence to examine those beliefs critically
4. make sure the student is permanently affected by the great ideas of the great minds of history
5. develop loyalty on the part of the faculty and staff to the university, rather than to their own jobs or professional concerns

Looking over this list, we see a relative dissatisfaction with goals which tend to be pushed to one side when the personal ambitions and the research careers of the faculty become dominant interest. There seems to be some feeling that top faculty (who are likely to be most mobile) do not have sufficient loyalty to the university. In the second neglected goal, there is probably being expressed a feeling on the part of persons who serve on committees and attempt to do their jobs that they are not sufficiently well recognized. We also see the familiar plaint of the liberal arts person that not enough attention is being given to the student's mind or to the attempt to get the student to develop insight into himself.

The "sins of goal commission" involve goals felt to be emphasized too much. Those goals, in order of discrepancy of ranks, are:

1. insure the favorable appraisal of those who validate the quality of the programs we offer
2. insure the continued confidence and support of those who contribute substantially to the finances and other material resource needs of the university
3. prepare students specifically for useful careers
4. carry on applied research
5. provide a full round of student activities

We see that although providing a full round of student activities is not emphasized as a goal (as we can see again by looking at Table 3), nevertheless there is a feeling that it is emphasized more than it ought to be. In addition persons resent the apparent emphasis on the need to satisfy outside organizations that validate programs. There is similar resistance to what might be construed as pressure from the outside in the emphasis on carrying on applied research. On the whole these are entirely consistent with the emphasis that we have already noticed on academic freedom, and on the needs and the concerns of the faculty and their own professional careers. In addition we note again that the only way in which students come into the picture here is that, while there is a general feeling that not much attention is being paid to them or should be, that in one area at least, mainly providing a full round of student activities, the relatively little attention paid is too much.

GOALS AND GLOBAL VARIABLES

In the attempt to secure further information on the utility of goal characterization as a descriptive component of universities, we sought answers to the question of whether types of universities differed from one another in goal structure. We characterized universities in terms of the following "global"[11] components: type of control (state or private), prestige, degree of emphasis on graduate work, volume of contract research, size (measured in two ways: number of faculty and number of students) and location (regional, and rural vs. urban). Of these the most productive by far of strong relationships were type of control and prestige. The others were considerably less productive (some, in fact, being only productive because they were related to type of control or prestige). Most interestingly size (measured by either of the two indices we used) was found to be almost completely unrelated to any goals.[12] Table 4 is illustrative of the type of analysis summed up in the gammas (Goodman and Kruskal, 1954 and 1963) in the tables which follow. In Table 4, state and private universities are compared with reference to their degree of emphasis on academic freedom. To make this possible, the average score of each university on that goal is calculated, and the scores for all 68 universities arranged in order from low to high. The distribution is then cut into approximate thirds, with each third being labelled "low," "medium" or "high." As can be seen, protecting academic freedom is emphasized as a goal to a markedly greater extent in private than in state universities: over half of private universities fall in the "high" third, whereas almost half of the state universities fall in the "low" third. A quite high gamma indicates that our impression from inspection is supported by that measure of strength of association. Further-

TABLE 4

Illustrative Table Showing Relationship Between Degree of Emphasis on Academic Freedom and Type of Control

	Type of Control		
	State	Private	Total
Low	20	3	23
Medium	13	9	22
High	9	14	23
Total	42	26	68

Gamma=.627.

more, the gamma is significant at the 5 per cent level, as is the case for all the gammas reported in this paper.[13] The number of relationships is, in all cases, far beyond what chance would lead one to expect.

Goals Related to Type of Control

The sample relationship examined in Table 4 deals with the question of whether one goal, protecting academic freedom, is related to type of control (state as compared to private). In Table 5, the findings from the comparison for all goals are presented. The goals are grouped in the categories described above. As can be seen, 24 out of the 47 comparisons made are significantly different in emphasis at the two kinds of university, with gammas as shown.

TABLE 5

Goals Related to Type of Control

Private	Size of Relationship		State	Size of Relationship
	(Gamma)			(Gamma)
		Student-Expressive		
Stud Intellect	(.788)			
Affect Stud Perm	(.784)			
Stud Objectivity	(.741)			
		Student-Instrumental		
Train Scholarship	(.500)		Stud Careers	(.603)
		Direct Service		
Dissem Ideas	(.531)		Assist Citizens	(.837)
		Research		
			Applied Research	(.552)
		Adaptation		
Accp Good Stud Only	(.874)		Educ to Utmost	(.941)
Ensur Confidnce	(.548)		Sat Area Needs	(.718)
			Keep Costs Down	(.626)
		Management		
Encour Grad Wk	(.602)		Keep Harmony	(.688)
			Stud Univ Gvt	(.801)
			Undergrad Inst	(.599)
		Motivation		
Acad Freedom	(.627)		Stud Activities	(.602)
Max Opportunity	(.535)			
Stud Inquire	(.566)			
		Positional		
Keep Up to Date	(.552)			
Pres Character	(.573)			
U Prestige	(.647)			

These gammas are large, suggesting large differences between the goals of private and state universities. In private universities the goals emphasized revolve about student-expressive matters such as the student intellect, affecting the student permanently with the great ideas, and helping the student to develop objectivity about himself (no expressive goals distinguish the state universities at all), training the student in methods of scholarship and creative research, serving as a center for the dissemination of ideas for the surrounding area, and encouraging graduate work. In contrast, state universities emphasize to a distinctly greater extent than the private universities preparing the students for useful careers, assisting citizens through extension and doing applied research. Academic freedom, although it is high everywhere turns out to be particularly high in the private universities reflecting their ability to maintain a greater degree of autonomy. Note that we are not speaking of how persons would like things to be but how they perceive that things actually are. There is also emphasis on the students' right to inquire into, investigate and examine critically any idea or program that they might get interested in, in contrast to state universities, where the emphasis is on involving students in the government of the university and providing a full round of student activities. One sees here a greater degree of responsiveness to students in a direct sense.

The private universities emphasize the needs of the faculty in the form of emphasis on making the university into a place in which faculty have maximum opportunity to pursue their careers in a matter satisfactory to them by their own criteria; they also emphasize the positional goals of keeping up to date, preserving the distinctive character of the university, and increasing or maintaining their prestige.

One of the striking differences is the extent to which the goal of accepting good students only is emphasized in private universities and by contrast the goal of educating to their utmost whoever can get in the state universities. This illustrates the traditional elitist goal of the private university in contrast to the land-grant, service goals of the state university and forms also a validation for the study. We notice also that it is in the state university that there is emphasis on satisfying the needs of the local area and keeping costs down as well as keeping harmony within the university.

On the whole, the data presented here strongly suggest that state and private universities differ from one another in type of goals. The claim of some students of the university that the differences between private and state universities are disappearing, as both respond to public needs and federal research grants, is not supported. Other data, not being reported here, further support this conclusion. Those data make the comparison in terms of power structure, values of faculty and administrators, internal organizational structure, and the backgrounds of personnel.

Goals and University Prestige

The second most "productive" variable was that of "quality." We made use of several measures of "quality": (1) a measure of "reputation with peers," or prestige, (2) a measure based on size and quality of library resources, and (3) a measure based on publications and other creative products of the faculty. All three turn out to be highly related to one another.[14] We shall report on our findings using the first measure only.

That measure was based on data provided for us by the American Council on Education.[15] Essentially, those data involve ratings made by peers of departments that they were familiar with. Our measure makes use of those ratings, weighted by number of areas in which a given university awards the Ph.D.[16]

A high proportion of our goals was found to be significantly related to prestige. It is one of the most distinctive characteristics of a university and may well be the one thing that marks it off from all other kinds of organizations. By this we mean that a university is judged not only in terms of any products that may come out of it (trained students, broadened citizens, solutions to research problems) nor only in terms of some job that it does for the society (socialization of the young, providing cultural leadership, symbolizing societal values), but to a great extent in terms of how it is seen by others. Universities are an excellent example of what Caplow (1964, Chap. 6) has called an "organizational set," in which members watch the members of other units in the set for any sign of a decline or rise in quality. Although it may certainly be questioned whether reputation or prestige is equivalent to "quality," the members of sets believe they can detect it or at least detect any change in it. In that sense, reputation is a measure of perception of quality, if not quality itself. The basic findings are presented in Table 6.

When we look at those universities that are in the top third—universities that might fairly be called the great American universities—we find a distinctive pattern of goals at such universities. They are universities which do emphasize student expressive goals. In them attention is given to producing a student who has had his intellect cultivated to the maximum, who has been permanently affected in mind and spirit by the great ideas of the great minds of history, and who has been assisted to develop objectivity about himself and examine his own beliefs critically. However, the most prestigious universities do not give any more attention than any other universities to producing the well-rounded student, nor to developing the inner character of students. This does not mean that these goals are neglected, but rather that they simply are not given any more special attention than they are given anywhere else. In a

TABLE 6

Prestige and University Goals

Student-Expressive	Gamma
Stud Intellect	0.516
Affect Stud Perm	0.473
Stud Objectivity	0.703
Student-Instrumental	
Stud Taste	—0.553
Train Scholarship	0.730
Stud Careers	—0.504
Direct Service	
Dissem Ideas	0.799
Preserve Heritage	0.651
Assist Citizens	—0.455
Research	
Pure Research	0.891
Adaptation	
Sat Area Needs	—0.628
Keep Costs Down	—0.448
Mntn Fav Apprsl	—0.583
Accp Good Stud Only	0.556
Management	
Encour Grad Wk	0.709
Reward Prof	0.772
Undrgrad Inst	—0.697
Motivation	
Acad Freedom	0.496
Opportunity	0.657
U Prestige	0.691
Top Qual Imp	0.756

sense then one can say that the parent who is interested in having his son's mind cultivated should send him to one of the top prestige universities; if he wants to make sure that he comes out a well-rounded student, then he has the same chance at such a university as he does at any other university. On the whole therefore, this adds up to a resounding vote in favor of the top prestige universities.

Student instrumental goals are not important except in a negative sense. Outside of the predictable goal of training students in scholarship and research, the only instrumental goals that come through are those of making a good consumer of the student and preparing him for a useful career, but these turn out to be correlated negatively with prestige. This means that they are positively de-emphasized in the better universities, which in turn means that they would be emphasized in the poorer universities. Of course this does not mean that there is any necessary causal relationship between preparing students for useful careers, for example, and prestige. A university does not attain top prestige by ignoring the attempt to prepare students for useful careers. On the contrary, we would guess that the top universities simply do not have to worry about the careers of their students, perhaps because of their selectivity of students. (Note that the goal of accepting good students only is positively correlated with prestige, gamma $= 0.556$). On the other hand the fact that there is a negative relationship rather than no relationship at all implies that this goal is always of little importance. Again we emphasize that we are talking about how goals *are* felt to be, not how people at the university feel they ought to be. In these universities in other words both administrators and faculty feel that this is a goal that is positively pushed into the background in comparison to other universities.

There is a similar lack of concern for satisfying a constituency in the negative relationship seen in the direct service goal of assisting citizens and in the adaptation goals of satisfying the area's needs, keeping costs down and maintaining the favorable appraisal of validating groups.

It is striking that the goal of emphasizing undergraduate instruction is negatively correlated (and very highly as can be seen) with prestige, at the same time the student expressive goals are positively related. The inference we would draw is that the student's mind is to be affected in ways other than through undergraduate instruction. The emphasis on pure research as well as other indications suggest to us that student expressive goals are to be reached primarily through encouraging the student to do research, through his exposure to outstanding professors and through his taking charge of a great deal of his education himself.

When we turn to the positive gammas, we see that the great universities are those concerned with disseminating new ideas, preserving the cultural heritage, training people in scholarship and research, doing pure research, encouraging graduate study, seeing to it that professors are rewarded according to their contribution to their disciplines, protecting academic freedom and providing a maximum opportunity for professors to develop in ways that they think they should develop, insisting on a student's right to inquire into things that interest him, and in most of the position goals (keeping up to date, maintaining quality in all things, and maintaining or increasing the prestige of the institution). This last would lead us to believe that the prestige is not simply something that lasts and lasts, but must be worked at all the time. There is more concern about prestige in the great universities than there is in the lesser ones, who may be on the make.

Power and University Goals

One of the motives for undertaking the research, as was stated above, was concern for the claimed split between faculty and administration, and for data on whether differences in power of the two groups might not be affecting the goals of the university. To that end, we developed measures of power and related them to goals, as well as global variables. We shall report only on the direct relationship between power and goals that we found.

We secured a measure of power by adapting a technique used (cf. Tannenbaum and Kahn, 1958; Tannenbaum, 1961, 1962) in studies of labor unions. The domain of power was restricted to "the major goals of the university." A list of power-holders (positions and categories) was provided and beside each, persons were asked to check whether they felt the indicated position or category has a "a great deal of say," "quite a bit of say," "some say," "very little say" or "no say at all." The positions and categories were: regents (or trustees), legislators, sources of large private grants or endowments, federal government agencies or offices, state government agencies or offices, the president, the vice-presidents (or provosts), dean of the graduate school, dean of liberal arts, deans of professional schools as a group, chairmen of departments (considered as a group), the faculty (as a group), the students (as a group), parents of students (as a group), the citizens of the state (as a group), alumni (as a group). The major findings, across all universities, are presented in Table 7.

The findings recorded in Table 7 are interesting in several respects. Some persons might be surprised that the regents score as high as they do (regents themselves usually were) since they rarely do more than rubberstamp the decisions of the president. But they do select the president and are often perceived as a rather shadowy, mysterious group. This perception applies mainly to the faculty, hardly at all to higher administrators. Those with a conspiratorial view of the power structure (who see large private donors,

TABLE 7

Who Make the Big Decisions

	Mean Score
President	4.65
Regents	4.37
Vice President	4.12
Deans of Profess Schools	3.62
Dean of Grad Sch	3.59
Dean of Liberal Arts	3.56
Faculty	3.31
Chairmen	3.19
Legislators	2.94
Federal Govt	2.79
State Govt	2.72
Large Private Donors	2.69
Alumni	2.61
Students	2.37
Citizens of State	2.08
Parents	1.91

alumni, influential citizens and the like pulling strings from behind) do not receive much support from the findings, as can be seen from the low ranking of such persons or groups. Of course we only have perceptions of power, but the perceptions represent the consensus of a large group of persons well-situated to perceive power, and including, surely, a large proportion of the major powerholders themselves.

Our major concern here is only to note the position of the faculty in comparison to the administrators. As can be seen, the faculty are ranked in general below all administrators, with the single exception of chairmen (and a chairman, some believe, is after all only a *primus inter pares*). The unease and concern of faculty on the question of who is running the university hence receive support from this finding. However, it is probably doubtful that most faculty are worried about power as such. Their concern is usually whether the power is being used in their interest or not. We made a number of tests of degree of consensus on the part of faculty and administrators on values, attitudes toward university goals, and various other measures. In particular, with regard to university goals, our findings suggest that there is a striking consensus on the part of administrators and faculty on what the goals are and on what they should be. By and large the split which many people have become alarmed about, and which to some extent was one of the reasons for our beginning this study, does not find support from our data. The faculty and administrators tend to see eye-to-eye. This result held both when we made gross comparisons of the faculty as a group with all administrators as a group and when we broke this down more finely and related the rank of the administrator to the point of view. That is, higher administrators tend to agree with the faculty quite as much as do lower administrators or chairmen. In sum, the findings show that although it is true that administrators in general have more power to affect the big decisions than do members of the faculty, they apparently see eye-to-eye with the faculty; consequently one might infer they will use this greater power to further the goals of the faculty, since they seem to share the same conceptions as the faculty about what the goals ought to be. However, this is only an inference.

The final type of analysis to which we turn is one in which we related the goals of universities to the power structure. The question is: Whatever the administrators *said* about the university and what it ought to be, how in fact do they behave when they get the power? For example, what are universities like in which, say, deans of professional schools have a lot of power as compared to those in which the faculty do? If they are different, then we may say that, whatever the professional school deans may *say,* one does not find the same kind of goal structure where they have power and consequently they do in fact act differently.

TABLE 8   Goals Related to Relative Powers Faculty and Administrators*

	Type of Powerholder			
Types of Goals	Faculty	Chairmen	Deans of Lib Arts	Deans of Prof Schools
Student-Expressive	Stud Intellect (.476) Stud Objectivity (.564)	Stud Intellect (.603) Stud Objectivity (.585)	Stud Intellect (.695) Stud Objectivity (.648) Affect Stud Perm (.605)	Stud Intellect (.523) Stud Objectivity (.528)
Student-Instrumental	Train Scholarship (.528) Stud Careers (—.544) Stud Taste (—.495)	Train Scholarship (.686) (—Stud Careers) (—Stud Taste)	Train Scholarship (.621) (—Stud Careers) (—Stud Taste)	Train Scholarship (.516) (—Stud Careers) (—Stud Taste)
Direct Service	Dissem Ideas (.537) Preserve Heritage (.452)	Dissem Ideas (.661) Preserve Heritage (.478)	Dissem Ideas (.500) Preserve Heritage (.565) Special Training (—.459) Assist Citizens (—.532)	(Dissem Ideas) (Preserve Heritage) (—Special Training) (—Assist Citizens)
Research	Pure Research (.589)	Pure Research (.568)	Pure Research (.544) Applied Research (—.498)	(Pure Research)
Adaptation	Accp Good Stud Only (.474) Keep Costs Down (—.526)	Accp Good Stud Only (.497) Keep Costs Down (—.510) Sat Area Needs (—.488)	Accp Good Stud Only (.524) Keep Costs Down (—.521) Sat Area Needs (—.487) Educ to Utmost (—.489)	Accp Good Stud Only (.579) Keep Costs Down (—.443) Educ to Utmost (—.440)
Management	(Encour Grad Wk) Ensure U Goals (.506) Reward Prof (.680) Will of Fac (.946) Fac U Govt (.878) Run U Demo (.821)	Encour Grad Wk (.537) Ensure U Goals (.672) Reward Prof (.811) Will of Fac (.750) Fac U Govt (.507) Run U Demo (.595)	Encour Grad Wk (.618) Ensure U Goals (.565) Reward Prof (.624) Undergrad Inst (—.473)	Encour Grad Wk (.572) Ensure U Goals (.571) Reward Prof (.583) (Will of Fac)
Motivation	Acad Freedom (.803) Max Opportunity (.775) Stud Pol Rights (.656) Stud Inquire (.766)	Acad Freedom (.664) Max Opportunity (.753) Stud Pol Rights (.524) Stud Inquire (.714)	Acad Freedom (.593) Max Opportunity (.634) Stud Inquire (.722)	Acad Freedom (.509) Max Opportunity (.566) Stud Inquire (.552)
Position	Top Qual All (.594) Top Qual Imp (.456) Up to Date (.446)	Top Qual All (.768) Top Qual Imp (.577) Up to Date (.606)	Top Qual All (.641) Top Qual Imp (.590) Up to Date (.563) U Prestige (.505)	Top Qual All (.570) Top Qual Imp (.489)

* Goals followed by decimal figures (Gammas) are those attaining the 5% level of significance only. In those cases where the level of significance was very close to the 5% (usually off in the 2nd decimal place only), the goal is listed in parentheses without any stated gamma, but with the direction shown by a minus or its absence (that is, plus).

TABLE 9

Goals Related to Relative Power: Legislature and State Government*

Type of Goals	Type of Powerholder	
	Legislature	State Government
Student-Expressive		
	Stud Intellect (−.704)	Stud Intellect (−.695)
	Stud Objectivity (−.628)	Stud Objectivity (−.676)
	Affect Stud Perm (−.674)	Affect Stud Perm (−.717)
		Stud Character (−.445)
Student-Instrumental		
	Train Scholarship (−.473)	Train Scholarship (−.602)
	Stud Careers (.566)	Stud Careers (.514)
Direct Service		
	Dissem Ideas (−.482)	Dissem Ideas (−.528)
	Preserve Heritage (−.496)	Preserve Heritage (−.496)
	Assist Citizens (.692)	Assist Citizens (.480)
Research		
	(−Pure Research)	(−Pure Research)
Adaptation		
	Accp Good Stud Only (−.782)	Accp Good Stud Only (−.627)
	Keep Costs Down (.546)	Keep Costs Down (.476)
	Sat Area Needs (.602)	Sat Area Needs (.506)
	Educ to Utmost (.804)	Educ to Utmost (.554)
Management		
	Encour Grad Wk (−.540)	Encour Grad Wk (−.615)
	Keep Harmony (.531)	Keep Harmony (.444)
	Stud U Govt (.567)	Stud U Govt (.532)
	Undergrad Inst (.605)	Undergrad Inst (.496)
Motivation		
	Acad Freedom (−.654)	Acad Freedom (−.583)
	Max Opportunity (−.588)	Max Opportunity (−.547)
	Stud Inquire (−.560)	Stud Inquire (−.577)
	Stud Activities (.501)	
Position		
	(−Top Qual All)	(−Top Qual Imp)
	(−Top Qual Imp)	Up to Date (−.483)
	U Prestige (−.656)	U Prestige (−.529)
	Pres Character (−.482)	

* Goals followed by decimal figures (Gammas) are those attaining the 5% level of significance (or better) only. In those cases where the level of significance was *very* close to the 5% level (usually off by the second decimal place only), the goal is listed in parentheses without any stated gamma, but with the direction shown by a minus sign, or its absence (for a plus).

The major findings are presented in Tables 8 and 9, which should be looked at together. What we have done is brought together those findings which are sufficiently strong to rule out chance findings. In the first column in Table 8 (with the heading of Faculty) are listed those goals which are emphasized in those places where the faculty are perceived to have most power. That is, we took the replies on the question dealing with faculty perceived power, calculated a mean score for the university, then arranged all 68 universities in sequence. The distribution was broken into thirds, and universities compared on this dimension. The first finding shown (Stud Intellect .476) reports that the higher the average score accorded the faculty as a power group, the more likely is the goal of cultivating the student's intellect to be emphasized. The figure in parentheses is the gamma. Occasionally, a goal came *very* close to reaching significance (off by only a point or two in the second decimal). Those goals are listed in parentheses without a gamma, but with the direction shown by a minus or no sign (for plus), as in the case, for example, of "Encour Grad Wk." The second column shows what goals are emphasized in those places where chairmen are perceived as having more power (than at other universities), and similarly for deans of liberal arts and professional schools.

If we read down the column headed "Faculty," we can characterize those universities where the faculty have (comparatively) more power than at other universities. At such places, the intellect of the student is emphasized and the importance of the student's developing objectively about himself is also emphasized. Students are to be trained in methods of scholarship, whereas student taste and student careers are to be de-emphasized. Direct service consists essentially of serving as a center for ideas, and preserving the cultural heritage, and not the land-grant goals. Pure rather than applied research is emphasized, and furthermore, when the faculty have power, they tend to be elitist in trying to select students. As could be expected, the will of the faculty is one of the important goals and strong effort is made to see to it that the university is run democratically and that professors themselves have a good deal to say about running the university. Predictably, academic freedom is a major goal, and the rights of students to inquire and even advocate whatever they think important is emphasized. The professors are concerned with making sure that the institution is up-to-date and that high quality is maintained. They are not concerned with keeping costs down. This finding is not quite so obvious as appears at first glance because we are not talking about the professors' opinions about what ought to be done but rather about what happens at universities in which faculty are perceived as having a high amount of power compared to the way in which they are perceived at other universities. Universities in which professors are so perceived, we are saying, are universities in which there is little concern with the university goal of keeping costs down.

When we look at the next column (in which the power of the chairmen in relation to university goals is examined), what comes through strongly is that practically the *same* set of goals is found with certain changes, though none of them is really very large. For example "Stud Careers" and "Stud Taste," while not quite reaching significance at the 5 per cent level, are in the same direction (negative). This general finding also holds up when one examines the situation for Deans of Liberal Arts *and* Deans of Professional Schools. Although in some cases some goals drop out, we find no cases of reversals, that is, situations where a goal is positive for one powerholder and negative for another. For example, places where deans of professional schools are powerful are places which tend to select only good students; the same thing is true of places where deans of liberal arts are powerful and where chairmen are powerful and where the faculty are powerful. So is the case with emphasis on graduate work, protecting academic freedom, maximum opportunity for the professor and so forth. The number of relationships is not as high but in general reversals do not occur.

It is when we turn to the relationship between legislatures and university goals, and state government and university goals (Table 9), that a real difference occurs, and here we get almost a complete reversal from the structure that tends to obtain when faculty and deans have power. Thus for example when the faculty have power the goal of student intellect receives strong emphasis. When legislatures have power, it is positively de-emphasized with a very high gamma. "Develop student objectivity" is similarly reversed when one looks at places where faculty have power. Such is also the case for training scholarship and research, student careers, disseminating ideas, preserving the heritage, accepting good students only, keeping costs down, maximum opportunity for the professors, student right to inquire, and, perhaps most disturbing, protecting academic freedom. For all of these goals there is a complete reversal of their relationship when legislatures have power as compared to the situation when faculty have power. The situation is similar where state governments are perceived as having power.

What these findings seem to add up to is that, in view of the consistency between the views and values of faculty as compared to administrators that we pointed to earlier, we now have the further result that the kind of university one has when the administrators have power is not very much different from what one has when the faculty have power (comparatively speaking, of course). What does make a difference is when legislatures and state government are perceived as having power compared to other universities where they are perceived as having less. It is in these universities that the goal structure really changes. In sum, the faculty and administrators find themselves in agreement, and with the kind of goal structure that both of them seem to find comfortable, at least it is the same goal structure whether one is talking about whether administrators or faculty are powerful. The split is between the university and outside influences particularly the state legislature and state government. Note too that these are local influences. We did not secure findings for the influence of the federal government or for sources of endowment funds. On the whole these results support the general picture that was suggested by our finding that academic freedom was the most important of all the goals of American universities. This suggests the importance to them of autonomy in doing their job as they see it. When that autonomy is severely breached, as it is apparently when state government or legislators begin to play a significant role in the power structure of a university, the goals of the university change in a profound way and it becomes something very different.

What, finally, of the effect of the most powerful man of all, the president? Here our findings are paradoxical and not what many would have predicted. We found that when we made comparisons between those universities in which the president was perceived as very powerful and those in which he was perceived as less powerful, there were almost no differences in the goal structures of such universities. This might be interpreted as meaning that the power of the president did not make a difference in the goal structure of the university, a conclusion we found hard to accept, precisely because he was considered to be the leading powerholder. Why should the power of persons perceived as having less power, such as deans of professional schools or the faculty, make a difference when the differences in the power of the president do not? This result appears to be a statistical artifact, but an interesting one. It says something about the power of presidents. When we arrange the average scores that presidents receive, the lowest score is 4.28 and the highest is 4.92. This means that the presidents, alone of all power-holders, occupy the unique position that *everywhere* they were perceived as having very high power, well over 4.00 on a five point scale. When we split the distribution into thirds, even this was not sufficient to produce any variation. This means that there simply is little variation between a person whose average score was 4.28 and a person whose average score was higher than that. They were all crowded over to the right end of the scale. Consequently our finding that the variations in the power of the president do not make any difference in the structure of university goals is simply a way of saying all presidents are so powerful that, even when one divides the presidents into the *very, very* powerful, as distinguished from the *very* powerful, no meaningful differences in goal structure emerge because even the least powerful are very powerful indeed. In order, therefore, to examine the effect of differences in the power of presidents, it is apparently necessary to move to a different kind of organization than the university as we have defined it. The president we have in the universities that we have studied is apparently so much a part of the structure of such universities that his impact cannot be detected in the general goal structure that universities share with one another.

NOTES

1. A metaphor of dubious authenticity. According to most authors, the phrase is attributed to President Garfield who, while a congressman, was said to have referred to the ideal university as one "with President Mark Hopkins at one end of a log and a student at the other." Eells (1962), remembering that Hopkins was at a college located

in New England, thought the metaphor inappropriate to the winter climate. His investigations lead to doubts that the precise phrase was ever used and that, at the very least, Garfield meant to place the log (or more likely bench) inside an enclosed building.

2. We shall use the phrase "organizational model" and the term "organization" without benefit of adjectives, such as "formal," "complex" or "large-scale," in order to avoid having to choose among them. While we agree with Blau's and Scott's (1962:6–7) criticism of such terms, we do not believe any one adjective avoids the problems they refer to.

3. The failure to do so was one of the earliest criticisms of the classic Hawthorne studies. (See Landsberger, 1958:Chap. 3).

4. Cf. the distinction between what Alvin W. Gouldner (1959) calls a "rational" and "natural system" model.

5. Daniel Katz and Robert L. Kahn (1966: Chap. 6) seek to conceptualize such maintenance in terms of "efficiency," or the amount of energy used up to maintain the system. However, as they are quick to point out, the word "energy" may be misleading in that it implies an ability to measure inputs in quantitative terms. Quite apart from difficulties of measurement, there is the central fact that much of an organization's inputs consist not of energies alone but also of information or signals. Katz and Kahn refer to D. R. Miller's (1963) approach to these matters. A treatment which seeks to generalize this discussion to all social systems is in Buckley (1967:Chaps. 3, 4).

6. Our study also included 10 denominational (mostly Catholic) universities, which fulfilled our test for "university" in all respects. However, preliminary findings suggested strongly that they made up a universe of their own and deserved separate tabulation and analysis. We are not reporting on them here.

7. Purdue University turned out to be an exception. It was not classified as a university by the editors of that volume, yet it was the feeling of the investigators that it was excluded by a minor technicality. Consequently, it was included. Such places as M.I.T. and Cal. Tech. are automatically excluded by our criteria.

8. Space forbids description of the tests of bias employed. Detailed information may be secured by writing to the author, or by examining Gross and Grambsch (1968).

9. In the above discussion the term "rank" has been used loosely to refer to what is, strictly speaking, a rating on a five-point scale. In this way, we have followed the procedure in the classic North-Hatt study of occupations, and for much the same reason, persons cannot rank a list of 47 items by comparing each with all others at the same time.

10. "Happy" in the sense implied in the Durkheimian conception of social integration as a state of a society in which people do willingly what they must do. For an organization, such a state is approximated when the actual goals are what members think they should be. It is obvious that we are speaking only of administrators and faculty. We have no data from students, and the possibility, for example, that assigning them a low place in university government is "happy" for them is quite dubious, according to the news of student campus activities at the time of this writing (June, 1968).

11. As the term is used by Lazarsfeld and Menzel (1961). See also Allen H. Barton (1961b) for illustrations from available research.

12. The role of size, as a determinant of organizational variation, is the subject of some controversy at present. See, for example, Blau, Heydebrand and Stauffer (1966) and Hall, Haas, and Johnson (1967). I do not believe that our non-findings on size are evidence one way or another on this controversy. We did get a large range: the smallest university had about 3,500 students, the largest well over 40,000. It may be, however,

that there is a "critical mass" phenomenon operating such that, once a university passes, say, 2,500, further increases are not correlated with other variations. Or perhaps a "university" in the full sense (by our definition) requires some minimum number which is already very large. Peter Blau, in personal conversation, expressed the view that size *is* important in all organizations, but that it must be "washed out"; that is, it is a reflection of other changes. If these other changes are examined, the impact of size as an independent variable may disappear.

13. Use was made of the description in Goodman and Kruskal (1963) of tests of significance for the measures described. Actually, the test of significance we used is the conservative one proposed in that article, based on an upper bound for the variance of the sampling distribution. It was programmed for calculation on an IBM 7090–7094 computer so that it could be read as a z-score. Gamma was used since we did not feel that actual scores, being no more than averages, represented any more precision than ranks. Gamma, in particular, served us well since our data were ordinal and since we had a large number of associations we wished to compare with one another. Gamma was used since it is what Costner (1965) shows is a "proportional reduction of error" measure having qualities similar to r_2; that is, a gamma of .800 can be said to be twice as strong as one of .400.

14. Partly this is due to the fact that we classified universities on four quality levels only. In effect, this resulted in an elite group of nine, a second-level group of nine, a third-level group of 21, and the remainder of 29. However, Cartter (1966) made use of actual "average scores" and found a Pearsonian correlation of .794 between his measure of quality and library resources.

15. Some of those data were reported in Cartter (1966).

16. Such a procedure is clearly necessary since universities in the American Council's list varied from those which gave Ph.D.'s in only 11 areas to some that gave them in 29.

REFERENCES

Bales, Robert F. "Task roles and social roles in problem-solving groups." Pp. 437–447 in Eleanor F. Maccoby, Theodore M. Newcomb and Eugene L. Hartley (eds.), *Readings in Social Psychology.* New York: Henry Holt, 1958.

Barton, Allen H. *Organizational Measurement.* New York: College Entrance Examination Board, 1961. (a)

_____. *Organizational Measurement and Its Bearing on the Study of College Environments.* New York: College Entrance Examination Board, 1961. (b)

Berelson, Bernard. *Graduate Education in the United States.* New York: McGraw-Hill, 1960.

Blau, Peter M., and W. Richard Scott. *Formal Organizations.* San Francisco: Chandler, 1962.

Blau, Peter M., Wolf V. Heydebrand and Robert E. Stauffer. "The structure of small bureaucracies." *American Sociological Review,* 31 (April, 1966), pp. 179–191.

Buckley, Walter. *Sociology and Modern Systems Theory.* Englewood Cliffs, N.J.: Prentice-Hall, 1967.

Capen, S. P. *The Management of Universities.* Buffalo: Foster and Stewart, 1953.

Caplow, Theodore. *Principles of Organization.* New York: Harcourt, Brace and World, 1964.

Cartter, Allen. *An Assessment of Quality in Graduate Education.* Washington, D.C.: American Council on Education, 1966.

Cartwright, Dorwin, and Alvin Zander (eds.). *Group Dynamics.* Evanston: Row Peterson, 1953.

Corson, J. J. *Governance of Colleges and Universities.* New York: McGraw Hill, 1960.

Costner, H. L. "Criteria for measures of association." *American Sociological Review,* 30 (June, 1965), pp. 341–353.

Cyert, Richard and James G. March. *A Behavioral Theory of the Firm.* Englewood Cliffs, N.J.: Prentice-Hall, 1963.

Downs, Anthony. *Inside Bureaucracy.* Boston: Little, Brown, 1967.

Eells, Walter Crosby. "Mark Hopkins and the log—fact or fiction?" *College and University,* 38 (1962), pp. 5–22.

Etzioni, Amitai. "Industrial sociology: the study of economic organizations." *Social Research,* 25 (1958), pp. 303–324.

———. *Modern Organizations.* Englewood Cliffs, N.J.: Prentice-Hall, 1964.

Georgopoulos, Basil S., and Arnold S. Tannenbaum. "A study of organizational effectiveness." *American Sociological Review,* 22 (1957), pp. 534–540.

Goodman, L. A., and W. H. Kruskal. "Measures of associations for cross-classifications." *Journal of the American Statistical Association,* 49 (1954), pp. 732–764.

———. "Measures of association for cross-classifications: III. Approximate sampling theory." *Journal of the American Statistical Association,* 58 (1963), pp. 310–364.

Gouldner, Alvin W. "Organizational analysis." Chap. 18 in Robert K. Merton et al. (eds.), *Sociology Today.* New York: Basic Books, 1959.

———. "Metaphysical pathos and the theory of bureaucracy." Pp. 71–82 in Amitai Etzioni (ed.), *Complex Organizations.* New York: Holt, Rinehart and Winston, 1961.

Gross, Edward, and Paul V. Grambsch. *Academic Administrators and University Goals.* Washington, D.C.: American Council on Education, 1968.

Hall, Richard H., J. Eugene Haas and Norman J. Johnson. "Organizational size, complexity, and formalization." *American Sociological Review,* 32 (December, 1967), pp. 901–912.

Katz, Daniel, and Robert L. Kahn. *The Social Psychology of Organizations.* New York: Wiley, 1966.

Knapp, R. H., and H. B. Goodrich. *Origins of American Scientists.* Chicago: University of Chicago Press, 1952.

Knapp, R. H., and J. J. Greenbaum. *The Younger American Scholar.* Chicago: University of Chicago Press, 1953.

Landsberger, Henry A. *Hawthorne Revisited.* Ithaca, New York: Cornell University, 1958.

Lazarsfeld, Paul F. and Herbert Menzel. "On the relation between individual and collective properties." Pp. 428–429 in Amitai Etzioni (ed.), *Complex Organizations.* New York: Holt, Rinehart and Winston, 1961.

March, James G., and Herbert Simon. *Organizations.* New York: Wiley, 1958.

Merton, Robert K., et al. (eds.). "Organizational analysis." *Sociology Today.* New York: Basic Books, 1959.

Miller, D. R. "The study of social relation: situation, identity and social interaction." Pp. 639–737 in S. Koch (ed.), *Psychology: A Study of a Science,* Vol. 5. New York: McGraw-Hill, 1963.

Parsons, Talcott. "A sociological approach to the theory of formal organizations." *Structure and Process in Modern Societies.* New York: Free Press, 1960.

Parsons, Talcott, *et al. Theories of Society.* New York: Free Press, 1961.

Price, James L. *Organizational Effectiveness: An Inventory of Propositions.* Homewood, Ill.: Richard D. Irwin, Inc., 1968.

Riesman, D. *Constraint and Variety in American Education.* New York: Doubleday, 1958.

Simon, Herbert. "On the concept of organization goal." *Administrative Science Quarterly,* 8 (1964), pp. 1–22.

Stroup, Herbert. *Bureaucracy in Higher Education.* New York: Free Press, 1966.

Tannenbaum, Arnold S. "Control and effectiveness in a voluntary organization." *American Journal of Sociology,* 47 (July, 1961), pp. 33–46.

————. "Control in organizations." *Administrative Science Quarterly,* 7 (1962), pp. 235–257.

Tannenbaum, Arnold S. and R. Kahn. *Participation in Union Locals.* New York: Harper and Row, 1958.

Thompson, James D. and William McEwen. "Organization goals and environment." *American Sociological Review,* 23 (1958), pp. 23–50.

Woodburne, L. S. *Principles of College and University Administration.* Stanford: Stanford University Press, 1958.

Part IV

The School as a Place of Work

Chapter Seven

Teaching and Administration: Careers and Conflict

Whatever else we might say about education, it is a field of employment for both teachers and administrators. This final chapter deals with education as an occupation, focusing on careers and the issue of teacher militancy and unionization.

One of the unique features of elementary and secondary school teaching is the absence of a "career line" that allows teachers to identify a meaningful series of career steps or stages to which they might aspire or which might serve as a basis for recognizing outstanding performance. In the first article of this chapter Cohen deals with this feature of teaching. The study presented here compares the effect of teaching in an "open-space" school with the conventional, self-contained school, on teachers' ambition and job satisfaction.

The second article, by Stimson and Forslund, deals with the careers of university presidents. The main focus here is on intergenerational mobility. While presidents have experienced considerable upward intergenerational mobility (i.e., compared to their fathers' occupations), their own careers appear to have been spent largely within the field of education.

A major issue and subject of debate both within and outside of education in recent years is that of the unionization of teachers. The final article of this chapter by Nagi and Pugh deals with determinants of teachers' membership in organizations that differ in terms of their militancy.

20.   ELIZABETH G. COHEN

Open-Space Schools:
The Opportunity To Become Ambitious

The fundamental peculiarity of the occupation of public elementary school teaching is the flatness of the reward structure. Whether teachers are more or less committed to their profession or more or less skillful in performance has little effect on the rewards they receive. Tenure and salary relate mainly to years of service rather than to skill and commitment. Indeed, evaluation by organizational superiors is infrequent for all but probationary teachers.

There are relatively few opportunities for professional advancement in elementary school teaching. Ambitious classroom teachers cannot look forward to an increase in responsibility and influence without somehow leaving the classroom. They may leave education altogether; they may return to schools of education in search of credits or advanced degrees; or they may move into the field of school administration. At this time, however, the possibility of moving into administration appears as a viable alternative to the small number of male elementary school teachers, but not to the female teachers who wish to have a wider impact on education. Examination of state directories of education reveals comparatively few women in the field of school administration, and graduate students in school administration are almost all male; indeed, very few women apply to such programs.

Lortie (1969) argues that teachers are not powerful figures in the organization of the school, being restricted to classrooms as "small universes of control." Teachers have few participation rights in school-wide decisions. Studies (cf. Corey, 1970) show that the limits of teachers' responsibility and influence are as important a source of teachers' dissatisfaction with work as are more obvious questions of salary.

Informal peer rewards for the elementary school teacher are as few and weak as are those available within the formal organization of the school. In most elementary schools, teachers are socially isolated from their colleagues; they

Reprinted from *Sociology of Education,* 46 (Spring, 1973), pp. 143–161, by permission of the author and the American Sociological Association.

This research is supported by funds from the United States Office of Education, Department of Health, Education, and Welfare. The opinions expressed in this publication do not necessarily reflect the position, policy or endorsement of the Office of Education. (Contract No. OEC 6-10-078, Project No. 5-0252-0307.)

do not see or hear each other in the act of teaching; they rarely meet for the purposes of planning or evaluation of teaching tasks. Indeed, there are very few mutual or common tasks. The traditional isolation of elementary school teachers is such that there are norms against visiting a fellow teacher while she is working with the children in the classroom. Teachers talk to one another, but their conversation rarely occurs in a formal occupational context where decisions are being made on school policies, discipline, curriculum or evaluation of the teaching process.

The effect of not being able to see and hear each other at work is profound; teachers have almost no basis for supporting and rewarding each other in the process of instruction. There is no opportunity for one teacher to tell another that she has carried out a lesson well, handled a difficult child with skill, or planned a clever curriculum unit. There are few opportunities for teachers to earn professional respect from other teachers on the basis of proven skill in teaching or skill in planning and evaluation within a collaborative teacher group.

Little visibility has still further effects on opportunities for teachers to make an impact on anyone but their own group of students. Without a chance to see and hear each other at work, teachers cannot form any sensible idea of who is relatively skilled and should act as a leader and model for other teachers. Even if teachers have no formal organizational rights to evaluate and control one another's behavior, they might still be able to function as highly influential in a colleague group. But, without a process of decision-making in collaborative teacher groups, there is no way to convince colleagues of the efficacy of one's techniques or curriculum ideas. If one teacher is unusually successful in planning small group work in classrooms, there is no way for her to influence other teachers to plan with her techniques.

In review, the elementary school is a formal organization giving few rewards for competence and loyalty to the teacher, there are few opportunities for promotion and pay is rarely related to competence. In addition, the teacher has very little power and authority outside her particular classroom. The same may be said of opportunities for playing an influential role or receiving professional rewards in the informal work organization; there is little chance to receive praise, respect and support from other teachers or for controlling the behavior of colleagues through a process of influence on professional matters.

The open-space school, an innovative form of school architecture, represents significant change in both the formal and informal organization of elementary school teaching. This paper reports partial results of a study of organizational innovation by the Environment for Teaching program, at the Stanford Center for Research and Development in Teaching. The larger study (Meyer, Cohen, et al., 1971) compared teachers from teams working in open-space elementary schools with teachers in conventionally organized schools.

The "open-space" school should not be confused with the concept of the "open classroom." A relatively recent innovation in school architecture, the "open-space school" lacks interior partitions; visual and acoustical separation between teaching stations and classroom areas is limited or eliminated.[1] The most common practice has been to create instructional areas by forming "pods," "classroom clusters" or "big rooms" that accommodate a definite number of teachers and class groups usually ranging from the equivalent of two to nine classrooms. According to a survey of 43 state directors of school planning, over 50 per cent of all new schools constructed within the last three years have been of open design.[2]

RESEARCH QUESTIONS ON AMBITION

Suspicion that the reward structure and powerlessness of elementary school teaching helps to drive out some of its most desirable members has often been voiced in educational literature (cf. Bush, 1970:112). A major question of this analysis was the relationship between ambition in teachers and job dissatisfaction. Was it true that more committed teachers were more dissatisfied than less committed and ambitious teachers? At the start of the larger study, we could not know what changes in formal organization these open-space schools entailed beyond delegation of decision-making powers to a team of teachers and the factor of increased visibility of a teacher's work to her colleagues. Nevertheless, we wished to examine the effect of working in open-space schools on the relationship of ambition to dissatisfaction. Would team teaching in open-space schools represent a major change for ambitious teachers, so that ambition might be positively associated with job satisfaction in the new setting? The third question was theoretical: If the relationship between ambition and job satisfaction changed in the open-space schools, what particular features of the new setting and organization of work were associated with this change? "Open-space school" is not a theoretical concept but an architectural term: we need to know how to abstract and characterize organizational sources of critical changes in the teacher's role.

As the study progressed, it became apparent that the open-space schools in the sample did not represent changes in the formal rewards available to competent teachers or increased opportunities for promotion to higher paying positions such as team leader. Principals' evaluations of teachers were infrequent in both types of schools. It was true that the authority structure of the two types of schools was different; the power to plan for and to schedule large groups of children had been delegated to teams in the open-space schools. But the teams were, formally speaking, equal status teams, so that the increase in decision-making power was a characteristic of the group rather than a competitive opportunity for an ambitious teacher.

What *had* changed radically was the nature of the interaction between teachers and their opportunity to teach in full view of each other. Unless the portable partitions were up, teachers in the open-space schools could see and hear each other at work. Time was usually set aside for team meetings where planning, decision-making and discussion of "problem" children and curriculum problems took place. In addition, teachers in open-space schools frequently conferred during the course of a working day.

Overall survey results revealed that interaction on the team is a necessary but not sufficient condition for an increased sense of influence and autonomy on the part of team teachers. For some teachers, the chance to become influential in a group of peers appears to lead to a general increase in a sense of autonomy and influence. Teachers in open-space schools were far more likely to perceive themselves as influential and autonomous than teachers in conventional schools.

Teams in open-space schools not only report increased interaction opportunities and an increased sense of influence, observations revealed that the teachers provided a source of reward and support to each other within team meetings. In the team situation, a teacher who reports the success of a classroom technique or the handling of a child who is defined by the team as a "problem" can and does receive the warm approbation of team members.

In discussions of curriculum decisions, the ideas of each teacher on at least some of the many tasks are likely to be agreed upon and favorably evaluated by peers. There are many chances for praise and social support. All favorable evaluation does not necessarily flow to one influential teacher (although some teams are dominated by one teacher); interaction patterns may vary over different meetings and different tasks (Molnar, 1971).

For the purposes of the analyses of this paper, then, the distinction between the open-space school and the conventional school becomes a rough indicator of differences in the probability of receiving praise and support from colleagues and differences in the probability of playing an influential role among colleagues. The architectural and work situation difference is *not* an indicator of a difference in the chance of favorable formal evaluation and possible reward based on competence, nor a difference in the availability of upward mobility within the ranks of the school.

The Ambitious Teacher

Two types of ambitious teachers were conceptualized for this study. One type of teacher wishes to become more influential and to receive differential reward and recognition for teaching competence, preferably without having to leave the classroom. This is a person committed to the profession of teaching. We have called this attitude and aspiration, Professional Ambition.

A second type of teacher also wishes to become more influential and to receive greater rewards than less competent teachers, but this person is willing to leave the classroom to achieve these rewards and increased status. This teacher desires some form of promotion in the ranks, such as a supervisory post. Such a teacher would be willing to leave the classroom for a return to school if this avenue held some hope for upward mobility. We have called this attitude-aspiration type, Vertical Ambition. It is entirely possible that a single subject would hold both these attitudes simultaneously. Because teaching supervisors and administrators sometimes see their role as "professional leader," teachers who want to enter supervisory or administrative ranks do not necessarily see themselves leaving behind direct professional concern with the students.

MEASUREMENT OF VARIABLES

Ambition

Two indices of ambition were constructed from attitude items included in the instrument. Ambitious teachers who were oriented toward clinical skills and the classroom were seen as distinct from ambitious teachers interested in promotion into administrative ranks. The first type of ambition is measured by an index called Professional Ambition, and the second is measured by an index called Vertical Ambition.

Professional Ambition. The items of this index show a substantial level of intercorrelation; each item is significantly correlated with every other item; the correlation coefficients range from .31 to .52. The content of these items centers on colleague leadership based upon high levels of professional skill:

Professional Ambition

Q 26. I would like the opportunity to help new young teachers develop classroom skills.

Q 32. I could see myself helping to lead a workshop on teaching techniques.

Q 34. I would be very interested in showing other teachers styles and techniques I've developed.

Q 35. I would be competent at making supervisory evaluations of the other teachers (Meyer, Cohen, *et al.,* 1970: 97).

Vertical Ambition.   Items in this index are more concerned with the lack of promotion opportunities in the hierarchy of the school. These items reflect more of a desire for upward occupational mobility than does the previous index. Of the items composed for this dimension, five showed a modest level of intercorrelation. These are as follows:

Vertical Ambition

Q   4. In comparison with other teachers, I would say that I am a very ambitious person.

Q   6. I personally really wish good teachers got more recognition.

Q 18. If my school encouraged me in acquiring a supervisory certificate by financing me, I would be extremely interested.

Q 22. I have often thought that I would like to return to school for at least a year to improve my professional abilities as a classroom teacher.

Q 29. It is very important to me to be in a school with many opportunities for advancement for the classroom teacher (Meyer, Cohen, *et al.*, 1971:101).

The items of this index show a low but statistically significant correlation with each other with the exception of Question 4 which is not significantly correlated with Question 22. The statistically significant correlation coefficients range from .11 to .38. In a future study some further item refinement is desirable. Questions 6, 22, and 29 do not clearly imply upward mobility only, but probably include some ideas of professional rewards for classroom competence.

Job Satisfaction.   This dimension was measured by a five-item index containing questions on satisfaction with present teaching job, with the choice of teaching as an occupation, and with the likelihood of accepting a job outside of education (Meyer, Cohen, *et al.*, 1971:50). All the correlation coefficients calculated on the relationship of each item to every other item were statistically significant; the size of the coefficients ranged from .18 to .63.

Calculation of Score Groups in Indices.   Scores were calculated for each subject for each index by simple addition of a score for each item. Each item had five Likert-type responses; and the most favorable response was given an item score of "five"; the next most favorable response was scored "four," etc. The distribution of the entire sample on the total index score was then trichotomized so that approximately one-third of the sample fell into each of three categories: High, Medium, or Low, on the particular index.

Restriction of Analysis to Women Teachers.   The results reported below are for women teachers only. This decision was made for the following reasons: (1) Perception of opportunities for advancement undoubtedly functions very differently in women than in men because of status differences between the sexes and because of the paucity of women in posts of educational administration. (2) There are comparatively few men in our sample: 16 men in open-space schools and 21 in self-contained classroom schools. Since we did not have enough men to analyze relationships separately, we decided to examine the predictions and associations for women teachers only.

RESULTS

School Setting and Job Satisfaction

Because the major research questions are in terms of job satisfaction, it is important to point out that there was a sharply increased level of job satisfaction among open-space school teachers. Forty-six per cent of the open-space school faculty had a high score on Job Satisfaction, while only 28 per cent of the self-contained classroom teachers had such a score.

Ambition and Job Satisfaction in Traditional Schools

The first research question concerned ambition and job satisfaction: Would more ambitious teachers show more job dissatisfaction in conventional schools than less ambitious teachers? Table 1 shows a clear negative association between each ambition index and job satisfaction with the self-contained classroom teachers. The higher the score on ambition as measured by either index, the lower is the probability of being highly satisfied by the job.

TABLE 1

Two Types of Ambition and Job Satisfaction: Self-Contained Classrooms

		Percentage High on Job Satisfaction	
Type of Ambition	Score	N	%
Professional	High	19	21%
	Medium	38	26
	Low	42	33
Vertical	High	33	21%
	Medium	37	30
	Low	29	35

Professional Ambition and Job Satisfaction

Would working in teams in an open-space school change this relationship between ambition and job satisfaction? Findings of the general study concerning the lack of differential rewards and authority awarded to individual teachers in the new schools, forced us to view the two indices of ambition quite differently. Obviously, teachers who had high scores on Vertical Ambition are no more likely to be promoted or given merit pay in the new setting than in the old. On the other hand, teachers with high scores on Professional Ambition are more likely to receive the reward of colleague respect and the chance to influence other teachers in the increased colleague interaction situation of the open-space school. At this stage in the analysis, we therefore predicted that job satisfaction would relate positively to ambition, only for the Professional Ambition Index, in the open-space school.

In testing this prediction of a more favorable response of the professionally ambitious teachers in the open-space school, we were surprised to find that there were quite a few more teachers with high scores on the Index of Professional Ambition in the open-space schools than in the self-contained classrooms. Table 2 shows the difference in percentage distributions of trichotomized scores on Professional Ambition. Thirty-two per cent of the women in open-space schools had high scores, whereas only 19 per cent of the women in self-contained classrooms had scores in this category.

A question concerning the possible self-selection of ambitious teachers into the open-space school is immediately obvious. It was therefore important to examine some of the background characteristics of the teachers to determine if open-space schools attracted and/or recruited a "special" kind of teacher, at least in terms of age, sex, years of teaching experience and education.

TABLE 2

Percentage Distribution of Trichotomized Scores of the Index of Professional Ambition in Open and Self-Contained Classroom Schools for Women Only

Professional Ambition	Open Schools	Self-Contained Classrooms
High	32%	19%
Medium	42%	38%
Low	27%	42%
Total	100%	100%
	(N=94)	(N=99)

TABLE 3

Professional Ambition and Job Satisfaction Among Women: For Open and Self-Contained Classroom Schools

	Percentage High on Job Satisfaction [a]			
Professional Ambition	Open Schools		Self-Contained Classrooms	
Score	N	%	N	%
High	30	53	19	21
Medium	39	49	38	26
Low	25	40	42	33

[a] The Index of Job Satisfaction was trichotomized with approximately one-third of all the teachers falling into "High," Medium," and "Low" categories.

Teachers in the two kinds of schools are virtually indistinguishable on the basis of sex or amount of formal education. In both samples, around 85 per cent of the teachers are female and around 45 per cent have more than a B.A. degree. Probably because the open-space schools are newer schools, there is a slight tendency for a higher proportion of the open-space school teachers to be in the 26–30 year age bracket and a higher probability that they have had less than three years experience. Personnel and recruitment policies were quite varied in the open-space schools; some teachers were selected by the building principal and others came through central district office decisions.

When the scores on Job Satisfaction are cross-tabulated with scores on Professional Ambition, it becomes clear that women with high scores on Professional Ambition are *more* satisfied with their jobs than are women with low scores on Professional Ambition, *in open-space schools only* (see Table 3). The reverse of this relationship holds for self-contained classrooms.

Vertical Ambition and Job Satisfaction

The score distributions on Vertical Ambition were similar in the two school settings. The positive association of Job Satisfaction and Professional Ambition seen in Table 3 turns out to be the single exception to the more general finding of a negative association between ambition and satisfaction. Table 4 shows that there is a strong negative relationship between scores on Vertical Ambition and Job Satisfaction *in both school settings.* Whether she teaches in open-space or in self-contained classroom schools, the more vertically ambitious a woman teacher declares herself to be, the more likely she is to be

TABLE 4

Vertical Ambition and Job Satisfaction in Open and Self-Contained Classroom Schools

| Vertical Ambition Score | Percentage High on Job Satisfaction [a] | | | |
| | Open Schools | | Self-Contained Classrooms | |
	N	%	N	%
High	26	31	33	21
Medium	37	49	37	30
Low	31	61	29	35

[a] The Index of Job Satisfaction was trichotomized with approximately one-third of all the teachers falling into "High," Medium," and "Low" categories.

dissatisfied with her job and the more likely she is to favor accepting a job outside education.

Although the relationship between Vertical Ambition and Job Satisfaction in the open-space school remains an inverse one, it is nonetheless true, in absolute terms, that vertically ambitious teachers in open-space schools were 10 per cent more likely to leave a high score on Job Satisfaction than vertically ambitious women in self-contained classrooms. The increased job satisfaction associated with open-space schools is much more marked with teachers scoring low on Vertical Ambition—61 per cent are highly satisfied in open-space schools compared to 35 per cent in self-contained classroom schools.

INTERPRETATION

In traditional schools there is evidence of job dissatisfaction among ambitious teachers, regardless of the index of ambition used. Although an index of job dissatisfaction does not necessarily predict dropping out of teaching altogether, this evidence is consistent with the supposition that the structure of teaching is not particularly satisfying for the more committed, ambitious woman.

The finding of a much higher proportion of professionally ambitious women in the open space school than in the self-contained classroom was not expected. Insofar as demographic characteristics of teachers might differ in the two settings, one might argue that this is the result of special selection procedures. Analysis reveals that the two samples of teachers appear very similar on background characteristics.

Another possible interpretation is that the experience of working on teams in open-space schools actually produces professionally ambitious responses to these items. Initially, ambition was not conceived of as an effect of the change in school organization, but as a prior characteristic brought by the person to the new work experience. From the wisdom of a *post hoc* point of view, it is clear that work in the open-space school does give women opportunities for activities similar to the ones described in the items. It hardly seems unreasonable, looking at these results, to suppose that people might *become ambitious* when given the opportunity to try out new skills and to achieve new recognition for competence.

Critical Features of Organizational Difference

As a result of this analysis, those of the larger study, as well as observational studies of teaching teams, we developed some theoretical propositions concerning abstract features of the work setting and their effects on the attitudes of individual workers. The first distinction is between the *formal work organization* and the *informal work organization*. Relevant concepts within the formal work organization are the differential evaluation and rewards given to workers and the authority rights vested in workers by virtue of assignment to a specific position or role. We refer to these aspects as the *chances for reward and influence in the formal work organization*. In many organizations an individual can look forward to promotion in rank with increased pay. With the promotion usually comes the right to supervise and evaluate subordinates, and therefore an increased chance to be influential. Although the open-space school did not increase the chances for reward and influence for the individual teacher in competition with others, it did delegate increased decision-making powers to the team as a whole. Thus one might argue that the group of teachers, called a team, had experienced increased influence in the work organization. If teachers who desire upward mobility do perceive teachers as very influential, they should show more job satisfaction than if they do not perceive teachers as influential.

Working relationships between team members are located in the informal work organization. The team is a relatively temporary sub-system of equal status workers. In the larger study it was found that unless teachers reported increased interaction within the team, as compared to the level of interaction in conventional schools, they did not report increased teacher influence. We theorize that team interaction, in some cases, proves highly rewarding to teachers and allows some of them to feel that they are being very influential on team decision-making. This increase in chances of reward and influence in

FIGURE 1

**The Theoretical Relationship Between Chances for Reward and
Influence in Formal and Informal Work Organizations and Ambition
and Satisfaction of Teachers**

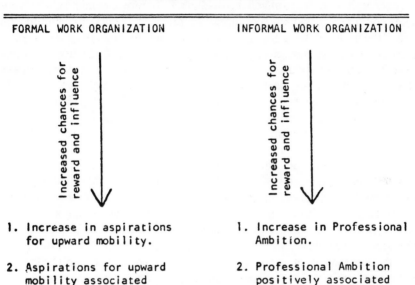

FORMAL WORK ORGANIZATION   INFORMAL WORK ORGANIZATION

Increased chances for reward and influence

Increased chances for reward and influence

1. Increase in aspirations
   for upward mobility.

2. Aspirations for upward
   mobility associated
   with job satisfaction.

1. Increase in Professional
   Ambition.

2. Professional Ambition
   positively associated
   with job satisfaction.

the informal work organization is the source of the growth in professional ambition and its associated increase in job satisfaction. It must be noted that teams are marked by variability as to whether or not they interact very frequently and whether or not they report teachers as influential.

Figure 1 diagrams the theoretical propositions developed as a result of the data analysis. Unfortunately, it is only possible to make a partial exploration in this body of data for support of these propositions. The measures are not uniquely constructed for the purpose of measuring some of the key concepts developed above. For example, we did not include a direct measure of how influential the individual teacher felt in decision-making on the team. Nor did we measure directly the extent to which the individual teacher found work on the team rewarding. Thus we can only speculate that the observed association between working on teams in open-space schools and an increase in job satisfaction associated with an increased professional ambition stems from reward and influence in the informal work organization. In the study currently under way, we are measuring influence and reward in team structure by questionnaire and by observing team interaction.

We did ask the following question: How much influence do individual teachers in this school have over ... (five specific task areas)? Responses to this question dealt with five task areas which were then combined into an index and dichotomized as High Perceived Teacher Influence and Low Perceived Teacher Influence. In terms of the diagram in Figure 1, a high score on this index could reflect two kinds of increased influence: (1) playing an influential role in the informal work organization of the team sub-system, or (2) increased decision-making powers of teams in the formal work organization; they now plan for over 100 children at a time. If this measure does reflect increased power and efficacy for teacher groups in the formal organization, vertically ambitious teachers who do perceive teachers as influential should exhibit increased job satisfaction in comparison to similarly ambitious teachers who do not see teachers as influential.

Table 5 shows the relationship between perceived teacher influence and job satisfaction, only for vertically ambitious teachers in the two school settings. A strong interaction effect is immediately visible in the open-space school, where perceived teacher influence is strongly associated with job satisfaction, but weakly if at all associated with job satisfaction in self-contained class-rooms. If a vertically ambitious teacher perceives teachers to be influential in the open-space school, she is twice as likely to have a high score on Job Satisfaction than if she does not have this perception. Secondly, vertically ambitious teachers in open-space schools who do not perceive teachers as influential are quite dissatisfied with their jobs; as a matter of fact, for this group the general increase in satisfaction of teachers working in the open-space schools as compared to self-contained classrooms disappears (29 per cent have high Job Satisfaction in both settings).

In absolute terms, the morale of ambitious women in open-space schools

TABLE 5

Perception of Teacher Influence and Job Satisfaction Among Women Teachers High in Vertical Ambition: For two School Settings

Vertical Ambition [a]	Perception of Teacher Influence [a]	Percentage High on Job Satisfaction [a]			
		Open Schools		Self-Contained Classrooms	
		N	%	N	%
High	High	37	60	30	33
	Low	21	29	41	29

[a] All three indices were dichotomized in order to preserve the number of cases falling into the different categories.

appears to be markedly improved if they perceive that teachers in general are influential in their school. The source of this improvement in job satisfaction in particular changes in formal and informal work organizations is not clear at this time; measures designed precisely for the theoretical concepts in Figure 1 are necessary in order to test the propositions of interest.

Organizational Gratification of Individual Needs

Initially we saw ambition as a characteristic which an individual brought with her to a work setting. If that work setting provided gratification for that ambition, we reasoned the individual teacher would show more job satisfaction. Contrary to our expectations, teachers in the open-space schools were much more likely to receive a high score on Professional Ambition than teachers in self-contained classrooms. As the analysis documented the increased professional interaction and attendant feelings of influence and autonomy of the open-space school teachers, we interpreted this finding as a function of the creation of an ambitious response by the new work setting itself. We reasoned that as teachers convinced team members of the best educational and instructional decisions, and as they were rewarded by praise and support for their teaching, in full view of each other, many teachers would develop professional ambition. It hardly seems unreasonable, when looking at this work setting, to suppose that people might become ambitious when given the opportunity to try out new skills and to achieve new recognition for competence. Although with cross-sectional data there is no way to tell with certainty whether or not the organization *created* the professionally ambitious response over time, a longitudinal study is in the planning stage to determine the answer to this among other questions. At this time, the best interpretation is that organizational change probably created the professionally ambitious response and the job satisfaction at one and the same time. It would not be too surprising to find that women who like to play these new roles also are satisfied with their jobs.

The original prediction was that more ambitious women would be more satisfied with their jobs in settings providing gratification for their goals. Table 3 confirmed this prediction for the index of Professional Ambition; women in the open-space schools with higher scores on Professional Ambition are more likely to be satisfied with their jobs than women who have low scores on Professional Ambition. The reverse is true for self-contained classrooms.

In self-contained classrooms the greater job dissatisfaction of the women with higher scores on Professional Ambition is a disquieting result. It certainly looks as though organizational arrangements for teaching can prove to be discouraging to the very people most educators would like to encourage.

The results of the Vertical Ambition Index indicate unequivocally that the more ambitious a woman declares herself to be, the more dissatisfied she is with her job. And that holds true in both kinds of school organizations. Sixty-one per cent of the low scorers in the open-space schools are satisfied with their jobs, while only 31 per cent of those who are more ambitious are satisfied. The ambitious women in the open-space schools are not much more satisfied than their counterparts in the self-contained classrooms.

This finding is interpreted as a function of the failure of open-space schools to provide any more opportunities for formal promotion than self-contained classrooms. And we do speak of this as a "failure" because it cannot be a desirable state of affairs when women with strongly expressed career orientations are so likely to be dissatisfied with their teaching jobs. Whether or not the job dissatisfaction expressed here turns into actual "dropout" from the occupation is an unanswerable question in this body of data, but is scheduled for investigation in the longitudinal study discussed above.

Ambition and Feelings Toward Children

All these "ambitious" women may be quite unsettling to the stereotype of the female elementary teacher deriving her major satisfaction from children themselves. Some may argue that women who are ambitious to get ahead cannot have the proper warm, loving attitude toward children. In this view, the nature of the reward and status structure in teaching with gratification stemming mainly from the client is turned into a virtue by which only women who are satisfied with these rewards and with this low status are *defined* as suitable for teaching because they are the only ones who care in a deep way about children.

The survey did include questions on the orientations of teachers to children. Especially relevant to this question are indices of maternal and child development orientations. Women with a high score on the Maternal Orientation Index feel so warmly toward children that they report they often "would like to take one home with them." Women with a high score on the Child Development Orientation Index are more interested in watching the progress in the growth of each child and in consciously building a good relationship with that child than they are in seeing how much of the required curriculum he has absorbed. The Child Development Orientation index reflects a professional philosophy of the child-centered elementary school approach, very much favored in schools of education in the recent period (Meyer, Cohen, *et al.*, 1971, Chapter 6).

TABLE 6

Probability of Having High Scores in Child and Maternal Orientations for High and Low Scorers on Professional Ambition: Women Only

Professional Ambition	Percentage High Score		N
	Child	Maternal	
High	49%	41%	49
Medium	25%	38%	77
Low	22%	30%	67

Tables 6 and 7 show that both indices of ambition are positively related to both the Maternal and Child Development Orientation Index. More ambitious women are more likely to have high scores on the indices of Maternal and Child Orientation than are less ambitious women. This finding offers some support for the general belief that one has to like children to want to stay in teaching and make it a lifelong career. The finding should also quiet the argument of the school administrator who might feel that "it was just as well for the profession" for dissatisfied ambitious women to leave teaching altogether.

TABLE 7

Probability of Having High Scores in Child and Maternal Orientations for High and Low Scorers of Vertical Ambition: Women Only

Vertical Ambition	Percentage High Score		N
	Child	Maternal	
High	44%	42%	59
Medium	28%	39%	74
Low	18%	30%	60

SUMMARY AND SPECULATION

The findings reported in this paper have strong implications for the status of the female elementary school teacher. They suggest that the low status of elementary school teaching and the high dropout figures characterizing the occupation until the very recent period result not only from the generally low standing of the occupation in social prestige but from at least three features of the structure of the occupation: (1) lack of power and influence of the teaching position within the organization of the school, (2) the lack of rewards for competence, and (3) the lack of promotion opportunities in the profession.

The open-space school has provided a chance to examine the relationship between teacher morale and an increased perception of teacher power and efficacy. Under conditions of organizational change, there is a marked rise in the perception of teachers as influential and in the tendency to see oneself as autonomous. And those teachers who respond to the new setting with perceptions of influence and autonomy are likely to be satisfied with their job. In other words, if teachers are made to feel more powerful as a result of changes in the organization of work, they will have higher morale.

The second feature of elementary school teaching, lack of differential reward for competence, was studied in the responses of teachers who felt sufficiently competent for demonstration teaching and supervision. There is a surprising increase in the percentage of professionally ambitious women in the open-space schools as compared to the traditional schools. Moreover, in the open-space schools, professional ambition was positively associated with job satisfaction, while in self-contained classrooms, the more ambitious a woman was, the more dissatisfied she was likely to be.

The increased occurrence of professional ambition and its associated improvement in teacher morale could not have occurred because of a formal change in the rewards and evaluation system—there were no such changes. Rather, these findings may indicate a *growth* of ambition and job satisfaction in response to certain informal rewards in the group interaction setting offered by the teaching team.

A final feature of elementary school teaching is the lack of opportunities for promotion into administration for women. Women who were oriented toward advancement, recognition, and supervisory responsibilities were markedly more dissatisfied than unambitious women in both settings. The inference can be made that the lack of opportunity for upward mobility is very frustrating to these ambitious teachers and may well drive them out of the profession. If we could find a school organization truly offering promotion opportunities to women, this relationship between ambition and dissatisfaction should change markedly.

Elementary school teaching is a traditional haven for women who work; rarely is this occupation used as an example of sex discrimination. Yet, most school administrators are men. And for women who have no wish to leave the classroom, but who are highly professionally oriented, there is a lack of reward and reinforcement for professional merit. There are many women in this sample who could be described as "ambitious" in an absolute sense by our attitude indices; they were typically highly dissatisfied with teaching. The structure of elementary school teaching may well drive some of these women out of the profession. Even if sex discrimination in school administration were eliminated, the dilemma of the professionally ambitious teacher would not be solved. More fundamental changes in the evaluation of teaching and rewards for competence will be necessary to alter the uniformly low status of women in elementary school teaching.

From a practical point of view, these findings suggest that if the status of teachers is raised by means of increasing their influence within the organization of the school, there will be an increase in job satisfaction among women teachers. Increased morale is of special concern because of the marked dissatisfaction among the more committed and ambitious teachers in the study, women likely to have desirable orientations toward children. Looking to the future, a most interesting question may be the long-range outcome of this kind of innovation with an attendant increase in professionally ambitious women and an increasing sense of teacher efficacy. Will team activities continue to provide gratification for these women as the years pass, or will they desire larger fields of operation such as influence over teacher trainees, shared power in school-wide decision-making, and more voice in school districts? A planned longitudinal study of the organizational innovations will examine longer-range consequences of increased ambition and efficacy among women teachers.

NOTES

1. School Planning Laboratory, School of Education. *Open-Space Schools,* Project Bulletin No. 1, March 1970. Stanford, California: Stanford University.
2. *Ibid.,* p. 5.

REFERENCES

Bush, R. N. "The Status of the Career Teacher: Its Effect upon the Teacher Dropout Problem" in T. M. Stinnett (Ed.), *The Teacher Dropout.* Itasca, Ill.: F. E. Peacock Publishers, 1970.
Corey, A. "Overview of Factors Affecting the Holding Power of the Teaching Profession," in T. M. Stinnett (Ed)., *The Teacher Dropout.* Itasca, Ill.: F. E. Peacock Publishers, 1970.
Lortie, D. C. "The Balance of Control and Autonomy in Elementary School Teaching" in A. Etzioni (Ed.), *The Semi-Professionals and Their Organization.* New York: The Free Press, 1964.
Meyer, J., E. Cohen, *et al.* "The Impact of the Open-Space School upon Teacher Influence and Autonomy: The Effects of an Organizational Innovation." Stanford, California: Stanford Center for Research and Development in Teaching, Technical Report No. 21, 1971.

Molnar, S. "Teachers in Teams: Interaction, Influence and Autonomy." Stanford,
    California: Stanford Center for Research and Development in Teaching, Technical
    Report No. 22, 1971.
School Planning Laboratory. *Open Space Schools.* Project Bulletin No. 1, Stanford,
    California: Stanford University, March 1970.

21.   JAMES STIMSON
and MORRIS A. FORSLUND

The Situs Dimension in the
Career Patterns of University Presidents

Although numerous studies have investigated the backgrounds of American
college and university presidents, little is known about the career patterns of
the individuals who occupy this vital position (see Kruse and Beck, 1928;
Chambers, 1932; Warren, 1938; Kohlbrenner, 1948; Lewis, 1954; Hughes,
1940; Gordon, 1951; Hawk, 1960; and King, 1967). In this study we are
concerned principally with exploring the utility of the stratum-situs schema
suggested by Morris and Murphy (1959)[1] in analyzing the career patterns of
the presidents[2] of various types of institutions of higher education.

    In the occupational career of any given individual, several types of moves
are possible. If the individual moves upward or downward between positions
differentiated by their rank in some formal or informal hierarchy of prestige,
influence, or income, he is making a vertical or stratum move. If, however, an
individual moves across hierarchies, he is making a situs move. Intrasitus
moves, then, are those changes of position that occur within a particular situs.
Intersitus moves are those that occur between situses. Stratum moves are those
that involve a change of position within some hierarchical ranking system to
one that is evaluated differently than that occupied originally.

    Five types of educational institutions were included in the study: publicly
funded junior colleges, publicly funded colleges offering at least a bachelor's

Reprinted from *Sociology of Education,* 43 (Spring, 1970), pp. 195–204, by permission of the
authors and the American Sociological Association.

degree but not a doctorate, privately financed colleges offering at least a bachelor's degree but not a doctorate, publicly funded colleges offering a doctorate, and privately financed universities offering a doctorate. Institutions were classified into these categories on the basis of information contained in the *Education Directory,* Part 3 (1968/69). Fifty institutions of each type were selected randomly for inclusion in the study. Denominational schools were not included unless they were listed as independent of church sponsorship. No proprietary institutions were included.

Much of the information necessary for the study was obtained from *Who's Who in America, Who's Who in Education,* and *Leaders in Education.* Other data were obtained through the use of mailed questionnaires, over 94 per cent of which were returned. Adequate data for the study were obtained from 45 junior college presidents, 50 private college presidents, 46 public college presidents, 45 private university presidents, and 50 public university presidents.

Four basic types of moves to the presidency were analyzed: (1) those consisting of an intrasitus move that did not involve a stratum advance; (2) those consisting of an intrasitus move that did involve a stratum advance; (3) those consisting of an intersitus move that did not involve a stratum advance; and, (4) those consisting of an intersitus move that did involve a stratum advance.[3]

In order to determine whether a change of position involved a change in stratum, it was necessary to use some measure of occupational prestige. The Socioeconomic Index developed by Otis Dudley Duncan and the NORC scale were considered (cf. Reiss, 1961:263–275). However, both measures were rejected because some distinctions seemed to be too fine for the purpose of this study. For example, college presidents were ranked 84 on the Socioeconomic Index and 83 on the NORC scale, while technical engineers were ranked 85 and 83 respectively on the same scales. When an invidious comparison is attempted, a move from technical engineer to college president would seem to involve no stratum move according to the NORC scale, a slight move downward according to the Socioeconomic Index. In order to escape the analytical difficulties produced by these fine distinctions, the variance of these two occupational prestige scales had to be sacrificed. The alternative was to employ a third measure. The measure utilized was the Population Decile Scale developed by Duncan (Reiss, 1961:263–275). Stratum mobility was measured by comparing the Population Decile Scale figure for college presidents (10) with that of the occupation from which the move to the presidency was made.

Given the basically exploratory nature of the research, the analysis of the data was guided by several questions rather than hypotheses: What proportion of moves to the university presidency were of each type described above? Does the usual type of move to the presidency differ among the various types of institutions of higher education included in the study? For those individuals who moved to the university presidency from a position within some situs other than Education and Research, from what situs was the move made? Does this differ by type of institution? Intergenerationally (i.e., compared with the occupations of their fathers), what type of move was made to the university presidency? Does this differ among types of institutions?

THE FINDINGS

The data concerning the kind of move made to the presidency are given by type of institution in Table 1. The overwhelming majority of moves (86.5 per cent) to the presidency were intrasitus in nature. By far the most typical move (76.3 per cent) was an intrasitus stratum advance. This move appears to be most usual for junior college and public university presidents, followed by those of public colleges, private colleges, and private universities. Thus, an intrasitus stratum advance seems to be more common for the presidents of public than of private institutions. On the other hand, the largest percentage of intersitus moves to the presidency was made by private college presidents, followed by those of private universities, public colleges, public universities, and junior colleges. In fact, no junior college president in the sample made an intersitus move to that position.

Data concerning the situs from which the move was made to the presidency are given in Table 2 by type of institution.

Intersitus moves were made from only five of the nine situses other than Education and Research. The most common intersitus move was from Finance

TABLE 1

Type of Move Made to the Presidency by Type of Institution
(Percentages)

Move Type*	Institution Type					
	Junior College	Private College	Public College	Private Univ.	Public Univ.	All Types
1	11.1	6.0	8.7	17.8	8.0	10.2
2	88.9	68.0	73.9	64.4	86.0	76.3
3	0.0	12.0	6.5	13.3	6.0	7.6
4	0.0	14.0	10.9	4.4	0.0	5.9
Total	100.0	100.0	100.0	99.9	100.0	100.0
N=	45	50	46	45	50	236

* Type 1 refers to an intrasitus move with no stratum advance, Type 2 to an intrasitus move with a stratum advance, Type 3 to an intersitus move with no stratum advance, and Type 4 to an intersitus move with a stratum advance.

TABLE 2

Distribution of Situses from Which the Move to the Presidency Was Made by Type of Institution

Situs	Institution Type					
	Junior College	Private College	Public College	Private Univ.	Public Univ.	All Types
Education and Research	45	37	38	38	47	205
Finance and Records	0	5	1	3	1	10
Health and Welfare	0	3	4	0	1	8
Commerce	0	2	3	1	0	6
Legal Authority	0	2	0	2	1	5
Manufacturing	0	1	0	1	0	2
Total	45	50	46	45	50	236

and Records, followed by Health and Welfare, Commerce, Legal Authority, and Manufacturing. The number of intersitus moves is too small to establish any definite pattern by type of institution. However, it is apparent that private colleges are most likely to select a president outside of the situs of Education and Research; when they do select a president from some other situs, private colleges appear most likely to select a person from Finance and Records, public colleges from Health and Welfare, and private universities from Finance and Records or Legal Authority.

From the data available it also was possible to establish the number of presidents who had *ever* had experience in some situs other than Education and Research since beginning their occupational experience, and the particular situses in which they had held positions. These data are presented in Tables

TABLE 3

Distribution of Presidents by the Number of Positions Ever Held in Situses Other than Education and Research, by Type of Institution

Institution Type	Number of Positions Ever Held in Situses Other than Education and Research				
	0	1	2	3	4
Junior College	42	1	2	0	0
Private College	24	19	5	1	1
Public College	36	6	3	1	0
Private University	24	12	8	1	0
Public University	32	8	8	2	0
Total	158	46	26	5	1

TABLE 4

Number of Presidents Who Have Ever Held Positions in Situses Other than Education and Research by Situs and Type of Institution

Situs	Institution Type					
	Junior College	Private College	Public College	Private Univ.	Public Univ.	All Types
Finance and Records	2	9	2	9	5	27
Health and Welfare	1	10	5	4	5	25
Legal Authority	0	6	0	5	7	18
Commerce	0	3	3	6	5	17
Manufacturing	0	5	0	6	2	13
Extraction	2	0	2	0	3	7
Aesthetics and Entertainment	0	0	0	0	1	1
Building and Maintenance	0	0	0	0	.0	0
Transportation	0	0	0	0	0	0
Total	5	33	12	30	28	108

3 and 4. Of the 236 presidents for whom data were available, only 78 (33.1 per cent) had ever had experience in some situs other than Education and Research. Of these, 40 had held a position in only one other situs, 26 in two, 5 in three, and only 1 in four. Twenty-seven persons had held positions in Finance and Records, 25 in Health and Welfare, 18 in Legal Authority, 17 in Commerce, 13 in Manufacturing, 7 in Extraction, and only 1 in Aesthetics and Entertainment. None of the presidents had held positions in Transportation.

It is clear that junior college presidents are less likely to have had any experience outside of the situs of Education and Research, while private college, private university, and public university presidents are more likely to have had such experience. However, while more private college presidents than presidents of any other type of institution have held at least one position in some other situs, a larger number of both private and public university presidents have held positions in at least two other situses.

The data concerning intergenerational mobility are presented in Tables 5 and 6. As can be seen, 82.2 per cent of the presidents hold positions in situses different from those in which their fathers held their principal occupational positions. In other words, over four-fifths of the presidents have been intergenerationally mobile across situses. However, a somewhat larger percentage of presidents of both private and public universities had fathers whose principal occupations were in the situses of Education and Research than was the case for any of the three types of colleges. On the whole, the presidents also appear to be occupationally upwardly mobile; 72.1 per cent of them hold positions that are higher on the Population Decile Scale than the principal occupations

TABLE 5

Type of Intergenerational Move Made to the Presidency by Type of Institution (Percentages)

| | Institution Type | | | | | |
Move Type	Junior College	Private College	Public College	Private Univ.	Public Univ.	All Types
1	2.2	4.0	2.2	2.2	0.0	2.1
2	11.1	12.0	8.7	20.0	26.0	15.7
3	15.6	26.0	21.7	40.0	26.0	25.8
4	71.1	58.0	67.4	37.8	48.0	56.4
Total	100.0	100.0	100.0	100.0	100.0	100.0
N=	45	50	46	45	50	236

of their fathers. This is true especially of the presidents of junior colleges, 82.2 per cent of whom hold higher positions than those of their fathers. It is least true of presidents of private universities. To put it another way, a higher percentage of private university presidents than presidents of the other four types of institutions had fathers whose occupational prestige equalled their own.

Overall, the largest number of presidents had fathers whose principal occupations were in Extraction, followed closely by Education and Research and Health and Welfare. There also is a substantial number of presidents whose

TABLE 6

Distribution by Situs of the Principal Occupations of the Presidents' Father by Type of Institution

| | Institution Type | | | | | |
Situs	Junior College	Private College	Public College	Private Univ.	Public Univ.	All Types
Extraction	14	4	16	1	10	45
Education and Research	6	8	5	10	13	42
Health and Welfare	6	15	5	7	5	38
Commerce	3	8	3	5	7	26
Finance and Records	2	2	7	6	4	21
Building and Maintenance	2	5	5	7	2	21
Manufacturing	5	1	3	4	4	17
Transportation	3	4	1	2	3	13
Legal Authority	2	3	1	3	2	11
Aesthetics and Entertainment	2	0	0	0	0	2
Total	45	50	46	45	50	236

fathers' principal occupations were in Commerce, Finance and Records, Building and Maintenance or Manufacturing. However, there are considerable differences in the principal occupations of the fathers of the presidents of the various types of institutions. The largest number of the fathers of junior college presidents held positions in Extraction, while the largest number of fathers of private college presidents held positions in Health and Welfare. For public colleges, the largest number of fathers also worked in Extraction, while for both private and public universities the largest number of fathers worked in Education and Research. It also should be noted that a large number of the fathers of public university presidents held their principal occupational positions in Extraction. Thus, all of the types of public institutions have a considerable number of presidents whose fathers' principal occupations were in Extraction; this is in sharp contrast to the presidents of private institutions. Like the private universities, the private colleges have a substantial number of presidents whose fathers were in Education and Research, while like the private colleges, a considerable number of the fathers of the presidents of private universities held positions in Health and Welfare. Thus, there appears to be some difference between the public and private institutions in terms of the principal occupations of the fathers of their presidents.

Of some interest is the question of the amount of previous administrative experience of persons selected for the presidency and the point in their careers at which they first entered administration. Of the individuals in the sample, each had held at least one administrative position prior to assuming his current presidency. The range was from one to nine such positions, with most persons having held between two and five previous administrative posts. Analysis revealed no significant differences among the types of institutions and the number of previous administrative positions held by their presidents. However, analysis of the points in their careers when they first entered administration did reveal differences among the types of institutions. The overwhelming majority of presidents of junior colleges (86.1 per cent) and public colleges (87.0 per cent) entered administration within five years after having received their last earned degrees. On the other hand, 60.0 per cent of private college presidents, 85.5 per cent of private university presidents, and 68.0 per cent of public university presidents entered administration more than five years after having received their last earned degrees; most of them did so between five and fifteen years after having received those degrees.

In terms of administrative experience, it is interesting to note that of the 236 presidents, 197 are serving in their first presidency, 32 in their second, 6 in their third, and only 1 in his fourth. Of the 47 moves from one presidency to another made by these men during their careers, 26 (55.3 per cent) were moves to institutions of the same type. Ten of the 21 moves to an institution of another type were made by persons now presidents of private universities. None of the presidents of private universities with previous presidential experience had ever been president of another private university; all had been presidents of either private or public colleges. However, when the other types of institutions choose a person with previous presidential experience as their president, they are likely to select a man with experience in the same type of institution.

The type of last earned degree, which may be considered as a prelude to an occupational career, differs considerably among the presidents of the different types of institutions. Only 17.8 per cent of the presidents of junior colleges hold the Ph.D. degree, in contrast to 74.0 per cent of the presidents of private colleges, 72.0 per cent of the presidents of public universities, and 68.9 per cent of the presidents of public colleges. On the other hand, 46.7 per cent of the presidents of junior colleges and 28.2 per cent of the presidents of public colleges hold the Ed.D. degree, while no private college presidents hold this degree, and only two private and two public university presidents hold the Ed.D. degree. The remaining presidents hold a wide variety of other degrees.

SUMMARY AND CONCLUSIONS

Intergenerationally, the great majority of the college and university presidents in the sample have been both horizontally and vertically mobile. That is, when compared with the principal occupations of their fathers, they have been mobile both across situses and upward in the occupational structure. Also it is clear that most began their occupational careers with the Ph.D. degree, held several administrative positions prior to assuming the presidency, and were selected from within the situs of Education and Research. The most typical move to the presidency, involving over three-fourths of the presidents in the sample, was an intrasitus stratum advance. Only about one-third of the presidents had ever had experience in some situs other than Education and Research. For the most part, these positions were in Finance and Records, Health and Welfare, Legal Authority, Commerce, and Manufacturing. Finally, it appears that the careers of private college and private university presidents differ considerably from those of the presidents of junior colleges: the careers of public university presidents are more like those of the presidents of the private institutions; and the careers of the presidents of public colleges are more like those of junior college presidents.

NOTES

1. Morris and Murphy suggested the existence of ten situses: (1) Legal Authority, (2) Finance and Records, (3) Manufacturing, (4) Transportation, (5) Extraction, (6) Building and Maintenance, (7) Commerce, (8) Aesthetics and Entertainment, (9) Education and Research, and (10) Health and Welfare.

2. In some instances the title of "Dean" is used for the administrative head of a junior college and the title "Chancellor" for the administrative head of a university. In cases where the title of Chancellor refers to the leader of a system of universities rather than a single institution, the leader of the individual institution rather than the leader of the system was included in the sample.

3. Moves involving either intersitus or intrasitus stratum declines also are empirically possible; however, these were not logically possible given the methodology of the study.

REFERENCES

Chambers, M. M. "Presidents of state teachers colleges." *School and Society,* 35(February, 1932), pp. 234–236.

Gordon, J. E. "The university presidents: a study of their background and educational concern in 1900 and 1950." Unpublished doctoral dissertation, University of Chicago, 1951.

Hatt, P. K. "Occupations and social stratification." *American Journal of Sociology,* 45(May, 1950), pp. 533–543.

Hawk, R. "A profile of junior college presidents." *Junior College Journal* (February, 1960), pp. 340–356.

Hughes, R. M. "A study of university and college presidents." *School and Society,* 51(May, 1940), pp. 317–320.

King, F. P. "Presidents' profile." *Liberal Education* (October, 1967), pp. 403–410.

Kohlbrenner, B. J. "Some elements of background among university presidents." *School and Society,* 68(October, 1948), pp. 283–285.

Kruse, S. A., and E. C. Beck. "A study of the presidents of state colleges and of state universities." *Peabody Journal of Education* (May, 1928), pp. 358–361.

Lewis, W. P. "Backgrounds of college presidents in the U.S., 1952–1953." Unpublished doctoral dissertation, Peabody College, 1954.

Morris, R. T., and R. J. Murphy. "The situs dimension in occupational structure." *American Sociological Review,* 24(April, 1959), pp. 231–239.

Warren, L. E. "A study of the presidents of four-year colleges in the United States." *Education* (March, 1938), pp. 427–428.

22. MOSTAFA H. NAGI and MEREDITH D. PUGH

Status Inconsistency and Professional Militancy in the Teaching Profession

Social scientists have shown a long-standing interest in status inconsistency as a predictor of human behavior. Status inconsistency may be conceived as a nonvertical configuration involving several dimensions—occupation, education, income, race, religion, and ethnicity—some of which are directly related to economic class attributes. Research in recent years has focused on the effect of two or more inconsistent status dimensions on patterns of behavior (Lenski, 1954; Jackson, 1962). Several studies cite an association between status inconsistency and liberal ideology (Lenski, 1954, 1956; Segal and Knoke, 1970); others have suggested that status inconsistency may lead individuals to seek conflict resolution through right-wing extremism (Rush, 1967; Hunt and Cushing, 1970–1971).

Methodological considerations in evaluating the sometimes contradictory findings of status inconsistency research abound (Treiman, 1966; Kasl, 1969). One problem concerns the question of reference. Inconsistency on various status dimensions can result from an individual's departure from reference group norms, or from his departure from national norms. The interjection of personal reference groups suggests that a person's subjective feelings of status inconsistency are perhaps more indicative of human behavior than the averaging of various status indicators based on national norms (Geschwender, 1967). Even though prestige is an important dimension of subjective status, few studies use it in determining status inconsistency (Rettig, 1958; Laumann, 1966; Tucker, 1969; Nagi, 1973). In the sociology of occupations the prestige of various professions has received considerable attention. Most of the studies of prestige are concerned with the methodological problems of measuring the variable, but there are some that demonstrate empirical relationships with other "sociological indicators" (Reiss, 1961; Hodge, 1962; Hodge, Siegel, and Rossi, 1964; Hodge, Treiman, and Rossi, 1966; Blau and Duncan, 1967).

Our concern is with the relationship between status inconsistency on two dimensions—prestige and income—and professional militancy among secondary school teachers. The literature reveals an increasing interest in theoretical analysis of the development and strength of union organizations among certain

Reprinted from *Education and Urban Society*, 5 (August, 1973), pp. 385–403, by permission of the authors and Sage Publications, Inc.

professions, and especially among public school teachers (Goldstein, 1955; Corwin, 1970; Cole, 1969). Nevertheless, the collection of data describing teachers' attitudes and values conducive to their membership in union organizations, rather than professional groups, is rare. Thus, most of the explanations regarding the subjective states that may significantly influence teachers to unionize remain imputative and speculative in nature.

UNIONISM, PROFESSIONAL MILITANCY AND STATUS INCONSISTENCY IN THE TEACHING PROFESSION

The development of unions in the teaching profession dates back as early as the first decade of the twentieth century with the emergence of AFT locals in the cities of Chicago and New York. However, the decade of the 1960s was one of great change in the teaching profession.

At the beginning of the decade, it would have been difficult to find a more conservative and acquiescent group than schoolteachers; in terms of participating in an illegal strike, perhaps no less likely group existed. Today, all that has changed. In cities across the United States, teachers are demanding a voice in the determination of their salaries and working conditions, and when these demands are ignored, teachers are using militant tactics, including strikes, to force compliance by school boards (Cole, 1969: 3).

Unionism is one of the collective means by which workers achieve success in the economic realm. As a social phenomenon, unionism has always been equated with the labor movement, since conflict between labor and management is recognized as the basic principle of its development. Consequently, unionism implies (1) "the separateness of workers' economic interest from that of employers," and (2) "a declaration of their collective independence from the employers and consequently collective dependence on the union." Although the union movement has undergone continuous change in America, unions have always been committed to collective bargaining as a means to achieving their goals. When necessary, they resorted to strikes. The conflicting theories behind unionism in modern industrial society and its changing character gives it a complex and diffuse nature.

Most researchers see unions as organizations (1) that arise from a variety of work dissatisfactions, (2) that deal with situations of interest conflict, and (3) that engage in collective bargaining as the most usual means of protecting and enhancing economic conditions. "The mere fact that collective bargaining would have little meaning were it not for the possibility of strikes," demonstrates the potential militancy of union action.

The professional association, as separable from professionalism as ideology, is characterized by two principal attitudes: (1) the professional association is a nonprofit, social unit predominantly occupied with the dual purpose of promoting proper professional conduct through a code of ethics and elevating the standards of competence of its members; and (2) since all professions serve the public, emphasis is placed on minimizing competition within the profession, as well as between professions, in securing material benefits for members.

A professional association as a formal body of an occupational group reflects these aspects in the following ways: (1) professional issues are of primary importance, and individual benefits of members are of secondary concern; and (2) a profession constitutes a pressure group on the matters concerning the profession itself. Outside these matters, they maintain a neutral attitude toward whatever segments exist in the larger society.

Because of basic theoretical and functional differences between unions and professional associations, it is somewhat misleading to deal with them in a dichotomous manner. The two do not represent opposite poles on a continuum, since they share overlapping attributes and since the gradual development of one does not necessarily exclude the other. One may note, for instance, developments of union organization in quasi-professional and technical occupations that are directly concerned with wages and working conditions. In many cases, but especially in that of teachers, professional associations continue to coexist with unions.

C. Wright Mills' celebrated analysis of white collar unionism rests on the assumption that if a union raises the wage level and security of employees, it may, at the same time, lower their prestige and its derivative sense of security. Central to Mills' analysis is his premise that public school teachers represent the economic proletariat of the professions. Stress is generated by the reality of their economic conditions on one hand, and their attitude toward unionization on the other (Mills, 1956). Providing a similar level of argument, Theodore Caplow (1954) sees the motives that favored unionization of the fringe professions to be substantial, especially in the case of teachers whose salaries tended to constantly lag behind the cost of living. Many writers have articulated explanations of the relatively underdeveloped state of professionalization in the teaching occupations. Myron Lieberman (1960: 179) felt that because "teachers' organizations are irrelevant in the national scene, they are weak and teachers are without power, and that power is exercised upon them to weaken and corrupt public education." Stephen Cole explains the unionization of teachers as an outcome of their dissatisfaction with salaries and loss of prestige. He sees the conditions of the teaching profession as favorable to channel such dissatisfaction into a union movement. His study (1969: 154) of the teacher's union suggests that

> the experience of a sharp decline in prestige provides strong motivation to participate in reform movements. High school teachers may have felt that their prestige was far less than that of doctors and lawyers; but, when they thought that what little prestige they had was slipping away because of the single-salary schedule, their discontent rose sharply. No other professional groups suited to unionization appear to have experienced a similar sudden decline in prestige, but it would seem likely that those groups that experience such a decline will be the most likely to turn to a union-type movement.

In summary, most analysts of unionization among public school teachers stress the relatively low salary and prestige levels accorded the teaching profession. Dissatisfaction seeks resolution in the union movement. Mills and Cole, however, differ in their interpretation of the importance of prestige. Cole explains the incipient unionization of teachers as a result of their perceived loss of prestige, while Mills views prestige as a secondary variable subordinate to salary. The disagreement is a matter of emphasis, and is ultimately an empirical rather than a theoretical question. Some teachers may feel comfortably satisfied with their salaries and still experience relative prestige deprivation. Others may feel relatively underpaid and experience little prestige deprivation. Some teachers, of course, are likely to feel that they are both underpaid and underprivileged. Status consistency in terms of both income and prestige can be contrasted with status inconsistency on the prestige and income dimensions. It is generally expected that status inconsistency is an especially important motive for militant behavior.

Our intention is to test this general assertion with regard to membership in the AFT or NEA. Theories of status consistency usually suggest that inconsistency on status dimensions is a more powerful motivating force than consistency. In this case, we would expect the highest proportion of AFT union members to experience inconsistency on the income and prestige dimensions. This expectation, however, disregards the type of inconsistency experienced by teachers. Relative prestige deprivation, by itself, is an unlikely predisposing force for joining a teachers' union. We would expect to find the highest proportion of AFT members among teachers who experience status inconsistency, rather than consistency, and who feel relatively satisfied in terms of professional prestige, but not satisfied in terms of income. The type of inconsistency experienced by individuals may account for the disparity in behavioral outcomes noted earlier by Rush (1967). Inconsistency resulting from perceived prestige deprivation may result in conservative rather than liberal militancy.

In this case, we should find that status "inconsistents" experiencing prestige deprivation are underrepresented in the liberal union organization.

FINDINGS

In the spring of 1966, 300 questionnaires were sent to high school teachers, members of the NEA and AFT locals in the city of Toledo, Ohio; 150 questionnaires were distributed to each. The return from the NEA members consisted of 90 questionnaires, and the return from AFT members was 136. After reviewing the data, 26 incomplete questionnaires and five subjects who held double membership were dropped. Seventy-seven completed questionnaires from the NEA members and 118 questionnaires from the AFT members were tabulated in the analysis.

The measure of status consistency used in the study was developed from a factor analysis of 12 items dealing with significant issues in the teaching profession. In the factor analysis the principle axes technique was combined with a varimax rotation to reach the terminal solution. All of the items were presented in the standard agree/disagree format. Relative satisfaction with the prestige accorded public school teachers was indexed as a summative scale consisting of four items: (1) Teachers do not get their fair share of prestige; (2) In many ways the public thinks teachers are little more than daytime babysitters; (3) Teachers are highly respected by the public (reverse scoring); and (4) Comparing teachers with lawyers, physicians and other professional people, teachers' prestige is somewhat lower than it should be. Relative satisfaction with teaching salaries was indexed by the following items: (1) Teachers are not paid enough; (2) Teachers are concerned too much about their salaries (reverse scoring); (3) What teachers need most is a greater increase in their salary; and (4) Comparing teachers with lawyers, physicians and other professional people, teachers' income is much lower than it should be. Each of the items on the two scales had factor loadings of at least .40 and a factorial complexity of one.

The prestige and income scales were dichotomized into high and low satisfaction. (The dichotomies were based on natural breaking points in bimodal distributions.) The low prestige and low income satisfaction category (Low Status Consistents) constituted the largest group of teachers (n = 85). The remaining cases divided nearly evenly between the high income satisfaction and low prestige satisfaction teachers (Low Prestige Inconsistents) and the low income satisfaction and high prestige satisfaction teachers (Low Income Inconsistents). The totals for the last two categories were 56 and 55, respectively.

TABLE 1

Organizational Membership by Prestige and Income Consistency (in percentages)

	Organization		
	NEA	AFT	n
Low Consistents	34	66	(83)
Low Prestige Inconsistents	48	52	(56)
Low Income Inconsistents	36	64	(55)
Total			(194)
$df = 2$; $x^2 = 2.80$; $p = .75$			

Not unexpectedly, teachers who felt satisfied with both their salary and prestige (3), were too few for analysis.

A majority of the secondary school teachers were members of the AFT (64 per cent), but as shown in Table 1, this proportion is considerably smaller among the Low Prestige Inconsistents (52 per cent). Those teachers who felt relatively deprived in terms of professional prestige, rather than salary, were least likely to join the AFT. Conversely, they were more likely to join the more professionally oriented NEA. Whereas only 34 per cent of the Low Status Consistents, and only 36 per cent of the Low Income Inconsistents were NEA members, fully 48 per cent of the Low Income Inconsistents had joined the NEA. The type of status inconsistency (prestige versus income) experienced by an individual, therefore, clearly has an effect on his choice of organizational membership. The data, however, do not confirm our expectation that status inconsistency, as opposed to low status consistency, predisposes teachers to join the AFT.

Introducing sex (Table 2) as a control variable yields mixed results. Males were more likely to join the AFT than were females (70 per cent versus 56 per cent). Among the men, the Low Status Consistents were again the most likely members of the AFT (75 per cent), but among the women the Low Income Inconsistents were the most likely AFT members. There is, then, some support for our expectation that Low Income Inconsistents would show greater preference for membership in the AFT than other teachers. More surprisingly, the membership patterns for Low Prestige Inconsistents diverge noticeably between males and females. The highest proportion of NEA members among the women is among the Low Prestige Inconsistents (54 per cent). The smallest proportion of female NEA members, as already implied, is among the Low Income Inconsistents (34 per cent).

TABLE 2

**Organizational Membership by Sex and Prestige and
Income Consistency (in percentages)**

| | Organization | | |
	NEA	AFT	n
Males			
Low Consistents	25	75	(36)
Low Prestige Inconsistents	31	69	(13)
Low Income Inconsistents	37	63	(17)
Total			(76)
df $= 2$; $x^2 = 1.23$; p $=$ N.S.			
Females			
Low Consistents	40	60	(47)
Low Prestige Inconsistents	54	46	(43)
Low Income Inconsistents	36	64	(28)
Total			(118)
df $= 2$; $x^2 = 2.50$; p $=$ N.S.			

The corresponding figures for the Low Prestige and Low Income Inconsistents among the men are 31 per cent and 37 per cent. The male teachers who felt deprived in terms of occupational prestige, unlike their female counterparts, were not more likely than others to join the NEA. Women were apparently more acutely affected by perceived prestige deprivation than were men. At least, the female Low Prestige Inconsistents were much more likely to join the NEA than were the Low Prestige Inconsistent males (54 per cent versus 31 per cent). Perhaps this result is because the men were slightly more likely to be liberals, and consequently reluctant to join the NEA, than were their female colleagues.

The data displayed in Table 3 introduce sex and political orientation as simultaneous control variables (McClosky's [1958] conservatism scale was used to measure political orientation). Among the male teachers the Low Status Consistents were still the most likely members of the AFT, and this fact is especially true among the liberals. Nearly 90 per cent of the liberal Low Status Consistents were AFT members as opposed to only 62 per cent of their conservative parallels. The type of status inconsistency experienced by teachers again seems to have small effect on organizational memberships. Among the liberals, Low Prestige Inconsistents were slightly less likely to join the AFT than were the Low Income Inconsistents (60 per cent versus 67 per cent). The same pattern is clearly evident in the data supplied by women.

The control for political orientation indicates that conservatives, as ex-

TABLE 3

Organizational Membership by Sex, Political Orientation, and Prestige and Income Consistency (in percentages)

	Organization		
	NEA	AFT	n
Males			
Conservatives			
Low Consistents	38	62	(18)
Low Prestige Inconsistents	—	—	(3)
Low Income Inconsistents	42	58	(12)
Total			(33)
df = 1; x^2 = 0.0; p = N.S.			
Liberals			
Low Consistents	11	89	(18)
Low Prestige Inconsistents	40	60	(10)
Low Income Inconsistents	33	67	(15)
Total			(43)
df = 2; x^2 = 3.30; p = .75			
Females			
Conservatives			
Low Consistents	36	64	(22)
Low Prestige Inconsistents	65	35	(26)
Low Income Inconsistents	50	50	(12)
Total			(60)
df = 2; x^2 = 4.08; p = .75			
Liberals			
Low Consistents	44	56	(25)
Low Prestige Inconsistents	35	65	(17)
Low Income Inconsistents	25	75	(16)
Total			(58)
df = 2; x^2 = 1.75; p = N.S.			

pected, are more likely to join the NEA rather than the AFT. Among the men, for example, 64 per cent of the conservatives are AFT members as compared to nearly 75 per cent of the liberals. Moreover, the conservative viewpoint apparently enhances the probability that Low Prestige Inconsistents will join the NEA, while a liberal viewpoint will encourage Low Income Inconsistents to join the AFT. The highest proportion of NEA members is found among the conservative women who feel relatively deprived in terms of occupational prestige.

Up to this point in our analysis, we have simply assumed that status inconsistency and political orientation predispose teachers to act in particular ways with respect to organizational membership. This may not be a realistic assumption. If Low Income Inconsistents feel nothing can be gained by joining the AFT, they may just as well join the more professionally oriented NEA. Joining

TABLE 4

Organizational Membership by Sex, Powerlessness, and Prestige and Income Consistency (in percentages)

| | Organization | | |
	NEA	AFT	n
Males			
High Powerlessness			
Low Consistents	28	72	(18)
Low Prestige Inconsistents	43	57	(7)
Low Income Inconsistents	—	—	(4)
Total			(29)
df = 1; x^2 = .94; p = N.S.			
Low Powerlessness			
Low Consistents	22	78	(18)
Low Prestige Inconsistents	17	83	(6)
Low Income Inconsistents	62	39	(13)
Total			(37)
df = 2; x^2 = 4.68; p = .90			
Females			
High Powerlessness			
Low Consistents	22	78	(23)
Low Prestige Inconsistents	46	55	(22)
Low Income Inconsistents	36	64	(14)
Total			(59)
df = 2; x^2 = 3.60; p = .75			
Low Powerlessness			
Low Consistents	58	42	(24)
Low Prestige Inconsistents	62	38	(21)
Low Income Inconsistents	36	64	(14)
Total			(59)
df = 2; x^2 = 2.60; p = N.S.			

the AFT to improve occupational salaries implies, at least, that only collective, rather than individual, efforts would be useful with respect to manipulating the external environment.

The data shown in Table 4 introduce sex and political alienation (powerlessness) as simultaneous control variables. The measurement of powerlessness used in this study is the scale developed and used by Neal and Seeman (1964). The data for the women reveal the clearest pattern of results. Approximately 65 per cent of the women who expressed a feeling of powerlessness were members of AFT. Only 46 per cent of the women who did not feel politically powerless joined the AFT. It may very well be that membership in the AFT is a power-seeking response of people who feel personally unable to control their environments as individuals.

Once again, the data indicate that the type of status inconsistency experienced by an individual is an important factor. Women who experienced prestige deprivation were most likely to join the NEA rather than the AFT. Powerlessness, however, does decrease their membership in the NEA. Only 42 per cent of the powerless, low prestige inconsistents were NEA members compared with 62 per cent of their female counterparts who experienced little feeling of powerlessness.

DISCUSSIONS AND CONCLUSIONS

In this article we have argued that a tension exists in the minds of public school teachers between the income and prestige factors of their jobs. We also argued that such tension is a factor creating a general feeling of dissatisfaction among teachers, and that such discontent provides strong motivation to participate in reform movements, as manifested in the unionization of teachers and the use of relatively militant tactics.

We hypothesized that a feeling of economic deprivation will dispose teachers to join a union type organization (AFT), and that a greater feeling of prestige deprivation will be more conducive for joining the traditionally less militant teacher organization (NEA). This hypothesis suggested that a status inconsistency framework needs to be considered to understand the complex relationship between the economic and prestige dimensions, and to assure their relative influence on teachers' decisions to join one or the other of these two organizations.

Our typology of status inconsistency was generated from a subjective point of view; that is, from the teachers' own feelings about their income and the ⁀restige accrued to their jobs in comparison to those of other well-established professions. Respondents were grouped in four types. The first group included teachers who were satisfied with both their prestige and income; these were labeled "High Consistent." As we expected, this type included only a very few cases that supported our basic contention that a general feeling of discontent exists among public school teachers. Teachers who expressed a feeling of dissatisfaction with both the income and prestige of their jobs were labeled "Low Consistent." Approximately 43 per cent of our sample fell into this group, the majority of whom were members of the AFT. The two groups of status inconsistency were termed "low on income" when they expressed dissatisfaction with the economic remuneration of the teaching job, and "low on prestige" when they evaluated the prestige of their job as low in comparison to other established professions, i.e., doctors or lawyers.

The data gave some support to our earlier expectation that dissatisfaction with the economic remuneration is a greater motivating force for joining the union type organization, it being mostly concerned with bread-and-butter issues. At the same time the findings also indicate that concern with professional prestige is a stronger force conducive to joining the traditionally more professionally oriented NEA. In part, these findings support the utility of using status inconsistency as a predictor of membership in teachers' organizations. They also show that a profile of status inconsistency can be ascertained from a purely subjective level even though objective criteria may be less incongruent in such cases.

This study, however, failed to show that status inconsistency per se is a more powerful motivating force than low status consistency, since teachers who were dissatisfied with both the income and prestige of their jobs tended to join the AFT more often than those who were satisfied with income alone. This fact, we believe, does not negate the utility of status inconsistency framework, and it should not be viewed as theoretically unsound.

By itself, income factors seem to be a more motivating drive than prestige concern. It is reasonable to believe that when combined, these two factors seem to have an additive affect influencing a favorable orientation toward joining the more militant group among teachers' organizations. For some teachers a concern for the low prestige accrued to the teacher's job may be an integral part of the low income remuneration of the teaching job compared to other professionals. They feel that an increase in income will automatically enhance the prestige of their job, and therefore they are probably willing to forego whatever loss of prestige may result from their membership in a union and the resulting association with a working class movement.

In sum, certain types of status discrepancy appear to be predisposed by distinct status dilemma rather than by discrepancy per se to either support or reject militancy as experienced in teachers' unions. Feelings of prestige deprivation seemed to be a more powerful force among female teachers than among males, usually causing them to join the traditionally more professionally oriented organization (NEA). This fact is probably due to the differing male and female perceptions of the teaching experience. Earlier evidence indicates that "insofar as teaching is a feminized occupation, and if it is assumed that teaching is a middle class occupation, then for males teaching becomes a mechanism of status change while for females, it is a mechanism of status maintenance."

Differing class origins of male and female teachers may very well be another factor explaining the relatively larger preoccupation of prestige among female teachers. The majority of males who become high school teachers came from lower class backgrounds, whereas the majority of females who became high school teachers came from middle and upper class backgrounds. (This data is based on a comparison between the respondent and his father's occupation.) Therefore, women teachers tend to be concerned with the prestige of public school teaching substantially more than are men.

We sought an interpretation of the specific linkages between subjective status inconsistency and professional militancy in two theoretically related variables: conservatism and feeling of powerlessness. We may ask first what kinds of interpretations may be made of the specific linkages found between subjectively defined discrepancy profiles and political attitudes. Assuming that conservatism implies individual resistance to change, the status dilemma that led to support or rejection of the relatively militant movement in the teaching profession (AFT) is probably related to the specific profile of the status discrepancy, and to the way the status discrepants are affected by the goals and the tactics of the different organizational groups.

The AFT's (the union movement) clearly identifiable preference for immediate economic gains and better economic conditions no doubt attracts the liberals among teachers who are, in general, politically disposed to favor social, political and economic change. Conversely, the status discrepant whose prestige concerns are high is not likely to be attracted to AFT, although some teachers in this category of prestige inconsistence may experience some ambivalence in relation to the present structure that fails to recognize his or her essential worth by appropriate financial rewards. For these groups, a situation of status dilemma would not be resolved by a loss of prestige that they feel they will experience if they join the AFT.

Our interpretation of the linkage between conservatism and professional militance received further support when we introduced sex as a control variable. The relatively conservative outlook characteristic of female teachers in conjunction with their apparent concern with prestige heightens their favorable inclination toward the traditionally more conservative organization (NEA). Conservatism of female teachers may be an expression of their middle class origin; it may also be an outcome of their concern for prestige.

In order to see the linkages between status discrepancy profile and the feeling of powerlessness, we have to focus finally on the different tactics and their success as used by the militant movement among teachers (AFT). Teachers' unions' strong stands on issues of immediate concern to their members, as well as their frequent strikes or threats of strikes, express the power that teachers can collectively exert. Since such a collective power can be individually felt in matters related to salaries and contract negotiations more so than in matters related to the prestige of the teaching profession, it is therefore reasonable to expect that Low Income Inconsistents will be inclined to join in a collectivity that seeks remedies for inadequate salaries. Individual teachers' feelings of powerlessness to do anything about correcting what they believe to be inadequate salaries is a greater motivating force for them to join the union.

In conclusion, we propose status consistency on the subjective level as an appropriate framework to explain the differing propensities of teachers toward joining militant occupational organizations. We also suggest that a feeling of status discrepancy predisposes an experience of status dilemma, and that status dilemma can be resolved to the satisfaction of the specific individuals depending on the person's political orientation and feeling of powerlessness. Future research on status inconsistency can profit not only from considering this experience from a subjective perspective, but also from specifying nonstructural correlates that heighten or possibly resolve the status dilemma implied by the conditions of discrepancy.

REFERENCES

Blau, P. M. and O. D. Duncan. *The American Occupational Structure.* New York: Wiley, 1967.

Caplow, T. *The Sociology of Work.* New York: McGraw-Hill, 1954.

Cole, S. *The Unionization of Teachers.* New York: Praeger, 1969.

Corwin, R. G. *Militant Professionalism: A Study of Organizational Conflict in High Schools.* New York: Appleton-Century-Crofts, 1970.

Goldstein, B. "Unionism among salaried professionals in industry." *Amer. Soc. Rev.,* 22 (April, 1955), pp. 199–206.

Geschwender, J. A. "Continuities of status consistency and cognitive dissonance." *Social Forces,* 41 (December, 1967), pp. 160–171.

Hodge, R. W. "The status consistency of occupational groups." *Amer. Soc. Rev.,* 27 (1962), pp. 336–343.

Hodge, R. W., P. M. Siegel, and P. H. Rossi. "Occupational prestige in the United States: 1925–1963." *Amer. J. of Sociology* 70 (November, 1964), pp. 286–302.

Hodge, R. W., D. J. Treiman, and P. H. Rossi. "A comparative study of occupational prestige," pp. 309–321 in R. Bendix and S. M. Lipset (eds.), *Class, Status and Power.* New York: Free Press, 1966.

Hunt, L. L. and R. G. Cushing. "Status discrepancy, interpersonal attachment and right-wing extremism." *Social Sci. Q.,* 51 (December–March, 1970–71), pp. 587–601.

Jackson, E. F. "Status consistency and symptoms of stress." *Amer. Soc. Rev.,* 27 (August, 1962), pp. 469–480.

Kasl, S. U. "Status inconsistency: some conceptual and methodological considerations," pp. 377–390 in J. D. Robinson, R. Athanasion, and K. Drabhead (eds.), *Measures of Occupational Attitudes and Occupational Characteristics.* Ann Arbor: Survey Research Center, Institute of Social Research, University of Michigan, 1969.

Laumann, E. O. *Prestige and Association in an Urban Community.* Indianapolis: Bobbs-Merrill, 1966.

Lenski, G. "Social participation and status crystallization." *Amer. Soc. Rev.,* 21 (August, 1956), pp. 458–464.

————. "Status crystallization: a non-vertical dimension of social status." *Amer. Soc. Rev.,* 19 (August, 1954), pp. 405–413.

Lieberman, M. *The Future of Public Education.* Chicago: Univ. of Chicago Press, 1960.

McClosky, H. "Conservatism and personality." *Amer. Pol. Sci. Rev.* 52 (March, 1958), pp. 27–45.

Mills, C. W. *White Collar.* London: Oxford Univ. Press, 1956.

Nagi, M. H. "Social psychological correlates of membership in teachers' organizations." *Teachers College Record,* 74 (February, 1973), pp. 369–378.

Neal, A. and M. Seeman. "Organization and powerlessness: a test of the mediation hypothesis." *Amer. Soc. Rev.,* 29 (April, 1964), pp. 216–226.

Reiss, A. J. Jr., et al. *Occupations and Social Status.* New York: Free Press, 1961.

Rettig, S., F. Jacobson, and B. Pasamanick. "Status overestimation, objective status, and job satisfaction among professions." *Amer. Soc. Rev.,* (February, 1958), pp. 75–81.

Rush, G. B. "Status consistency and right wing extremism." *Amer. Soc. Rev.,* 32 (February, 1967), pp. 86–93.

Segal, D. R. and D. Knoke. "Social and economic basis of political partisanship in the United States." *Amer. J. of Economics and Sociology,* 29 (July, 1970), pp. 253–262.

Treiman, D. "Status discrepancy and prejudice." *Amer. J. of Sociology* (May, 1966), pp. 651–664.

Tucker, C. "Occupational prestige and self-designation: a critical examination." *Soc. Forces,* 2 (Summer, 1969), pp. 107–116.

AUTHOR INDEX

SUBJECT INDEX

THE BOOK MANUFACTURE

Sociology of Education: A Book of Readings, Second Edition, was typeset by Datagraphics of Phoenix, Arizona. Printing and binding were by the George Banta Company, Menasha, Wisconsin. Cover design was by Charles Kling. The type is Times Roman with Eterna Bold display.